T0382644

A Hands-On Introduction to Data Science

This book introduces the field of data science in a practical and accessible manner, using a hands-on approach that assumes no prior knowledge of the subject. The foundational ideas and techniques of data science are provided independently from technology, allowing students to easily develop a firm understanding of the subject without a strong technical background, as well as being presented with material that will have continual relevance even after tools and technologies change. Using popular data science tools such as Python and R, the book offers many examples of real-life applications, with practice ranging from small to big data. A suite of online material for both instructors and students provides a strong supplement to the book, including datasets, chapter slides, solutions, sample exams, and curriculum suggestions. This entry-level textbook is ideally suited to readers from a range of disciplines wishing to build a practical, working knowledge of data science.

Chirag Shah is Associate Professor at University of Washington in Seattle. Before, he was a faculty member at Rutgers University, where he also served as the Coordinator of Data Science concentration for Master of Information. He has been teaching data science and machine learning courses to undergraduate, masters, and Ph.D. students for more than a decade. His research focuses on issues of search and recommendations using data mining and machine learning. Dr. Shah received his M.S. in Computer Science from the University of Massachusetts Amherst, and his Ph.D. in Information Science from the University of North Carolina Chapel Hill. He directs the InfoSeeking Lab, supported by awards from the National Science Foundation (NSF), the National Institute of Health (NIH), the Institute of Museum and Library Services (IMLS), as well as Amazon, Google, and Yahoo!. He was a Visiting Research Scientist at Spotify and has served as a consultant to the United Nations Data Analytics on various data science projects. He is currently working at Amazon in Seattle on large-scale e-commerce data and machine learning problems as Amazon Scholar.

A Hands-On Introduction to Data Science

CHIRAG SHAH
University of Washington

Shaftesbury Road, Cambridge CB2 8EA, United Kingdom

One Liberty Plaza, 20th Floor, New York, NY 10006, USA

477 Williamstown Road, Port Melbourne, VIC 3207, Australia

314–321, 3rd Floor, Plot 3, Splendor Forum, Jasola District Centre, New Delhi – 110025, India

103 Penang Road, #05–06/07, Visioncrest Commercial, Singapore 238467

Cambridge University Press is part of Cambridge University Press & Assessment, a department of the University of Cambridge.

We share the University's mission to contribute to society through the pursuit of education, learning and research at the highest international levels of excellence.

www.cambridge.org
Information on this title: www.cambridge.org/9781108472449

DOI: 10.1017/9781108560412

First published 2020 (version 3, October 2024)

Printed in Great Britain by CPI Group (UK) Ltd, Croydon CR0 4YY, October 2024

A catalogue record for this publication is available from the British Library

ISBN 978-1-108-47244-9 Hardback

Additional resources for this publication at www.cambridge.org/shah.

To my amazingly smart and sweet daughters – Sophie, Zoe, and Sarah – for adding colors and curiosity back to doing science and living life!

Contents

Preface

Data science is one of the fastest-growing disciplines at the university level. We see more job postings that require training in data science, more academic appointments in the field, and more courses offered, both online and in traditional settings. It could be argued that data science is nothing novel, but just statistics through a different lens. What matters is that we are living in an era in which the kind of problems that could be solved using data are driving a huge wave of innovations in various industries – from healthcare to education, and from finance to policy-making. More importantly, data and data analysis are playing an increasingly large role in our day-to-day life, including in our democracy. Thus, knowing the basics of data and data analysis has become a fundamental skill that everyone needs, even if they do not want to pursue a degree in computer science, statistics, or data science. Recognizing this, many educational institutions have started developing and offering not just degrees and majors in the field but also minors and certificates in data science that are geared toward students who may not become data scientists but could still benefit from data literacy skills in the same way every student learns basic reading, writing, and comprehension skills.

This book is not just for data science majors but also for those who want to develop their data literacy. It is organized in a way that provides a very easy entry for almost anyone to become introduced to data science, but it also has enough fuel to take one from that beginning stage to a place where they feel comfortable obtaining and processing data for deriving important insights. In addition to providing basics of data and data processing, the book teaches standard tools and techniques. It also examines implications of the use of data in areas such as privacy, ethics, and fairness. Finally, as the name suggests, this text is meant to provide a hands-on introduction to these topics. Almost everything presented in the book is accompanied by examples and exercises that one could try – sometimes by hand and other times using the tools taught here. In teaching these topics myself, I have found this to be a very effective method.

The remainder of this preface explains how this book is organized, how it could be used for fulfilling various teaching needs, and what specific requirements a student needs to meet to make the most out of it.

Requirements and Expectations

This book is intended for advanced undergraduates or graduate students in information science, computer science, business, education, psychology, sociology, and related fields who are interested in data science. It is not meant to provide in-depth treatment of any programming language, tool, or platform. Similarly, while the book covers topics such as machine learning and data mining, it is not structured to give detailed theoretical instruction on them; rather, these topics are covered in the context of applying them to solving various data problems with hands-on exercises.

The book assumes very little to no prior exposure to programming or technology. It does, however, expect the student to be comfortable with computational thinking (see Chapter 1) and the basics of statistics (covered in Chapter 3). The student should also have general computer literacy, including skills to download, install, and configure software, do file operations, and use online resources. Each chapter lists specific requirements and expectations, many of which can be met by going over some other parts of the book (usually an earlier chapter or an appendix).

Almost all the tools and software used in this book are free. There is no requirement of a specific operating system or computer architecture, but it is assumed that the student has a relatively modern computer with reasonable storage, memory, and processing power. In addition, a reliable and preferably high-speed Internet connection is required for several parts of this book.

Structure of the Book

The book is organized in four parts. Part I includes three chapters that serve as the foundations of data science. Chapter 1 introduces the field of data science, along with various applications. It also points out important differences and similarities with related fields of computer science, statistics, and information science. Chapter 2 describes the nature and structure of data as we encounter today. It initiates the student about data formats, storage, and retrieval infrastructures. Chapter 3 introduces several important techniques for data science. These techniques stem primarily from statistics and include correlation analysis, regression, and introduction to data analytics.

Part II of this book includes chapters to introduce various tools and platforms such as UNIX (Chapter 4), Python (Chapter 5), R (Chapter 6), and MySQL (Chapter 7). It is important to keep in mind that, since this is not a programming or database book, the objective here is not to go systematically into various parts of these tools. Rather, we focus on learning the basics and the relevant aspects of these tools to be able to solve various data problems. These chapters therefore are organized around addressing various data-driven problems. In the chapters covering Python and R, we also introduce basic machine learning.

But machine learning is a crucial topic for data science that cannot be treated just as an afterthought, which is why Part III of this book is devoted to it. Specifically, Chapter 8 provides a more formal introduction to machine learning and includes a few techniques that are basic and broadly applicable at the same time. Chapter 9 describes in some depth supervised learning methods, and Chapter 10 presents unsupervised learning. It should be noted that, since this book is focused on data science and not core computer science or mathematics, we skip much of the underlying math and formal structuring while discussing and applying machine learning techniques. The chapters in Part III, however, do present machine learning methods and techniques using adequate math in order to discuss the theories and intuitions behind them in detail.

Finally, Part IV of this book takes the techniques from Part I, as well as the tools from Parts II and III to start applying them to problems of real-life significance. In Chapter 11, we take this opportunity by applying various data science techniques to several real-life problems, including those involving social media, finance, and social good. Finally, Chapter 12 provides additional coverage into data collection, experimentation, and evaluation.

The book is full of extra material that either adds more value and knowledge to your existing data science theories and practices, or provides broader and deeper treatment of some of the topics. Throughout the book, there are several FYI boxes that provide important and relevant information without interrupting the flow of the text, allowing the student to be aware of various issues such as privacy, ethics, and fairness without being overwhelmed by them. The appendices of this book provide quick reference to various formulations relating to differential calculus and probability, as well as helpful pointers and instructions for installing and configuring various tools used in the book. For those interested in using cloud-based platforms and tools, there is also an appendix that shows how to sign up, configure, and use them. Another appendix provides listing of various sources for obtaining small to large datasets for more practice and even participate in data challenges to win some cool prizes and recognition. There is also an appendix that provides helpful information related to data science jobs in various fields and what skills one should have to target those calls. Finally, a couple of appendices introduce the ideas of data ethics and data science for social good to inspire you to be a responsible and socially aware *data citizen*.

The book also has an online appendix (OA), accessible through the book's website at www.cambridge.org/shah, which is regularly updated to reflect any changes in data and other resources. The primary purpose for this online appendix is to provide you with the most current and updated datasets or links to datasets that you can download and use in the dozens of examples and try-it-yourself exercises in the chapters, as well as data problems at the end of the chapters. Look for the icon at various places that inform you that you need to find the needed resource from OA. In the description of that exercise, you will see the specific number (e.g., OA 3.2) that tells you where exactly you should go in the online appendix.

Using This Book in Teaching

The book is quite deliberately organized around teaching data science to beginner computer science (CS) students or intermediate to advanced non-CS students. The book is modular, making it easier for both students and teachers to cover topics to the desired depth. This makes it quite suitable for the book to be used as a main reference book or textbook for a data science curriculum. The following is a suggested curriculum path in data science using this book. It contains five courses, each lasting a semester or a quarter.

- Introduction to data science: Chapters 1 and 2, with some elements from Part II as needed.
- Data analytics: Chapter 3, with some elements from Part II as needed.
- Problem solving with data or programming for data science: Chapters 4–7.
- Machine learning for data science: Chapters 8–10.
- Research methods for data science: Chapter 12, with appropriate elements from Chapter 3 and Part II.

At the website for this book is a Resources tab with a section labeled "For Instructors." This section contains sample syllabi for various courses that could be taught using this book, PowerPoint slides for each chapter, and other useful resources such as sample mid-term and final exams. These resources make it easier for someone teaching this course for the first time to adapt the text as needed for his or her own data science curriculum.

Each chapter also has several conceptual questions and hands-on problems. The conceptual questions could be used in either in-class discussions, for homework, or for quizzes. For each new technique or problem covered in this book, there are at least two hands-on problems. One of these could be used in the class and the other one could be given for homework or exam. Most hands-on exercises in chapters are also immediately followed by hands-on homework exercises that a student could try for further practice, or an instructor could assign as homework or in-class practice assignment.

Strengths and Unique Features of This Book

Data science has a very visible presence these days, and it is not surprising that there are currently several available books and much material related to the field. *A Hands-On Introduction to Data Science* is different from the other books in several ways.

- It is targeted to students with very basic experience with technology. Students who fit in that category are majoring in information science, business, psychology, sociology, education, health, cognitive science, and indeed any area in which data can be applied. The study of data science should not be limited to those studying computer science or statistics. This book is intended for those audiences.
- The book starts by introducing the field of data science without any prior expectation of knowledge on the part of the reader. It then introduces the reader to some foundational ideas and techniques that are independent of technology. This does two things: (1) it provides an easier access point for a student without strong technical background; and (2) it presents material that will continue to be relevant even when tools and technologies change.
- Based on my own teaching and curriculum development experiences, I have found that most data science books on the market are divided into two categories: they are either too technical, making them suitable only for a limited audience, or they are structured to be

simply informative, making it hard for the reader to actually use and apply data science tools and techniques. *A Hands-On Introduction to Data Science* is aimed at a nice middle ground: On the one hand, it is not simply describing data science, but also teaching real hands-on tools (Python, R) and techniques (from basic regression to various forms of machine learning). On the other hand, it does not require students to have a strong technical background to be able to learn and practice data science.

- *A Hands-On Introduction to Data Science* also examines implications of the use of data in areas such as privacy, ethics, and fairness. For instance, it discusses how unbalanced data used without enough care with a machine learning technique could lead to biased (and often unfair) predictions. There is also an introduction to the newly formulated General Data Protection Regulations (GDPR) in Europe.
- The book provides many examples of real-life applications, as well as practices ranging from small to big data. For instance, Chapter 4 has an example of working with housing data where simple UNIX commands could extract valuable insights. In Chapter 5, we see how multiple linear regression can be easily implemented using Python to learn how advertising spending on various media (TV, radio) could influence sales. Chapter 6 includes an example that uses R to analyze data about wines to predict which ones are of high quality. Chapters 8–10 on machine learning have many real-life and general interest problems from different fields as the reader is introduced to various techniques. Chapter 11 has hands-on exercises for collecting and analyzing social media data from services such as Twitter and YouTube, as well as working with large datasets (Yelp data with more than a million records). Many of the examples can be worked by hand or with everyday software, without requiring specialized tools. This makes it easier for a student to grasp a concept without having to worry about programming structures. This allows the book to be used for non-majors as well as professional certificate courses.
- Each chapter has plenty of in-chapter exercises where I walk the reader through solving a data problem using a new technique, homework exercises to do more practice, and more hands-on problems (often using real-life data) at the end of the chapters. There are 37 hands-on solved exercises, 46 hands-on try-it-yourself exercises, and 55 end-of-chapter hands-on problems.
- The book is supplemented by a generous set of material for instructors. These instructor resources include curriculum suggestions (even full-length syllabuses for some courses), slides for each chapter, datasets, program scripts, answers and solutions to each exercise, as well as sample mid-term exams and final projects.

About the Author

Dr. Chirag Shah is Associate Professor at University of Washington in Seattle. Before, he was a faculty member at Rutgers University. He is a Senior Member of the Association for Computing Machinery (ACM). He received his Ph.D. in Information Science from University of North Carolina at Chapel Hill and a M.S. in Computer Science from the University of Massachusetts at Amherst.

His research interests include studies of interactive information seeking and retrieval, with applications to personalization and recommendation, as well as applying machine learning and data mining techniques to both big data and tiny data problems. He has published several books and peer-reviewed articles in the areas of information seeking and social media. He has developed Coagmento system for collaborative and social searching, IRIS (Information Retrieval and Interaction System) for investigating and implementing interactive IR activities, as well as several systems for collecting and analyzing data from social media channels, including award winning ContextMiner, InfoExtractor, TubeKit, and SOCRATES. He directs the InfoSeeking Lab, where he investigates issues related to information seeking, social media, and neural information retrieval. These research projects are supported by grants from the National Science Foundation (NSF), the National Institute of Health (NIH), the Institute of Museum and Library Services (IMLS), Amazon, Google, and Yahoo!. He also serves as a consultant to the United Nations Data Analytics on various data science projects involving social and political issues, peacekeeping, climate change, and energy. He spent his last sabbatical at Spotify as a Visiting Research Scientist and is currently consulting to Amazon on personalization and recommendation problems as an Amazon Scholar.

Dr. Shah has taught extensively to both undergraduate and graduate (masters and Ph.D.) students on topics of data science, machine learning, information retrieval (IR), human–computer interaction (HCI), and quantitative research methods. He has also delivered special courses and tutorials at various international venues, and created massive open online courses (MOOCs) for platforms such as Coursera. He has developed several courses and curricula for data science and advised dozens of undergraduate and graduate students pursuing data science careers. This book is a result of his many years of teaching, advising, researching, and realizing the need for such a resource.

chirags@uw.edu
http://chiragshah.org
@chirag_shah

Acknowledgments

A book like this does not happen without a lot of people's help and it would be rude of me to not acknowledge at least some of those people here.

As is the case with almost all of my projects, this one would not have been possible without the love and support of my wife Lori. She not only understands late nights and long weekends working on a project like this, but also keeps me grounded on what matters the most in life – my family, my students, and the small difference that I am trying to make in this world through the knowledge and skills I have.

My sweet and smart daughters – Sophie, Zoe, and Sarah – have also kept me connected to the reality while I worked on this book. They have inspired me to look beyond data and information to appreciate the human values behind them. After all, why bother doing anything in this book if it is not helping human knowledge and advancement in some way? I am constantly amazed by my kids' curiosity and sense of adventure, because those are the qualities one needs in doing any kind of science, and certainly data science. A lot of the analyses and problem solving presented in this book fall under this category, where we are not simply processing some data, but are driven by a sense of curiosity and a quest to derive new knowledge.

This book, as I have noted in the Preface, happened organically over many years through developing and teaching various data science classes. And so I need to thank all of those students who sat in my classes or joined online, went through my material, asked questions, provided feedback, and helped me learn more. With every iteration of every class I have taught in data science, things have gotten better. In essence, what you are holding in your hands is the result of the best iteration so far.

In addition to hundreds (or thousands, in the case of MOOCs) of students over the years, there are specific students and assistants I need to thank for their direct and substantial contributions to this book. My InfoSeeking Lab assistants Liz Smith and Catherine McGowan have been tremendously helpful in not only proofreading, but also helping with literature review and contributing several pieces of writings. Similarly, Dongho Choi and Soumik Mandal, two of my Ph.D. students, have contributed substantially to some of the writings and many of the examples and exercises presented in this book. If it was not for the help and dedication of these four people, this book would have been delayed by at least a year.

I am also thankful to my Ph.D. students Souvick Ghosh, who provided some writeup on misinformation, and Ruoyuan Gao, for contributing to the topic of fairness and bias.

Finally, I am eternally grateful to the wonderful staff of Cambridge University Press for guiding me through the development of this book from the beginning. I would specifically call out Lauren Cowles, Lisa Pinto, and Stefanie Seaton. They have been an amazing team helping me in almost every aspect of this book, ensuring that it meets the highest standards of quality and accessibility that one would expect from the Press. Writing a book is often a painful endeavor, but when you have a support team like this, it becomes possible and even a fun project!

I am almost certain that I have forgotten many more people to thank here, but they should know that it was a result of my forgetfulness and not ungratefulness.

PART I

CONCEPTUAL INTRODUCTIONS

This part includes three chapters that serve as the foundations of data science. If you have never done anything with data science or statistics, I highly recommend going through this part before proceeding further. If, on the other hand, you have a good background in statistics and a basic knowledge of data storage, formats, and processing, you can easily skim through most of the material here.

Chapter 1 introduces the field of data science, along with various applications. It also points out important differences and similarities with related fields of computer science, statistics, and information science.

Chapter 2 describes the nature and structure of data as we encounter it today. It initiates the student about data formats, storage, and retrieval infrastructures.

Chapter 3 introduces several important techniques for data science. These techniques stem primarily from statistics and include correlation analysis, regression, and introduction to data analytics.

No matter where you come from, I would still recommend paying attention to some of the sections in Chapter 1 that introduce various basic concepts of data science and how they are related to other disciplines. In my experience, I have also found that various aspects of data pre-processing are often skipped in many data science curricula, but if you want to develop a more comprehensive understanding of data science, I suggest you go through Chapter 2 as well. Finally, even if you have a solid background in statistics, it would not hurt to at least skim through Chapter 3, as it introduces some of the statistical concepts that we will need many times in the rest of the book.

1 Introduction

"It is a capital mistake to theorize before one has data.
Insensibly, one begins to twist the facts to suit theories, instead of theories to suit facts."

— Sherlock Holmes

What do you need?

- A general understanding of computer and data systems.
- A basic understanding of how smartphones and other day-to-day life devices work.

What will you learn?

- Definitions and notions of data science.
- How data science is related to other disciplines.
- Computation thinking – a way to solve problems systematically.
- What skills data scientists need.

1.1 What Is Data Science?

Sherlock Holmes would have loved living in the twenty-first century. We are drenched in **data**, and so many of our problems (including a murder mystery) can be solved using large amounts of data existing at personal and societal levels.

These days it is fair to assume that most people are familiar with the term "data." We see it everywhere. And if you have a cellphone, then chances are this is something you have encountered frequently. Assuming you are a "connected" person who has a smartphone, you probably have a data plan from your phone service provider. The most common cellphone plans in the USA include unlimited talk and text, and a limited amount of data – 5 GB, 20 GB, etc. And if you have one of these plans, you know well that you are "using data" through your phone and you get charged per usage of that data. You understand that checking your email and posting a picture on a social media platform consumes data. And if you are a curious (or thrifty) sort, you calculate how much data you consume monthly and pick a plan that fits your needs.

You may also have come across terms like "data sharing," when picking a family plan for your phone(s). But there are other places where you may have encountered the notion of data sharing. For instance, if you have concerns about privacy, you may want to know if your cellphone company "shares" data about you with others (including the government).

And finally, you may have heard about "data warehouses," as if data is being kept in big boxes on tall shelves in middle-of-nowhere locations.

In the first case, the individual is consuming data by retrieving email messages and posting pictures. In the second scenario concerning data sharing, "data" refers to information *about* you. And third, data is used as though it represents a physical object that is being stored somewhere. The nature and the size of "data" in these scenarios vary enormously – from personal to institutional, and from a few kilobytes (kB) to several petabytes (PB).

In this book, we will consider these and more scenarios and learn about defining, storing, cleaning, retrieving, and analyzing data – all for the purpose of deriving meaningful insights toward making decisions and solving problems. And we will use systematic, verifiable, and repeatable processes; or in other words, we will apply scientific approaches and techniques. Finally, we will do almost all of these processes with a hands-on approach. That means we will look at data and situations that generate or use data, and we will manipulate data using tools and techniques. But before we begin, let us look at how others describe data science.

FYI: Datum, Data, and Science

Webster's dictionary (https://www.merriam-webster.com/dictionary/datum) defines *data* as a plural form of *datum* as "something given or admitted especially as a basis for reasoning or inference." For the purpose of this book, as is common these days, we will use *data* for both plural and singular forms. For example, imagine a table containing birthdays of everyone in your class or office. We can consider this whole table (a collection of birthdays) as data. Each birthday is a single point of data, which could be called *datum*, but we will call that *data* too.

There is also often a debate about what is the difference between *data* and *information.* In fact, it is common to use one to define the other (e.g., "data is a piece of information"). We will revisit this later in this chapter when we compare data science and information science.

Since we are talking about sciences, it is also important to clarify here what exactly is *science*. According to the Oxford dictionary (https://en.oxforddictionaries.com/definition/science), science is "systematic study of the structure and behaviour of the physical and natural world through observation and experiment." When we talk about science, we are interested in using a systematic approach that can allow us to study a phenomenon, often giving us the ability to explain and derive meaningful insights.

Frank Lo, the Director of Data Science at Wayfair, says this on datajobs.com: "Data science is a multidisciplinary blend of data inference, algorithm development, and technology in order to solve analytically complex problems."[1] He goes on to elaborate that data science, at its core, involves uncovering insights from mining data. This happens through exploration of the data using various tools and techniques, testing hypotheses, and creating conclusions with data and analyses as evidence.

In one famous article, Davenport and Patil[2] called data science "the sexiest job of the twenty-first century." Listing data-driven companies such as (in alphabetical order) Amazon, eBay, Google, LinkedIn, Microsoft, Twitter, and Walmart, the authors see a data scientist as a hybrid of data hacker, analyst, communicator, and trusted adviser; a Sherlock Holmes for the twenty-first century. As data scientists face technical limitations and make discoveries to address these problems, they communicate what they have learned and suggest implications for new business directions. They also need to be creative in visually displaying information, and clearly and compellingly showing the patterns they find. One of the data scientist's most important roles in the field is to advise executives and managers on the implications of the data for their products, services, processes, and decisions.

In this book, we will consider **data science** as a field of study and practice that involves the collection, storage, and processing of data in order to derive important insights into a problem or a phenomenon. Such data may be generated by humans (surveys, logs, etc.) or machines (weather data, road vision, etc.), and could be in different formats (text, audio, video, augmented or virtual reality, etc.). We will also treat data science as an independent field by itself rather than a subset of another domain, such as statistics or computer science. This will become clearer as we look at how data science relates to and differs from various fields and disciplines later in this chapter.

Why is data science so important now? Dr. Tara Sinclair, the chief economist at indeed.com since 2013, said, "the number of job postings for 'data scientist' grew 57%" year-over-year in the first quarter of 2015.[3] Why have both industry and academia recently increased their demand for data science and data scientists? What changed within the past several years? The answer is not surprising: we have a lot of data, we continue to generate a staggering amount of data at an unprecedented and ever-increasing speed, analyzing data wisely necessitates the involvement of competent and well-trained practitioners, and analyzing such data can provide actionable insights.

The "3V model" attempts to lay this out in a simple (and catchy) way. These are the three Vs:

1. Velocity: The speed at which data is accumulated.
2. Volume: The size and scope of the data.
3. Variety: The massive array of data and types (structured and unstructured).

Each of these three Vs regarding data has dramatically increased in recent years. Specifically, the increasing volume of heterogeneous and unstructured (text, images, and video) data, as well as the possibilities emerging from their analysis, renders data science ever more essential. Figure 1.1[4] shows the expected volumes of data to reach 40 zettabytes (ZB) by the end of 2020, which is a 50-fold increase in volume than what was available at the beginning of 2010. How much is that really? If your computer has 1 terabytes (TB) hard drive (roughly 1000 GB), 40 ZB is 40 billion times that. To provide a different perspective, the world population is projected to be close to 8 billion by the end of 2020, which means, if we think about data per person, each individual in the world (even the newborns) will have 5 TB of data.

1.2 Where Do We See Data Science?

The question should be: Where do we not see data science these days? The great thing about data science is that it is not limited to one facet of society, one domain, or one department of a university; it is virtually everywhere. Let us look at a few examples.

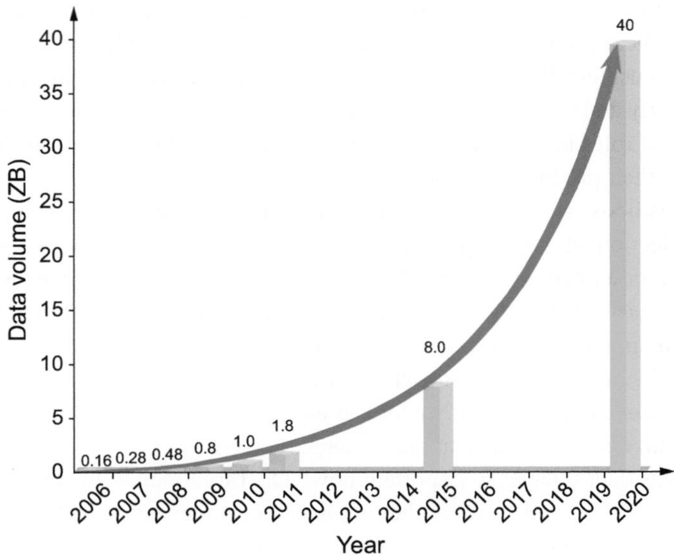

Figure 1.1 Increase of data volume in last 15 years. (Source: IDC's Digital Universe Study, December 2012.[5])

1.2.1 Finance

There has been an explosion in the velocity, variety, and volume (that is, the 3Vs) of financial data, just as there has been an exponential growth of data in almost most fields, as we saw in the previous section. Social media activity, mobile interactions, server logs, real-time market feeds, customer service records, transaction details, and information from existing databases combine to create a rich and complex conglomeration of information that experts (*cough, cough*, data scientists!) must tackle.

What do financial data scientists do? Through capturing and analyzing new sources of data, building predictive models and running real-time simulations of market events, they help the finance industry obtain the information necessary to make accurate predictions.

Data scientists in the financial sector may also partake in fraud detection and risk reduction. Essentially, banks and other loan sanctioning institutions collect a lot of data about the borrower in the initial "paperwork" process. Data science practices can minimize the chance of loan defaults via information such as customer profiling, past expenditures, and other essential variables that can be used to analyze the probabilities of risk and default. Data science initiatives even help bankers analyze a customer's purchasing power to more effectively try to sell additional banking products.[6] Still not convinced about the importance of data science in finance? Look no further than your credit history, one of the most popular types of risk management services used by banks and other financial institutions to identify the creditworthiness of potential customers. Companies use machine learning algorithms in analyzing past spending behavior and patterns to decide the creditworthiness of customers. The credit score, along with other factors, including length of credit history and customer's age, are in turn used to predict the approximate lending amount that can be safely forwarded to the customer when applying for a new credit card or bank loan.

Let us look at a more definitive example. Lending Club is one of the world's largest online marketplaces that connects borrowers with investors. An inevitable outcome of lending that every lender would like to avoid is default by borrowers. A potential solution to this problem is to build a predictive model from the previous loan dataset that can be used to identify the applicants who are relatively risky for a loan. Lending Club hosts its loan dataset in its data repository (https://www.lendingclub.com/info/download-data.action) and can be obtained from other popular third-party data repositories[7] as well. There are various algorithms and approaches that can be applied to create such predictive models. A simple approach of creating such a predictive model from Lending Club loan dataset is demonstrated at KDnuggets[8] if you are interested in learning more.

1.2.2 Public Policy

Simply put, public policy is the application of policies, regulations, and laws to the problems of society through the actions of government and agencies for the good of a citizenry. Many branches of social sciences (economics, political science, sociology, etc.) are foundational to the creation of public policy.

Data science helps governments and agencies gain insights into citizen behaviors that affect the quality of public life, including traffic, public transportation, social welfare, community wellbeing, etc. This information, or data, can be used to develop plans that address the betterment of these areas.

It has become easier than ever to obtain useful data about policies and regulations to analyze and create insights. The following open data repositories are examples:

(1) US government (https://www.data.gov/)
(2) City of Chicago (https://data.cityofchicago.org/)
(3) New York City (https://nycopendata.socrata.com/)

As of this writing, the data.gov site had more than 200,000 data repositories on diverse topics that anyone can browse, from agriculture to local government, to science and research. The City of Chicago portal offers a data catalog with equally diverse topics, organized in 16 categories, including administration and finance, historic preservation, and sanitation. NYC OpenData encompasses datasets organized into 10 categories. Clicking on the category City Government, for instance, brings up 495 individual results. NYC OpenData also organizes its data by city agency, of which 94 are listed, from the Administration for Children's Services to the Teachers Retirement System. The data is available to all interested parties.

A good example of using data to analyze and improve public policy decisions is the Data Science for Social Good project, where various institutions including Nova SBE, Municipality of Cascais, and the University of Chicago will participate in the program for three months, and which will bring together 25 data analytics experts from several countries who will be working on using the open public policy dataset to find clues to solve relevant problems with impact on society, such as: how does an NGO use data to estimate the size of a temporary refugee camp in war zones to organize the provision of help, how to successfully develop and maintain systems that use data to produce social good and inform public policy, etc. The project usually organizes new events in June of every year.[9]

1.2.3 Politics

Politics is a broad term for the process of electing officials who exercise the policies that govern a state. It includes the process of getting policies enacted and the action of the officials wielding the power to do so. Much of the financial support of government is derived from taxes.

Recently, the real-time application of data science to politics has skyrocketed. For instance, data scientists analyzed former US President Obama's 2008 presidential campaign success with Internet-based campaign efforts.[10] In this *New York Times* article, the writer quotes Ariana Huffington, editor of *The Huffington Post*, as saying that, without the Internet, Obama would not have been president.

Data scientists have been quite successful in constructing the most accurate voter targeting models and increasing voter participation.[11] In 2016, the campaign to elect Donald Trump was a brilliant example of the use of data science in social media to tailor individual messages to individual people. As Twitter has emerged as a major digital PR tool for politics over the last decade, studies[12] analyzing the content of tweets from both candidates' (Trump and Hillary Clinton) Twitter handles as well as the content of their websites found significant difference in the emphasis on traits and issues, main content of tweet, main source of retweet, multimedia use, and the level of civility. While Clinton emphasized her masculine traits and feminine issues in her election campaign more than her feminine traits and masculine issues, Trump focused more to masculine issues, paying no particular attention to his traits. Additionally, Trump used user-generated content as sources of his tweets significantly more often than Clinton. Three-quarters of Clinton's tweets were original content, in comparison to half of Trump's tweets, which were retweets of and replies to citizens. Extracting such characteristics from data and connecting them to various outcomes (e.g., public engagement) falls squarely under data science. In fact, later in this book we will have hands-on exercises for collecting and analyzing data from Twitter, including extracting sentiments expressed in those tweets.

Of course, we have also seen the dark side of this with the infamous Cambridge Analytica data scandal that surfaced in March 2018.[13] This data analytics firm obtained data on approximately 87 million Facebook users from an academic researcher in order to target political ads during the 2016 US presidential campaign. While this case brought to public attention the issue of privacy in data, it was hardly the first one. Over the years, we have witnessed many incidents of advertisers, spammers, and cybercriminals using data, obtained legally or illegally, for pushing an agenda or a rhetoric. We will have more discussion about this later when we talk about ethics, bias, and privacy issues.

1.2.4 Healthcare

Healthcare is another area in which data scientists keep changing their research approach and practices.[14] Though the medical industry has always stored data (e.g., clinical studies, insurance information, hospital records), the healthcare industry is now awash in an unprecedented amount of information. This includes biological data such as gene expression, next-generation DNA sequence data, proteomics (study of proteins), and metabolomics (chemical "fingerprints" of cellular processes).

While diagnostics and disease prevention studies may seem limited, we may see data from or about a much larger population with respect to clinical data and health outcomes data contained in ever more prevalent electronic health records (EHRs), as well as in longitudinal drug and medical claims. With the tools and techniques available today, data scientists can work on massive datasets effectively, combining data from clinical trials with direct observations by practicing physicians. The combination of raw data with necessary resources opens the door for healthcare professionals to better focus on important, patient-centered medical quandaries, such as what treatments work and for whom.

The role of data science in healthcare does not stop with big health service providers; it has also revolutionized personal health management in the last decade. Personal wearable health trackers, such as Fitbit, are prime examples of the application of data science in the personal health space. Due to advances in miniaturizing technology, we can now collect most of the data generated by a human body through such trackers, including information about heart rate, blood glucose, sleep patterns, stress levels and even brain activity. Equipped with a wealth of health data, doctors and scientists are pushing the boundaries in health monitoring.

Since the rise of personal wearable devices, there has been an incredible amount of research that leverages such devices to study personal health management space. Health trackers and other wearable devices provide the opportunity for investigators to track adherence to physical activity goals with reasonable accuracy across weeks or even months, which was almost impossible when relying on a handful of self-reports or a small number of accelerometry wear periods. A good example of such study is the use of wearable sensors to measure adherence to a physical activity intervention among overweight or obese, postmenopausal women,[15] which was conducted over a period of 16 weeks. The study found that using activity-measuring trackers, such as those by Fitbit, high levels of self-monitoring were sustained over a long period. Often, even being aware of one's level of physical activities could be instrumental in supporting or sustaining good behaviors.

Apple has partnered with Stanford Medicine[16] to collect and analyze data from Apple Watch to identify irregular heart rhythms, including those from potentially serious heart conditions such as atrial fibrillation, which is a leading cause of stroke. Many insurance companies have started providing free or discounted Apple Watch devices to their clients, or have reward programs for those who use such devices in their daily life.[17] The data collected through such devices are helping clients, patients, and healthcare providers to better monitor, diagnose, and treat health conditions not possible before.

1.2.5 Urban Planning

Many scientists and engineers have come to believe that the field of urban planning is ripe for a significant – and possibly disruptive – change in approach as a result of the new methods of data science. This belief is based on the number of new initiatives in "informatics" – the acquisition, integration, and analysis of data to understand and improve urban systems and quality of life.

The Urban Center for Computation and Data (UrbanCCD), at the University of Chicago, traffics in such initiatives. The research center is using advanced computational methods to understand the rapid growth of cities. The center brings together scholars and scientists from the University of Chicago and Argonne National Laboratory[18] with architects, city planners, and many others.

The UrbanCCD's director, Charlie Catlett, stresses that global cities are growing quickly enough to outpace traditional tools and methods of urban design and operation. "The consequences," he writes on the center's website,[19] "are seen in inefficient transportation networks belching greenhouse gases and unplanned city-scale slums with crippling poverty and health challenges. There is an urgent need to apply advanced computational methods and resources to both explore and anticipate the impact of urban expansion and find effective policies and interventions."

On a smaller scale, chicagoshovels.org provides a "Plow Tracker" so residents can track the city's 300 snow plows in real time. The site uses online tools to help organize a "Snow Corps" – essentially neighbors helping neighbors, like seniors or the disabled – to shovel sidewalks and walkways. The platform's app lets travelers know when the next bus is arriving. Considering Chicago's frigid winters, this can be an important service. Similarly, Boston's Office of New Urban Mechanics created a SnowCOP app to help city managers respond to requests for help during snowstorms. The Office has more than 20 apps designed to improve public services, such as apps that mine data from residents' mobile phones to address infrastructure projects. But it is not just large cities. Jackson, Michigan, with a population of about 32,000, tracks water usage to identify potentially abandoned homes. The list of uses and potential uses is extensive.

1.2.6 Education

According to Joel Klein, former Chancellor of New York Public Schools, "when it comes to the intersection of education and technology, simply putting a computer in front of a student, or a child, doesn't make their lives any easier, or education any better."[20] Technology will definitely have a large part to play in the future of education, but how exactly that happens is still an open question. There is a growing realization among educators and technology evangelists that we are heading toward more data-driven and personalized use of technology in education. And some of that is already happening.

The Brookings Institution's Darrell M. West opened his 2012 report on big data and education by comparing present and future "learning environments." According to West, today's students improve their reading skills by reading short stories, taking a test every other week, and receiving graded papers from teachers. But in the future, West postulates that students will learn to read through "a computerized software program," the computer constantly measuring and collecting data, linking to websites providing further assistance, and giving the student instant feedback. "At the end of the session," West says, "his teacher will receive an automated readout on [students in the class] summarizing their reading time, vocabulary knowledge, reading comprehension, and use of supplemental electronic resources."[21]

So, in essence, teachers of the future will be data scientists!

Big data may be able to provide much-needed resources to various educational structures. Data collection and analysis have the potential to improve the overall state of education. West says, "So-called 'big data' make it possible to mine learning information for insights regarding student performance and learning approaches. Rather than rely on periodic test performance, instructors can analyze what students know and what techniques are most effective for each pupil. By focusing on data analytics, teachers can study learning in far more nuanced ways. Online tools enable evaluation of a much wider range of student actions, such as how long they devote to readings, where they get electronic resources, and how quickly they master key concepts."

1.2.7 Libraries

Data science is also frequently applied to libraries. Jeffrey M. Stanton has discussed the overlap between the task of a data science professional and that of a librarian. In his article, he concludes, "In the near future, the ability to fulfill the roles of citizenship will require finding, joining, examining, analyzing, and understanding diverse sources of data [...] Who but a librarian will stand ready to give the assistance needed, to make the resources accessible, and to provide a venue for knowledge creation when the community advocate arrives seeking answers?"[22]

Mark Bieraugel echoes this view in his article on the website of the Association of College and Research Libraries.[23] Here, Bieraugel advocates for librarians to create taxonomies, design metadata schemes, and systematize retrieval methods to make big datasets more useful. Even though the role of data science in future libraries as suggested here seems too rosy to be true, in reality it is nearer than you think. Imagine that Alice, a scientist conducting research on diabetes, asks Mark, a research librarian, to help her understand the research gap in previous literature. Armed with the digital technologies, Mark can automate literature reviews for any discipline by reducing ideas and results from thousands of articles into a cohesive bulleted list and then apply data science algorithms, such as network analysis, to visualize trends in emerging lines of research on similar topics. This will make Alice's job far easier than if she had to painstakingly read all the articles.

1.3 How Does Data Science Relate to Other Fields?

While data science has emerged as a field in its own right, as we saw before it is often considered a subdiscipline of a field such as statistics. One could certainly study data science as a part of one of the existing, well-established fields. But, given the nature of data-driven problems and the momentum at which data science has been able to tackle them, a separate slot is warranted for data science – one that is different from those well-established fields, and yet connected to them. Let us look at how data science is similar to and different from other fields.

1.3.1 Data Science and Statistics

Priceonomics (a San Francisco-based company that claims to "turn data into stories") notes that, not long ago, the term "data science" meant nothing to most people, not even to those who actually worked with data.[24] A common response to the term was: "Isn't that just statistics?"

Nate Silver does not seem to think data science differs from statistics. The well-known number cruncher behind the media site FiveThirtyEight – and the guy who famously and correctly predicted the electoral outcome of 49 of 50 states in the 2008 US Presidential election, and a perfect 50 for 50 in 2012 – is more than a bit skeptical of the term. However, the performance of his 2016 election prediction model was a dud. The model predicted Democrat-nominee Hillary Clinton's chance of winning the presidency at 71.4% over Republican-nominee Donald Trump's 28.6%.[25] The only silver lining in his 2016 prediction was that it gave Trump a higher chance of winning the electoral college than almost anyone else.[26]

"I think data-scientist is a sexed up term for a statistician," Silver told an audience of statisticians in 2013 at the Joint Statistical Meeting.[27]

The difference between these two closely related fields lies in the invention and advancements of modern computers. Statistics was primarily developed to help people deal with pre-computer "data problems," such as testing the impact of fertilizer in agriculture, or figuring out the accuracy of an estimate from a small sample. Data science emphasizes the data problems of the twenty-first century, such as accessing information from large databases, writing computer code to manipulate data, and visualizing data.

Andrew Gelman, a statistician at Columbia University, writes that it is "fair to consider statistics … as a subset of data science" and probably the "least important" aspect.[28] He suggests that the administrative aspects of dealing with data, such as harvesting, processing, storing, and cleaning, are more central to data science than is hard-core statistics.

So, how does the knowledge of these fields blend together? Statistician and data visualizer Nathan Yau of Flowing Data suggests that data scientists should have at least three basic skills:[29]

1. A strong knowledge of basic statistics (see Chapter 3) and machine learning (see Chapters 8–10) – or at least enough to avoid misinterpreting correlation for causation or extrapolating too much from a small sample size.
2. The computer science skills to take an unruly dataset and use a programming language (like R or Python, see Chapters 5 and 6) to make it easy to analyze.
3. The ability to visualize and express their data and analysis in a way that is meaningful to somebody less conversant in data (see Chapters 2 and 11).

As you can see, this book that you are holding has you covered for most, if not all, of these basic skills (and then some) for data science.

1.3.2 Data Science and Computer Science

Perhaps this seems like an obvious application of data science, but computer science involves a number of current and burgeoning initiatives that involve data scientists. Computer scientists have developed numerous techniques and methods, such as (1) database (DB) systems that can handle the increasing volume of data in both structured and unstructured formats, expediting data analysis; (2) visualization techniques that help people make sense of data; and (3) algorithms that make it possible to compute complex and heterogeneous data in less time.

In truth, data science and computer science overlap and are mutually supportive. Some of the algorithms and techniques developed in the computer science field – such as machine learning algorithms, pattern recognition algorithms, and data visualization techniques – have contributed to the data science discipline.

Machine learning is certainly a very crucial part of data science today, and it is hard to do meaningful data science in most domains without at least basic knowledge of machine learning. Fortunately for us, the third part of this book is dedicated to machine learning. While we will not go into so much theoretical depth as a computer scientist would, we are going to see many of the popular and useful machine learning algorithms and techniques applied to various data science problems.

1.3.3 Data Science and Engineering

Broadly speaking, engineering in various fields (chemical, civil, computer, mechanical, etc.) has created demand for data scientists and data science methods.

Engineers constantly need data to solve problems. Data scientists have been called upon to develop methods and techniques to meet these needs. Likewise, engineers have assisted data scientists. Data science has benefitted from new software and hardware developed via engineering, such as the CPU (central processing unit) and GPU (graphic processing unit) that substantially reduce computing time.

Take the example of jobs in civil engineering. The trend has drastically changed in the construction industry due to use of technology in the last few decades. Now it is possible to use "smart" building techniques that are rooted in collecting and analyzing large amounts of heterogeneous data. Thanks to predictive algorithms, it has become possible to estimate the likely cost of construction from the unit price for a specific item, like a guardrail, that contractors are likely to bid given a contractor's location, time of year, total value, relevant cost indices, etc.

In addition, "smart" building techniques have been introduced by use of various technologies. From 3D printing of models that can help predict the weak spots in construction, to use of drones in monitoring the building site during the actual construction phase, all these technologies generate volumes of data that need to be analyzed to engineer the construction design and activity. Thus, through increase in the use of technology for any engineering design and applications, it is inevitable that the role of data science will expand in the future.

1.3.4 Data Science and Business Analytics

In general, we can say that the main goal of "doing business" is turning a profit – even with limited resources – through efficient and sustainable manufacturing methods, and effective service models, etc. This demands decision-making based on objective evaluation, for which data analysis is essential.

Whether it concerns companies or customers, data related to business is increasingly cheap (easy to obtain, store, and process) and ubiquitous. In addition to the traditional types of data, which are now being digitized through automated procedures, new types of data from mobile devices, wearable sensors, and embedded systems are providing businesses with rich information. New technologies have emerged that seek to help us organize and understand this increasing volume of data. These technologies are employed in business analytics.

Business analytics (BA) refers to the skills, technologies, and practices for continuous iterative exploration and investigation of past and current business performance to gain insight and be strategic. BA focuses on developing new perspectives and making sense of performance based on data and statistics. And that is where data science comes in. To fulfill the requirements of BA, data scientists are needed for statistical analysis, including explanatory and predictive modeling and fact-based management, to help drive successful decision-making.

There are four types of analytics, each of which holds opportunities for data scientists in business analytics:[30]

1. Decision analytics: supports decision-making with visual analytics that reflect reasoning.
2. Descriptive analytics: provides insight from historical data with reporting, score cards, clustering, etc.
3. Predictive analytics: employs predictive modeling using statistical and machine learning techniques.
4. Prescriptive analytics: recommends decisions using optimization, simulation, etc.

We will revisit these in Chapter 3.

1.3.5 Data Science, Social Science, and Computational Social Science

It may sound weird that social science, which began almost four centuries ago and was primarily concerned with society and relationships among individuals, has anything to do with data science. Enter the twenty-first century, and not only is data science helping social science, but it is also shaping it, even creating a new branch called computational social science.

Since its inception, social science has spread into many branches, including but not limited to anthropology, archaeology, economics, linguistics, political science, psychology, public health, and sociology. Each of these branches has established its own standards, procedures, and modes of collecting data over the years. But connecting theories or results from one discipline to another has become increasingly difficult. This is where computational social science has revolutionized social science research in the last few decades. With the help of data science, computational social science has connected results from multiple disciplines to explore the key urgent question: how will the information revolution in this digital age transform society?

Since its inception, computational social science has made tremendous strides in generating arrays of interdisciplinary projects, often in partnership with computer scientists, statisticians, mathematicians, and lately with data scientists. Some of these projects include leveraging tools and algorithms of prediction and machine learning to assist in tackling stubborn policy problems. Others entail applying recent advances in image, text, and speech recognition to classic issues in social science. These projects often demand methodological breakthroughs, scaling proven methods to new levels, as well as designing new metrics and interfaces to make research findings intelligible to scholars, administrators, and policy-makers who may lack computational skill but have domain expertise.

After reading the above paragraph, if you think computational social science has only borrowed from data science but has nothing to return, you would be wrong. Computational social science raises inevitable questions about the politics and ethics often embedded in data science research, particularly when it is based on sociopolitical problems with real-life applications that have far-reaching consequences. Government policies, people's mandates in elections, and hiring strategies in the private sector, are prime examples of such applications.

1.4 The Relationship between Data Science and Information Science

While this book is broad enough to be useful for anyone interested in data science, some aspects are targeted at people interested in or working in information-intensive domains. These include many contemporary jobs that are known as "knowledge work," such as those in healthcare, pharmaceuticals, finance, policy-making, education, and intelligence. The field of **information science**, which often stems from computing, computational science, informatics, information technology, or library science, often represents and serves such application areas. The core idea here is to cover people studying, accessing, using, and producing information in various contexts. Let us think about how data science and information science are related.

Data is everywhere. Yes, this is the third time I am stating this in this chapter, but this point is that important. Humans and machines are constantly creating new data. Just as natural science focuses on understanding the characteristics and laws that govern natural phenomena, data scientists are interested in investigating the characteristics of data – looking for patterns that reveal how people and society can benefit from data. That perspective often misses the processes and people behind the data, as most researchers and professionals see data from the system side and subsequently focus on quantifying phenomena; they lack an understanding of the users' perspective. Information scientists, who look at data in the *context* they are generated and used, can play an important role that bridges the gap between quantitative analysis and an examination of data that tells a story.

1.4.1 Information vs. Data

In an FYI box earlier, we alluded to some connections and differences between **data** and **information**. Depending on who you consult, you will get different answers – from seeming differences to a blurred-out line between data and information. To make matters worse, people often use one to mean the other. A traditional view used to be that data is something raw, meaningless, an object that, when analyzed or converted to a *useful* form, becomes information. Information is also defined as "data that are endowed with meaning and purpose."[31]

For example, the number "480,000" is a data point. But when we add an explanation that it represents the number of deaths per year in the USA from cigarette smoking,[32] it becomes information. But in many real-world scenarios, the distinction between a *meaningful* and a *meaningless* data point is not clear enough for us to differentiate *data* and *information.* And therefore, for the purpose of this book, we will not worry about drawing such a line. At the same time, since we are introducing various concepts in this chapter, it is useful for us to at least consider how they are defined in various conceptual frameworks.

Let us take one such example. The Data, Information, Knowledge, and Wisdom (DIKW) model differentiates the meaning of each concept and suggests a hierarchical system among them.[33] Although various authors and scholars offer several interpretations of this model, the model defines *data* as (1) fact, (2) signal, and (3) symbol. Here, information is differentiated from data in that it is "useful." Unlike conceptions of *data* in other disciplines, information science demands and presumes a thorough understanding of information, considering different contexts and circumstances related to the data that is created, generated, and shared, mostly by human beings.

1.4.2 Users in Information Science

Studies in information science have focused on the human side of data and information, in addition to the system perspective. While the system perspective typically supports users' ability to observe, analyze, and interpret the data, the former allows them to make the data into useful information for their purposes. Different users may not agree on a piece of information's relevancy depending on various factors that affect judgment, such as "usefulness."[34] Usefulness is a criterion that determines how useful is the interaction between the user and the information object (data) in accomplishing the task or goal of the user. For example, a general user who wants to figure out if drinking coffee is injurious to health may find information in the search engine result pages (SERP) to be useful, whereas a dietitian who needs to decide if it is OK to recommend a patient to consume coffee may find the same result in SERP worthless. Therefore, operationalization of the criterion of usefulness will be specific to the user's task.

Scholars in information science tend to combine the user side and the system side to understand how and why data is generated and the information they convey, given a context. This is often then connected to studying people's behaviors. For instance, information scientists may collect log data of one's browser activities to understand one's search behaviors (the search terms they use, the results they click, the amount of time they spend on various sites, etc.). This could allow them to create better methods for personalization and recommendation.

1.4.3 Data Science in Information Schools (iSchools)

There are several advantages to studying data science in information schools, or iSchools. Data science provides students a more nuanced understanding of individual, community, and society-wide phenomena. Students may, for instance, apply data collected from a particular community to enhance that locale's wellbeing through policy change and/or urban planning. Essentially, an iSchool curriculum helps students acquire diverse perspectives on data and information. This becomes an advantage as students transition into full-fledged data scientists with a grasp on the big (data) picture. In addition to all the required data science skills and knowledge (including understanding computer science, statistics, machine learning, etc.), the focus on the human factor gives students distinct opportunities.

An iSchool curriculum also provides a depth of contextual understanding of information. Studying data science in an iSchool offers unique chances to understand data in contexts including communications, information studies, library science, and media research. The difference between studying data science in an iSchool, as opposed to within a computer science or statistics program, is that the former tends to focus on analyzing data and extracting insightful information grounded in *context*. This is why the study of "where information comes from" is as equally important as "what it represents," and "how it can be turned into a valuable resource in the creation of business and information technology strategies." For instance, in the case of analyzing electronic health records, researchers at iSchools are additionally interested in investigating how corresponding patients perceive and seek health-related information and support from both professionals and peers. In short, if you are interested in combining the technical with the practical, as well as the human, you would be right at home in an iSchool's data science department.

1.5 Computational Thinking

Many skills are considered "basic" for everyone. These include reading, writing, and thinking. It does not matter what gender, profession, or discipline one belongs to; one should have all these abilities. In today's world, **computational thinking** is becoming an essential skill, not reserved for computer scientists only.

What is computational thinking? Typically, it means thinking like a computer scientist. But that is not very helpful, even to computer scientists! According to Jeannette Wing,[35] "Computational thinking is using abstraction and decomposition when attacking a large complex task or designing a large complex system" (p. 33). It is an iterative process based on the following three stages:

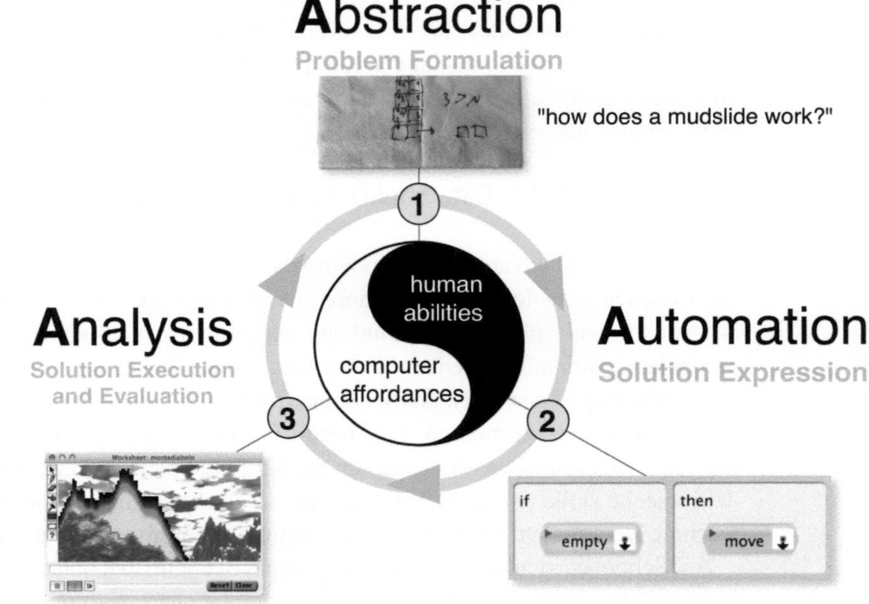

Figure 1.2 Three-stage process describing computational thinking. From Repenning, A., Basawapatna, A., & Escherle, N. (2016). Computational thinking tools. In *2016 IEEE Symposium on Visual Languages and Human-Centric Computing (VL/HCC)* (pp. 218–222), September.

1. Problem formulation (abstraction)
2. Solution expression (automation)
3. Solution execution and evaluation (analyses).

The three stages and the relationship between them are schematically illustrated in Figure 1.2.

Hands-On Example 1.1: Computational Thinking

Let us consider an example. We are given the following numbers and are tasked with finding the largest of them: 7, 24, 62, 11, 4, 39, 42, 5, 97, 54. Perhaps you can do it just by looking at it. But let us try doing it "systematically."

Rather than looking at all the numbers at the same time, let us look at two at a time. So, the first two numbers are 7 and 24. Pick the larger of them, which is 24. Now we take that and look at the next number. It is 62. Is it larger than 24? Yes, which means, as of now, 62 is our largest number. The next number is 11. Is it larger than the largest number we know so far, that is, 62? No. So we move on.

If you continue this process until you have seen all the remaining numbers, you will end up with 97 as the largest. And that is our answer.

What did we just do? We broke down a complex problem (looking through 10 numbers) into a set of small problems (comparing two numbers at a time). This process is called *decomposition*, which refers to identifying small steps to solve a large problem.

More than that, we derived a process that could be applied to not just 10 numbers (which is not that complex), but to 100 numbers, 1000 numbers, or a billion numbers! This is called *abstraction* and *generalization*. Here, *abstraction* refers to treating the actual object of interest (10 numbers) as a series of numbers, and *generalization* refers to being able to devise a process that is applicable to the abstracted quantity (a series of numbers) and not just the specific objects (the given 10 numbers).

And there you have an example of computational thinking. We approached a problem to find a solution using a systematic process that can be expressed using clear, feasible computational steps. And that is all. You do not need to know any programming language to do this. Sure, you could write a computer program to carry out this process (an algorithm). But here, our focus is on the thinking behind this.

Let us take one more step with the previous example. Assume you are interested not just in the largest number, but also the second largest, third largest, and so on. One way to do this is to sort the numbers in some (increasing or decreasing) order. It looks easy when you have such a small set of numbers. But imagine you have a huge unsorted shelf of books that you want to alphabetize. Not only is this a tougher problem than the previous one, but it becomes increasingly challenging as the number of items increases. So, let us step back and try to think of a systematic approach.

A natural way to solve the problem would be just to scan the shelf and look for out-of-order pairs, for instance Rowling, J. K., followed by Lee, Stan, and flipping them around. Flip out-of-order pairs, then continue your scan of the rest of the shelf, and start again at the beginning of the shelf each time you reach the end until you make a complete pass without finding a single out-of-order pair on the entire shelf. That will get your job done. But depending on the size of your collection and how unordered the books are at the beginning of the process, it will take a lot of time. It is not a very efficient tactic.

Here is an alternative approach. Let us pick any book at random, say Lee, Stan, and reorder the shelf so that all the books that are earlier (letters to the left of "L" in the dictionary, A–K) than Lee, Stan, are on the left-hand side of it, and the later ones (M–Z) are on the right. At the end of this step, the Lee, Stan, is in its final position, probably near the middle. Next you perform the same steps to the subshelf of the books on the left, and separately to the subshelf of books on the right. Continue this effort until every book is in its final position, and thus the shelf is sorted.

Now you might be wondering, what is the easiest way to sort the subshelves? Let us take the same set of numbers from the last example and see how it works. Assume that you have picked the first number, 7, as the chosen one. So, you want all the numbers that are smaller than 7 on the left-hand side of it and the larger ones on the right. You can start by assuming 7 is the lowest number in the queue and therefore its final position will be first, in its current position. Now you compare the rest of the numbers with 7 and adjust its position accordingly. Let us start at the beginning. You have 24 at the beginning of the rest, which is larger than 7. Therefore, the tentative position of 7 remains at the beginning. Next, is 62, which is, again, larger than 7, therefore, no change in the tentative position of 7. Same for the next number, 11. Next, the comparison is between 4 and 7. Unlike the previous three numbers, 4 is smaller than 7. Here, your assumption of 7 as the smallest number in the queue is rendered incorrect. So, you need to readjust your assumption of 7 from smallest to second smallest.

Here is how to perform the readjustment. First, you have to switch the place of 4 and the number in second position, 24. As a result the queue becomes 7, 4, 62, 11, 24, 39, 42, 5, 97, 54. And the tentative position of 7 has shifted to the second position, right after 4, making the queue 4, 7, 62, 11, 24, 39, 42, 5, 97, 54.

Now you might be thinking, why not swap between 7 and 4 instead of 24 and 4. The reason is that you started with the assumption that 7 is the smallest number in the queue. And so far during comparisons you have found just one violation of the assumption; that is, with 4. Therefore, it is logical that at the end of the current comparison you will adjust your assumption to 7 as the second smallest element and 4 as the smallest one, which is reflected by the current queue.

Moving on with comparisons, the next numbers in the queue are 39 and 42, both of them are larger than 7, and thus no change in our assumption. The next number is 5, which is, again, smaller than 7. So, you follow the same drill as you did with 4. Swap the third element of the queue with 5 to readjust your assumption as 7 as the third smallest element in the queue and continue the process until you reach the end of the queue. At the end of this step, your queue is transformed into 4, 5, 7, 11, 24, 39, 42, 62, 97, 54, and the initial assumption has evolved, as now 7 is the third smallest number in the queue. So now, 7 has been placed in its final position. Notice that, all the elements to the left (4, 5) of 7 are smaller than 7, and the larger ones are on the right.

If you now perform the same set of previous steps with the numbers on the left and separately to the numbers on the right, every number will fall into the right place and you will have a perfectly ordered list of ascending numbers.

Once again, a nice characteristic that all these approaches share is that the process for finding a solution is clear, systematic, and repeatable, regardless of the size of the input (number of numbers or books). That is what makes it computationally feasible.

Now that you have seen these examples, try finding more problems around you and see if you can practice your computational thinking by devising solutions in this manner. Below are some possibilities to get you started.

Try It Yourself 1.1: Computational Thinking

For each of the following problem-solving situations, explain how you apply computational thinking, that is, how you abstract the situation, break the complex problem into small subproblems, and bring together subsolutions to solve the problem.

1. Find a one-hour slot in your schedule when the preceding or following event is not at home.
2. Visit five different places while you are running errands with the least amount of travel time and not crossing any road, sidewalk, or location more than once.

3. Strategize your meetings with potential employers at a job fair so that you can optimize connecting with both high-profile companies (long lines) and startups (short lines).

1.6 Skills for Data Science

By now, hopefully you are convinced that: (1) data science is a flourishing and a fantastic field; (2) it is virtually everywhere; and (3) perhaps you want to pursue it as a career! OK, maybe you are still pondering the last one, but if you are convinced about the first two and still holding this book, you may be at least curious about what you should have in your toolkit to be a data scientist. Let us look at carefully what data scientists are, what they do, and what kinds of skills one may need to make their way in and through this field.

One Twitter quip[36] about data scientists captures their skill set particularly well: "Data Scientist (n.): Person who is better at statistics than any software engineer and better at software engineering than any statistician."

In her *Harvard Business Review* article,[37] noted academic and business executive Jeanne Harris listed some skills that employers expect from data scientists: willing to experiment, proficiency in mathematical reasoning, and data literacy. We will explore these concepts in relation to what business professionals are seeking in a potential candidate and why.

1. ***Willing to Experiment.*** A data scientist needs to have the drive, intuition, and curiosity not only to solve problems as they are presented, but also to identify and articulate problems on her own. Intellectual curiosity and the ability to experiment require an amalgamation of analytical and creative thinking. To explain this from a more technical perspective, employers are seeking applicants who can ask questions to define intelligent hypotheses and to explore the data utilizing basic statistical methods and models. Harris also notes that employers incorporate questions in their application process to determine the degree of curiosity and creative thinking of an applicant – the purpose of these questions is not to elicit a specific correct answer, but to observe the approach and techniques used to discover a possible answer. "Hence, job applicants are often asked questions such as 'How many golf balls would fit in a school bus?' or 'How many sewer covers are there in Manhattan?'."
2. ***Proficiency in Mathematical Reasoning.*** Mathematical and statistical knowledge is the second critical skill for a potential applicant seeking a job in data science. We are not suggesting that you need a Ph.D. in mathematics or statistics, but you do need to have a strong grasp on the basic statistical methods and how to employ them. Employers are seeking applicants who can demonstrate their ability in reasoning, logic, interpreting data, and developing strategies to perform analysis. Harris further notes that,

"interpretation and use of numeric data are going to be increasingly critical in business practices. As a result, an increasing trend in hiring for most companies is to check if applicants are adept at mathematical reasoning."

3. ***Data Literacy.*** Data literacy is the ability to extract meaningful information from a dataset, and any modern business has a collection of data that needs to be interpreted. A skilled data scientist plays an intrinsic role for businesses through an ability to assess a dataset for relevance and suitability for the purpose of interpretation, to perform analysis, and create meaningful visualizations to tell valuable data stories. Harris observes that "data literacy training for business users is now a priority. Managers are being trained to understand which data is suitable, and how to use visualization and simulation to process and interpret it." Data-driven decision-making is a driving force for innovation in business, and data scientists are integral to this process. Data literacy is an important skill, not just for data scientists, but for all. Scholars and educators have started arguing that, similar to the abilities of reading and writing that are essential in any educational program, data literacy is a basic, fundamental skill, and should be taught to all. More on this can be found in the FYI box that follows.

FYI: Data Literacy

People often complain when there was a 10% chance of raining and it starts pouring down. This disappointment stems from their lack of understanding of how data is translated to information. In this case, the data comes from prior observations related to weather. Essentially, if there were 100 days observed before (over probably decades) with the same weather conditions (temperature, humidity, pressure, wind, etc.), it rained 10 of those days. And that is conveyed as 10% chance of rain. When people mistake that information as a binary decision (since there is 90% chance of not raining, it will not rain at all), it is as a result of lack of data literacy.

There are many other day-to-day life incidents that we encounter in which information is conveyed to us based on some data analysis. Some other examples include ads we see when visiting websites, the way political messages are structured, and resource allocation decisions your town makes. Some of these may look questionable and others affect us in subtle ways that we may not comprehend. But most of these could be resolved if only we had a better understanding of how data turns into information.

As we rely more and more on capturing and leveraging large amounts of data for making important decisions that affect every aspect of our lives – from personalized recommendations about what we should buy and who we should date, to self-driving cars and reversing climate change – this issue of data literacy becomes increasingly important. And this is not just for the data scientists, but for everyone who is subjected to such experiences. In fact, in a way, this is more important for everyone other than a data scientist because at least a data scientist will be required to learn this as a part of their training, whereas others may not even realize that they lack such an important skill.

If you are an educator, I strongly encourage you to take these ideas – from this book or from other places – and use your position and power to integrate data literacy in whichever way possible. It does not matter if your students are high-schoolers or graduates, whether they are majoring in biology or political science, they all could use a discussion on data literacy.

In another view, Dave Holtz blogs about specific skill sets desired by various positions to which a data scientist may apply. He lists basic types of data science jobs:[38]

1. ***A Data Scientist Is a Data Analyst Who Lives in San Francisco!*** Holtz notes that, for some companies, a data scientist and a data analyst are synonymous. These roles are typically entry-level and will work with pre-existing tools and applications that require the basics skills to retrieve, wrangle, and visualize data. These digital tools may include MySQL databases and advanced functions within Excel such as pivot tables and basic data visualizations (e.g., line and bar charts). Additionally, the data analyst may perform the analysis of experimental testing results or manage other pre-existing analytical toolboxes such as Google Analytics or Tableau. Holtz further notes that, "jobs such as these are excellent entry-level positions, and may even allow a budding data scientist to try new things and expand their skillset."
2. ***Please Wrangle Our Data!*** Companies will discover that they are drowning in data and need someone to develop a data management system and infrastructure that will house the enormous (and growing) dataset, and create access to perform data retrieval and analysis. "Data engineer" and "data scientist" are the typical job titles you will find associated with this type of required skill set and experience. In these scenarios, a candidate will likely be one of the company's first data hires and thus this person should be able to do the job without significant statistics or machine-learning expertise. A data scientist with a software engineering background might excel at a company like this, where it is more important that they make meaningful data-like contributions to the production code and provide basic insights and analyses. Mentorship opportunities for junior data scientists may be less plentiful at a company like this. As a result, an associate will have great opportunities to shine and grow via trial by fire, but there will be less guidance and a greater risk of flopping or stagnating.
3. ***We Are Data. Data Is Us.*** There are a number of companies for whom their data (or their data analysis platform) *is* their product. These environments offer intense data analysis or machine learning opportunities. Ideal candidates will likely have a formal mathematics, statistics, or physics background and hope to continue down a more academic path. Data scientists at these types of firms would focus more on producing data-driven products than answering operational corporate questions. Companies that fall into this group include consumer-facing organizations with massive amounts of data and companies that offer a data-based service.
4. ***Reasonably Sized Non-Data Companies Who Are Data-Driven.*** This categorizes many modern businesses. This type of role involves joining an established team of other data scientists. The company evaluates data but is not entirely concerned about data. Its data scientists perform analysis, touch production code, visualize data, etc. These companies are either looking for generalists or they are looking to fill a specific niche where they feel their team is lacking, such as data visualization or machine learning. Some of the more important skills when interviewing at these firms are familiarity with tools designed for "big data" (e.g., Hive or Pig), and experience with messy, *real-life* datasets.

These skills are summarized in Figure 1.3.

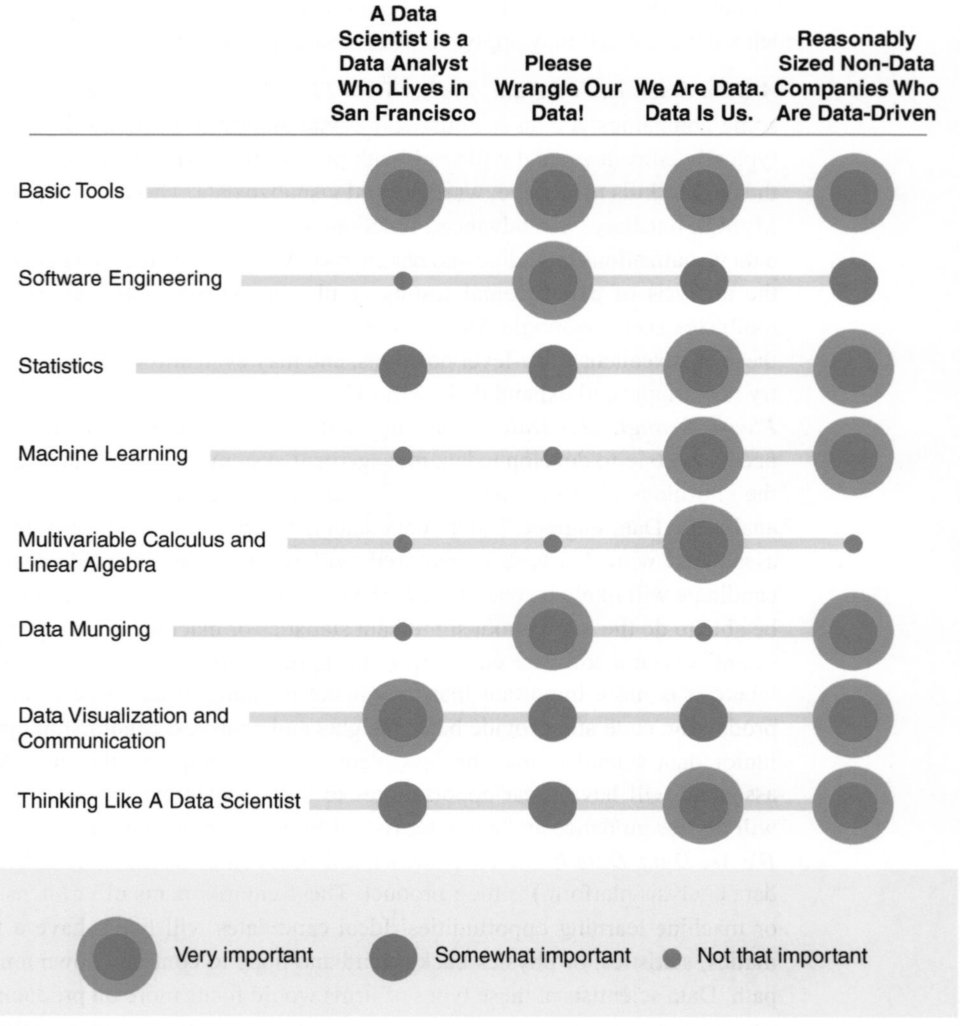

Figure 1.3 Types of data science roles.[39]

Hands-On Example 1.2: Analyzing Data

Although we have not yet covered any theory, techniques, or tools, we can still get a taste of what it is like to work on a data-driven problem.

We will look at an example that gives a glimpse of what kinds of things people do as a data scientist. Specifically, we will start with a data-driven problem, identify a data source, collect data, clean the data, analyze the data, and present our findings. At this point, since I am assuming no prior background in programming, statistics, or data science techniques, we are going to follow a very simple process and walk through an easy example. Eventually, as you develop a stronger technical background and understand the ins and outs of data science methods, you will be able to tackle problems with bigger datasets and more complex analyses.

For this example, we will use the dataset of average heights and weights for American women available from OA 1.1.

This file is in comma-separated values (CSV) format – something that we will revisit in the next chapter. For now, go ahead and download it. Once downloaded, you can open this file in a spreadsheet program such as Microsoft Excel or Google Sheets.

For your reference, this data is also provided in Table 1.1. As you can see, the dataset contains a sample of 15 observations. Let us consider what is present in the dataset. At the first look, it is clear that the data is already sorted – both the height and weight numbers range from small to large. That makes it easier to see the boundaries of this dataset – height ranges from 58 to 72, and weight ranges from 115 to 164.

Next, let us consider averages. We can easily compute average height by adding up the numbers in the "Height" column and dividing by 15 (because that is how many observations we have). That yields a value of 65. In other words, we can conclude that the average height of an American woman is 65 inches, at least according to these 15 observations. Similarly, we can compute the average weight – 136 pounds in this case.

The dataset also reveals that an increase in height correlates with the value of weight. This may be clearer using a visualization. If you know any kind of a spreadsheet program (e.g., Microsoft Excel, Google Sheets), you easily generate a plot of values. Figure 1.4 provides an example. Look at the curve. As we move from left to right (Height), the line increases in value (Weight).

Table 1.1 Average height and weight of American women.

Observation	Height (inches)	Weight (lbs)
1	58	115
2	59	117
3	60	120
4	61	123
5	62	126
6	63	129
7	64	132
8	65	135
9	66	139
10	67	142
11	68	146
12	69	150
13	70	154
14	71	159
15	72	164

Now, let us ask a question: On average, how much increase can we expect in weight with an increase of one inch in height?

Think for a moment how you would address this question.

Do not proceed until you have figured out a solution yourself.

A simple method is to compute the differences in height ($72 - 58 = 14$ inches) and weight ($164 - 115 = 49$ pounds), then divide the weight difference by the height difference, that is, 49/14, leading to 3.5. In other words, we see that, on average, one inch of height difference leads to a difference of 3.5 pounds in weight.

If you want to dig deeper, you may discover that the weight change with respect to the height change is not that uniform. On average, an increase of an inch in height results in an increase of less than 3 pounds in weight for height between 58 and 65 inches (remember that 65 inches is the average). For values of height greater than 65 inches, weight increases more rapidly (by 4 pounds mostly until 70 inches, and 5 pounds for more than 70 inches).

Here is another question: What would you expect the weight to be of an American woman who is 57 inches tall? To answer this, we will have to extrapolate the data we have. We know from the previous paragraph that in the lower range of height (less than the average of 65 inches), with each inch of height change, weight changes by about 3 pounds. Given that we know for someone who is 58 inches in height, the corresponding weight is 115 pounds; if we deduct an inch from the height, we should deduct 3 pounds from the weight. This gives us the answer (or at least our guess), 112 pounds.

What about the end of the data with the larger values for weight and height? What would you expect the weight of someone who is 73 inches tall to be?

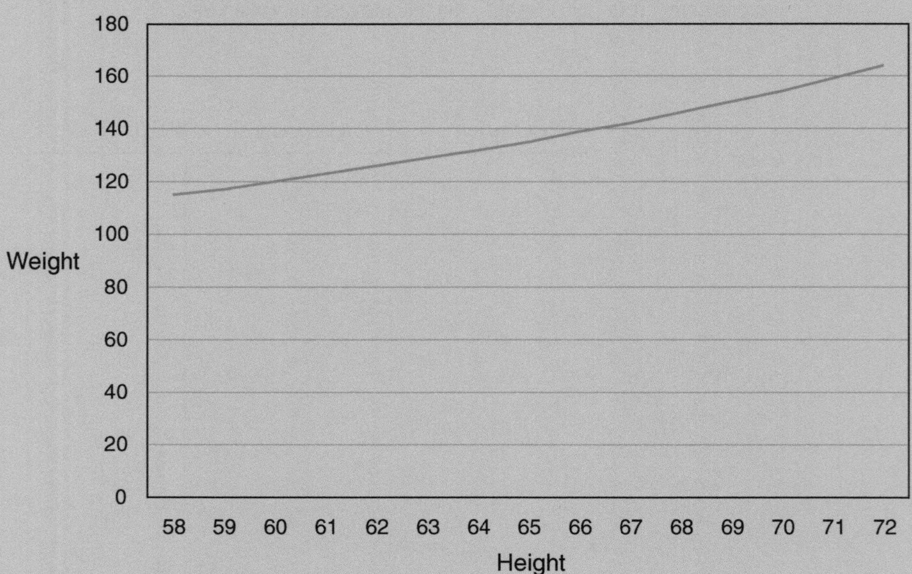

Figure 1.4 Visualization of height vs. weight data.

The correct estimate is 169 pounds. Students should verify this answer.

More than the answer, what is important is the process. Can you explain that to someone? Can you document it? Can you repeat it for the same problem but with different values, or for similar problems, in the future? If the answer to these questions is "yes," then you just practiced some science. Yes, it is important for us not only to solve data-driven problems, but to be able to explain, verify, and repeat that process.

And that, in short, is what we are going to do in data science.

Try It Yourself 1.2: Analyzing Data

Let us practice data analysis methods. For this work, you are going to use a dataset that describes list price (*X*) and best price (*Y*) in $1000 for a new GMC pickup truck. The dataset is available from OA 1.2.

Use this dataset to predict the best price of a pickup track that has been listed at $24,000 by a dealer.

1.7 Tools for Data Science

A couple of sections ago, we discussed what kind of skills one needs to have to be a successful data scientist. We also know by now that a lot of what data scientists do involves processing data and deriving insights. An example was given above, along with a hands-on practice problem. These things should at least give you an idea of what you may expect to do in data science. Going forward, it is important that you develop a solid foundation in statistical techniques (covered in Chapter 3) and computational thinking (covered in an earlier section). And then you need to pick up a couple of programing and data processing tools. A whole section of this book is devoted to such tools (Part II) and covers some of the most used tools in data science – Python, R, and SQL. But let us quickly review these here so we understand what to expect when we get to those chapters.

Let me start by noting that there are no special tools for doing data science; there just happen to be some tools that are more suitable for the kind of things one does in data science. And so, if you already know some programing language (e.g., C, Java, PHP) or a scientific data processing environment (e.g., Matlab), you could use them to solve many or most of the problems and tasks in data science. Of course, if you go through this book, you would also find that Python or R could generate a graph with one line of code – something that could take you a lot more effort in C or Java. In other words, while Python or R were not specifically designed for people to do data science, they provide excellent environments for quick implementation, visualization, and testing for most of what one would want to do in data science – at least at the level in which we are interested in this book.

Python is a scripting language. It means that programs written in Python do not need to be compiled as a whole like you would do with a program in C or Java; instead, a Python program runs line by line. The language (its syntax and structure) also provides a very easy learning curve for the beginner, yet giving very powerful tools for advanced programmers.

Let us see this with an example. If you want to write the classic "Hello, World" program in Java, here is how it goes:

Step 1: Write the code and save as HellowWorld.java.

```
public class HelloWorld {
    public static void main(String[] args) {
        System.out.println("Hello, World");
    }
}
```

Step 2: Compile the code.

```
% javac HelloWorld.java
```

Step 3: Run the program.

```
% java HelloWorld
```

This should display "Hello, World" on the console. Do not worry if you have never done Java (or any) programming before and all this looks confusing. I hope you can at least see that printing a simple message on the screen is quite complicated (we have not even done any data processing!).

In contrast, here is how you do the same in Python:

Step 1: Write the code and save as hello.py

```
print("Hello, World")
```

Step 2: Run the program.

```
% python hello.py
```

Again, do not worry about actually trying this now. We will see detailed instructions in Chapter 5. For now, at least you can appreciate how easy it is to code in Python. And if you want to accomplish the same in R, you type the same – `print("Hello, World")` – in R console.

Both Python and R offer a very easy introduction to programming, and even if you have never done any programming before, it is possible to start solving data problems from day 1 of using either of these. Both of them also offer plenty of packages that you can import or call into them to accomplish more complex tasks such as machine learning (see Part III of this book).

Most times in this book we will see data available to us in simple text files formatted as CSV (comma-separated values) and we can load up that data into a Python or R environment. However, such a method has a major limit – the data we could store in a file or load in a computer's memory cannot be beyond a certain size. In such cases (and for some other reasons), we may need to use a better storage of data in something called an SQL (Structured Query Language) database. The field of this database is very rich with lots of tools, techniques, and methods for addressing all kinds of data problems. We will, however, limit ourselves to working with SQL databases through Python or R, primarily so that we could work with large and remote datasets.

In addition to these top three most used tools for data science (see Appendix G), we will also skim through basic UNIX. Why? Because a UNIX environment allows one to solve many data problems and day-to-day data processing needs without writing any code. After all, there is no perfect tool that could address all our data science needs or meet all of our preferences and constraints. And so, we will pick up several of the most popular tools in data science in this book, while solving data problems using a hands-on approach.

1.8 Issues of Ethics, Bias, and Privacy in Data Science

This chapter (and this book) may give an impression that data science is all good, that it is the ultimate path to solve all of society's and the world's problems. First of all, I hope you do not buy such exaggerations. Second, even at its best, data science and, in general, anything that deals with data or employs data analysis using a statistical-computation technique, bears several issues that should concern us all – as users or producers of data, or as data scientists. Each of these issues is big and serious enough to warrant their own separate books (and such books exist), but lengthy discussions will be beyond the scope of this book. Instead, we will briefly mention these issues here and call them out at different places throughout this book when appropriate.

Many of the issues related to privacy, bias, and ethics can be traced back to the origin of the data. Ask – how, where, and why was the data collected? Who collected it? What did they intend to use it for? More important, if the data was collected from people, did these people know that: (1) such data was being collected about them; and (2) how the data would be used? Often those collecting data mistake availability of data as the right to use that data. For instance, just because data on a social media service such as Twitter is available on the Web, it does not mean that one could collect and sell it for material gain without the consent of the users of that service. In April 2018, a case surfaced that a data analytics firm, Cambridge Analytica, obtained data about a large number of Facebook users to use for political campaigning. Those Facebook users did not even know that: (1) such data about them was collected and shared by Facebook to third parties; and (2) the data was used to target political ads to them. This incident shed light on something that was not really new; for many years, various companies such as Facebook and Google have collected enormous amounts of data about and from their users in order not only to improve and market their products, but also to share and/or sell it to other entities for profit. Worse, most people don't know about these practices. As the old saying goes, "there is no free lunch." So, when you are getting an email service or a social media account for "free," ask why? As it is often understood, "if you are not paying for it, you are the product." Sure enough, for Facebook, each user is worth \$158. Equivalent values for other major companies are: \$182/user for Google and \$733/user for Amazon.[40]

There are many cases throughout our digital life history where data about users have been intentionally or unintentionally exposed or shared that caused various levels of harm to the users. And this is just the tip of the iceberg in terms of ethical or privacy violations.

What we are often not aware of is how even ethically collected data could be highly biased. And if a data scientist is not careful, such inherent bias in the data could show up in the analysis and the insights developed, often without anyone actively noticing it.

Many data and technology companies are trying to address these issues, often with very little to no success. But it is admirable that they are trying. And while we also cannot be successful at fending off biases and prejudices or being completely fair, we need to try. So, as we proceed in this book with data collection and analysis methods, keep these issues at the back of your mind. And, wherever appropriate, I will present some pointers in FYI boxes, such as the one below.

FYI: Fairness

Understanding the gravity of ethics in practicing data analytics, Google, a company that has thrived during the last two decades guided by machine learning, recently acknowledged the biases in traditional machine learning approaches in one of its blog posts. You can read more about this announcement here: https://developers.google.com/machine-learning/fairness-overview/.

In this regard, computational social science has a long way to go to adequately deal with ordinary human biases. Just as with the field of genomics, to which computational social sciences has often been compared, it may well take a generation or two before researchers combine high-level competence in data science with equivalent expertise in anthropology, sociology, political science, and other social science disciplines.

There is a community, called Fairness, Accountability, and Transparency (FAT), that has emerged in recent years that is trying to address some of these issues, or at least is shedding a light on them. This community, thankfully, has scholars from fields of data science, machine learning, artificial intelligence, education, information science, and several branches of social sciences.

This is a very important topic in data science and machine learning, and, therefore, we will continue discussions throughout this book at appropriate places with such FYI boxes.

Summary

Data science is new in some ways and not new in other ways. Many would argue that statisticians have already been doing a lot of what today we consider data science. On the other hand, we have an explosion of data in every sector, with data varying a great deal in its nature, format, size, and other aspects. Such data has also become substantially more important in our daily lives – from connecting with our friends and family to doing business. New problems and new opportunities have emerged and we have only scratched the surface of possibilities. It is not enough to simply solve a data problem; we also need to create new tools, techniques, and methods that offer verifiability, repeatability, and generalizability. This is what data science covers, or at least is meant to cover. And that's how we are going to present data science in this book.

The present chapter provided several views on how people think and talk about data science, how it affects or is connected to various fields, and what kinds of skills a data scientist should have.

Using a small example, we practiced (1) data collection, (2) descriptive statistics, (3) correlation, (4) data visualization, (5) model building, and (6) extrapolation and regression analysis. As we progress through various parts of this book, we will dive into all of these and more in detail, and learn scientific methods, tools, and techniques to tackle data-driven problems, helping us derive interesting and important insights for making decisions in various fields – business, education, healthcare, policy-making, and more.

Finally, we touched on some of the issues in data science, namely, privacy, bias, and ethics. More discussions on these issues will be considered as we proceed through different topics in this book.

In the next chapter, we will learn more about data – types, formats, cleaning, and transforming, among other things. Then, in Chapter 3, we will explore various techniques – most of them statistical in nature. We can learn about them in theory and practice by hand using small examples. But of course, if we want to work with *real* data, we need to develop some technical skills. For this, we will acquire several tools in Chapters 4–7, including UNIX, R, Python, and MySQL. By that time, you should be able to build your own models using various programming tools and statistical techniques to solve data-driven problems. But today's world needs more than that. So, we will go a few steps further with three chapters on machine learning. Then, in Chapter 11, we will take several real-world examples and applications and see how we can apply all of our data science knowledge to solve problems in various fields and derive decision-making insights. Finally, we will learn (at least on the surface) some of the core methodologies for collecting and analyzing data, as well as evaluating systems and analyses, in Chapter 12. Keep in mind that the appendices discuss much of the background and basic materials. So, make sure to look at appropriate sections in the appendices as you move forward.

Key Terms

- **Data:** Information that is factual, such as measurements or statistics, which can be used as a basis for reasoning, discussion, or prediction.
- **Information:** Data that are endowed with meaning and purpose.
- **Science:** The systematic study of the structure and behavior of the physical and natural world through observations and experiments.
- **Data science:** The field of study and practice that involves collection, storage, and processing of data in order to derive important insights into a problem or a phenomenon.

- **Information science:** A thorough understanding of information considering different contexts and circumstances related to the data that is created, generated, and shared, mostly by human beings.
- **Business analytics:** The skills, technologies, and practices for continuous iterative exploration and investigation of past and current business performance to gain insight and be strategic.
- **Computational thinking:** This is a process of using abstraction and decomposition when attacking a large complex task or designing a large complex system.

Conceptual Questions

1. What is data science? How does it relate to and differ from statistics?
2. Identify three areas or domains in which data science is being used and describe how.
3. If you are allocated 1 TB data to use on your phone, how many years will it take until you run out of your quota of 1 GB/month consumption?
4. We saw an example of bias in predicting future crime potential due to misrepresentation in the available data. Find at least two such instances where an analysis, a system, or an algorithm exhibited some sort of bias or prejudice.

Hands-On Problems

Problem 1.1

Imagine you see yourself as the next Harland Sanders (founder of KFC) and want to learn about the poultry business at a much earlier age than Mr. Sanders did. You want to figure out what kind of feed can help grow healthier chickens. Below is a dataset that might help. The dataset is sourced from OA 1.3.

#	Weight (lbs)	Feed
1	179	Horsebean
2	160	Horsebean
3	136	Horsebean
4	227	Horsebean
5	217	Horsebean
6	168	Horsebean
7	108	Horsebean
8	124	Horsebean

#	Weight (lbs)	Feed
9	143	Horsebean
10	140	Horsebean
11	309	Linseed
12	229	Linseed
13	181	Linseed
14	141	Linseed
15	260	Linseed
16	203	Linseed
17	148	Linseed
18	169	Linseed
19	213	Linseed
20	257	Linseed
21	244	Linseed
22	271	Linseed
23	243	Soybean
24	230	Soybean
25	248	Soybean
26	327	Soybean
27	329	Soybean
28	250	Soybean
29	193	Soybean
30	271	Soybean
31	316	Soybean
32	267	Soybean
33	199	Soybean
34	171	Soybean
35	158	Soybean
36	248	Soybean
37	423	Sunflower
38	340	Sunflower
39	392	Sunflower
40	339	Sunflower
41	341	Sunflower
42	226	Sunflower
43	320	Sunflower
44	295	Sunflower
45	334	Sunflower
46	322	Sunflower
47	297	Sunflower
48	318	Sunflower
49	325	Meatmeal
50	257	Meatmeal
51	303	Meatmeal

#	Weight (lbs)	Feed
52	315	Meatmeal
53	380	Meatmeal
54	153	Meatmeal
55	263	Meatmeal
56	242	Meatmeal
57	206	Meatmeal
58	344	Meatmeal
59	258	Meatmeal
60	368	Casein
61	390	Casein
62	379	Casein
63	260	Casein
64	404	Casein
65	318	Casein
66	352	Casein
67	359	Casein
68	216	Casein
69	222	Casein
70	283	Casein
71	332	Casein

Based on this dataset, which type of chicken food appears the most beneficial for a thriving poultry business?

Problem 1.2

The following table contains an imaginary dataset of auto insurance providers and their ratings as provided by the latest three customers. Now if you had to choose an auto insurance provider based on these ratings, which one would you opt for?

#	Insurance provider	Rating (out of 10)
1	GEICO	4.7
2	GEICO	8.3
3	GEICO	9.2
4	Progressive	7.4
5	Progressive	6.7
6	Progressive	8.9
7	USAA	3.8
8	USAA	6.3
9	USAA	8.1

Problem 1.3

Imagine you have grown to like Bollywood movies recently and started following some of the well-known actors from the Hindi film industry. Now you want to predict which of these actor's movies you should watch when a new one is released. Here is a movie review dataset from the past that might help. It consists of three attributes: movie name, leading actor in the movie, and its IMDB rating. [Note: assume that a better rating means a more watchable movie.]

Leading actor	Movie name	IMDB rating (out of 10)
Irfan Khan	Knock Out	6.0
Irfan Khan	New York	6.8
Irfan Khan	Life in a ... metro	7.4
Anupam Kher	Striker	7.1
Anupam Kher	Dirty Politics	2.6
Anil Kapoor	Calcutta Mail	6.0
Anil Kapoor	Race	6.6

Notes

1. What is data science? https://datajobs.com/what-is-data-science
2. Davenport, T. H., & Patil, D. J. (2012). Data scientist: the sexiest job of the 21st century. *Harvard Business Review*, October: https://hbr.org/192012/10/data-scientist-the-sexiest-job-of-the-21st-century
3. Fortune.com: Data science is still white hot: http://fortune.com/2015/05/21/data-science-white-hot/
4. Dhar, V. (2013). Data science and prediction. *Communications of the ACM*, 56(12), 64–73.
5. Computer Weekly: Data to grow more quickly says IDC's Digital Universe study: https://www.computerweekly.com/news/2240174381/Data-to-grow-more-quickly-says-IDCs-Digital-Universe-study
6. Analytics Vidhya Content Team. (2015). 13 amazing applications/uses of data science today, Sept. 21: https://www.analyticsvidhya.com/blog/2015/09/applications-data-science/
7. Kaggle: Lending Club loan data: https://www.kaggle.com/wendykan/lending-club-loan-data
8. Ahmed, S. Loan eligibility prediction: https://www.kdnuggets.com/2018/09/financial-data-analysis-loan-eligibility-prediction.html
9. Data Science for Social Good: https://dssg.uchicago.edu/event/using-data-for-social-good-and-public-policy-examples-opportunities-and-challenges/
10. Miller, C. C. (2008). How Obama's internet campaign changed politics. *The New York Times*, Nov. 7: http://bits.blogs.nytimes.com/2008/11/07/how-obamas-internet-campaign-changed-politics/
11. What you can learn from data science in politics: http://schedule.sxsw.com/2016/events/event_PP49570
12. Lee, J., & Lim, Y. S. (2016). Gendered campaign tweets: the cases of Hillary Clinton and Donald Trump. Public Relations Review, 42(5), 849–855.
13. Cambridge Analytica: https://en.wikipedia.org/wiki/Cambridge_Analytica

14. O'Reilly, T., Loukides, M., & Hill, C. (2015). How data science is transforming health care. O'Reilly. May 4: https://www.oreilly.com/ideas/how-data-science-is-transforming-health-care
15. Cadmus-Bertram, L., Marcus, B. H., Patterson, R. E., Parker, B. A., & Morey, B. L. (2015). Use of the Fitbit to measure adherence to a physical activity intervention among overweight or obese, post-menopausal women: self-monitoring trajectory during 16 weeks. JMIR mHealth and uHealth, 3(4).
16. Apple Heart Study: http://med.stanford.edu/appleheartstudy.html
17. Your health insurance might score you an Apple Watch: https://www.engadget.com/2016/09/28/your-health-insurance-might-score-you-an-apple-watch/
18. Argonne National Laboratory: http://www.anl.gov/about-argonne
19. Urban Center for Computation and Data: http://www.urbanccd.org/#urbanccd
20. Forbes Magazine. Fixing education with big data: http://www.forbes.com/sites/gilpress/2012/09/12/fixing-education-with-big-data-turning-teachers-into-data-scientists/
21. Brookings Institution. Big data for education: https://www.brookings.edu/research/big-data-for-education-data-mining-data-analytics-and-web-dashboards/
22. Syracuse University iSchool Blog: https://ischool.syr.edu/infospace/2012/07/16/data-science-whats-in-it-for-the-new-librarian/
23. ACRL. Keeping up with big data: http://www.ala.org/acrl/publications/keeping_up_with/big_data
24. Priceonomics. What's the difference between data science and statistics?: https://priceonomics.com/whats-the-difference-between-data-science-and/
25. FiveThirtyEight. 2016 election forecast: https://projects.fivethirtyeight.com/2016-election-forecast/
26. New York Times. 2016 election forecast: https://www.nytimes.com/interactive/2016/upshot/presidential-polls-forecast.html?_r=0#other-forecasts
27. Mixpanel. This is the difference between statistics and data science: https://blog.mixpanel.com/2016/03/30/this-is-the-difference-between-statistics-and-data-science/
28. Andrew Gelman. Statistics is the least important part of data science: http://andrewgelman.com/2013/11/14/statistics-least-important-part-data-science/
29. Flowingdata. Rise of the data scientist: https://flowingdata.com/2009/06/04/rise-of-the-data-scientist/
30. Wikipedia. Business analytics: https://en.wikipedia.org/wiki/Business_analytics
31. Wallace, D. P. (2007). Knowledge Management: Historical and Cross-Disciplinary Themes. Libraries Unlimited. pp. 1–14. ISBN 978-1-59158-502-2.
32. CDC. Smoking and tobacco use: https://www.cdc.gov/tobacco/data_statistics/fact_sheets/fast_facts/index.htm
33. Rowley, J., & Hartley, R. (2006). Organizing Knowledge: An Introduction to Managing Access to Information. Ashgate Publishing. pp. 5–6. ISBN 978-0-7546-4431-6: https://en.wikipedia.org/wiki/DIKW_Pyramid
34. Belkin, N. J., Cole, M., & Liu, J. (2009). A model for evaluation of interactive information retrieval. In *Proceedings of the SIGIR 2009 Workshop on the Future of IR Evaluation* (pp. 7–8), July.
35. Wing, J. M. (2006). Computational thinking. *Communications of the ACM*, 49(3), 33–35.
36. @Josh_Wills Tweet on Data scientist: https://twitter.com/josh_wills/status/198093512149958656
37. Harris, J. (2012). Data is useless without the skills to analyze it. *Harvard Business Review*, Sept. 13: https://hbr.org/2012/09/data-is-useless-without-the-skills
38. https://blog.udacity.com/2014/11/data-science-job-skills.html
39. Udacity chart on data scientist skills: http://1onjea25cyhx3uvxgs4vu325.wpengine.netdna-cdn.com/wp-content/uploads/2014/11/blog_dataChart_white.png
40. You are worth $182 to Google, $158 to Facebook and $733 to Amazon! https://arkenea.com/blog/big-tech-companies-user-worth/

2 Data

"Data is a precious thing and will last longer than the systems themselves."
— Tim Berners-Lee

What do you need?
- A basic understanding of data sizes, storage, and access.
- Introductory experience with spreadsheets.
- Familiarity with basic HTML.

What will you learn?
- Data types, major data sources, and formats.
- How to perform basic data cleaning and transformation.

2.1 Introduction

"Just as trees are the raw material from which paper is produced, so too, can data be viewed as the raw material from which information is obtained."[1] To present and interpret information, one must start with a process of gathering and sorting data. And for any kind of data analysis, one must first identify the right kinds of information sources.

In the previous chapter, we discussed different forms of data. The height–weight data we saw was numerical and structured. When you post a picture using your smartphone, that is an example of multimedia data. The datasets mentioned in the section on public policy are government or open data collections. We also discussed how and where this data is stored – from as small and local as our personal computers, to as large and remote as data warehouses. In this chapter, we will look at these and more variations of data in a more formal way. Specifically, we will discuss data types, data collection, and data formats. We will also see and practice how data is cleaned, stored, and processed.

2.2 Data Types

One of the most basic ways to think about data is whether it is structured or not. This is especially important for data science because most of the techniques that we will learn depend on one or the other inherent characteristic.

Most commonly, **structured data** refers to highly organized information that can be seamlessly included in a database and readily searched via simple search operations; whereas **unstructured data** is essentially the opposite, devoid of any underlying structure. In structured data, different values – whether they are numbers or something else – are labeled, which is not the case when it comes to unstructured data. Let us look at these two types in more detail.

2.2.1 Structured Data

Structured data is the most important data type for us, as we will be using it for most of the exercises in this book. Already we have seen it a couple of times. In the previous chapter we discussed an example that included height and weight data. That example included structured data because the data has defined fields or labels; we know "60" to be height and "120" to be weight for a given record (which, in this case, is for one person).

But structured data does not need to be strictly numbers. Table 2.1 contains data about some customers. This data includes numbers (age, income, num.vehicles), text (housing. type), Boolean type (is.employed), and categorical data (sex, marital.stat). What matters for us is that any data we see here – whether it is a number, a category, or a text – is labeled. In other words, we know what that number, category, or text means.

Pick a data point from the table – say, third row and eighth column. That is "22." We know from the structure of the table that that data is a number; specifically, it is the age of a customer. Which customer? The one with the ID 2848 and who lives in Georgia. You see how easily we could interpret and use the data since it is in a structured format? Of course, someone would have to collect, store, and present the data in such a format, but for now we will not worry about that.

2.2.2 Unstructured Data

Unstructured data is data without labels. Here is an example:

"It was found that a female with a height between 65 inches and 67 inches had an IQ of 125–130. However, it was not clear looking at a person shorter or taller than this

Table 2.1 Customer data sample.

custid	sex	is.employed	income	marital.stat	housing.type	num.vehicles	age	state.of.res
2068	F	NA	11300	Married	Homeowner free and clear	2	49	Michigan
2073	F	NA	0	Married	Rented	3	40	Florida
2848	M	True	4500	Never married	Rented	3	22	Georgia
5641	M	True	20000	Never married	Occupied with no rent	0	22	New Mexico
6369	F	True	12000	Never married	Rented	1	31	Florida

observation if the change in IQ score could be different, and, even if it was, it could not be possibly concluded that the change was solely due to the difference in one's height."

In this paragraph, we have several data points: 65, 67, 125–130, female. However, they are not clearly labeled. If we were to do some processing, as we did in the first chapter to try to associate height and IQ, we would not be able to do that easily. And certainly, if we were to create a systematic process (an algorithm, a program) to go through such data or observations, we would be in trouble because that process would not be able to identify which of these numbers corresponds to which of the quantities.

Of course, humans have no difficulty understanding a paragraph like this that contains unstructured data. But if we want to do a systematic process for analyzing a large amount of data and creating insights from it, the more structured it is, the better. As I mentioned, in this book for the most part we will work with structured data. But at times when such data is not available, we will look to other ways to convert unstructured data to structured data, or process unstructured data, such as text, directly.

2.2.3 Challenges with Unstructured Data

The lack of structure makes compilation and organizing unstructured data a time- and energy-consuming task. It would be easy to derive insights from unstructured data if it could be instantly transformed into structured data. However, structured data is akin to machine language, in that it makes information much easier to be parsed by computers. Unstructured data, on the other hand, is often how humans communicate ("natural language"); but people do not interact naturally with information in strict, database format.

For example, email is unstructured data. An individual may arrange their inbox in such a way that it aligns with their organizational preferences, but that does not mean the data is structured. If it were truly fully structured, it would also be arranged by exact subject and content, with no deviation or variability. In practice, this would not work, because even focused emails tend to cover multiple subjects.

Spreadsheets, which are arranged in a relational database format and can be quickly scanned for information, are considered structured data. According to Brightplanet®, "The problem that unstructured data presents is one of volume; most business interactions are of this kind, requiring a huge investment of resources to sift through and extract the necessary elements, as in a Web-based search engine."[2] And here is where data science is useful. Because the pool of information is so large, current data mining techniques often miss a substantial amount of available content, much of which could be game-changing if efficiently analyzed.

2.3 Data Collections

Now, if you want to find datasets like the one presented in the previous section or in the previous chapter, where would you look? There are many places online to look for sets or collections of data. Here are some of those sources.

2.3.1 Open Data

The idea behind open data is that some data should be freely available in a public domain that can be used by anyone as they wish, without restrictions from copyright, patents, or other mechanisms of control.

Local and federal governments, non-government organizations (NGOs), and academic communities all lead open data initiatives. For example, you can visit data repositories produced by the US Government[3] or the City of Chicago.[4] To unlock the true potential of "information as open data," the White House developed Project Open Data in 2013 – a collection of code, tools, and case studies – to help agencies and individuals adopt the Open Data Policy. To this extent, the US Government released a policy, M-13-3,[5] that instructs agencies to manage their data, and information more generally, as an asset from the start, and, wherever possible, release it to the public in a way that makes it open, discoverable, and usable. Following is the list of principles associated with open data as observed in the policy document:

- ***Public.*** Agencies must adopt a presumption in favor of openness to the extent permitted by law and subject to privacy, confidentiality, security, or other valid restrictions.
- ***Accessible.*** Open data are made available in convenient, modifiable, and open formats that can be retrieved, downloaded, indexed, and searched. Formats should be machine-readable (i.e., data are reasonably structured to allow automated processing). Open data structures do not discriminate against any person or group of persons and should be made available to the widest range of users for the widest range of purposes, often by providing the data in multiple formats for consumption. To the extent permitted by law, these formats should be non-proprietary, publicly available, and no restrictions should be placed on their use.
- ***Described.*** Open data are described fully so that consumers of the data have sufficient information to understand their strengths, weaknesses, analytical limitations, and security requirements, as well as how to process them. This involves the use of robust, granular metadata (i.e., fields or elements that describe data), thorough documentation of data elements, data dictionaries, and, if applicable, additional descriptions of the purpose of the collection, the population of interest, the characteristics of the sample, and the method of data collection.
- ***Reusable.*** Open data are made available under an open license[6] that places no restrictions on their use.
- ***Complete.*** Open data are published in primary forms (i.e., as collected at the source), with the finest possible level of granularity that is practicable and permitted by law and other requirements. Derived or aggregate open data should also be published but must reference the primary data.
- ***Timely.*** Open data are made available as quickly as necessary to preserve the value of the data. Frequency of release should account for key audiences and downstream needs.
- ***Managed Post-Release.*** A point of contact must be designated to assist with data use and to respond to complaints about adherence to these open data requirements.

2.3.2 Social Media Data

Social media has become a gold mine for collecting data to analyze for research or marketing purposes. This is facilitated by the Application Programming Interface (API) that social media companies provide to researchers and developers. Think of the API as a set of rules and methods for asking and sending data. For various data-related needs (e.g., retrieving a user's profile picture), one could send API requests to a particular social media service. This is typically a programmatic call that results in that service sending a response in a structured data format, such as an XML. We will discuss about XML later in this chapter.

The Facebook Graph API is a commonly used example.[7] These APIs can be used by any individual or organization to collect and use this data to accomplish a variety of tasks, such as developing new socially impactful applications, research on human information behavior, and monitoring the aftermath of natural calamities, etc. Furthermore, to encourage research on niche areas, such datasets have often been released by the social media platform itself. For example, Yelp, a popular crowd-sourced review platform for local businesses, released datasets that have been used for research in a wide range of topics – from automatic photo classification to natural language processing of review texts, and from sentiment analysis to graph mining, etc. If you are interested in learning about and solving such challenges, you can visit the Yelp.com dataset challenge[8] to find out more. We will revisit this method of collecting data in later chapters.

2.3.3 Multimodal Data

We are living in a world where more and more devices exist – from lightbulbs to cars – and are getting connected to the Internet, creating an emerging trend of the Internet of Things (IoT). These devices are generating and using much data, but not all of which are "traditional" types (numbers, text). When dealing with such contexts, we may need to collect and explore multimodal (different forms) and multimedia (different media) data such as images, music and other sounds, gestures, body posture, and the use of space.

Once the sources are identified, the next thing to consider is the kind of data that can be extracted from those sources. Based on the nature of the information collected from the sources, the data can be categorized into two types: structured data and unstructured data. One of the well-known applications of such multimedia data is analysis of brain imaging data sequences – where the sequence can be a series of images from different sensors, or a time series from the same subject. The typical dataset used in this kind of application is a multimodal face dataset, which contains output from different sensors such as EEG, MEG, and fMRI (medical imaging techniques) on the same subject within the same paradigm. In this field, statistical parametric mapping (SPM) is a well-known statistical technique, created by Karl Friston,[9] that examines differences in brain activity recorded during functional neuroimaging experiments. More on this can be found at the UCL SPM website.[10]

If you still need more pointers for obtaining datasets, check out Appendix E, which covers not just some of the contemporary sources of datasets, but also active challenges for processing data, and creating and solving real-life problems.

2.3.4 Data Storage and Presentation

Depending on its nature, data is stored in various formats. We will start with simple kinds – data in text form. If such data is structured, it is common to store and present it in some kind of delimited way. That means various fields and values of the data are separated using delimiters, such as commas or tabs. And that gives rise to two of the most commonly used formats that store data as simple text – comma-separated values (CSV) and tab-separated values (TSV).

1. **CSV (Comma-Separated Values)** format is the most common import and export format for spreadsheets and databases. There is no "CSV standard," so the format is operationally defined by the many applications that read and write it. For example, *Depression.csv* is a dataset that is available at UF Health, UF Biostatistics[11] for downloading. The dataset represents the effectiveness of different treatment procedures on separate individuals with clinical depression. A snippet of the file is shown below:

```
treat,before,after,diff
No Treatment,13,16,3
No Treatment,10,18,8
No Treatment,16,16,0
Placebo,16,13,-3
Placebo,14,12,-2
Placebo,19,12,-7
Seroxat (Paxil),17,15,-2
Seroxat (Paxil),14,19,5
Seroxat (Paxil),20,14,-6
Effexor,17,19,2
Effexor,20,12,-8
Effexor,13,10,-3
```

   In this snippet, the first row mentions the variable names. The remaining rows each individually represent one data point. It should be noted that, for some data points, values of all the columns may not be available. The "Data Pre-processing" section later in this chapter describes how to deal with such missing information.

   An advantage of the CSV format is that it is more generic and useful when sharing with almost anyone. Why? Because specialized tools to read or manipulate it are not required. Any spreadsheet program such as Microsoft Excel or Google Sheets can readily open a CSV file and display it correctly most of the time. But there are also several disadvantages. For instance, since the comma is used to separate fields, if the data contains a comma, that could be problematic. This could be addressed by escaping the comma (typically adding a backslash before that comma), but this remedy could be frustrating because not everybody follows such standards.

2. **TSV (Tab-Separated Values)** files are used for raw data and can be imported into and exported from spreadsheet software. Tab-separated values files are essentially text files, and the raw data can be viewed by text editors, though such files are often used when

moving raw data between spreadsheets. An example of a TSV file is shown below, along with the advantages and disadvantages of this format.
Suppose the registration records of all employees in an office are stored as follows:

```
Name<TAB>Age<TAB>Address
Ryan<TAB>33<TAB>1115 W Franklin
Paul<TAB>25<TAB>Big Farm Way
Jim<TAB>45<TAB>W Main St
Samantha<TAB>32<TAB>28 George St
```

where <TAB> denotes a TAB character.[12]

An advantage of TSV format is that the delimiter (tab) will not need to be avoided because it is unusual to have the tab character within a field. In fact, if the tab character is present, it may have to be removed. On the other hand, TSV is less common than other delimited formats such as CSV.

3. **XML (eXtensible Markup Language)** was designed to be both human- and machine-readable, and can thus be used to store and transport data. In the real world, computer systems and databases contain data in incompatible formats. As the XML data is stored in plain text format, it provides a software- and hardware-independent way of storing data. This makes it much easier to create data that can be shared by different applications.
XML has quickly become the default mechanism for sharing data between disparate information systems. Currently, many information technology departments are deciding between purchasing native XML databases and converting existing data from relational and object-based storage to an XML model that can be shared with business partners.
Here is an example of a page of XML:

```
<?xml version="1.0" encoding="UTF-8"?>
<bookstore>
    <book category="information science" cover="hardcover">
        <title lang="en">Social Information Seeking</title>
        <author>Chirag Shah</author>
        <year>2017</year>
        <price>62.58</price>
    </book>
    <book category="data science" cover="paperback">
        <title lang="en">Hands-On Introduction to Data
          Science</title>
        <author>Chirag Shah</author>
        <year>2019</year>
        <price>50.00</price>
    </book>
</bookstore>
```

If you have ever worked with HTML, then chances are this should look familiar. But as you can see, unlike HTML, we are using custom tags such as <book> and <price>.

That means whosoever reads this will not be able to readily format or process it. But in contrast to HTML, the markup data in XML is not meant for direct visualization. Instead, one could write a program, a script, or an app that specifically parses this markup and uses it according to the context. For instance, one could develop a website that runs in a Web browser and uses the above data in XML, whereas someone else could write a different code and use this same data in a mobile app. In other words, the data remains the same, but the presentation is different. This is one of the core advantages of XML and one of the reasons XML is becoming quite important as we deal with multiple devices, platforms, and services relying on the same data.

4. **RSS (Really Simple Syndication)** is a format used to share data between services, and which was defined in the 1.0 version of XML. It facilitates the delivery of information from various sources on the Web. Information provided by a website in an XML file in such a way is called an RSS feed. Most current Web browsers can directly read RSS files, but a special RSS reader or aggregator may also be used.[13]

The format of RSS follows XML standard usage but in addition defines the names of specific tags (some required and some optional), and what kind of information should be stored in them. It was designed to show selected data. So, RSS starts with the XML standard, and then further defines it so that it is more specific.

Let us look at a practical example of RSS usage. Imagine you have a website that provides several updates of some information (news, stocks, weather) per day. To keep up with this, and even to simply check if there are any updates, a user will have to continuously return to this website throughout the day. This is not only time-consuming, but also unfruitful as the user may be checking too frequently and encountering no updates, or, conversely, checking not often enough and missing out on crucial information as it becomes available. Users can check your site faster using an RSS aggregator (a site or program that gathers and sorts out RSS feeds). This aggregator will ensure that it has the information as soon as the website provides it, and then it pushes that information out to the user – often as a notification.

Since RSS data is small and fast loading, it can easily be used with services such as mobile phones, personal digital assistants (PDAs), and smart watches.

RSS is useful for websites that are updated frequently, such as:

- News sites – Lists news with title, date and descriptions.
- Companies – Lists news and new products.
- Calendars – Lists upcoming events and important days.
- Site changes – Lists changed pages or new pages.

Do you want to publish your content using RSS? Here is a brief guideline on how to make it happen.

First, you need to register your content with RSS aggregator(s). To participate, first create an RSS document and save it with an .xml extension (see example below). Then, upload the file to your website. Finally, register with an RSS aggregator. Each day (or with a frequency you specify) the aggregator searches the registered websites for RSS documents, verifies the link, and displays information about the feed so clients can link to documents that interest them.[14]

Here is a sample RSS document.

```
<?xml version="1.0" encoding="UTF-8" ?>
<rss version="2.0">
    <channel>
          <title>Dr. Chirag Shah's Home Page</title>
          <link>http://chiragshah.org/</link>
          <description> Chirag Shah's webhome
          </description>
          <item>
                <title>Awards and Honors</title>
                <link>http://chiragshah.org/awards
                .php</link>
                <description>Awards and Honors
                Dr. Shah received</description>
          </item>
    </channel>
</rss>
```

Here, the `<channel>` element describes the RSS feed, and has three required "child" elements: `<title>` defines the title of the channel (e.g., Dr. Chirag Shah's Home Page); `<link>` defines the hyperlink to the channel (e.g., http://chiragshah.org/); and `<description>` describes the channel (e.g., About Chirag Shah's webhome).

The `<channel>` element usually contains one or more `<item>` elements. Each `<item>` element defines an article or "story" in the RSS feed.

Having an RSS document is not useful if other people cannot reach it. Once your RSS file is ready, you need to get the file up on the Web. Here are the steps:

1. Name your RSS file. Note that the file must have an .xml extension.
2. Validate your RSS file (a good validator can be found at FEED Validator[15]).
3. Upload the RSS file to your Web directory on your Web server.
4. Copy the little orange RSS or XML button to your Web directory.
5. Put the little orange "RSS" or "XML" button on the page where you will offer RSS to the world (e.g., on your home page). Then add a link to the button that links to the RSS file.
6. Submit your RSS feed to the RSS Feed Directories (you can search on Google or Yahoo! for "RSS Feed Directories"). Note that the URL to your feed is not your home page; it is the URL to your feed.
7. Register your feed with the major search engines:
    - Google[16]
    - Bing[17]
8. Update your feed. After registering your RSS feed, you must update your content frequently and ensure that your RSS feed is constantly available to those aggregators.

And that is it. Now, as new information becomes available on your website, it will be noticed by the aggregators and pushed to the users who have subscribed to your feed.

5. **JSON (JavaScript Object Notation)** is a lightweight data-interchange format. It is not only easy for humans to read and write, but also easy for machines to parse and generate. It is based on a subset of the JavaScript Programming Language, Standard ECMA-262, 3rd Edition – December 1999.[18]

   JSON is built on two structures:

   - A collection of name–value pairs. In various languages, this is realized as an *object*, *record*, *structure*, *dictionary*, *hash table*, *keyed list,* or *associative array.*
   - An ordered list of values. In most languages, this is realized as an *array*, *vector*, *list*, or *sequence*.

   When exchanging data between a browser and a server, the data can be sent only as text.[19] JSON is text, and we can convert any JavaScript object into JSON, and send JSON to the server. We can also convert any JSON received from the server into JavaScript objects. This way we can work with the data as JavaScript objects, with no complicated parsing and translations.

   Let us look at examples of how one could send and receive data using JSON.

   1. Sending data: If the data is stored in a JavaScript object, we can convert the object into JSON, and send it to a server. Below is an example:

```
<!DOCTYPE html>
  <html>
  <body>
  <p id="demo"></p>
  <script>
    var obj = {"name":"John", "age":25, "state": "New Jersey"};
    var obj_JSON = JSON.stringify(obj);
    window.location = "json_Demo.php?x=" + obj_JSON;
  </script>
  </body>
  </html>
```

   2. Receiving data: If the received data is in JSON format, we can convert it into a JavaScript object. For example:

```
<!DOCTYPE html>
   <html>
   <body>
   <p id="demo"></p>
   <script>
     var obj_JSON = "{"name":"John", "age":25, "state":
     "New Jersey"}";
     var obj = JSON.parse(obj_JSON);
     document.getElementById("demo").innerHTML=obj.name;
</script>
</body>
</html>
```

Now that we have seen several formats of data storage and presentation, it is important to note that these are by no means the only ways to do it, but they are some of the most preferred and commonly used ways.

Having familiarized ourselves with data formats, we will now move on with manipulating the data.

2.4 Data Pre-processing

Data in the real world is often *dirty*; that is, it is in need of being cleaned up before it can be used for a desired purpose. This is often called data pre-processing. What makes data "dirty"? Here are some of the factors that indicate that data is not clean or ready to process:

- **Incomplete.** When some of the attribute values are lacking, certain attributes of interest are lacking, or attributes contain only aggregate data.
- **Noisy.** When data contains errors or outliers. For example, some of the data points in a dataset may contain extreme values that can severely affect the dataset's range.
- **Inconsistent.** Data contains discrepancies in codes or names. For example, if the "Name" column for registration records of employees contains values other than alphabetical letters, or if records do not start with a capital letter, discrepancies are present.

Figure 2.1 shows the most important tasks involved in data pre-processing.[20]

In the subsections that follow, we will consider each of them in detail, and then work through an example to practice these tasks.

FYI: Bias in Data

It is worth noting here that when we use the term *dirty* to describe data, we are only referring to the syntactical, formatting, and structural issues with the data, and ignoring all other ways the data could be "muddled up." What do I mean by this? Take, for instance, data used in a now famous study of facial recognition. The study showed that the operative algorithm performed better for white males than for women and non-white males. Why? Because the underlying data, which included many more instances of white males than black females, was imbalanced. Perhaps this was intentional, perhaps not. But bias is a real issue with many datasets and data sources that are blindly used in analyses. Read more about this study in the *NY Times* article from February 9, 2018: https://www.nytimes.com/2018/02/09/technology/facial-recognition-race-artificial-intelligence.html

It is important to start with data from a reputable source, but every decision you make in handling data could add subtle errors, adding bias. Introducing errors will tend to be systemic (throughout) and will tend to overemphasize or underemphasize outcomes. Scrutinize your choices so that you are relatively free of favoring a certain outcome.

Data Cleaning

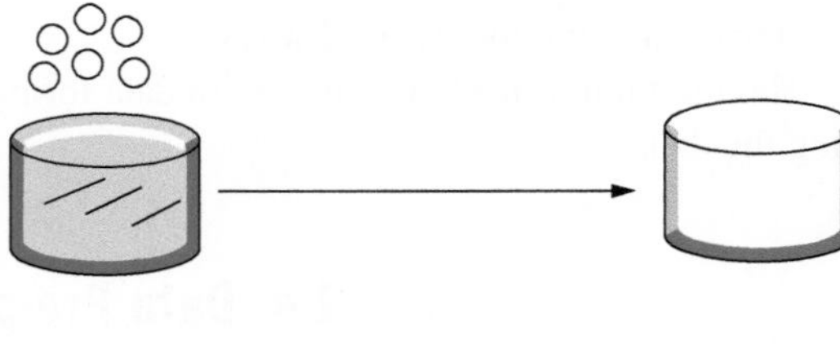

Data Integration

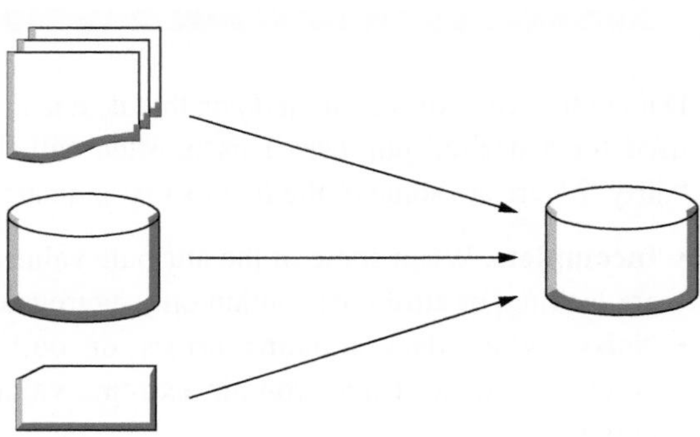

Data Transformation −17, 25, 39, 128, −39 → 0.17, 0.25, 0.39, 1.28, −0.39

Data Reduction

	A1	A2	A3	....	A200
T1					
T2					
T3					
....					
T200					

→

	A1	A2	A3	...	A120
T1					
T2					
T3					
....					
T150					

Figure 2.1 Forms of data pre-processing (N.H. Son, Data Cleaning and Data Pre-processing[21]).

2.4.1 Data Cleaning

Since there are several reasons why data could be "dirty," there are just as many ways to "clean" it. For this discussion, we will look at three key methods that describe ways in which data may be "cleaned," or better organized, or scrubbed of potentially incorrect, incomplete, or duplicated information.

2.4.1.1 Data Munging

Often, the data is not in a format that is easy to work with. For example, it may be stored or presented in a way that is hard to process. Thus, we need to convert it to something more

Table 2.2 Wrangled data for a recipe.

Ingredient	Quantity	Unit/size
Tomato	2	Diced
Garlic	3	Cloves
Salt	1	Pinch

suitable for a computer to understand. To accomplish this, there is no specific scientific method. The approaches to take are all about manipulating or wrangling (or munging) the data to turn it into something that is more convenient or desirable. This can be done manually, automatically, or, in many cases, semi-automatically.

Consider the following text recipe.

"Add two diced tomatoes, three cloves of garlic, and a pinch of salt in the mix."

This can be turned into a table (Table 2.2).

This table conveys the same information as the text, but it is more "analysis friendly." Of course, the real question is – How did that sentence get turned into the table? A not-so-encouraging answer is "using whatever means necessary"! I know that is not what you want to hear because it does not sound systematic. Unfortunately, often there is no better or systematic method for *wrangling*. Not surprisingly, there are people who are hired to do specifically just this – wrangle ill-formatted data into something more manageable.

2.4.1.2 Handling Missing Data

Sometimes data may be in the right format, but some of the values are missing. Consider a table containing customer data in which some of the home phone numbers are absent. This could be due to the fact that some people do not have home phones – instead they use their mobile phones as their primary or only phone.

Other times data may be missing due to problems with the process of collecting data, or an equipment malfunction. Or, comprehensiveness may not have been considered important at the time of collection. For instance, when we started collecting that customer data, it was limited to a certain city or region, and so the area code for a phone number was not necessary to collect. Well, we may be in trouble once we decide to expand beyond that city or region, because now we will have numbers from all kinds of area codes.

Furthermore, some data may get lost due to system or human error while storing or transferring the data.

So, what to do when we encounter missing data? There is no single good answer. We need to find a suitable strategy based on the situation. Strategies to combat missing data include ignoring that record, using a global constant to fill in all missing values, imputation, inference-based solutions (Bayesian formula or a decision tree), etc. We will revisit some of these *inference* techniques later in the book in chapters on machine learning and data mining.

2.4.1.3 Smooth Noisy Data

There are times when the data is not missing, but it is corrupted for some reason. This is, in some ways, a bigger problem than missing data. Data corruption may be a result of faulty data collection instruments, data entry problems, or technology limitations. For example, a digital thermometer measures temperature to one decimal point (e.g., 70.1°F), but the storage system ignores the decimal points. So, now we have 70.1°F and 70.9°F both stored as 70°F. This may not seem like a big deal, but for humans a 99.4°F temperature means you are fine, and 99.8°F means you have a fever, and if our storage system represents both of them as 99°F, then it fails to differentiate between healthy and sick persons!

Just as there is no single technique to take care of missing data, there is no one way to remove noise, or smooth out the noisiness in the data. However, there are some steps to try. First, you should identify or remove outliers. For example, records of previous students who sat for a data science examination show all students scored between 70 and 90 points, barring one student who received just 12 points. It is safe to assume that the last student's record is an outlier (unless we have a reason to believe that this anomaly is really an unfortunate case for a student!). Second, you could try to resolve inconsistencies in the data. For example, all entries of customer names in the sales data should follow the convention of capitalizing all letters, and you could easily correct them if they are not.

2.4.2 Data Integration

To be as efficient and effective for various data analyses as possible, data from various sources commonly needs to be integrated. The following steps describe how to integrate multiple databases or files.

1. Combine data from multiple sources into a coherent storage place (e.g., a single file or a database).
2. Engage in schema integration, or the combining of metadata from different sources.
3. Detect and resolve data value conflicts. For example:
   a. A conflict may arise; for instance, such as the presence of different attributes and values from various sources for the same real-world entity.
   b. Reasons for this conflict could be different representations or different scales; for example, metric vs. British units.
4. Address redundant data in data integration. Redundant data is commonly generated in the process of integrating multiple databases. For example:
   a. The same attribute may have different names in different databases.
   b. One attribute may be a "derived" attribute in another table; for example, annual revenue.
   c. Correlation analysis may detect instances of redundant data.

If this has begun to appear confusing, hang in there – some of these steps will become clearer as we take an example in the next section.

2.4.3 Data Transformation

Data must be transformed so it is consistent and readable (by a system). The following five processes may be used for data transformation. For the time being, do not worry if these seem too abstract. We will revisit some of them in the next section as we work through an example of data pre-processing.

1. Smoothing: Remove noise from data.
2. Aggregation: Summarization, data cube construction.
3. Generalization: Concept hierarchy climbing.
4. Normalization: Scaled to fall within a small, specified range and aggregation. Some of the techniques that are used for accomplishing normalization (but we will not be covering them here) are:
   a. Min–max normalization.
   b. Z-score normalization.
   c. Normalization by decimal scaling.
5. Attribute or feature construction.
   a. New attributes constructed from the given ones.

Detailed explanation of all of these techniques are out of scope for this book, but later in this chapter we will do a hands-on exercise to practice some of these in simpler forms.

2.4.4 Data Reduction

Data reduction is a key process in which a reduced representation of a dataset that produces the same or similar analytical results is obtained. One example of a large dataset that could warrant reduction is a data cube. Data cubes are multidimensional sets of data that can be stored in a spreadsheet. But do not let the name fool you. A data cube could be in two, three, or a higher dimension. Each dimension typically represents an attribute of interest. Now, consider that you are trying to make a decision using this multidimensional data. Sure, each of its attributes (dimensions) provides some information, but perhaps not all of them are equally useful for a given situation. In fact, often we could reduce information from all those dimensions to something much smaller and manageable without losing much. This leads us to two of the most common techniques used for data reduction.

1. **Data Cube Aggregation.** The lowest level of a data cube is the aggregated data for an individual entity of interest. To do this, use the smallest representation that is sufficient to address the given task. In other words, we reduce the data to its more meaningful size and structure for the task at hand.
2. **Dimensionality Reduction.** In contrast with the data cube aggregation method, where the data reduction was with the consideration of the task, dimensionality reduction method works with respect to the nature of the data. Here, a dimension or a column in your data spreadsheet is referred to as a "feature," and the goal of the process is to identify which features to remove or collapse to a combined feature. This requires identifying redundancy

in the given data and/or creating composite dimensions or features that could sufficiently represent a set of raw features. Strategies for reduction include sampling, clustering, principal component analysis, etc. We will learn about clustering in multiple chapters in this book as a part of machine learning. The rest are outside the scope of this book.

2.4.5 Data Discretization

We are often dealing with data that are collected from processes that are continuous, such as temperature, ambient light, and a company's stock price. But sometimes we need to convert these continuous values into more manageable parts. This mapping is called discretization. And as you can see, in undertaking discretization, we are also essentially reducing data. Thus, this process of discretization could also be perceived as a means of data reduction, but it holds particular importance for numerical data. There are three types of attributes involved in discretization:

a. Nominal: Values from an unordered set
b. Ordinal: Values from an ordered set
c. Continuous: Real numbers

To achieve discretization, divide the range of continuous attributes into intervals. For instance, we could decide to split the range of temperature values into cold, moderate, and hot, or the price of company stock into above or below its market valuation.

Hands-On Example 2.1: Data Pre-processing

In the previous section, we looked at theoretical (and that often means abstract) explanations of various stages of data processing. Now, let us use a sample dataset and walk through those stages step by step. For this example, we will use a modified version of a dataset of the number of deaths from excessive wine consumption, available from OA 2.1, which we have tweaked (Table 2.3) to explain the pre-processing stages. The dataset consists of the following attributes:

a. Name of the country from which sample obtained
b. Alcohol consumption measured as liters of wine, per capita
c. Number of deaths from alcohol consumption, per 100,000 people
d. Number of heart disease deaths, per 100,000 people
e. Number of deaths from liver diseases, also per 100,000 people

Now, we can use this dataset to test for various hypotheses or the relation between various attributes, such as the relation between number of deaths and the amount of alcohol consumption, the relation between the number of fatal heart disease cases and the amount of wine consumed, etc. But, to build an effective analysis (more on this in later chapters), first we need to prepare the dataset. Here is how we are going to do it:

1. **Data Cleaning.** In this stage, we will go through the following pre-processing steps:

Table 2.3 Excessive wine consumption and mortality data.

#	Country	Alcohol	Deaths	Heart	Liver
1	Australia	2.5	785	211	15.30000019
2	Austria	3.000000095	863	167	45.59999847
3	Belg. and Lux.	2.900000095	883	131	20.70000076
4	Canada	2.400000095	793	NA	16.39999962
5	Denmark	2.900000095	971	220	23.89999962
6	Finland	0.800000012	970	297	19
7	France	9.100000381	751	11	37.90000153
8	Iceland	−0.800000012	743	211	11.19999981
9	Ireland	0.699999988	1000	300	6.5
10	Israel	0.600000024	−834	183	13.69999981
11	Italy	27.900000095	775	107	42.20000076
12	Japan	1.5	680	36	23.20000076
13	Netherlands	1.799999952	773	167	9.199999809
14	New Zealand	1.899999976	916	266	7.699999809
15	Norway	0.0800000012	806	227	12.19999981
16	Spain	6.5	724	NA	NA
17	Sweden	1.600000024	743	207	11.19999981
18	Switzerland	5.800000191	693	115	20.29999924
19	UK	1.299999952	941	285	10.30000019
20	US	1.200000048	926	199	22.10000038
21	West Germany	2.700000048	861	172	36.70000076

- ***Smooth Noisy Data.*** We can see that the wine consumption value for Iceland per capita is −0.800000012. However, wine consumption values per capita cannot be negative. Therefore, it must be a faulty entry and we should change the alcohol consumption for Iceland to 0.800000012. Using the same logic, the number of deaths for Israel should be converted from −834 to 834.
- ***Handling Missing Data.*** As we can see in the dataset, we have missing values (represented by NA – not available) of the number of cases of heart disease for Canada and number of cases of heart and liver disease for Spain. A simple workaround for this is to replace all the NAs with some common values, such as zero or average of all the values for that attribute. Here, we are going to use the average of the attribute for handling the missing values. So, for both Canada and Spain, we will use the value of 185 as number of heart diseases. Likewise, the number of liver diseases for Spain is replaced by 20.27. It is important to note: depending on the nature of the problem, it may not be a good idea to replace all of the NAs with the same value. A better solution would be to derive the value of the missing attribute from the values of other attributes of that data point.
- ***Data Wrangling.*** As previously discussed, data wrangling is the process of manually converting or mapping data from one "raw" form into another format. For example, it may happen that, for a country, we have the value of the number of deaths as per 10,000, and not per 100,000, as other countries. In that case, we need to transform the value of the number of deaths for that country into per 100,000, or the same for every other country into 10,000. Fortunately for us, this dataset does not involve any data wrangling steps. So, at the end of this stage the dataset would look like what we see in Table 2.4.

2. **Data Integration.** Now let us assume we have another dataset (fictitious) collected from a different source, which is about alcohol consumption and number of related fatalities across various states of India, as shown in Table 2.5.

Table 2.4 Wine consumption vs. mortality data after data cleaning.

#	Country	Alcohol	Deaths	Heart	Liver
1	Australia	2.5	785	211	15.30000019
2	Austria	3.000000095	863	167	45.59999847
3	Belg. and Lux.	2.900000095	883	131	20.70000076
4	Canada	2.400000095	793	185	16.39999962
5	Denmark	2.900000095	971	220	23.89999962
6	Finland	0.800000012	970	297	19
7	France	9.100000381	751	11	37.90000153
8	Iceland	0.800000012	743	211	11.19999981
9	Ireland	0.699999988	1000	300	6.5
10	Israel	0.600000024	834	183	13.69999981
11	Italy	27.900000095	775	107	42.20000076
12	Japan	1.5	680	36	23.20000076
13	Netherlands	1.799999952	773	167	9.199999809
14	New Zealand	1.899999976	916	266	7.699999809
15	Norway	0.0800000012	806	227	12.19999981
16	Spain	6.5	724	185	20.27
17	Sweden	1.600000024	743	207	11.19999981
18	Switzerland	5.800000191	693	115	20.29999924
19	UK	1.299999952	941	285	10.30000019
20	US	1.200000048	926	199	22.10000038
21	West Germany	2.700000048	861	172	36.70000076

Table 2.5 Data about alcohol consumption and health from various States in India.

#	Name of the State	Alcohol consumption	Heart disease	Fatal alcohol-related accidents
1	Andaman and Nicobar Islands	1.73	20,312	2201
2	Andhra Pradesh	2.05	16,723	29,700
3	Arunachal Pradesh	1.98	13,109	11,251
4	Assam	0.91	8532	211,250
5	Bihar	3.21	12,372	375,000
6	Chhattisgarh	2.03	28,501	183,207
7	Goa	5.79	19,932	307,291

Here is what the dataset contains:

A. Name of the State.
B. Liters of alcohol consumed per capita.
C. Number of fatal heart diseases, measured per 1,000,000 people.
D. Number of fatal accidents related to alcohol per 1,000,000 people.

Now we can use this dataset to integrate the attributes for India into our original dataset. To do this, we calculate the total alcohol consumption for the country of India as an average of alcohol consumption for all the states, which is 2.95. Similarly, we can calculate the fatal heart diseases per 100,000 people for India as 171 (approximated to the nearest integer value). Since we do not have any source for the number of total deaths or the number of fatal liver diseases for India, we are going to handle these the same way we previously addressed any missing values. The resultant dataset is shown in Table 2.6.

Note that some of the assumptions we have made here before using this external dataset are for our own cause. First, when we are using the average of the alcohol consumption for these States as the amount of alcohol consumption for India, we are assuming that: (a) the populations of these States are the same or

Table 2.6 Wine consumption and associated mortality after data integration.

#	Country	Alcohol	Deaths	Heart	Liver
1	Australia	2.5	785	211	15.30000019
2	Austria	3.000000095	863	167	45.59999847
3	Belg. and Lux.	2.900000095	883	131	20.70000076
4	Canada	2.400000095	793	185	16.39999962
5	Denmark	2.900000095	971	220	23.89999962
6	Finland	0.800000012	970	297	19
7	France	9.100000381	751	11	37.90000153
8	Iceland	0.800000012	743	211	11.19999981
9	Ireland	0.699999988	1000	300	6.5
10	Israel	0.600000024	834	183	13.69999981
11	Italy	27.900000095	775	107	42.20000076
12	Japan	1.5	680	36	23.20000076
13	Netherlands	1.799999952	773	167	9.199999809
14	New Zealand	1.899999976	916	266	7.699999809
15	Norway	0.0800000012	806	227	12.19999981
16	Spain	6.5	724	185	20.27
17	Sweden	1.600000024	743	207	11.19999981
18	Switzerland	5.800000191	693	115	20.29999924
19	UK	1.299999952	941	285	10.30000019
20	US	1.200000048	926	199	22.10000038
21	West Germany	2.700000048	861	172	36.70000076
22	India	2.950000000	750	171	20.27

at least similar; (b) the sample of these States is similar to the whole population of India; and (c) the wine consumption is roughly equivalent to the total alcohol consumption value in India; even though in reality, the wine consumption per capita should be less than the total alcohol consumption per capita, as there are other kinds of alcoholic beverages in the market.

3. **Data Transformation.** As previously mentioned, the data transformation process involves one or more of smoothing, removing noise from data, summarization, generalization, and normalization. For this example, we will employ smoothing, which is simpler than summarization and normalization. As we can see, in our data the wine consumption per capita for Italy is unusually high, whereas the same for Norway is unusually low. So, chances are these are outliers. In this case we will replace the value of wine consumption for Italy with 7.900000095. Similarly, for Norway we will use the value of 0.800000012 in place of 0.0800000012. We are treating both of these potential errors as "equipment error" or "entry error," which resulted in an extra digit for both of these countries (extra "2" in front for Italy and extra "0" after the decimal point for Norway). This is a reasonable assumption given the limited context we have about the dataset. A more practical approach would be to look at the nearest geolocation for which we have the values and use that value to make predictions about the countries with erroneous entries. So, at the end of this step the dataset will be transformed into what is shown in Table 2.7.

Table 2.7 Wine consumption and associated mortality dataset after data transformation.

#	Country	Alcohol	Deaths	Heart	Liver
1	Australia	2.5	785	211	15.30000019
2	Austria	3.000000095	863	167	45.59999847
3	Belg. and Lux.	2.900000095	883	131	20.70000076
4	Canada	2.400000095	793	185	16.39999962
5	Denmark	2.900000095	971	220	23.89999962
6	Finland	0.800000012	970	297	19
7	France	9.100000381	751	11	37.90000153
8	Iceland	0.800000012	743	211	11.19999981
9	Ireland	0.699999988	1000	300	6.5
10	Israel	0.600000024	834	183	13.69999981
11	Italy	7.900000095	775	107	42.20000076
12	Japan	1.5	680	36	23.20000076
13	Netherlands	1.799999952	773	167	9.199999809
14	New Zealand	1.899999976	916	266	7.699999809
15	Norway	0.800000012	806	227	12.19999981
16	Spain	6.5	724	185	20.27
17	Sweden	1.600000024	743	207	11.19999981
18	Switzerland	5.800000191	693	115	20.29999924
19	UK	1.299999952	941	285	10.30000019
20	US	1.200000048	926	199	22.10000038
21	West Germany	2.700000048	861	172	36.70000076
22	India	2.950000000	750	171	20.27

4. **Data Reduction.** The process of data reduction is aimed at producing a reduced representation of the dataset that can be used to obtain the same or similar analytical results. For our example, the sample is relatively small, with only 22 rows. Now imagine that we have values for all 196 countries in the world, and the geospatial values, for which the attribute values are available, are stated. In that case, the number of rows is large, and, depending on the limited processing and storage capacity you have at your disposal, it may make more sense to round up the alcohol consumption per capita to two decimal places. Each extra decimal place for every data point in such a large dataset will need a significant amount of storage capacity. Thus, reducing the liver column to one decimal place and the alcohol consumption column to two decimal places would result in the dataset shown in Table 2.8.

   Note that data reduction does not mean just reducing the size of attributes – it also may involve removing some attributes, which is known as **feature space selection**. For example, if we are interested in the relation between the wine consumed and number of casualties from heart disease, we may opt to remove the attribute "number of liver diseases" if we assume that there is no relation between number of heart disease fatalities and number of lung disease fatalities.

Table 2.8 Wine consumption and associated mortality dataset after data reduction.

#	Country	Alcohol	Deaths	Heart	Liver
1	Australia	2.50	785	211	15.3
2	Austria	3.00	863	167	45.6
3	Belg. and Lux.	2.90	883	131	20.7
4	Canada	2.40	793	185	16.4
5	Denmark	2.90	971	220	23.9
6	Finland	0.80	970	297	19.0
7	France	9.10	751	11	37.9
8	Iceland	0.80	743	211	11.2
9	Ireland	0.70	1000	300	6.5
10	Israel	0.60	834	183	13.7
11	Italy	7.90	775	107	42.2
12	Japan	1.50	680	36	23.2
13	Netherlands	1.80	773	167	9.2
14	New Zealand	1.90	916	266	7.7
15	Norway	0.80	806	227	12.2
16	Spain	6.50	724	185	20.3
17	Sweden	1.60	743	207	11.2
18	Switzerland	5.80	693	115	20.3
19	UK	1.30	941	285	10.3
20	US	1.20	926	199	22.1
21	West Germany	2.70	861	172	36.7
22	India	2.95	750	171	20.3

Table 2.9 Wine consumption and mortality dataset at the end of pre-processing.

#	Country	Alcohol	Deaths	Heart	Liver
1	Australia	2	785	211	15.3
2	Austria	2	863	167	45.6
3	Belg. and Lux.	2	883	131	20.7
4	Canada	2	793	185	16.4
5	Denmark	2	971	220	23.9
6	Finland	0	970	297	19.0
7	France	3	751	11	37.9
8	Iceland	0	743	211	11.2
9	Ireland	0	1000	300	6.5
10	Israel	0	834	183	13.7
11	Italy	3	775	107	42.2
12	Japan	1	680	36	23.2
13	Netherlands	1	773	167	9.2
14	New Zealand	1	916	266	7.7
15	Norway	0	806	227	12.2
16	Spain	3	724	185	20.3
17	Sweden	1	743	207	11.2
18	Switzerland	3	693	115	20.3
19	UK	1	941	285	10.3
20	US	1	926	199	22.1
21	West Germany	2	861	172	36.7
22	India	2	750	171	20.3

5. **Data Discretization.** As we can see, all the attributes involved in our dataset are continuous type (values in real numbers). However, depending on the model you want to build, you may have to discretize the attribute values into binary or categorical types. For example, you may want to discretize the wine consumption per capita into four categories – less than or equal to 1.00 per capita (represented by 0), more than 1.00 but less than or equal to 2.00 per capita (1), more than 2.00 but less than or equal to 5.00 per capita (2), and more than 5.00 per capita (3). The resultant dataset should look like that shown in Table 2.9.

And that is the end result of this exercise. Yes, it may seem that we did not conduct *real* data processing or analytics. But through our pre-processing techniques, we have managed to prepare a much better and meaningful dataset. Often, that itself is half the battle. Having said that, for most of the book we will focus on the other half of the battle – processing, visualizing, analyzing the data for solving problems, and making decisions. Nonetheless, I hope the sections on data pre-processing and the hands-on exercise we did here has given some insights into what needs to occur before you get your hands on nice-looking data for processing.

Try It Yourself 2.1: Data Pre-processing

Imagine you want to open a new bakery, and you are trying to figure out which item in the menu will help you to keep maximum profit margin. You have the following few options:

- For cookies, you would need flour, chocolate, butter, and other ingredients, which comes at $3.75 per pound (lb). The initial setup cost is $1580, while the labor charge is another $30 per hour. In one hour you can serve two batches of cookies, while making 250 cookies per batch. Each batch requires 15 lb of ingredients, and each cookie can be priced at $2.
- For your second option, you can make cake with the same ingredients. However, the ratio of the ingredients being different, it will cost you $4 per lb. The initial setup cost is $2000, while the labor charge remains the same. However, baking two batches of cake will require 3 hours in total, with five cakes in each batch. Each cake when baked with 2 lb of ingredient can be sold at $34.
- In the third option, you can make bagels in your shop, which will require flour, butter and other ingredients, which will cost you $2.50 per lb. The initial setup cost is low, at $680, as is the labor cost, $25 per hour. In one batch, using 20 lb of ingredients, you can make 300 bagels in 45 minutes. Each bagel can be sold at $1.75.
- For the fourth and final option, you can bake loaves of bread, where you will need only flour and butter for the ingredients, which will cost you $3 per lb. The initial setup cost is marginal between $270 and $350; however, the labor charge is high, $40 per hour. However, you can bake as many as 1000 loaves in 2 hours; each can be priced at $3.

Use this information to create a dataset that can be used to decide the menu for your bakery.

Summary

Many of the examples of data we have seen so far have been in nice tables, but it should be clear by now that data appears in many forms, sizes, and formats. Some are stored in spreadsheets, and others are found in text files. Some are structured, and some are unstructured. In this book, most data we will deal with are found in text format, but there are plenty of data out there in image, audio, and video formats.

As we saw, the process of data processing is more complicated if there is missing or corrupt data, and some data may need cleaning or converting before we can even begin to do any processing with it. This requires several forms of pre-processing.

Some data cleaning or transformation may be required, and some may depend on our purpose, context, and availability of analysis tools and skills. For instance, if you know SQL (a program covered in Chapter 7) and want to take advantage of this effective and efficient query language, you may want to import your CSV-formatted data into a MySQL database, even if that CSV data has no "issues."

Data pre-processing is so important that many organizations have specific job positions just for this kind of work. These people are expected to have the skills to do all the stages described in this chapter: from cleaning to transformation, and even finding or approximating the missing or corrupt values in a dataset. There is some technique, some science, and much engineering involved in this process. But it is a very important job, because, without having the right data in the proper format, almost all that follows in this book would be impossible. To put it differently – before you jump to any of the "fun" analyses here, make sure you have at least thought about whether your data needs any pre-processing, otherwise you may be asking the right question of the wrong data!

Key Terms

- **Structured data:** Structured data is highly organized information that can be seamlessly included in a database and readily searched via simple search operations.
- **Unstructured data:** Unstructured data is information devoid of any underlying structure.
- **Open data:** Data that is freely available in a public domain that can be used by anyone as they wish, without restrictions from copyright, patents, or other mechanisms of control.
- **Application Programming Interface (API):** A programmatic way to access data. A set of rules and methods for asking and sending data.
- **Outlier:** A data point that is markedly different in value from the other data points of the sample.
- **Noisy data:** The dataset has one or more instances of errors or outliers.
- **Nominal data:** The data type is nominal when there is no natural order between the possible values, for example, colors.
- **Ordinal data:** If the possible values of a data type are from an ordered set, then the type is ordinal. For example, grades in a mark sheet.
- **Continuous data:** A continuous data is a data type that has an infinite number of possible values. For example, real numbers.
- **Data cubes:** They are multidimensional sets of data that can be stored in a spreadsheet. A data cube could be in two, three, or higher dimensions. Each dimension typically represents an attribute of interest.
- **Feature space selection:** A method for selecting a subset of features or columns from the given dataset as a way to do data reduction.

Conceptual Questions

1. List at least two differences between structured and unstructured data.
2. Give three examples of structured data formats.
3. Give three examples of unstructured data formats.
4. How will you convert a CSV file to a TSV file? List at least two different strategies.

5. You are looking at employee records. Some have no middle name, some have a middle initial, and others have a complete middle name. How do you explain such inconsistency in the data? Provide at least two explanations.

Hands-On Problems

Problem 2.1

The following dataset, obtained from OA 2.2, contains statistics in arrests per 100,000 residents for assault and murder, in each of the 50 US states, in 1973. Also given is the percentage of the population living in urban areas.

	Murder	Assault	Urban population (%)
Alabama	13.2	236	58
Alaska	10	263	48
Arizona	8.1	294	80
Arkansas	8.8	190	50
California	9	276	91
Colorado	7.9	204	78
Connecticut	3.3	110	77
Delaware	5.9	238	72
Florida	15.4	335	80
Georgia	17.4		60
Hawaii	5.3	46	83
Idaho	2.6	120	54
Illinois	10.4	249	83
Indiana	7.2	113	65
Iowa	2.2	56	570
Kansas	6	115	66
Kentucky	9.7	109	52
Louisiana	15.4	249	66
Maine	2.1	83	51
Maryland	11.3	300	67
Massachusetts	4.4	149	85
Michigan	12.1	255	74
Minnesota	2.7	72	66
Mississippi	16.1	259	44
Missouri	9	178	70
Montana	6	109	53
Nebraska	4.3	102	62
Nevada	12.2	252	81

	Murder	Assault	Urban population (%)
New Hampshire	2.1	57	56
New Jersey	7.4	159	89
New Mexico	11.4	285	70
New York	11.1	254	6
North Carolina	13	337	45
North Dakota	0.8	45	44
Ohio	7.3	120	75
Oklahoma	6.6	151	68
Oregon	4.9	159	67
Pennsylvania	6.3	106	72
Rhode Island	3.4	174	87
South Carolina	14.4	879	48
South Dakota	3.8	86	45
Tennessee	13.2	188	59
Texas	12.7	201	80
Utah	3.2	120	80
Vermont	2.2	48	32
Virginia	8.5	156	63
Washington	4	145	73
West Virginia	5.7	81	39
Wisconsin	2.6	53	66
Wyoming	6.8	161	60

Now, use the pre-processing techniques at your disposal to prepare the dataset for analysis.

a. Address all the missing values.
b. Look for outliers and smooth noisy data.
c. Prepare the dataset to establish a relation between an urban population category and a crime type. [Hint: Convert the urban population percentage into categories, for example, small (<50%), medium (<60%), large (<70%), and extra-large (70% and above) urban population.]

Problem 2.2

The following is a dataset of bridges in Pittsburgh. The original dataset was prepared by Yoram Reich and Steven J. Fenves, Department of Civil Engineering and Engineering Design Research Center, Carnegie Mellon University, and is available from OA 2.3.

ID	Purpose	Length	Lanes	Clear	T or D	Material	Span	Rel-L
E1	Highway	?	2	N	Through	Wood	Short	S

ID	Purpose	Length	Lanes	Clear	T or D	Material	Span	Rel-L
E2	Highway	1037	2	N	Through	Wood	Short	S
E3	Aqueduct	?	1	N	Through	Wood	?	S
E5	Highway	1000	2	N	Through	Wood	Short	S
E6	Highway	?	2	N	Through	Wood	?	S
E7	Highway	990	2	N	Through	Wood	Medium	S
E8	Aqueduct	1000	1	N	Through	Iron	Short	S
E9	Highway	1500	2	N	Through	Iron	Short	S
E10	Aqueduct	?	1	N	Deck	Wood	?	S
E11	Highway	1000	2	N	Through	Wood	Medium	S
E12	RR	?	2	N	Deck	Wood	?	S
E14	Highway	1200	2	N	Through	Wood	Medium	S
E13	Highway	?	2	N	Through	Wood	?	S
E15	RR	?	2	N	Through	Wood	?	S
E16	Highway	1030	2	N	Through	Iron	Medium	S-F
E17	RR	1000	2	N	Through	Iron	Medium	?
E18	RR	1200	2	N	Through	Iron	Short	S
E19	Highway	1000	2	N	Through	Wood	Medium	S
E20	Highway	1000	2	N	Through	Wood	Medium	S
E21	RR	?	2	?	Through	Iron	?	?
E23	Highway	1245	?	?	Through	Steel	Long	F
E22	Highway	1200	4	G	Through	Wood	Short	S
E24	RR	?	2	G	?	Steel	?	?
E25	RR	?	2	G	?	Steel	?	?
E27	RR	?	2	G	Through	Steel	?	F
E26	RR	1150	2	G	Through	Steel	Medium	S
E30	RR	?	2	G	Through	Steel	Medium	F
E29	Highway	1080	2	G	Through	Steel	Medium	?
E28	Highway	1000	2	G	Through	Steel	Medium	S
E32	Highway	?	2	G	Through	Iron	Medium	F
E31	RR	1161	2	G	Through	Steel	Medium	S
E34	RR	4558	2	G	Through	Steel	Long	F
E33	Highway	1120	?	G	Through	Iron	Medium	F
E36	Highway	?	2	G	Through	Iron	Short	F
E35	Highway	1000	2	G	Through	Steel	Medium	F

Use this dataset to complete the following tasks:

a. Address all the missing values.
b. Look for outliers and smooth noisy data.
c. Prepare the dataset to establish a relation among:
    i. Length of the bridge and its purpose.
    ii. Number of lanes and its materials.
    iii. Span of the bridge and number of lanes.

Problem 2.3

The following is a dataset that involves child mortality rate and is inspired by data collected from UNICEF. The original dataset is available from OA 2.4. According to the report, the world has achieved substantial success in reducing child mortality during the last few decades. According to the UNICEF report, globally the under-five age mortality rate has decreased from 93 deaths per 1000 live births in 1990 to less than 50 in 2016.

Year	Under-five mortality rate	Infant mortality rate	Neonatal mortality rate
1990	93.4	64.8	36.8
1991	92.1	63.9	36.3
1992	90.9	63.1	35.9
1993	89.7	62.3	35.4
1994	88.7	61.4	
1995	87.3	60.5	34.4
1996	85.6	59.4	33.7
1997		58.2	33.1
1998	82.1	56.9	32.3
1999	79.9	55.4	31.5
2000	77.5	53.9	30.7
2001	74.8	52.1	29.8
2002	72		28.9
2003	69.2	48.6	28
2004	66.7	46.9	
2005		45.1	26.1
2006	61.1	43.4	25.3
2007	58.5		24.4
2008	56.2	40.3	23.6
2009	53.7	38.8	22.9
2010		37.4	22.2
2011	49.3	36	21.5
2012	47.3	34.7	20.8
2013	45.5	33.6	20.2
2014	43.7		19.6
2015	42.2	31.4	19.1
2016	40.8	30.5	18.6

However, as you can see, the dataset has a number of missing instances, which need to be fixed before a clear progress on child mortality can be explained from the year of 1990 to 2016. Use this dataset to complete the following tasks:

a. Address all the missing values using the techniques at your disposal.
b. Prepare the dataset to establish the following relations:
   i. Under-five mortality rate and neonatal mortality rate.

ii. Infant mortality late and neonatal mortality rate.
iii. Year and infant mortality rate.

[Hints: You may think of converting the mortality rates into five-point Likert scale values. You may count the year before this dataset (i.e., 1989) as the starting point of this program, to assess the progress we have made as the years have passed.]

Further Reading and Resources

- Bellinger, G., Castro, D., & Mills, A. Data, information, knowledge, and wisdom: http://www.systems-thinking.org/dikw/dikw.htm
- US Government Open Data Policy: https://project-open-data.cio.gov/
- Developing insights from social media data: https://sproutsocial.com/insights/social-media-data/
- Social Media Data Analytics course on Coursera by the author: https://www.coursera.org/learn/social-media-data-analytics

Notes

1. Statistics Canada. Definitions: http://www.statcan.gc.ca/edu/power-pouvoir/ch1/definitions/5214853-eng.htm
2. BrightPlanet®. Structured vs. unstructured data definition: https://brightplanet.com/2012/06/structured-vs-unstructured-data/
3. US Government data repository: https://www.data.gov/
4. City of Chicago data repository: https://data.cityofchicago.org/
5. US Government policy M-13-3: https://project-open-data.cio.gov/policy-memo/
6. Project Open Data "open license": https://project-open-data.cio.gov/open-licenses/
7. Facebook Graph API: https://developers.facebook.com/docs/graph-api/
8. Yelp dataset challenge: https://www.yelp.com/dataset/challenge
9. SPM created by Karl Friston: https://en.wikipedia.org/wiki/Karl_Friston
10. UCL SPM website: http://www.fil.ion.ucl.ac.uk/spm/
11. UF Health. UF Biostatistics open learning textbook: http://bolt.mph.ufl.edu/2012/08/02/learn-by-doing-exploring-a-dataset/
12. An actual tab will appear as simply a space. To aid clarity, in this book we are explicitly spelling out `<TAB>`. Therefore, wherever you see in this book `<TAB>`, in reality an actual tab would appear as a space.
13. XUL.fr. Really Simple Syndication definition: http://www.xul.fr/en-xml-rss.html
14. w3schools. XML RSS explanation and example: https://www.w3schools.com/xml/xml_rss.asp
15. FEED Validator: http://www.feedvalidator.org
16. Google: submit your content: http://www.google.com/submityourcontent/website-owner
17. Bing submit site: http://www.bing.com/toolbox/submit-site-url
18. JSON: http://www.json.org/
19. w3schools. JSON introduction: http://www.w3schools.com/js/js_json_intro.asp
20. KDnuggets™ introduction to data mining course: http://www.kdnuggets.com/data_mining_course/
21. Data cleaning and pre-processing presentation: http://www.mimuw.edu.pl/~son/datamining/DM/4-preprocess.pdf

3 Techniques

"Information is the oil of the 21st century, and analytics is the combustion engine."
— Peter Sondergaard, Senior Vice President, Gartner Research

What do you need?

- Computational thinking (refer to Chapter 1).
- Knowledge of basic math operations, including exponents and roots.
- A basic understanding of linear algebra (e.g., line representation and line equation).
- Access to a spreadsheet program such as Microsoft Excel or Google Sheets.

What will you learn?

- Various forms of data analysis and analytics techniques.
- A simple introduction to correlation and regression.
- How to undertake simple summaries and presentation of numerical and categorical data.

3.1 Introduction

There are many tools and techniques that a data scientist is expected to know or acquire as problems arise. Often, it is hard to separate tools and techniques. One whole section of this book (four chapters) is dedicated to teaching how to use various tools, and, as we learn about them, we also pick up and practice some essential techniques. This happens for two reasons. The first one is already mentioned here – it is hard to separate tools from techniques. Regarding the second reason – since our main purpose is not necessarily to master any programming tools, we will learn about programming languages and platforms in the context of solving data problems.

That said, there are aspects of data science-related techniques that are better studied without worrying about any particular tool or programming language. And that is the approach we will pursue. In this chapter, we will review some basic techniques used in data science and see how they are used for performing analytics and data analyses.

We will begin by considering some differences and similarities between data analysis and data analytics. Often, it is not critical to ignore their differences, but here we will see how distinguishing the two might be important. For the rest of the chapter we will look at various forms of analyses: descriptive, diagnostic, predictive, prescriptive, exploratory, and mechanistic. In the process we will be reviewing basic statistics. That should not surprise you, as data science is often considered just a fancy term for statistics! As we learn about these tools and techniques, we will also look at some examples and gain experience using real data analysis (though it will be limited due to our lack of knowledge about any programming or specialized tools as of this chapter).

3.2 Data Analysis and Data Analytics

These two terms – **data analysis** and **data analytics** – are often used interchangeably and could be confusing. Is a job that calls for data analytics really talking about data analysis and vice versa? Well, there are some subtle but important differences between analysis and analytics. A lack of understanding can affect the practitioner's ability to leverage the data to their best advantage.[1]

According to Dave Kasik, Boeing's Senior Technical Fellow in visualization and interactive techniques, "In my terminology, data analysis refers to hands-on data exploration and evaluation. Data analytics is a broader term and includes data analysis as [a] necessary subcomponent. Analytics defines the science behind the analysis. The science means understanding the cognitive processes an analyst uses to understand problems and explore data in meaningful ways."[2]

One way to understand the difference between analysis and analytics is to think in terms of past and future. Analysis looks backwards, providing marketers with a historical view of what has happened. Analytics, on the other hand, models the future or predicts a result.

Analytics makes extensive use of mathematics and statistics and the use of descriptive techniques and predictive models to gain valuable knowledge from data. These insights from data are used to recommend action or to guide decision-making in a business context. Thus, analytics is not so much concerned with individual analysis or analysis steps, but with the entire methodology.

There is no clear agreeable-to-all classification scheme available in the literature to categorize all the analysis techniques that are used by data science professionals. However, based on their application on various stages of data analysis, I have categorized analysis techniques into six classes of analysis and analytics: descriptive analysis, diagnostic analytics, predictive analytics, prescriptive analytics, exploratory analysis, and mechanistic analysis. Each of these and their applications are described below.

3.3 Descriptive Analysis

Descriptive analysis is about: "What is happening now based on incoming data." It is a method for quantitatively describing the main features of a collection of data. Here are a few key points about **descriptive analysis**:

- Typically, it is the first kind of data analysis performed on a dataset.
- Usually it is applied to large volumes of data, such as census data.
- Description and interpretation processes are different steps.

Descriptive analysis can be useful in the sales cycle, for example, to categorize customers by their likely product preferences and purchasing patterns. Another example is the Census Data Set, where descriptive analysis is applied on a whole population (see Figure 3.1).

Researchers and analysts collecting quantitative data or translating qualitative data into numbers are often faced with a large amount of raw data that needs to be organized and summarized before it can be analyzed. Data can only reveal patterns and allow observers to draw conclusions when it is presented as an organized summary. Here is where descriptive statistics come into play: they facilitate analyzing and summarizing the data and are thus instrumental to processes inherent in data science.

Data cannot be properly used if it is not correctly interpreted. This requires appropriate statistics. For example, should we use the mean, median, or mode, two of these, or all three?[4] Each of these measures is a summary that emphasizes certain aspects of the data and overlooks others. They all provide information we need to get a full picture of the world we are trying to understand.

The process of describing something requires that we extract its important parts: to paint a scene, an artist must first decide which features to highlight. Similarly, humans often point out significant aspects of the world with numbers, such as the size of a room, the population of a State (as in Figure 3.1), or the Scholastic Aptitude Test (SAT) score of a high-school senior. Nouns name these things, or characteristic areas, populations, and verbal learning abilities. To describe these features, English speakers use adjectives, for example, decent-sized room, small-town population, bright high-school senior. But numbers can replace these words: 100 sq. ft. room, Florida population of 18,801,318, or a senior with a verbal score of 800.

Numerical representation can hold a considerable advantage over words. Numbers allow humans to more precisely differentiate between objects or concepts. For example, two rooms may be described as "small," but numbers distinguish a 9-foot expanse from a 10-foot expanse. One could argue that even imperfect measuring instruments afford more levels of differentiation than adjectives. And, of course, numbers can modify words by providing a count of units (2500 persons), indicating a rank (third most populated city in the country, as shown in the inset box in Figure 3.1), or placing the characteristics on some scale (SAT score of 800, with a mean of 600).

3.3.1 Variables

Before we process or analyze any data, we have to be able to capture and represent it. This is done with the help of variables. A variable is a label we give to our data. For instance, you can write down age values of all your cousins in a table or a spreadsheet and label that column with "age." Here, "age" is a variable and it is of type numeric (and "ratio" type as we will soon see). If we then want to identify who is a student or not, we can create another column, and next to each cousin's name we can write down "yes" or "no" under a new column called "student." Here, "student" is a variable and it is of type categorical (more on that soon).

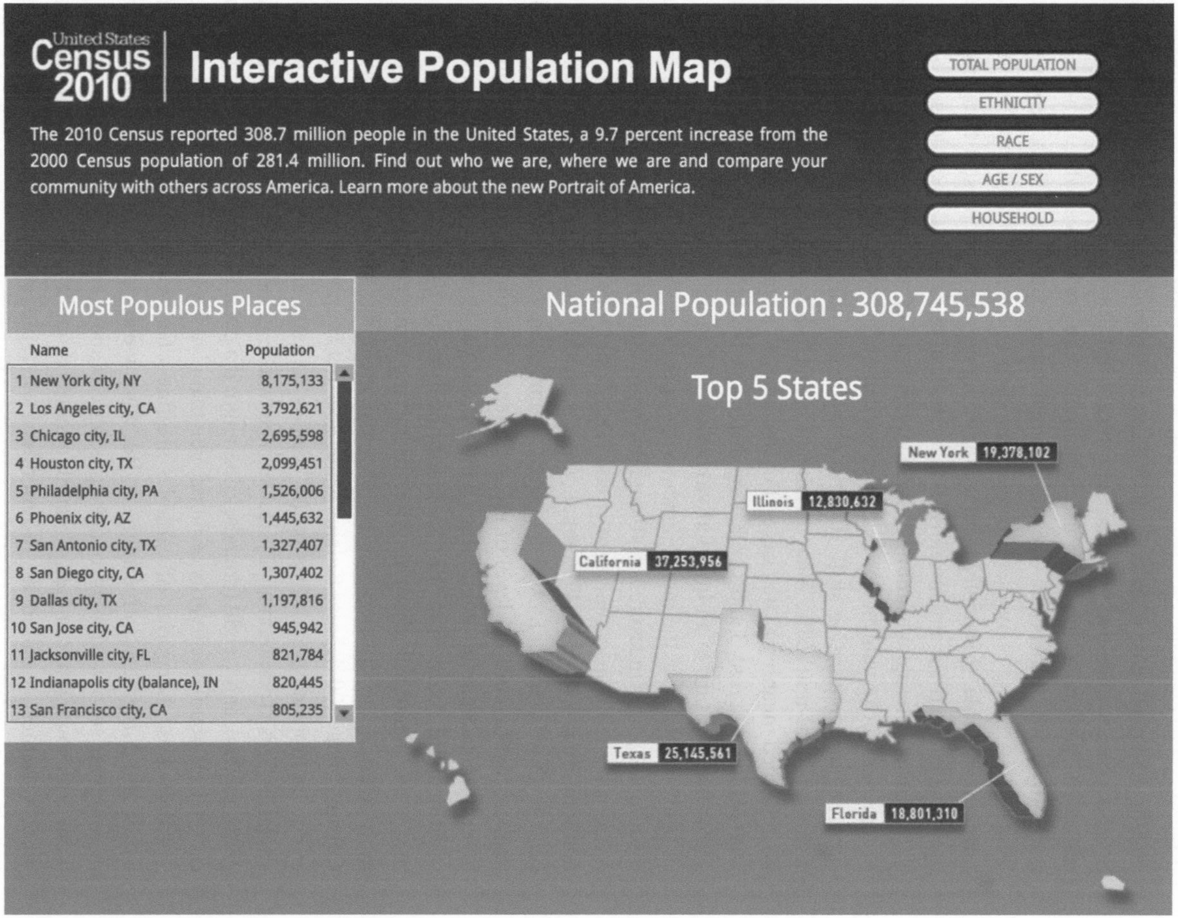

United States Census 2010

Interactive Population Map

The 2010 Census reported 308.7 million people in the United States, a 9.7 percent increase from the 2000 Census population of 281.4 million. Find out who we are, where we are and compare your community with others across America. Learn more about the new Portrait of America.

TOTAL POPULATION
ETHNICITY
RACE
AGE / SEX
HOUSEHOLD

Most Populous Places

Name	Population
1 New York city, NY	8,175,133
2 Los Angeles city, CA	3,792,621
3 Chicago city, IL	2,695,598
4 Houston city, TX	2,099,451
5 Philadelphia city, PA	1,526,006
6 Phoenix city, AZ	1,445,632
7 San Antonio city, TX	1,327,407
8 San Diego city, CA	1,307,402
9 Dallas city, TX	1,197,816
10 San Jose city, CA	945,942
11 Jacksonville city, FL	821,784
12 Indianapolis city (balance), IN	820,445
13 San Francisco city, CA	805,235

National Population : 308,745,538

Top 5 States

New York 19,378,102
Illinois 12,830,632
California 37,253,956
Texas 25,145,561
Florida 18,801,310

Figure 3.1 Census data as a way to describe the population.[3]

Since a lot of what we will do in this book (and perhaps what you will do in a data science job) will deal with different forms of numerical information, let us look further into such variables. Numeric information can be separated into distinct categories that can be used to summarize data. The first stage of summarizing any numeric information is to identify the category to which it belongs. For example, the above section covered three operations for numbers: counting, ranking, and placing on a scale. Each of these corresponds to different levels of measurement. So, if people are classified based on their racial identities, statisticians can name the categories and count their contents. Such use defines the **categorical variable**. Think about animal taxonomy that biologists use – the one with mammals, reptiles, etc. Those represent categorical levels. If we find it convenient to represent such categories using numbers, this becomes a **nominal variable**. Essentially here, we are using numbers to represent categories, but cannot use those numbers for any meaningful mathematical or statistical operations.

If we can differentiate among individuals within a group, we can use an **ordinal variable** to represent those values. For example, we can rank a selection of people in terms of their apparent communication skill. But this statistic can only go so far; it cannot, for example, create an equal-unit scale. What this means is that, while we could order the entities, there is no enhanced meaning to that order. For instance, we cannot just subtract someone at rank 5 with someone at rank 3 and say that the difference is what is represented by someone at rank 2. For that, we turn to an **interval variable**.

Let us think about the measurement of temperature. We do it in Fahrenheit or Celsius. If the temperature is measured as 40 degrees Fahrenheit on a given day, that measure is placed on a scale with an actual zero point (i.e., 0 degrees Fahrenheit). If the next day the temperature is 45 degrees Fahrenheit, we can say that the temperature has risen by 5 degrees (that is the difference). And 5 degrees Fahrenheit has physical meaning, unlike what happens with an ordinal level of measurement. This kind of scenario describes an interval level of measurement. Put another way, an interval level of measurement allows us to do additions and subtractions but not multiplications or divisions. What does that mean? It means we cannot talk about doubling or halving temperature. OK, well, we could, but that multiplication or division has no physical meaning. Water evaporates at 100 degrees Celsius, but at 200 degrees Celsius water does not evaporate twice as much or twice as fast.

For multiplication and division (as well as addition and subtraction), we turn to a **ratio variable**. This is common in physical sciences and engineering. Examples include length (feet, yards, meters), and weight (pounds, kilograms). If a pound of grapes costs $5, two pounds will cost $10. If you have 4 yards of fabric, you can give 2 yards each to two of your friends.

All of these categories of variables are fine when we are dealing with one variable at a time and doing descriptive analysis. But when we are trying to connect multiple variables or using one set of variables to make predictions about another set, we may want to classify them with some other names. A variable that is thought to be controlled or not affected by other variables is called an **independent variable**. A variable that depends on other variables (most often other independent variables) is called a **dependent variable**. In the case of a prediction problem, an independent variable is also called a **predictor variable** and a dependent variable is called an **outcome variable**.

For instance, imagine we have data about tumor size for some patients and whether the patients have cancer or not. This could be in a table with two columns: "tumor size" and "cancer," the former being a ratio type variable (we can talk about one tumor being twice the size of another), and the latter being a categorical type variable ("yes", "no" values). Now imagine we want to use the "tumor size" variable to say something about the "cancer" variable. Later in this book we will see how something like this could be done under a class of problems called "classification." But for now, we can think of "tumor size" as an independent or a predictor variable and "cancer" as a dependent or an outcome variable.

3.3.2 Frequency Distribution

Of course, data needs to be displayed. Once some data has been collected, it is useful to plot a graph showing how many times each score occurs. This is known as a frequency distribution. Frequency distributions come in different shapes and sizes. Therefore, it is important to have some general descriptions for common types of distribution. The following are some of the ways in which statisticians can present numerical findings.

Histogram. Histograms plot values of observations on the horizontal axis, with a bar showing how many times each value occurred in the dataset. Let us take a look at an example of how a histogram can be crafted out of a dataset. Table 3.1 represents *Productivity* measured in terms of output for a group of data science professionals. Some of them went through extensive statistics training (represented as "Y" in the *Training* column) while others did not (N). The dataset also contains the work experience (denoted as *Experience*) of each professional in terms of number of working hours.

Table 3.1 Productivity dataset.

Productivity	Experience	Training
5	1	Y
2	0	N
10	10	Y
4	5	Y
6	5	Y
12	15	Y
5	10	Y
6	2	Y
4	4	Y
3	5	N
9	5	Y
8	10	Y
11	15	Y
13	19	Y
4	5	N
5	7	N
7	12	Y
8	15	N
12	20	Y
3	5	N
15	20	Y

Table 3.1 (cont.)

Productivity	Experience	Training
8	16	N
4	9	N
6	17	Y
9	13	Y
7	6	Y
5	8	N
14	18	Y
7	17	N
6	6	Y

Try It Yourself 3.1: Variables

Before we continue with generating a histogram, let us use this table and make sure we have grasped the concepts about the variables from before.

Answer the following questions using Table 3.1.

1. What kind of variable is "Productivity"?
2. What kind of variable is "Experience"?
3. What kind of variable is "Training"?
4. We are trying to understand if, by looking at "Productivity" and "Experience," we could predict if someone went through training or not. In this scenario, identify independent or predictor variable(s) and dependent or outcome variable(s).

Hands-On Example 3.1: Histogram

A histogram can be created from the numbers in the *Productivity* column, as shown in Figure 3.2. Any spreadsheet program, for example, Microsoft Excel or Google Sheets, supports a host of visualization options,

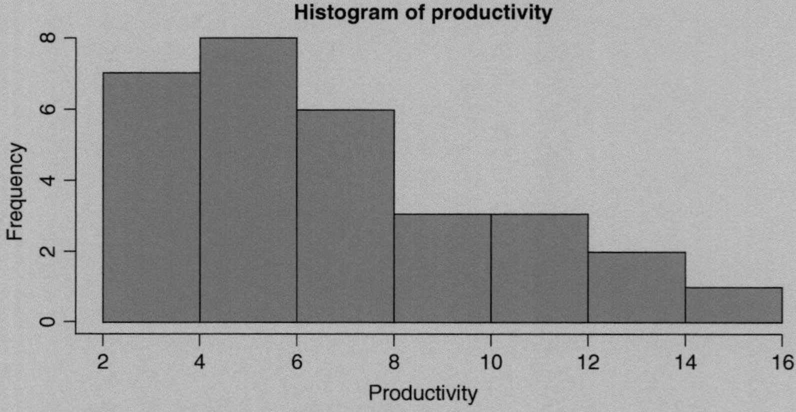

Figure 3.2 Histogram using the Productivity data.

such as charts, plots, line graphs, maps, etc. If you are using a Google Sheet, the procedure to create the histogram is first to select the intended column, followed by selecting the option of "insert chart", denoted by the icon in the toolbar, which will present you with the chart editor. In the editor, select the option of histogram chart in the chart type dropdown and it will create a chart like that in Figure 3.2. You can further customize the chart by specifying the color of the chart, the *X*-axis label, *Y*-axis label, etc.

Try It Yourself 3.2: Histogram

Let us test your understanding of histogram and related concepts on the pizza franchise dataset from the Business Opportunity Handbook. The dataset is available from OA 3.1, where *X* represents annual franchise fee in $100 and *Y* represents the startup cost in the same numeration. Using this data and your favorite spreadsheet program, plot the data to visualize the startup cost changes with the franchise cost.

Hands-On Example 3.2: Pie Chart

A histogram worked fine for numerical data, but what about categorical data? In other words, how do we visualize the data when it's distributed in a few finite categories? We have such data in the third column called "Training." For that, we can create a pie chart, as shown in Figure 3.3.

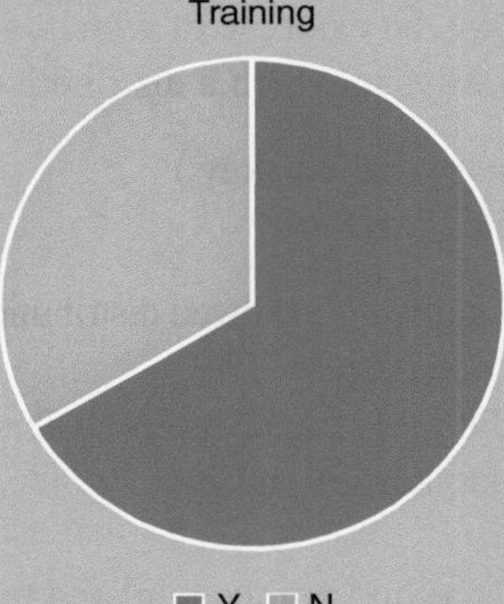

Figure 3.3 Pie chart showing the distribution of "Training" in the Productivity data.

You can follow the same process as for a histogram if you are using a Google Sheet. The key difference is here you have to select the pie chart as chart type from the chart editor.

We will often be working with data that are numerical and we will need to understand how those numbers are spread. For that, we can look at the nature of that distribution. It turns out that, if the data is normally distributed, various forms of analyses become easy and straightforward. What is a normal distribution?

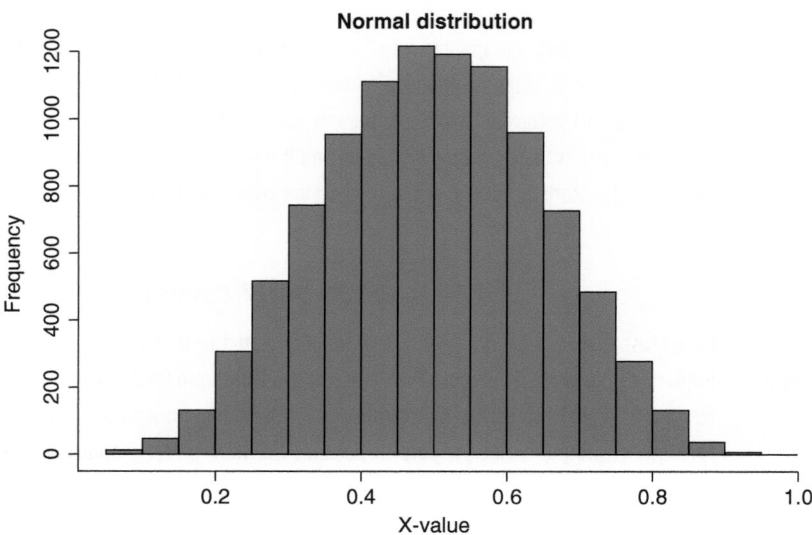

Figure 3.4 Example of a normal distribution.

Normal Distribution. In an ideal world, data would be distributed symmetrically around the center of all scores. Thus, if we drew a vertical line through the center of a distribution, both sides should look the same. This so-called *normal distribution* is characterized by a bell-shaped curve, an example of which is shown in Figure 3.4.

There are two ways in which a distribution can deviate from normal:

- Lack of symmetry (called **skew**)
- Pointiness (called **kurtosis**)

As shown in Figure 3.5, a skewed distribution can be either positively skewed (Figure 3.5a) or negatively skewed (Figure 3.5b).

Kurtosis, on the other hand, refers to the degree to which scores cluster at the end of a distribution (platykurtic) and how "pointy" a distribution is (leptokurtic), as shown in Figure 3.6.

There are ways to find numbers related to these distributions to give us a sense of their skewedness and kurtosis, but we will skip that for now. At this point, we will leave the judgment of the normality of a distribution to our visual inspection of it using the histograms as shown here. As we acquire appropriate statistical tools in the next section of this book, we will see how to run some tests to find out if a distribution is normal or not.

Try It Yourself 3.3: Distributions

What does the shape of the histogram distribution from Try it Yourself 3.2 look like? What does this kind of shape inform us about the underlying data?

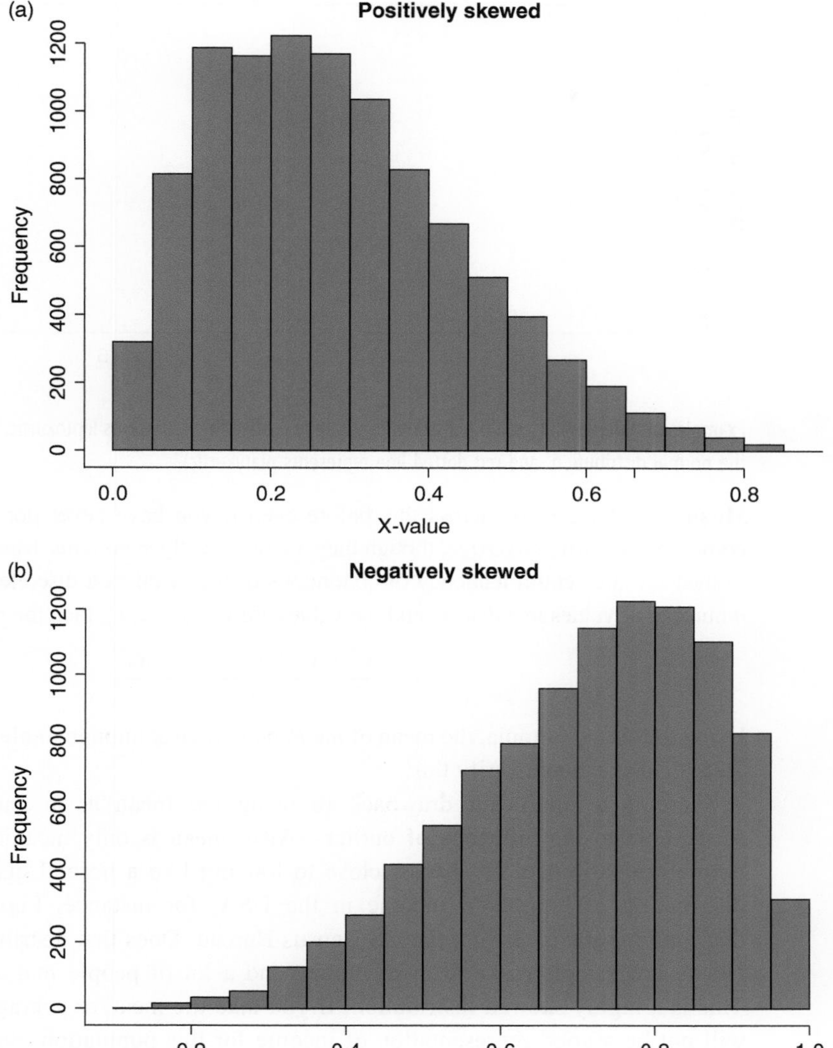

Figure 3.5 Examples of skewed distributions.

3.3.3 Measures of Centrality

Often, one number can tell us enough about a distribution. This is typically a number that points to the "center" of a distribution. In other words, we can calculate where the "center" of a frequency distribution lies, which is also known as the central tendency. We put "center" in quotes because it depends how it is defined. There are three measures commonly used: mean, median, and mode.

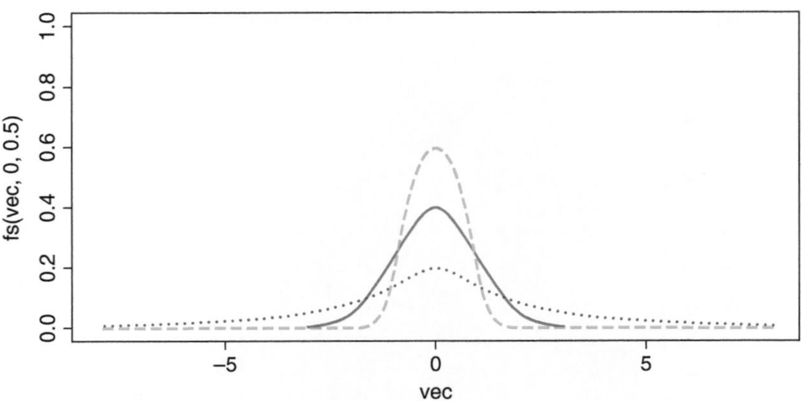

Figure 3.6 Examples of different kurtosis in a distribution (orange dashed line represents leptokurtic, blue solid line represents the normal distribution, and red dotted line represents platykurtic).

Mean. You have come across this before even if you have never done statistics. Mean is commonly known as *average*, though they are not exactly synonyms. Mean is most often used to measure the central tendency of continuous data as well as a discrete dataset. If there are n number of values in a dataset and the values are $x_1, x_2, \ldots, x_n$, then the mean is calculated as

$$\overline{x} = \frac{x_1 + x_2 + x_3 + \cdots + x_n}{n}. \tag{3.1}$$

Using the above formula, the mean of the *Productivity* column in Table 3.1 comes out to be 7.267. Go ahead and verify this.

There is a significant drawback to using the mean as a central statistic: it is susceptible to the influence of outliers. Also, mean is only meaningful if the data is normally distributed, or at least close to looking like a normal distribution. Take the distribution of household income in the USA, for instance. Figure 3.7 shows this distribution, obtained from the US Census Bureau. Does that distribution look normal? No. A few people make a lot of money and a lot of people make very little money. This is a highly skewed distribution. If you take the mean or average from this data, it will not be a good representation of income for this population. So, what can we do? We can use another measure of central tendency: median.

Median. The median is the middle score for a dataset that has been sorted according to the values of the data. With an even number of values, the median is calculated as the average of the middle two data points. For example, for the Productivity dataset, the median of *Experience* is 9.5. What about the US household income? The median income in the USA, as of 2014, is $53,700. That means half the people in the USA are making $53,700 or less and the other half are on the other side of that threshold.

Mode. The mode is the most frequently occurring value in a dataset. On a histogram representation, the highest bar denotes the mode of the data. Normally, mode is used for categorical data; for example, for the *Training* component in the Productivity dataset, the most common category is the desired output.

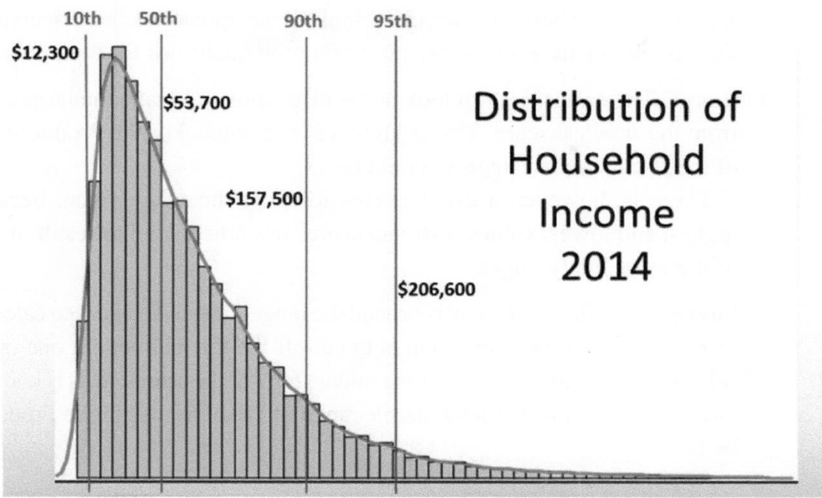

Figure 3.7 Income distribution in the United States based on the latest census data available.[5]

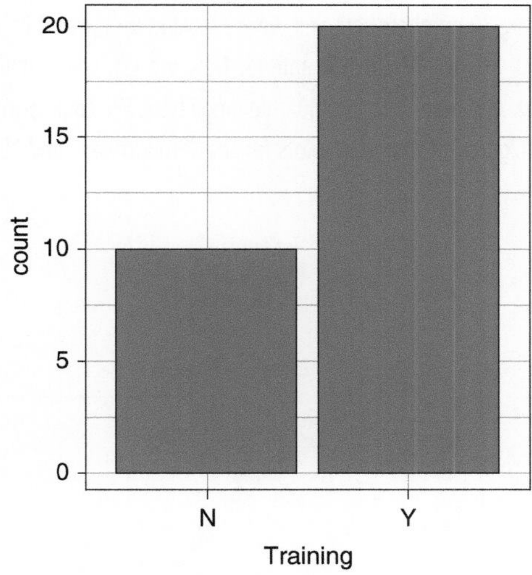

Figure 3.8 Visualizing mode for the Productivity data.

As depicted in Figure 3.8, in the Productivity dataset, there are 10 instances of N and 20 instances of Y values in *Training*. So, in this case, the mode for *Training* is Y. [Note: If the number of instances of Y and N are the same, then there would be no mode for *Training*.]

3.3.4 Dispersion of a Distribution

We saw in section 3.3.2 that distributions come in all shapes and sizes. Simply looking at a central point (mean, median, or mode) may not help in understanding the actual shape of a distribution. Therefore, we often look at the spread, or the dispersion, of a distribution. The following are some of the most common quantities for measures of dispersion.

Range. The easiest way to look at the dispersion is to take the largest score and subtract it from the smallest score. This is known as the range. For the Productivity dataset, the range of the *Productivity* category would be 13.

There is, however, a disadvantage to using the range value: because it uses only the highest and lowest values, extreme scores or outliers tend to result in an inaccurate picture of the more likely range.

Interquartile Range. One way around the range's disadvantage is to calculate it after removing extreme values. One convention is to cut off the top and bottom one-quarter of the data and calculate the range of the remaining middle 50% of the scores. This is known as the interquartile range. For example, the interquartile range of "Experience" in the Productivity dataset would be 10.

Hands-On Example 3.3: Interquartile Range

Can we easily find out interquartile range, and even visualize it? The answer is "yes." Let us revisit the data in Table 3.1 and focus on the "Experience" column. If we sort it, we get Table 3.2.

There are 30 numbers here and we are looking for the middle 15 numbers. That gives us numbers 5, 5, 5, 6, 6, 7, 8, 9, 10, 10, 10, 12, 13, 15, and 15. Now we can see that the range of these numbers is 10 (min = 5 to max = 15). And that is our interquartile range here. We could also visualize this whole process in something called boxplots. Figure 3.9 shows boxplots for the "Productivity" and "Experience" columns.

Table 3.2 Sorted "Experience" column from the Productivity dataset.

Experience
0
1
2
4
5
5
5
5
5
5
6
6
7
8
9

Table 3.2 (cont.)

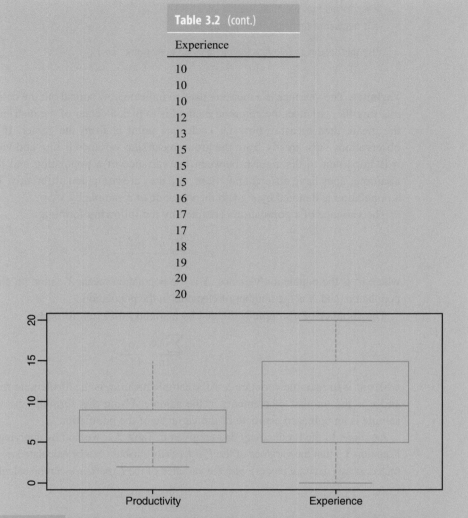

Experience
10
10
10
12
13
15
15
15
16
17
17
18
19
20
20

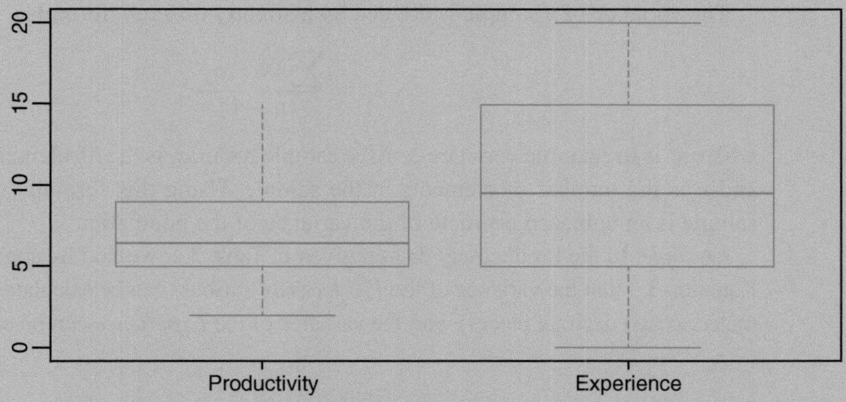

Figure 3.9 Boxplot for the "Productivity" and "Experience" columns of the Productivity dataset.

As shown in the boxplot for the "Experience" attribute, after removing the top one-fourth values (between 15 and 20) and bottom one-fourth (close to zero to 5), the range of the remaining data can be calculated as 10 (from 5 to 15). Likewise, the interquartile range of the "Productivity" attribute can be calculated as 5.

Try It Yourself 3.4: Interquartile Range

For this exercise, you are going to use the fire and theft data from same zip code of Chicago metropolitan area (reference: US Commission on Civil Rights). The dataset available from OA 3.2 has observations in pairs:

X represents fires per 1000 housing units.
Y is number of thefts per 1000 population.

Use this dataset to calculate the interquartile ranges of *X* and *Y*.

Variance. The variance is a measure used to indicate how spread out the data points are. To measure the variance, the common method is to pick a center of the distribution, typically the mean, then measure how far each data point is from the center. If the individual observations vary greatly from the group mean, the variance is big; and vice versa. Here, it is important to distinguish between the variance of a population and the variance of a sample. They have different notations, and they are computed differently. The variance of a population is denoted by σ^2; and the variance of a sample by s^2.

The variance of a population is defined by the following formula:

$$\sigma^2 = \frac{\sum (X_i - X)^2}{N}, \tag{3.2}$$

where σ^2 is the population variance, X is the population mean, X_i is the ith element from the population, and N is the number of elements in the population.

The variance of a sample is defined by a slightly different formula:

$$s^2 = \frac{\sum (x_i - x)^2}{(n-1)}, \tag{3.3}$$

where s^2 is the sample variance, x is the sample mean, x_i is the ith element from the sample, and n is the number of elements in the sample. Using this formula, the variance of the sample is an unbiased estimate of the variance of the population.

Example: In the Productivity dataset given in Table 3.1, we find by applying the formula in Equation 3.3 that the variance of the *Productivity* attribute can be calculated as 11.93 (approximated to two decimal places), and the variance of the *Experience* can be calculated as 36.

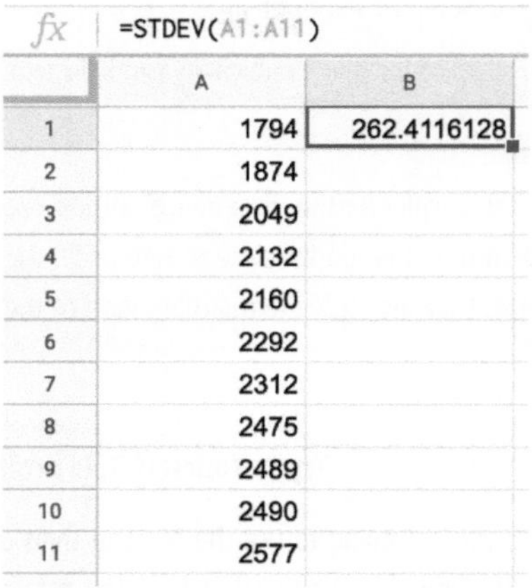

fx =STDEV(A1:A11)

	A	B
1	1794	262.4116128
2	1874	
3	2049	
4	2132	
5	2160	
6	2292	
7	2312	
8	2475	
9	2489	
10	2490	
11	2577	

Figure 3.10 A snapshot from Google Sheets showing how to compute the standard deviation.

Standard Deviation. There is one issue with the variance as a measure. It gives us the measure of spread in units squared. So, for example, if we measure the variance of age (measured in years) of all the students in a class, the measure we will get will be in *years*^{2}. However, practically, it would make more sense if we got the measure in *years* (not years squared). For this reason, we often take the square root of the variance, which ensures the measure of average spread is in the same units as the original measure. This measure is known as the standard deviation (see Figure 3.10).

The formula to compute the standard deviation of a sample is

$$s = \sqrt{\frac{\sum (x_i - x)^2}{(n-1)}}. \tag{3.4}$$

FYI: Comparing Distributions and Hypothesis Testing

Often there is a need to compare different distributions to derive some important insights or make decisions. For instance, we want to see if our new strategy for marketing is changing our customers' spending behaviors from the last month to this month. Let us assume that we have data about each customer's spending amounts for both of these months. Using that data, we can plot a histogram per month that shows on the *x*-axis the number of customers and on the *y*-axis the amount they spent in that month. Now the question is: Are these two plots different enough to say that the new marketing strategy is effective? This is not something that can be easily answered by visual inspection. For this, there are several statistical tests that one could run that compare the two distributions and tell us if they are different.

Normally, for this, we begin by stating our hypotheses. A **hypothesis** is a way to state our assumption or belief that could be tested. The default knowledge or assumption could be stated as a **null hypothesis** and the opposite of that is called the **alternative hypothesis.** So, in this case, our null hypothesis could say that there is no difference between the two distributions, and the alternative hypothesis will state that there is indeed a difference.

Next, we run one (or several) of those statistical tests. Almost any statistical package that you use will have in-built functions or packages to run such tests. Often, they are very easy to do. Typically, the result of a test would be some score and more importantly a confidence or probability value (frequently referred to as *p*-value) that indicates how much we believe the two distributions are the same. If this value is very small (typically less than 0.05 or 5%), we can reject the null hypothesis (that the distributions are the same) and accept the alternative hypothesis (that they are not). And that gives us our conclusion. In short, if we run a statistical test and the *p*-value comes out less than or equal to 0.05, we can conclude that the new marketing strategy did indeed have the effect (considering that no other variables were changed).

Try It Yourself 3.5: Standard Deviation

For this exercise, use the ANAEROB dataset that is available for download from OA 3.3. The dataset has 53 observations (numbers) of oxygen uptake and expired ventilation. Use this data to calculate the standard deviation for both attributes individually.

3.4 Diagnostic Analytics

Diagnostic analytics are used for discovery, or to determine why something happened. Sometimes this type of analytics when done hands-on with a small dataset is also known as **causal analysis**, since it involves at least one cause (usually more than one) and one effect.

This allows a look at past performance to determine what happened and why. The result of the analysis is often referred to as an analytic dashboard.

For example, for a social media marketing campaign, you can use descriptive analytics to assess the number of posts, mentions, followers, fans, page views, reviews, or pins, etc. There can be thousands of online mentions that can be distilled into a single view to see what worked and what did not work in your past campaigns.

There are various types of techniques available for diagnostic or causal analytics. Among them, one of the most frequently used is correlation.

3.4.1 Correlations

Correlation is a statistical analysis that is used to measure and describe the *strength* and *direction* of the relationship between two variables. Strength indicates how closely two variables are related to each other, and direction indicates how one variable would change its value as the value of the other variable changes.

Correlation is a simple statistical measure that examines how two variables change together over time. Take, for example, "umbrella" and "rain." If someone who grew up in a place where it never rained saw rain for the first time, this person would observe that, whenever it rains, people use umbrellas. They may also notice that, on dry days, folks do not carry umbrellas. By definition, "rain" and "umbrella" are said to be correlated! More specifically, this relationship is strong and positive. Think about this for a second.

An important statistic, the **Pearson's *r* correlation**, is widely used to measure the degree of the relationship between linear related variables. When examining the stock market, for example, the Pearson's r correlation can measure the degree to which two commodities are related. The following formula is used to calculate the Pearson's r correlation:

$$r = \frac{N\sum xy - \sum x \sum y}{\sqrt{\left[N\sum x^2 - \left(\sum x\right)^2\right]\left[N\sum y^2 - \left(\sum y\right)^2\right]}}, \tag{3.5}$$

where

r = Pearson's r correlation coefficient,
N = number of values in each dataset,
$\sum xy$ = sum of the products of paired scores,
$\sum x$ = sum of x scores,
$\sum y$ = sum of y scores,

$\sum x^2$ = sum of squared x scores, and
$\sum y^2$ = sum of squared y scores.[6]

Hands-On Example 3.4: Correlation

Let us use the formula in Equation 3.5 and calculate Pearson's r correlation coefficient for the height–weight pair with the data provided in Table 3.3.

First we will calculate various quantities needed for solving Pearson's r correlation formula:

N = number of values in each dataset = 10
$\sum xy$ = sum of the products of paired scores = 98,335.30
$\sum x$ = sum of x scores = 670.70
$\sum y$ = sum of y scores = 1463
$\sum x^2$ = sum of squared x scores = 45,058.21
$\sum y^2$ = sum of squared y scores = 218,015

Plugging these into the Pearson's r correlation formula gives us 0.39 (approximated to two decimal places) as the correlation coefficient. This indicates two things: (1) "height" and "weight" are positively related, which means that, as one goes up, so does the other; and (2) the strength of their relation is medium.

Table 3.3 Height–weight data.

Height	Weight
64.5	118
73.3	143
68.8	172
65	147
69	146
64.5	138
66	175
66.3	134
68.8	172
64.5	118

Try It Yourself 3.6: Correlation

For this exercise, you are going to use the nasal data of male gray kangaroos (*Australian Journal of Zoology*, **28**, 607–613). The dataset can be downloaded from OA 3.4. It has two attributes. In each pair, the X represents the nasal length in 10 mm, whereas the corresponding Y represents nasal width. Use this dataset to test the correlation between X and Y.

3.5 Predictive Analytics

As you may have guessed, **predictive analytics** has its roots in our ability to predict what might happen. These analytics are about understanding the future using the data and the trends we have seen in the past, as well as emerging new contexts and processes. An example is trying to predict how people will spend their tax refunds based on how consumers normally behave around a given time of the year (past data and trends), and how a new tax policy (new context) may affect people's refunds.

Predictive analytics provides companies with actionable insights based on data. Such information includes estimates about the likelihood of a future outcome. It is important to remember that no statistical algorithm can "predict" the future with 100% certainty because the foundation of predictive analytics is based on probabilities. Companies use these statistics to forecast what might happen. Some of the software most commonly used by data science professionals for predictive analytics are SAS predictive analytics, IBM predictive analytics, RapidMiner, and others.

As Figure 3.11 suggests, predictive analytics is done in stages.

1. First, once the data collection is complete, it needs to go through the process of cleaning (refer to Chapter 2 on data).
2. Cleaned data can help us obtain *hindsight* in relationships between different variables. Plotting the data (e.g., on a scatterplot) is a good place to look for *hindsight*.
3. Next, we need to confirm the existence of such relationships in the data. This is where regression comes into play. From the regression equation, we can confirm the pattern of distribution inside the data. In other words, we obtain *insight* from *hindsight*.
4. Finally, based on the identified patterns, or *insight*, we can predict the future, i.e., *foresight*.

The following example illustrates a use for predictive analytics.[8] Let us assume that Salesforce kept campaign data for the last eight quarters. This data comprises total sales generated by newspaper, TV, and online ad campaigns and associated expenditures, as provided in Table 3.4.

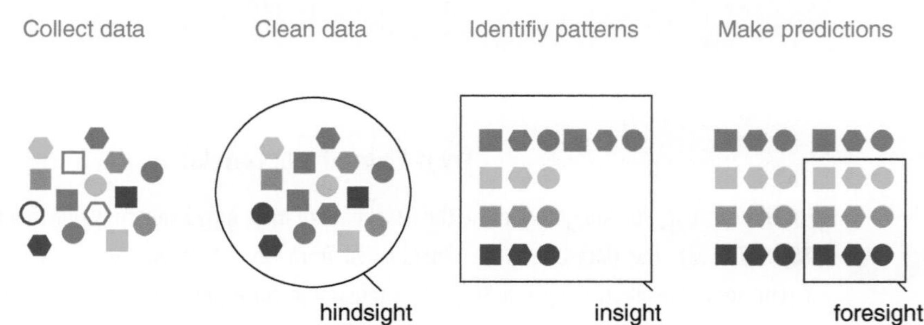

Figure 3.11 Process of predictive analytics.[7]

Table 3.4 Data for doing predictive analytics.

Serial	Sales	Newspaper	TV	Online
1	16,850	1000	500	1500
2	12,010	500	500	500
3	14,740	2000	500	500
4	13,890	1000	1000	1000
5	12,950	1000	500	500
6	15,640	500	1000	1000
7	14,960	1000	1000	1000
8	13,630	500	1500	500

With this data, we can predict the sales based on the expenditures of ad campaigns in different media for Salesforce.

Like data analytics, predictive analytics has a number of common applications. For example, many people turn to predictive analytics to produce their credit scores. Financial services use such numbers to determine the probability that a customer will make their credit payments on time. FICO, in particular, has extensively used predictive analytics to develop the methodology to calculate individual FICO scores.[9]

Customer relationship management (CRM) classifies another common area for predictive analytics. Here, the process contributes to objectives such as marketing campaigns, sales, and customer service. Predictive analytics applications are also used in the healthcare field. They can determine which patients are at risk for developing certain conditions such as diabetes, asthma, and other chronic or serious illnesses.

3.6 Prescriptive Analytics

Prescriptive analytics[10] is the area of business analytics dedicated to finding the best course of action for a given situation. This may start by first analyzing the situation (using descriptive analysis), but then moves toward finding connections among various parameters/variables, and their relation to each other to address a specific problem, more likely that of prediction.

A process-intensive task, the prescriptive approach analyzes potential decisions, the interactions between decisions, the influences that bear upon these decisions, and the bearing all of this has on an outcome to ultimately prescribe an optimal course of action in real time.[11]

Prescriptive analytics can also suggest options for taking advantage of a future opportunity or mitigate a future risk and illustrate the implications of each. In practice, prescriptive analytics can continually and automatically process new data to improve the accuracy of predictions and provide advantageous decision options.

Specific techniques used in prescriptive analytics include optimization, simulation, game theory,[12] and decision-analysis methods.

Prescriptive analytics can be really valuable in deriving insights from given data, but it is largely not used.[13] According to Gartner,[14] 13% of organizations are using predictive analytics, but only 3% are using prescriptive analytics. Where big data analytics in general sheds light on a subject, prescriptive analytics gives you laser-like focus to answer specific questions.

For example, in healthcare, we can better manage the patient population by using prescriptive analytics to measure the number of patients who are clinically obese, then add filters for factors like diabetes and LDL cholesterol levels to determine where to focus treatment.

There are two more categories of data analysis techniques that are different from the above-mentioned four categories – exploratory analysis and mechanistic analysis.

3.7 Exploratory Analysis

Often when working with data, we may not have a clear understanding of the problem or the situation. And yet, we may be called on to provide some insights. In other words, we are asked to provide an answer without knowing the question! This is where we go for an exploration.

Exploratory analysis is an approach to analyzing datasets to find previously unknown relationships. Often such analysis involves using various data visualization approaches. Yes, sometimes seeing is believing! But more important, when we lack a clear question or a hypothesis, plotting the data in different forms could provide us with some clues regarding what we may find or want to find in the data. Such insights can then be useful for defining future studies/questions, leading to other forms of analysis.

Usually not the definitive answer to the question at hand but only the start, exploratory analysis should not be used alone for generalizing and/or making predictions from the data.

Exploratory data analysis is an approach that postpones the usual assumptions about what kind of model the data follows with the more direct approach of allowing the data itself to reveal its underlying structure in the form of a model. Thus, exploratory analysis is not a mere collection of techniques; rather, it offers a philosophy as to how to dissect a dataset; what to look for; how to look; and how to interpret the outcomes.

As exploratory analysis consists of a range of techniques; its application is varied as well. However, the most common application is looking for patterns in the data, such as finding groups of similar genes from a collection of samples.[15]

Let us consider the US census data available from the US census website.[16] This data has dozens of variables; we have already seen some of them in Figures 3.1 and 3.7. If you are looking for something specific (e.g., which State has the highest population), you could go with descriptive analysis. If you are trying to predict something (e.g., which city will have the lowest influx of immigrant population), you could use prescriptive or predictive analysis. But, if someone gave you this data and asks you to find *interesting* insights, then what do you do? You could still do descriptive or prescriptive analysis, but given that there are lots of variables with massive amounts of data, it may be futile to do all possible combinations of those variables. So, you need to go exploring. That could mean a number of things. Remember, exploratory analysis is about the methodology or philosophy of doing the analysis, rather than a specific technique. Here, for instance, you could take a small sample (data and/or variables) from the entire dataset and plot some of the variables (bar chart, scatterplot). Perhaps you see something interesting. You could go ahead and organize some of the data points along one or two dimensions (variables) to see if you find any patterns. The list goes on. We are not going to see these approaches/techniques right here. Instead, you will encounter them (e.g., clustering, visualization, classification, etc.) in various parts of this book.

3.8 Mechanistic Analysis

Mechanistic analysis involves understanding the exact changes in variables that lead to changes in other variables for individual objects. For instance, we may want to know how the number of free doughnuts per employee per day affects employee productivity. Perhaps by giving them one extra doughnut we gain a 5% productivity boost, but two extra doughnuts could end up making them lazy (and diabetic)!

More seriously, though, think about studying the effects of carbon emissions on bringing about the Earth's climate change. Here, we are interested in seeing how the increased amount of CO_2 in the atmosphere is causing the overall temperature to change. We now know that, in the last 150 years, the CO_2 levels have gone from 280 parts per million to 400 parts per million.[17] And in that time, the Earth has heated up by 1.53 degrees Fahrenheit (0.85 degrees Celsius).[18] This is a clear sign of climate change, something that we all need to be concerned about, but I will leave it there for now. What I want to bring you back to thinking about is the kind of analysis we presented here – that of studying a relationship between two variables. Such relationships are often explored using regression.

3.8.1 Regression

In statistical modeling, **regression** analysis is a process for estimating the relationships among variables. Given this definition, you may wonder how regression differs from correlation. The answer can be found in the limitations of correlation analysis. Correlation by itself does not provide any indication of how one variable can be predicted from another. Regression provides this crucial information.

Beyond estimating a relationship, regression analysis is a way of predicting an outcome variable from one predictor variable (simple linear regression) or several predictor variables (multiple linear regression). Linear regression, the most common form of regression used in data analysis, assumes this relationship to be linear. In other words, the relationship of the predictor variable(s) and outcome variable can be expressed by a straight line. If the predictor variable is represented by x, and the outcome variable is represented by y, then the relationship can be expressed by the equation

$$y = \beta_0 + \beta_1 x, \tag{3.6}$$

where β_1 represents the slope of the x, and β_0 is the intercept or error term for the equation. What linear regression does is estimate the values of β_0 and β_1 from a set of observed data points, where the values of x, and associated values of y, are provided. So, when a new or previously unobserved data point comes where the value of y is unknown, it can fit the values of x, β_0, and β_1 into the above equation to predict the value of y.

From statistical analysis, it has been shown that the slope of the regression β_1 can be expressed by the following equation:

$$\beta_1 = r\frac{\mathrm{sd}_y}{\mathrm{sd}_x}, \tag{3.7}$$

where r is the Pearson's correlation coefficient, and sd represents the standard deviation of the respective variable as calculated from the observed set of data points. Next, the value of the error term can be calculated from the following formula:

$$\beta_0 = \overline{y} - \beta_1\overline{x}, \tag{3.8}$$

where $\overline{y}$ and $\overline{x}$ represent the means of the y and x variables, respectively. (More on these equations can be found in later chapters.) Once you have these values calculated, it is possible to estimate the value of y from the value of x.

Hands-On Example 3.5: Regression

We use the attitude dataset in Table 3.5. The first variable, *attitude*, represents the amount of positive attitude of the students who have taken an examination, and the *score* represents the marks scored by the participants in the examination.

Table 3.5 Attitude and score data.

#	Attitude	Score
1	65	129
2	67	126
3	68	143
4	70	156
5	71	161
6	72	158
7	72	168
8	73	166
9	73	182
10	75	201

Here *attitude* is going to be the predictor variable, and what regression would be able to do is to estimate the value of *score* from *attitude*. As explained above, first let us calculate the value of the slope, β_1.

From the data, Pearson's correlation coefficient r can be calculated as 0.94. The standard deviations of x (*attitude*) and y (*score*) are 3.10 and 22.80, respectively. Therefore, the value of the slope is

$$\beta_1 = 0.94 \times \frac{22.80}{3.10} = 6.91.$$

Next, the calculation of the error term β_0 requires the mean values of x and y. From the given dataset, $\overline{y}$ and $\overline{x}$ are derived as 159 and 70.6, respectively. Therefore, the value of β_0 will be

$$\beta_0 = 159 - (6.91 \times 70.6) = -328.85$$

Now, say you have a new participant whose positive attitude before taking the examination is measured at 78. His score in the examination can be estimated at 210.13:

$$y = -328.85 + (6.91 \times 78) = 210.13.$$

Regression analysis has a number of salient applications to data science and other statistical fields. In the business realm, for example, powerful linear regression can be used to generate insights on consumer behavior, which helps professionals understand business and factors related to profitability. It can also help a corporation understand how sensitive its sales are to advertising expenditures, or it can examine how a stock price is affected by changes in interest rates. Regression analysis may even be used to look to the future; an equation may forecast demand for a company's products or predict stock behaviors.[19]

Try It Yourself 3.7: Regression

Obtain the Container Crane Controller Data Set available from OA 3.5. A container crane is used to transport containers from one place to another. The difficulty of this task lies in the fact that the bridge crane is connected to the container by cables, causing an opening angle when the container is being transported. Interfering with the operation at high speeds due to oscillation that occurs at the end-point could cause accidents.

Use regression analysis to predict the power from speed and angle.

Summary

In this chapter, we reviewed some of the techniques and approaches used for data science. As should be evident, a lot of this revolves around statistics. And there is no way we could even introduce all of the statistics in one chapter. Therefore, this chapter focused on providing broader strokes of what these approaches and analyses are, with a few concrete examples and applications. As we proceed, many of these broad strokes will become more precise. Another reason for skimping on the details here is our lack of knowledge (or assumption about) any specific programming tool. You will soon see that, while it is possible to have a theoretical understanding of statistical analysis, for a hands-on data science approach it makes more sense to actually do stuff and gain an understanding of such analysis. And so, in the next part of the book, we are going to cover a bunch of tools and, while doing so, we will come back to most of these techniques. Then, we will have a chance to really understand different kinds of analysis and analytics as we apply them to solve various data problems.

Almost all the real-life data science-related problems use more than one category of the analysis techniques described above. The number and types of categories used for analysis can be an indicator of the quality of the analysis. For example, in social science-related problems:

- A *weak* analysis will only tell a story or describe the topic.
- A *good* analysis will go beyond a mere description by engaging in several of the types of analysis listed above, but it will be weak on sociological analysis, the future orientation, and the development of social policy.
- An *excellent* analysis will engage in many of the types of analyses we have discussed and will demonstrate an aggressive sociological analysis which develops a clear future orientation and offers social policy changes to address problems associated with the topic.

There is no clear agreeable-to-all classification scheme available in the literature to categorize all the analysis techniques that are used by data science professionals. However, based on their application to various stages of data analysis, we categorized analysis techniques into certain classes. Each of these categories and their application were described – some at length and some less so – with an understanding that we will revisit them later when we are addressing various data problems.

I hope that with this chapter you can see that familiarity with various statistical measures and techniques is an integral part of being a data scientist. Armed with this arsenal of tools, you can take your skills and make important discoveries for a number of people in a number of areas.

FYI: Algorithmic Bias

Bias is caused not only by the data we use, as we saw in the previous chapter, but also by the algorithms and the techniques we use.

We see biases introduced by algorithms all around us. For instance, automated decision-making (ADM) systems run on algorithms and are present in processes that can affect whether one person gets a good credit score or another person gets parole. The systems making these predictions are based on assumptions that are programmed into algorithms. And what are assumptions? Well, these are human-created perceptions and preconceived notions. And since they are created by humans, they are prone to problems of any such creation; they could be false, faulty, or simply a form of prejudice.

For example, a June 2017 study by Matthias Spielkamp (Spielkamp, M. (2017). Inspecting algorithms for bias. *MIT Technology Review*) showed that the stop-and-frisk practice that the New York City Police

Department used from 2004 to 2012 to temporarily detain, question, and search individuals on the street whom they deemed suspicious turned out to have been a gross miscalculation based on human bias. The actual data revealed that 88% of those stopped were not and did not become offenders.

Moral of the story? Do not trust the data or the technique blindly; they may be perpetuating the inherent biases and prejudices we already have.

Key Terms

- **Data analysis:** This is a process that refers to hands-on data exploration and evaluation. Analysis looks backwards, providing marketers with a historical view of what has happened. Analytics, on the other hand, models the future or predicts a result.
- **Data analytics:** This defines the science behind the analysis. The science means understanding the cognitive processes an analyst uses to understand problems and explore data in meaningful ways. It is used to model the future or predict a result.
- **Nominal variable:** The variable type is nominal when there is no natural order between the possible values that it stores, for example, colors.
- **Ordinal variable:** If the possible values of a data type are from an ordered set, then the type is ordinal. For example, grades in a mark sheet.
- **Interval variable:** A kind of variable that provides numerical storage and allows us to do additions and subtractions on them but not multiplications or divisions. Example: temperature.
- **Ratio variable:** A kind of variable that provides numerical storage and allows us to do additions and subtractions, as well as multiplications or divisions, on them. Example: weight.
- **Independent /predictor variable:** A variable that is thought to be controlled or not affected by other variables.
- **Dependent /outcome /response variable:** A variable that depends on other variables (most often other independent variables).
- **Mean:** Mean is the average of continuous data found by the summation of the given data and dividing by the number of data entries.
- **Median:** Median is the middle data point in any ordinal dataset.
- **Mode:** Mode of a dataset is the value that occurs most frequently.
- **Normal distribution:** A normal distribution is a type of distribution of data points in which, when ordered, most values cluster in the middle of the range and the rest of the values symmetrically taper off toward both extremes.
- **Correlation:** This indicates how closely two variables are related and ranges from −1 (negatively related) to +1 (positively related). A correlation of 0 indicates no relation between the variables.

- **Regression:** Regression is a measure of functional relationship between two or more correlated variables, in which typically the relation is used to estimate the value of outcome variable from the predictor(s).
- **Descriptive analysis:** This is a method for quantitatively describing the main features of a collection of data.
- **Diagnostic analytics:** Also known as **causal analysis**, it is used for discovery, or to determine why something happened. It often involves at least one cause (usually more than one) and one effect.
- **Predictive analytics:** This involves understanding the future using the data and the trends we have seen in the past, as well as emerging new contexts and processes.
- **Prescriptive analytics:** This is the area of business analytics dedicated to finding the best course of action for a given situation.
- **Exploratory analysis:** This is an approach to analyzing datasets to find previously unknown relationships. Often such analysis involves using various data visualization approaches.
- **Mechanistic analysis:** This involves understanding the exact changes in variables that lead to changes in other variables for individual objects.

Conceptual Questions

1. How do data analysis and data analytics differ?
2. Name three measures of centrality and describe how they differ.
3. You are looking at data about tax refunds people get. Which measure of centrality would you use to describe this data? Why?
4. In this chapter we saw that the distribution of household income is a skewed distribution. Find two more examples of skewed distributions.
5. Describe how exploratory analysis differs from predictive analysis.
6. List two differences between correlation analysis and regression analysis.
7. What is a predictor variable?

Hands-On Problems

Problem 3.1

Imagine 10 years down the line, in a dark and gloomy world, your data science career has failed to take off. Instead, you have settled for the much less glamorous job of a community librarian.

Now, to simplify the logistics, the library has decided to limit all future procurement of books either to hardback or to softback copies. The library also plans to convert all the existing books to one cover type later. Fortunately, to help you decide, the library has gathered a small sample of data that gives measurements on the volume, area (only the cover of the book), and weight of 15 existing books, some of which are softback ("Pb") and the rest are hardback ("Hb") copies. The dataset is shown in the table and can be obtained from OA 3.6.

	Volume	Area	Weight	Cover
1	885	382	800	Hb
2	1016	468	950	Hb
3	1125	387	1050	Hb
4	239	371	350	Hb
5	701	371	750	Hb
6	641	367	600	Hb
7	1228	396	1075	Hb
8	412	257	250	Pb
9	953	300	700	Pb
10	929	301	650	Pb
11	1492	403	975	Pb
12	419	213	350	Pb
13	1010	432	950	Pb
14	595	262	425	Pb
15	1034	380	725	Pb

The above table represents that the dataset has 15 instances of the following four attributes:

- Volume: Book volumes in cubic centimeters
- Area: Total area of the book in square centimeters
- Weight: Book weights in grams
- Cover: A factor with levels; Hb for hardback, and Pb for paperback

Now use this dataset to decide which type of book you want to procure in the future. Here is how you are going to do it. Determine:

a. The median of the book covers.

b. The mean of the book weights.

c. The variance in book volumes.

Use the above values to decide which book cover types the library should opt for in the future.

Problem 3.2

Following is a small dataset of list price vs. best price for a new GMC pickup truck in \$1000s. You can obtain it from OA 3.7. The x represents the list price, whereas the y represents the best price values.

x	y
12.4	11.2
14.3	12.5
14.5	12.7
14.9	13.1
16.1	14.1
16.9	14.8
16.5	14.4
15.4	13.4
17	14.9
17.9	15.6
18.8	16.4
20.3	17.7
22.4	19.6
19.4	16.9
15.5	14
16.7	14.6
17.3	15.1
18.4	16.1
19.2	16.8
17.4	15.2
19.5	17
19.7	17.2
21.2	18.6

Now, use this dataset to complete the following tasks:

a. Determine the Pearson's correlation coefficient between the list price and best price.
b. Establish a linear regression relationship between list price and best price.
c. Based on the relationship you found, determine the best price of a pickup whose list price is 25.2 in $1000s.

Problem 3.3

The following is a fictional dataset on the number of visitors to Asbury Park, NJ, in hundreds a day, the number of tickets issued for parking violations, and the average temperate (in degrees Celsius) for the same day.

Number of visitors (in hundreds a day)	Number of parking tickets	Average temperature
15.8	8	35
12.3	6	38
19.5	9	32

Number of visitors (in hundreds a day)	Number of parking tickets	Average temperature
8.9	4	26
11.4	6	31
17.6	9	36
16.5	10	38
14.7	3	30
3.9	1	21
14.6	9	34
10.0	7	36
10.3	6	32
7.4	2	25
13.4	6	37
11.5	7	34

Now, use this dataset to complete the following tasks:

a. Determine the relationship between number of visitors and number of parking tickets issued.
b. Find out the regression coefficient between the temperature and number of visitors.
c. Look for any possible relationship between the temperature of the day and number of parking tickets issued.

Further Reading and Resources

There are plenty of good (and some mediocre) books on statistics. If you want to develop your techniques in data science, I suggest you pick up a good statistics book at the level you need. A couple of such books are listed below.

- Salkind, N. (2016). *Statistics for People Who (Think They) Hate Statistics*. Sage.
- Krathwohl, D. R. (2009). *Methods of Educational and Social Science Research: The Logic of Methods*. Waveland Press.
- Field, A., Miles, J., & Field, Z. (2012). *Discovering Statistics Using R*. Sage.
- A video by IBM describing the progression from descriptive analytics, through predictive analytics to prescriptive analytics: https://www.youtube.com/watch?v=VtETirgVn9c

Notes

1. Analysis vs. analytics: What's the difference? Blog by Connie Hill: http://www.1to1media.com/data-analytics/analysis-vs-analytics-whats-difference
2. KDnuggets™: Interview: David Kasik, Boeing, on Data analysis vs. data analytics: http://www.kdnuggets.com/2015/02/interview-david-kasik-boeing-data-analytics.html
3. Population map showing US census data: https://www.census.gov/2010census/popmap/

4. Of course, we have not covered these yet. But have patience; we are getting there.
5. Income distribution from US Census: https://www.census.gov/library/visualizations/2015/demo/distribution-of-household-income-2014.html
6. Pearson correlation: http://www.statisticssolutions.com/correlation-pearson-kendall-spearman/
7. Process of predictive analytics: http://www.amadeus.com/blog/07/04/5-examples-predictive-analytics-travel-industry/
8. Use for predictive analytics: https://www.r-bloggers.com/predicting-marketing-campaign-with-r/
9. Understanding predictive analytics: http://www.fico.com/en/predictive-analytics
10. A company called Ayata holds the trademark for the term "Prescriptive Analytics". (*Ayata* is the Sanskrit word for *future*.)
11. Process of prescriptive analytics: http://searchcio.techtarget.com/definition/Prescriptive-analytics
12. Game theory: http://whatis.techtarget.com/definition/game-theory
13. Use of prescriptive analytics: http://www.ingrammicroadvisor.com/data-center/four-types-of-big-data-analytics-and-examples-of-their-use
14. Gartner predicts predictive analytics as next big business trend: http://www.enterpriseappstoday.com/business-intelligence/gartner-taps-predictive-analytics-as-next-big-business-intelligence-trend.html
15. Six types of analyses: https://datascientistinsights.com/2013/01/29/six-types-of-analyses-every-data-scientist-should-know/
16. Census data from US government: https://www.census.gov/data.html.
17. Climate change causes: https://climate.nasa.gov/causes/
18. Global temperature in the last 100 years: https://www2.ucar.edu/climate/faq/how-much-has-global-temperature-risen-last-100-years
19. How businesses use regression analysis statistics: http://www.dummies.com/education/math/business-statistics/how-businesses-use-regression-analysis-statistics/

PART II

TOOLS FOR DATA SCIENCE

This part includes chapters to introduce various tools and platforms such as UNIX (Chapter 4), Python (Chapter 5), R (Chapter 6), and MySQL (Chapter 7).

It is important to keep in mind that, since this is not a programming or database book, the objective here is not to go systematically into various parts of these tools. Rather, we focus on learning the basics and the relevant aspects of these tools to be able to solve various data problems. These chapters therefore are organized around addressing various data-driven problems. In the chapters covering Python and R, we also introduce basic machine learning.

Before beginning with this part, make sure you are comfortable with the basic terminology concerning data, information technology, and statistics. It is also important that you review our discussion on computational thinking from Chapter 1, especially if you have never done any programming before.

In some respects, Chapter 5 (Python) and Chapter 6 (R) offer very similar content; they each start out by introducing the fundamentals of programming in their respective environment, show how basic statistical and data operations can be done, and then extend it by working on some machine learning problems. In other words, you could jump to Chapter 6 without going through Chapter 5 if you are not interested in Python. However, you will find that Chapter 5 provides more detailed discussions on some of the concepts in statistics and machine learning, and, since Chapter 6 has less of it, we do not have to repeat so much of the conceptual material.

I should also note that, while there is introduction to applied machine learning for solving data problems in both the Python and R chapters, this is kept at the surface level, with not enough depth for someone who really wants to use machine leaning in data science. For that, you will need to move to the next part of this book. Keep in mind that when we do go deeper in machine learning in that part, we will be using only R, so make sure to go through Chapter 6 first, if you have not done R in the past.

4 UNIX

"Torture the data, and it will confess to anything."
— Ronald Coase, Nobel Prize Laureate for Economics

What do you need?

- A basic understanding of operating systems.
- Being able to install and configure software.

What will you learn?

- Basics of the UNIX environment.
- Running commands, utilities, and operations in UNIX.
- Using UNIX to solve small data problems without programming.

4.1 Introduction

While there are many powerful programming languages that one could use for solving data science problems, people forget that one of the most powerful *and* simplest tools to use is right under their noses. And that is UNIX. The name may generate images of old-time hackers hacking away on monochrome terminals. Or, it may hearken the idea of UNIX as a mainframe system, taking up lots of space in some warehouse. But, while UNIX is indeed one of the oldest computing platforms, it *is* quite sophisticated and supremely capable of handling almost any kind of computational and data problem. In fact, in many respects, UNIX is leaps and bounds ahead of other operating systems; it can do things of which others can only dream!

Alas, when people think of tools for data science or data analytics, UNIX does not come to mind. Most books on these topics do not cover UNIX. But I think this is a missed opportunity, as UNIX allows one to do many data science tasks, including data cleaning, filtering, organizing (sorting), and even visualization, often using no more than its built-in commands and utilities. That makes it appealing to people who have not mastered a programming language or a statistics tool.

So, we are not going to pass up this wonderful opportunity. In this chapter, we will see some basics of working in the UNIX environment. This involves running commands, piping and redirecting outputs, and editing files. We will also see several shortcuts that make it easier and faster to work on UNIX. Ultimately, of course, our goal is not mastering UNIX, but solving data-driven problems, and so we will see how UNIX is useful in solving many problems without writing any code.

4.2 Getting Access to UNIX

UNIX is everywhere. Well, it is if you look for it.

If you are on a Linux machine, you are on a UNIX platform. Open your console or a terminal and you are good to go (Figure 4.1).

If you have a Mac, you are working on a UNIX platform. Go to Applications > Utilities in your Finder window, and open the Terminal app. A window should open up and you should be at a command prompt (Figure 4.2).

If you are on a PC, it is a little tricky, but there is hope. There are a few options that allow you to create a UNIX-like environment on a Windows machine. One such option is Cygwin, available for free.[2] (See Figure 4.3; and see Appendix C for instructions to install and use it.)

Finally, if you do not have a UNIX-like environment on your computer or do not want to install something like Cygwin, you can get a couple of basic utilities and connect to a UNIX server. This will be covered in the next section.

For the rest of this chapter, I am assuming that you are connecting to a UNIX server (even if you are already on a Linux or a Mac platform) and working on the server. This server could be provided by your organization, school, or a Web hosting company. You could also look into free online UNIX server services.[4] Another sure way to have access to a UNIX

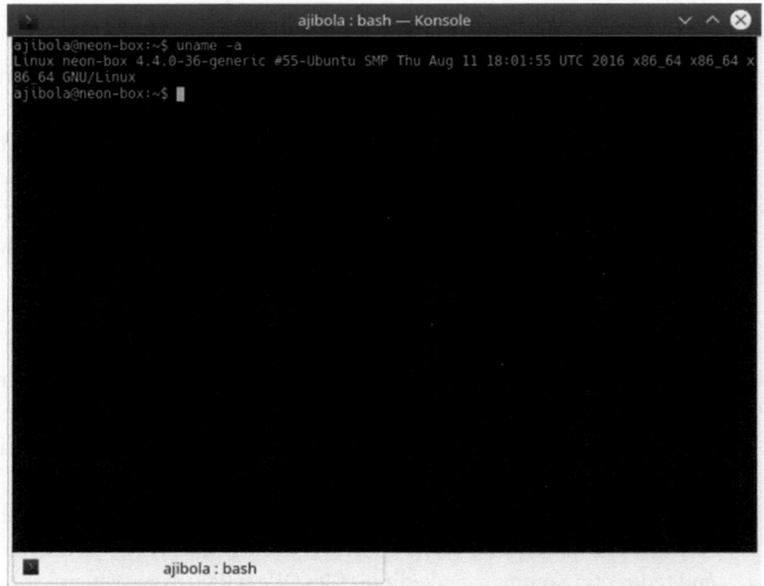

Figure 4.1 Console window on a Linux KDE desktop.[1]

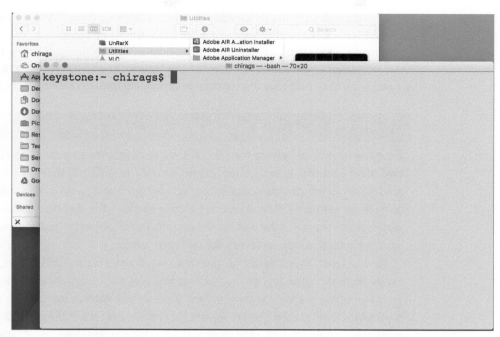

Figure 4.2 Terminal app on a Mac.

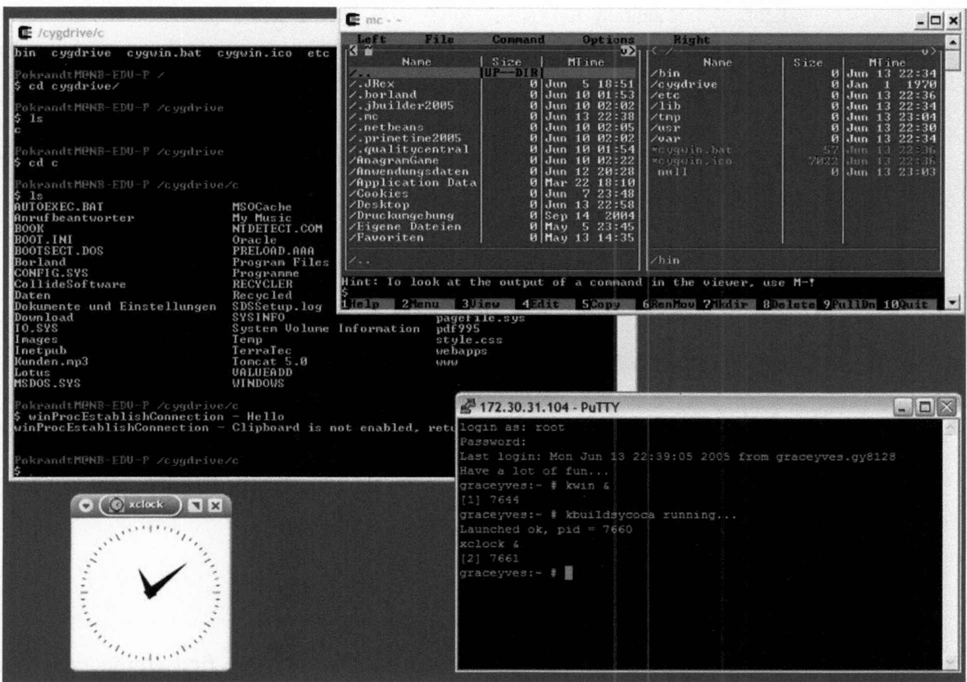

Figure 4.3 Cygwin running on a Windows desktop.[3]

server is through a cloud service such as Amazon Web Services (AWS) or Google Cloud. See the FYI box below and Appendix F for more details on them.

No matter what UNIX environment you end up using (whether you have a Linux or Mac machine, install Cygwin on a Windows PC, or connect to a UNIX server remotely), all that we are trying to do here (running commands, processing files, etc.) should work just the same.

FYI: There Are More Ways to Access UNIX

If you have never worked with anything like UNIX, it is important to take a pause at this point and really think about what UNIX is and, specifically, what we really need from it. While UNIX is a wonderful, powerful, networked operating system, we are not interested in that part of it. We simply want to get access to one of its shells (think about it as a cover or interface). This shell could give us access to the myriads of apps and utilities that UNIX has. Of course, this shell is covering the "real" UNIX, so while we are interested in the shell only, we have to find the "inner" part too.

There are several ways to do this, but since we are not interested in actual UNIX so much, let us just do the one that is the easiest. Start with your local machine. Does your computer have some form of UNIX? If you are on a Linux or a Mac, the answer is "yes." If you are on a Windows machine, then ask: Will it be easier for you to install a few pieces of software and configure them or find an external UNIX machine to connect to? If it is the latter, you can typically find such a machine (often called "server") at your education institute or your company.

But what if you are not in any school or do not have such a server at work? You can rent a server! That is right. Well, technically, it is called cloud services, but the idea is the same. You can go to Google, Amazon, or Microsoft and ask to create a virtual machine for you. Once created, you can log on to it just like you would to a physical server. Check out Appendix F, which takes you through the steps to set this up.

If you are using UNIX just to get through this chapter, then look for the easiest solution. If you want to dive into it further, look for a more stable solution, including one of the cloud-based services. Do not worry; most services have a free tier.

4.3 Connecting to a UNIX Server

If you have access to a UNIX, Linux, or Mac computer, you are in luck. Because then all you need are a couple of freely available tools on your machine. Here, that is what we are going to do. The two things you need are a way to connect to the server, and a way to transfer files between your machine and that server.

4.3.1 SSH

Since we are going with the assumption that you are first connecting to a UNIX server before doing any of the UNIX operations, we need to learn how to connect to such a server.

The plain vanilla method is the use of Telnet service, but since that plain vanilla Telnet is often insecure, many UNIX servers do not support that connection.

Instead, we will use **SSH**, which stands for "secure shell." This essentially refers to two parts: the server part and the client part. The former is something we are not going to worry about because, if we have access to a UNIX server, that server will have the necessary server part of SSH. What we need to figure out is the client part – a tool or a utility that we will run on our computers. To connect a UNIX server using SSH, you need to be running some kind of shell (a program that provides you a command-line interface to your operating system) with SSH client service on your own machine.

Again, if you have a Linux or a Mac, all you have to do is open your terminal or console.

On the other hand, if you are using a PC, you need software that has SSH client service. A couple of (free, of course) software options are WinSCP[5] and PuTTY.[6] (You can find instructions for using them at WinSCP and Using PuTTY in Windows,[7] respectively.)

Whichever option you choose, you will need three pieces of information: hostname, username, and password. Figure 4.4 shows what it looks like with PuTTY.

Hostname is the full name or IP (Internet Protocol) address of the server. The name could be something like example.organization.com and the IP address could be something like

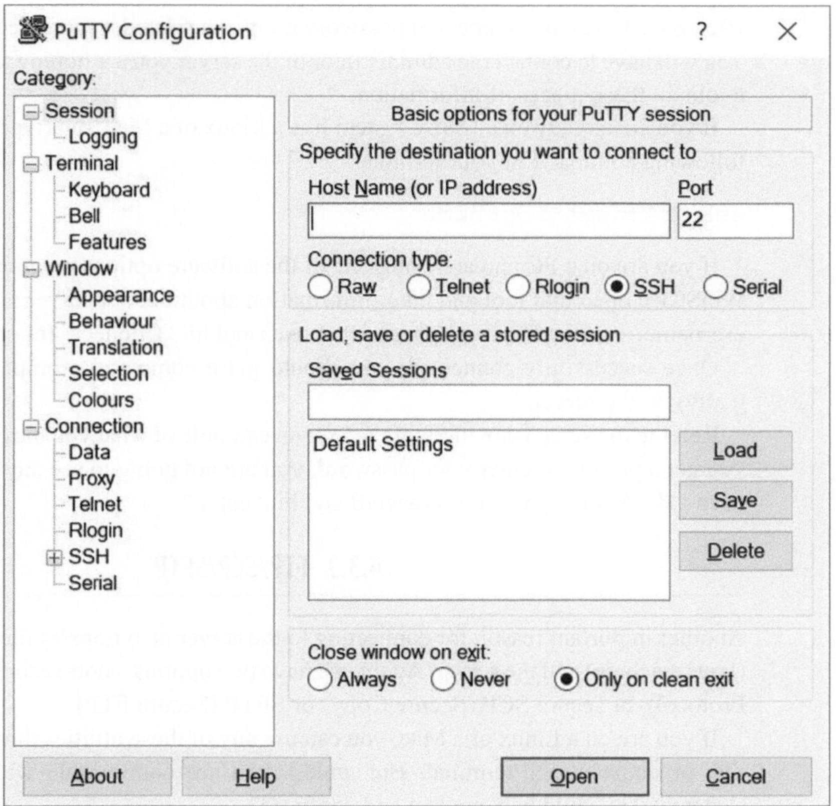

Figure 4.4 A screenshot of PuTTY.

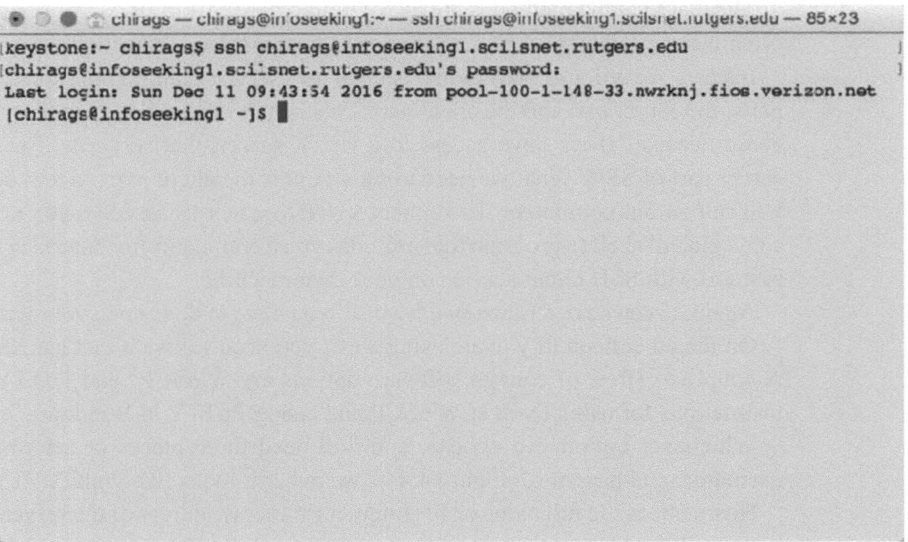
chirags — chirags@infoseeking1:~ — ssh chirags@infoseeking1.scilsnet.rutgers.edu — 85×23
keystone:~ chirags$ ssh chirags@infoseeking1.scilsnet.rutgers.edu
chirags@infoseeking1.scilsnet.rutgers.edu's password:
Last login: Sun Dec 11 09:43:54 2016 from pool-100-1-148-33.nwrknj.fios.verizon.net
[chirags@infoseeking1 ~]$

Figure 4.5 Example of getting connected to a UNIX server using SSH.

192.168.2.1. The username and password are those related to your account on that server. You will have to contact the administrator of the server you are hoping to connect to in order to obtain these pieces of information.

If you are already on a UNIX system like a Linux or a Mac, run (type and hit "enter") the following command in your terminal.[8]

```
ssh username@hostname
```

If you are on a PC and are using one of the software options mentioned earlier (PuTTY, WinSCP), open that tool and enter information about host or server name (or IP address), username, and password in appropriate boxes and hit "Connect" (or equivalent).

Once successfully connected, you should get a command prompt. You are now (virtually) on the server.

Refer to the screenshot in Figure 4.5 for an example of what you may see. Note that when you get a prompt to enter your password, you are not going to see anything you type – not even "*". So just type your password and hit "enter."

4.3.2 FTP/SCP/SFTP

Another important reason for connecting to the server is to transfer files between the client (your machine) and the server. Again, we have two options – non-secure **FTP** (File Transfer Protocol), or secure SCP (Secure Copy) or SFTP (Secure FTP).

If you are on a Linux or a Mac, you can use any of these utilities through your command line or console/shell/terminal. But, unless you are comfortable with UNIX paths and systems, you could become lost and confused.

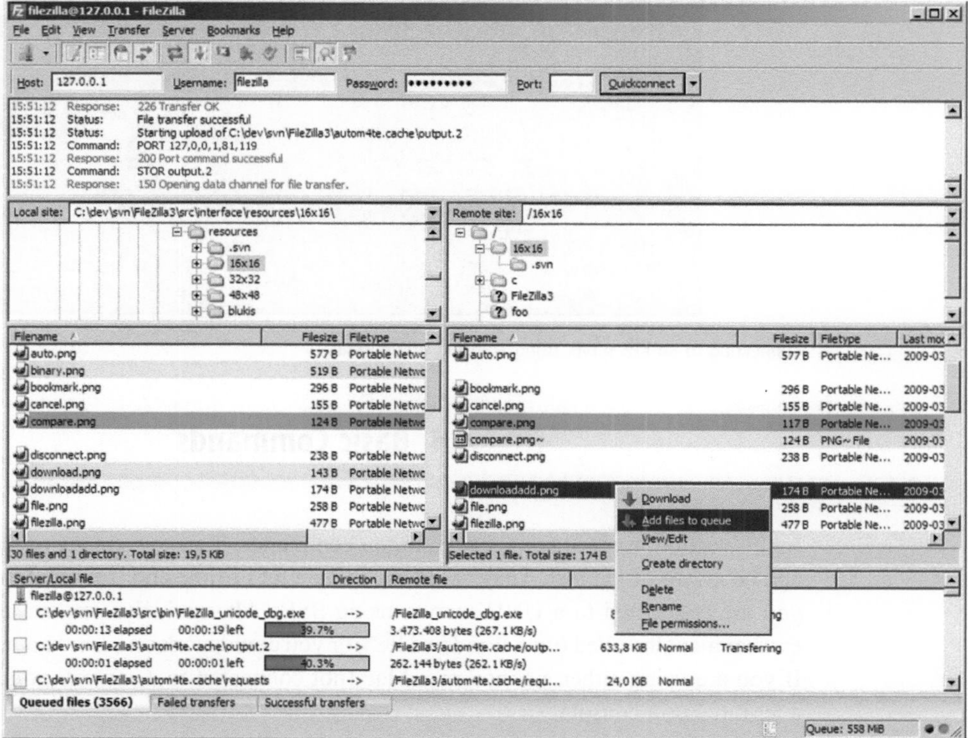

Figure 4.6 File transfer using FileZilla on Windows.

So, we will use more intuitive file transfer packages. FileZilla happens to be a good one (free and easy to use) that is available for all platforms, but I am sure you can search online and find one that you prefer. In the end, they all offer similar functionalities.

Whatever tool you have, you will once again need those three pieces of information: hostname, username, and password. Refer to the screenshot in Figure 4.6 from the FileZilla project site to give you an idea of what you might see. Here, the connection information that you need to enter are at the top ("Host," "Username," "Password," and "Port"). Leave "Port" empty unless you have specific instructions about it from your system administrator.

Figure 4.7 offers another example – this time from a different FTP tool, but as you can see, you need to enter the same kind of information: the server name (hostname), your username, and password.

Go ahead and enter those details and connect to the server. Once connected, you will be in the home directory on the server. Most file transfer software applications provide a two-pane view, where one pane shows your local machine and the other shows the server. Transferring files then becomes an easy drag-and-drop operation.

Figure 4.7 Connecting to an FTP server using Transmit app on Mac.

4.4 Basic Commands

In this section, we will see a few common commands. Try out as many of them as possible and be aware of the rest. They could save you a lot of time and trouble. I will assume that you are connected to a UNIX server using SSH. Alternatively, you can have a Cygwin environment installed (on a Windows PC), or you could work on a Linux or a Mac machine. If you are using either a Linux or a Mac (not connected to a server), go ahead and open a terminal or a console.

4.4.1 File and Directory Manipulation Commands

Let us look at some of the basic file- and directory-related commands you can use with UNIX. Each of these is only briefly explained here and perhaps some of them may not make much sense until you really need them. But go ahead and try as much as you can for now and make a note of the others. In the examples below, whenever you see "filename", you should enter the actual filename such as "test.txt".

1. ***pwd*:** Present working directory. By default, when you log in to a UNIX server or open a terminal on your machine, you will be in your home directory. From here, you can move around to other directories using the "cd" command (listed below). If you ever get lost, or are not sure where you are, just enter "pwd". The system will tell you the full path of where you are.
2. ***rm*:** Remove or delete a file (e.g., "rm filename"). Be careful. Deleting a file may get rid of that file permanently. So, if you are used to having a "Recycle Bin" or "Trash" icon on your machine from where you can recover deleted files, you might be in for an unpleasant surprise!
3. ***rmdir*:** Remove or delete a directory (e.g., "rmdir myfolder"). You need to make sure that the directory/folder you are trying to delete is empty. Otherwise the system will not let you delete it. Alternatively, you can say "rm -f myfolder", where "-f" is for forcing the deletion.

4. ***cd***: Change directory (e.g., "cd data" to move into "data" directory). Simply entering "cd" will bring you to your home directory. Entering a space and two dots or full points after "cd" (i.e., "cd ..") will take you up a level.
5. ***ls***: List the files in the current directory. If you want more details of the files, use the "-l" option (e.g., "ls -l").
6. ***du***: Disk usage. To find out how much space a directory is taking up, you can issue a "du" command, which will display space information in bytes. To see things in MB and GB, use the "-h" option (e.g., "du -h").
7. ***wc***: Reports file size in lines, words, and characters (e.g., "wc myfile.txt").
8. ***cat***: Types the file content on the terminal (e.g., "cat myfile.txt"). Be careful about which file type you use it with. If it is a binary file (something that contains other than simple text), you may not only get weird characters filling up your screen, but you may even get weird sounds and other things that start happening, including freezing up the machine.
9. ***more***: To see more of a file. You can say something like "more filename", which is like "cat filename", but it pauses after displaying a screenful of the file. You can hit Enter or the space-bar to continue displaying the file. Once again, use this only with text files.
10. ***head***: Print the first few lines of a file (e.g., "head filename"). If you want to see the top three lines, you can use "head -3 filename". Should I repeat that this needs to be tried only with text files?!

Figure 4.8 shows some of these commands running in a terminal window. Note that "keystone:data chirags$" is my command prompt. For you, it is going to be something different.

```
data — -bash — 80×24
keystone:data chirags$ rm edoc.txt~
keystone:data chirags$ mkdir myfolder
keystone:data chirags$ rm myfolder/
rm: myfolder/: is a directory
keystone:data chirags$ rmdir myfolder/
keystone:data chirags$ wc mydocument.txt
      16      40     207 mydocument.txt
keystone:data chirags$ cat mydocument.txt
Here is an example
of typing a document
in vi editor.

Currently I'm in 'insert' mode.
To save the file, type:

ESC (the escape key)
: (colon)
w (for write)

To quit, type:
ESC (the escape key)
: (colon)
q
```

Figure 4.8 Sample commands run on a terminal.

4.4.2 Process-Related Commands

While most operating systems hide what is going on behind the scene of a nice-looking interface, UNIX gives unprecedented access to not only viewing those background processes, but also manipulating them. Here we will list some of the basic commands you may find useful for understanding and interacting with various processes.

1. ***Ctrl+c*:** Stop an ongoing process. If you are ever stuck in running a process or a command that does not give your command prompt back, this is your best bet. You may have to press Ctrl+c multiple times.
2. ***Ctrl+d*:** Logout. Enter this on a command prompt and you will be kicked out of your session. This may even close your console window.
3. ***ps*:** Lists the processes that run through the current terminal.
4. ***ps aux*:** Lists the processes for everyone on the machine. This could be spooky since in a multiuser environment (multiple users logging into the same server) one could essentially see what others are doing! Of course, that also means someone else could spy on you as well.
5. ***ps aux | grep daffy*:** List of processes for user "daffy." Since there are likely to be lots of processes going on in a server environment, and most of them are of no relevance to you, you can use this combination to filter out only those processes that are running under your username. We will soon revisit the "|" (pipe) character you see here.
6. ***top*:** Displays a list of top processes in real time (Figure 4.9). This could be useful to see which processes are consuming considerable resources at the time. Note the PID column

```
data — top — 80×23
Processes: 385 total, 2 running, 383 sleeping, 1842 threads            15:48:51
Load Avg: 1.49, 1.60, 1.67  CPU usage: 1.31% user, 2.27% sys, 96.40% idle
SharedLibs: 270M resident, 56M data, 73M linkedit.
MemRegions: 86210 total, 4860M resident, 122M private, 2495M shared.
PhysMem: 13G used (2310M wired), 3353M unused.
VM: 1033G vsize, 633M framework vsize, 9242825(0) swapins, 10149161(0) swapouts.
Networks: packets: 42817434/44G in, 37488351/29G out.
Disks: 17939995/379G read, 7161597/195G written.

PID    COMMAND      %CPU TIME     #TH  #WQ  #PORTS MEM   PURG  CMPRS  PGRP
28748  top          3.8  00:03.09 1/1  0    20     5132K 0B    0B     28748
28747  helpd        0.0  00:00.02 2    1    36     1136K 0B    0B     28747
28744  mdworker     0.0  00:00.05 3    1    49     3212K 0B    0B     28744
28742  mdworker     0.0  00:00.09 4    1    55     6464K 0B    0B     28742
28739  mdworker     0.0  00:00.08 3    1    53     3300K 0B    0B     28739
28738  mdworker     0.0  00:00.06 3    1    46     3232K 0B    0B     28738
28737  mdworker     0.0  00:00.06 4    2    47     3348K 0B    0B     28737
28735  com.apple.sp 0.0  00:00.03 2    1    52     2724K 0B    0B     28735
28729  bash         0.0  00:00.02 1    0    16     856K  0B    0B     28729
28728  login        0.0  00:00.01 2    1    29     968K  0B    0B     28728
28725  ocspd        0.0  00:00.02 2    1    32     1344K 0B    0B     28725
28724  com.apple.iC 0.0  00:00.09 3    2    57     5036K 0B    0B     28724
28708- SnapNDrag    3.9  00:05.13 11   8    252    61M   25M   0B     28708
```

Figure 4.9 Output of "top" command.

at the left. This is where each process is reported with a unique process ID. You will need this in case you want to terminate that process. Press “q” to get out of this display.

7. ***kill***: To kill or terminate a process. Usage: “kill -9 1234”. Here, “-9” indicates forced kill and “1234” is the process ID, which can be obtained from the second column of “ps” or the first column of “top” command outputs.

4.4.3 Other Useful Commands

1. ***man***: Help (e.g., “man pwd”). Ever wanted to know more about using a command? Just use “man” (refers to manual pages). You may be surprised (and overwhelmed) to learn about all the possibilities that go with a command.
2. ***who***: Find out who is logged in to the server. Yes, spooky!

Try It Yourself 4.1: Basic UNIX

Once connected to a UNIX server or a shell, answer the following questions using appropriate UNIX commands.

1. List the contents of the current directory and ensure there is no directory named “test”.
2. Create a new directory named “test”.
3. Move inside the new directory. Verify where you are by finding out the exact path of your current location.
4. Find out details of a UNIX command called “touch”. Learn how to use it to create a new file.
5. Create a new file using “touch” command. Verify it by listing the content in the current directory.
6. Delete the newly created file. Verify it is removed by listing the content in the current directory.
7. Move out of “test” directory.
8. Remove the “test” directory.
9. Logout using “Ctrl+d”.

4.4.4 Shortcuts

Those who are intimidated by it probably do not know the fantastic shortcuts that UNIX offers. Here are some of them to make your life easier.

1. ***Auto-complete***: Any time you are typing a command, a filename, or a path on the terminal, type part of it and hit the “tab” key. The system will either complete the rest of it or show you options.
2. ***Recall***: UNIX saves a history of the commands you used. Simply pressing the up and down arrow keys on the terminal will bring them up in the order they were executed.
3. ***Search and recall***: Do not want to go through pressing the up arrow so many times to find that command? Hit Ctrl+r and start typing part of that command. The system will

search through your command history. When you see what you were looking for, simply hit enter (and you may have to hit enter again).

4. ***Auto-path*:** Tired of typing the full path to some program or file you use frequently? Add it to your path by following these steps.
   1. Go to your home directory on the server.
   2. Open .bash_profile in an editor (notice the dot or full point before "bash_profile").
   3. Let us assume that the program you want to have direct access to is at /home/user/daffy/MyProgram. Replace the line $PATH=$PATH:$HOME/bin with the following line: PATH=$PATH:$HOME/bin:/home/user/daffy/MyProgram
   4. Save the file and exit the editor.
   5. On the command line, run ". .bash_profile" (dot space dot bash_profile). This will set the path environment for your current session. For all future sessions, it will be set the moment you log in.

Now, whenever you need to run /home/user/daffy/MyProgram, you can simply type "MyProgram".

And that is about it in terms of basic commands for UNIX. I know this could be a lot if you have never used UNIX/Linux before, but keep in mind that there is no need to memorize any of this. Instead, try practicing some of them and come back to others (or the same ones) later. In the end, nothing works better than practice. So, do not feel bad if these things do not sound intuitive – trust me, not all of them are! – or accessible enough at first.

It may also help to practice these commands with a goal in mind. Look for a section later in this chapter where we see how these commands, processes, and their combinations can be used for solving data problems. But for now, let us move on to learn how to edit text files in a UNIX environment.

4.5 Editing on UNIX

4.5.1 The vi Editor

One of the most basic and powerful editors on UNIX is called vi, short for "visual display." I would not recommend it until you are comfortable with UNIX. But sometimes you may not have a choice – vi is omnipresent on UNIX. So even if some other editor may not be available, chances are, on a UNIX system, you will have vi.

To edit or create a file using vi, type:

```
vi filename
```

at the command prompt. This will open up that file in the vi editor. If the file already exists, vi will load its content and now you can edit the file. If the file does not exist, you will have a blank editor.

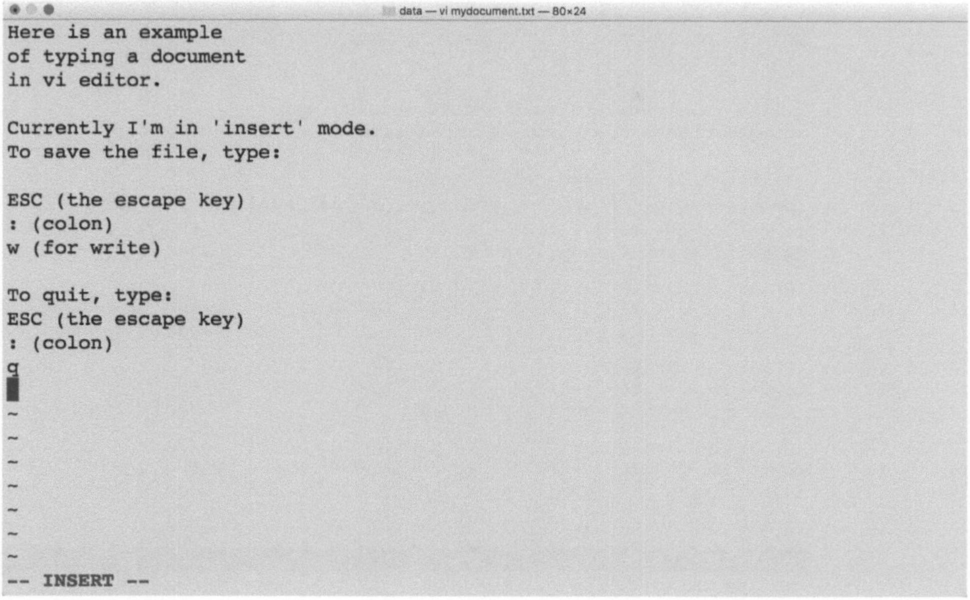

```
data — vi mydocument.txt — 80×24
Here is an example
of typing a document
in vi editor.

Currently I'm in 'insert' mode.
To save the file, type:

ESC (the escape key)
: (colon)
w (for write)

To quit, type:
ESC (the escape key)
: (colon)
q

~
~
~
~
~
~
~
-- INSERT --
```

Figure 4.10 A vi editor screenshot.

Here is the tricky part. You cannot simply start typing to edit the file. You have to first enter the "insert" (editing) mode. To do so, simply press "i". You will notice "-- INSERT --" appear at the bottom of your screen. Now you can start typing as you would normally in any text editor.

To save the file, you need to enter the command mode. Hit "esc" (the escape key at the top-left of your keyboard), then ":" (colon), and then "w". You should see a message at the bottom of your screen that the file was saved. To exit, once again enter the command mode by pressing "esc", then ":", and finally "q" for quit. Figure 4.10 shows a screenshot of what editing with vi looks like.

I know all of this may sound daunting if you have never used UNIX. But if you keep up with it, there are some tremendous benefits that only UNIX can provide. For instance, vi can run quite an effective search in your file using regular expressions (pattern matching in strings).

4.5.2 The Emacs Editor

I would recommend using Emacs as an easy-to-use alternative to vi. On the terminal, enter "emacs file.txt" to edit or create the file.txt file. Start typing as you would normally. To save, press the combination of Ctrl+x and Ctrl+s (hold down Ctrl key and press "x" and then "s"). To quit, enter the combination Ctrl+x and Ctrl+c. See Figure 4.11 for an example of what Emacs looks like.

Alternatively, you can create/edit a file on your computer and "FTP it" to the server. If you decide to do this, make sure you are creating a simple text file and not a Word doc or some other non-text format. Any time you want to read a file on the server, you can type "cat filename".

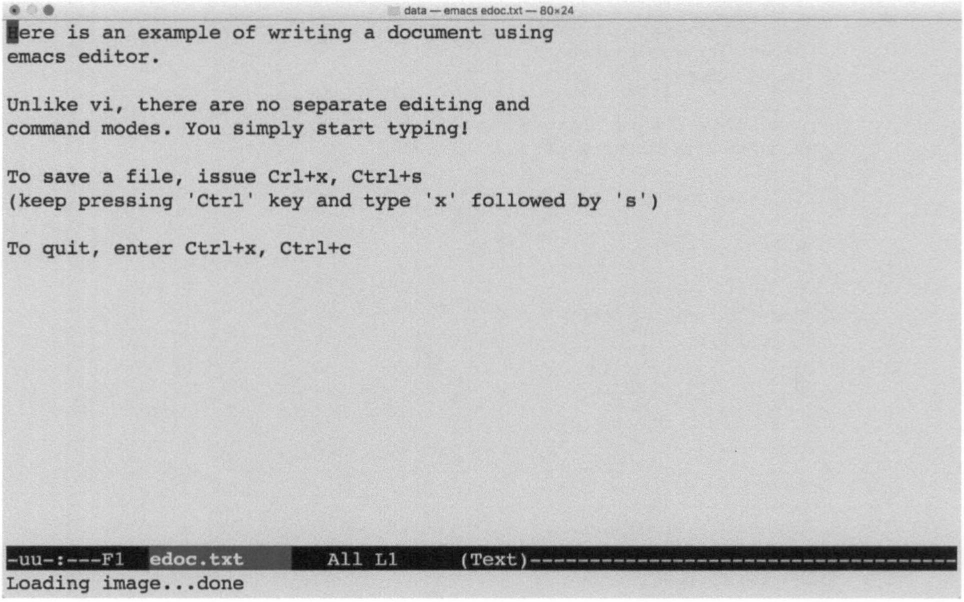

```
data — emacs edoc.txt — 80×24
Here is an example of writing a document using
emacs editor.

Unlike vi, there are no separate editing and
command modes. You simply start typing!

To save a file, issue Crl+x, Ctrl+s
(keep pressing 'Ctrl' key and type 'x' followed by 's')

To quit, enter Ctrl+x, Ctrl+c

-uu-:---F1  edoc.txt      All L1      (Text)-----------------------------------
Loading image...done
```

Figure 4.11 An Emacs editor screenshot.

Try It Yourself 4.2: Editing

Start a new file in Emacs editor. Type in your name, address, phone number, and email. Save the file and exit out of Emacs. Use an appropriate UNIX command to print the content of this file on your terminal, as well as count the number of characters.

Now open that file in vi editor. Delete your phone number. Save the file and exit vi. Use an appropriate UNIX command to print the content of this file on your terminal. Use an appropriate UNIX command to print the content of this file on your terminal, as well as count the number of characters.

What is the difference you see in this output compared to before? Was there a reduction in the number of characters in this file? By how much?

4.6 Redirections and Piping

Many programs and utilities (system-provided or user-created) can produce output, which is usually displayed on the console. However, if you like, you can redirect that output.

For instance, the "ls" command lists all the files available in a given directory. If you want this listing stored in a file instead of displayed on the console, you can run "ls > output". Here, ">" is a redirection operator and "output" is the name of the file where the output of the "ls" command will be stored.

Here we assumed that the "output" file does not already exist. If it does, its content will be overwritten by what "ls" generated. So be careful – check that you are not wiping out an existing file before redirecting the output to it.

Sometimes you want to append new output to an existing file instead of overwriting it or creating a new file. For that, you can use operator ">>". Example: "ls >> output". Now, the new output will be added at the end of the "output" file. If the file does not exist, it will be created just like before.

Redirection also works the other way. Let us take an example. We know that "wc -l xyz.txt" can count the number of lines in xyz.txt and display on the console; specifically, it lists the number of lines followed by the filename (here, xyz.txt). What if you want only the number of lines? You can redirect the file to "wc -l" command like this: "wc -l < xyz.txt". Now you should see only a number.

Let us extend this further. Imagine you want to store this number in another file (instead of displaying on the console). You can accomplish this by combining two redirection operators, like this: "wc -l < xyz.txt > output". Now, a number will be calculated and it will be stored in a file named "output." Go ahead and do "cat output" to read that file.

Redirection is primarily done with files, but UNIX allows other ways to connect different commands or utilities. And that is done using pipes. Looking for a pipe symbol "|" on your keyboard? It is that character above the "\" character.

Let us say you want to read a file. You can run "cat xyz.txt". But it has too many lines and you care about only the first five. You can pipe the output of "cat xyz.txt" command to another command, "head -5", which shows only the top five lines. And thus, the whole command becomes "cat xyz.txt | head -5".

Now imagine you want to see only the fifth line of that file. No problem. Pipe the above output to another command "tail -1", which shows only the last (1) line of whatever is passed to it. So, the whole command becomes "cat xyz.txt | head -5 | tail -1".

And what if you want to store that one line to a file instead of just seeing it on the console? You guessed it – "cat xyz.txt | head -5 | tail -1 > output".

In the next section, we will see more examples of how redirections and pipes can be used for solving simple problems.

Try It Yourself 4.3: Redirection and Piping

For this exercise, use the file you created earlier for the last hands-on homework. First, use the appropriate UNIX command to print the number of lines in the file to the console. Next, use the redirection operator(s) that you just learned to add this number at the end of the same file. Finally, print the last line of the file in the console. If you have done this correctly, the first and the last step will print the same output in the console.

4.7 Solving Small Problems with UNIX

UNIX provides an excellent environment for problem solving. We will not be able to go into every kind of problem and related details, but we will look at a few examples here.

1. Display Content of a File

```
cat 1.txt
```

2. Combining Multiple Files in One File

```
cat 1.txt 2.txt 3.txt > all.txt
```

3. Sorting a File

Let us say we have a file numbers.txt with one number per line and we want to sort them. Just run:

```
sort numbers.txt
```

Want them sorted in descending order (reverse order)? Run:

```
sort -r numbers.txt
```

We can do the same with non-numbers. Let us create a file text.txt with "the quick brown fox jumps over the lazy dog," as text written one word per line. And now run the sorting command:

```
sort text.txt
```

to get those words sorted alphabetically.

How about sorting multicolumn data? Say your file, test.txt, has three columns and you want to sort the dataset according to the values in the second column. Just run the following commands:

```
sort -k2 test.txt
```

4. Finding Unique Tokens

First, we need to make sure the words or tokens in the file are sorted, and then run the command for finding unique tokens. How do we do two things at the same time? Time to bring out the pipes:

```
sort text.txt | uniq
```

5. Counting Unique Tokens

And now, what if we want to find out how many unique tokens are in a file? Add another pipe:

```
sort text.txt | uniq | wc -l
```

6. Searching for Text

There are many ways one can search for text on UNIX. One option is "grep". Let us search for the word "fox" in text.txt:

```
grep 'fox' text.txt
```

If the word exists in that file, it will be printed on the console, otherwise the output will be nothing. But it does not end here. Let us say we want to search for "fox" in all the text files in the current directory. That can be done using:

```
grep 'fox' *.txt
```

Here, "`*.txt`" indicates all the text files, with "*" being the wildcard. In the output, you can see all the .txt files that have the word "fox".

7. Search and Replace

Just like searching for text, there are several ways one can substitute text on UNIX. It often depends on where you are doing this search and replacement. If it is inside a text editor like vi or Emacs, you can use those editor-specific commands. But let us go with doing this on the console. We will use the "sed" command to replace "fox" with "sox" in our text.txt file and save it to text2.txt.

```
sed 's/fox/sox/' text.txt > text2.txt
```

Here, 's/fox/sox' means search for "fox" and replace it with "sox". Notice the use of redirection in this command.

8. Extracting Fields from Structured Data

Let us first create a text file with a couple of fields for this experiment. Here is a file called "names.txt":

```
Bugs Bunny
Daffy Duck
Porky Pig
```

Now, let us say we want to get everyone's first name. We use the "cut" command like this:

```
cut -d ' ' -f1 names.txt
```

Here, the "-d" option is for specifying a delimiter, which is a space (see the option right after "-d") and "-f1" indicates the first field. Let us create another file with phone numbers, called phones.txt:

```
123 456 7890
456 789 1230
789 123 4560
```

How do we get last four digits of all phone numbers from this file?

```
cut -d ' ' -f3
```

9. More Text Operations

If you want to perform more textual operations, you can look at the "fmt" command. It is a simple text formatter, often used for limiting the width of lines in a file. Paired with a -width flag (where width is a positive integer denoting the number of words to go on each output line and words are sequences of non-white-space characters), the "fmt" command can be used to display individual words in a sentence. For example:

```
fmt -1 phones.txt
```

Running the above command in the previous phone.txt data will print the following:

```
123
456
7890
456
789
1230
789
123
4560
```

If your dataset is too large you can use "head" to print the first 10 lines. So, the above line of code can be rewritten as:

```
fmt -1 phones.txt | head
```

10. Merging Fields from Different Files

Now let us combine our names and phone numbers. For this, we will use the "paste" command. This command takes at least two arguments.[9] In this case, we will pass two arguments – names of the two files that we want to merge horizontally:

```
paste names.txt phones.txt
```

And voilà! Here is what you get:

```
Bugs Bunny   123 456 7890
Daffy Duck   456 789 1230
Porky Pig   789 123 4560
```

And of course, you can store that output to a file using redirection, like this:

```
paste names.txt phones.txt > phonebook.txt
```

If you print out this file on the console using the "cat" command, you will be able to see the content of it, which will, of course, be the same as what you just saw above.

11. Arithmetic Operations

UNIX can help you do small arithmetic operations without really writing any program. You just need to follow a few simple rules. For instance, we could easily assign values to variables "a" and "b" as follows.

```
a = 10
b = 5
```

Now, let us add them.

```
total=`expr $a + $b`
echo $total
```

Make sure you enter the above command exactly as it is shown here: those are back-ticks (on US keyboards, the character under the tilde character; yours may be elsewhere) and not single quotes, and there needs to be spaces around the "+" sign. This should print the result (15).

Similarly, `` `expr $a \* $b` `` is for multiplication, `` `expr $b / $a` `` is for division, and `` `expr $b % $a` `` is for modulus operation.

Try It Yourself 4.4: Small Data Problems

1. Execute a simple arithmetic operation
   Use UNIX commands to multiply 3 and 10, followed by divide by 2, and finally modulo 5.
2. Write the output to a file
   Write the output of all three steps in the last problem to a new file, numbers.txt in different lines.
3. Sorting a file
   Next, sort all the numbers in numbers.txt in ascending order.
4. Add more numbers to the end of a file
   Use UNIX commands to modify the file by adding the output of the last step to the end of the file.
5. Counting the number of unique numbers
   Count the number of unique numbers in the file.
6. Count the frequency of numbers
   Count the number of times each unique number appears in the same file.
7. Search and replace
   Using the UNIX commands find the largest number that appears in the file and the line number(s) in which it appears in the file. Add the text "Maximum: " at the beginning of the line(s). For example, if the largest number is 10 and it appears at the third line, at the end of this step the same line should appear as following:

   ```
   Maximum: 10
   ```

Hands-On Example 4.1: Solving Data Problems with UNIX

Let us take a data problem. We will work with housing.txt, which is a text file containing housing data. It is pretty big for a text file (53 MB) and available for download from OA 4.1. That size is easy to find. But can you find out how many records it has? This is a CSV file (field values separated using commas), so potentially you can load it into a spreadsheet program like Excel. OK, then go ahead and do it. It may take a while for that program to load this data. After that, see how quickly you can figure out the answer to that question.

Alternatively, we can use UNIX. If you are already on a UNIX-based machine or have a UNIX-based environment, open a console and navigate to where this file is using "cd" commands. Or you can upload this file to a UNIX server using FTP or SFTP and then log in to the machine using SSH. Either way, I am assuming that you have a console or a terminal open to the place where this file is stored. Now simply issue:

```
wc housing.txt
```

That should give you an output like this:

```
64536 3256971 53281106 housing.txt
```

The first number represents the number of lines, the second one refers to the number of words, and the third one reports the number of characters in this file. In other words, we can immediately see from this output that we have 64,535 records (one less because the first line has field names and not actual data). See how easy this was?!

Next, can you figure out what fields this data has? It is easy using the "head" command on UNIX:

```
head -1 housing.txt
```

The output will list a whole bunch of fields, separated by commas. While some of them will not make sense, some are easy to figure out. For instance, you can see a column listing the age (AGE1), value (VALUE), number of rooms (ROOMS), and number of bedrooms (BEDRMS). Try some of the UNIX commands you know to explore this data. For instance, you can use "head" to see the first few lines and "tail" to see the last few lines.

Now, let us ask: What is the maximum number of rooms in any house in this data? To answer this, we need to first extract the column that has information about the number of rooms (ROOMS) and then sort it in descending order.

OK, so where is the ROOMS column? Using "head -1" command shown above, we can find the names of all the fields or columns. Here, we can see that ROOMS is the nineteenth field. To extract it, we will split the data into fields and ask for field #19. Here is how to do it:

```
cut -d ',' -f19 housing.txt
```

Here, the "cut" command allows us to split the data using delimiter (that is the -d option), which is a comma here. And finally, we are looking for field #19 (-f19). If you happened to run this command (oh, did I not tell you not to run it just yet?!), you perhaps saw a long list of numbers flying across your screen. That is simply the nineteenth field (all 64,535 values) being printed on your console. But we need to print it in a certain order. That means we can pipe with a "sort" command, like this:

```
cut -d ',' -f19 housing.txt | sort -nr
```

Can you figure out what all those new things mean? Well, the first is the pipe "|" symbol. Here it allows us to channel the output of one command (here, "cut") to another one (here, "sort"). Now we are looking at the "sort" command, where we indicate that we want to sort numerical values in descending or reverse order (thus, -nr).

Once again, if you had no patience and went ahead to try this, you saw a list of numbers flying by, but in a different order. To make this output feasible to see, we can do one more piping – this time to "head":

```
cut -d ',' -f19 housing.txt | sort -nr | head
```

Did you run it? Yes, this time I do want you to run this command. Now you can see only the first few values. And the largest value is 15, which means in our data the highest number of rooms any house has is 15.

What if we also want to see how much these houses cost? Sure. For that, we need to extract field #15 as well. If we do that, here's what the above command looks like:

```
cut -d ',' -f15 -f19 housing.txt | sort -nr | head
```

Here are the top few lines in the output:

```
2520000,15
2520000,14
2520000,13
2520000,13
2520000,13
```

Do you see what is happening here? The "sort" command is taking the whole thing like "2520000,15" for sorting. That is not what we really want. We want it to sort the data using only the number of rooms. To make that happen, we need to have "sort" do its own splitting of the data passed to it by the "cut" command and apply sorting to a specific field. Here is what that looks like:

```
cut -d ',' -f15 -f19 housing.txt | sort -t ',' -k2 -nr | head
```

Here we added the "-t" option to indicate we are going to split the data using a delimiter ("," in this case), and once we do that, we will use the second field or key to apply sorting (thus, -k2). And now the output looks something like the following:

```
450000,15
2520000,15
990000,14
700000,14
600000,14
```

Try It Yourself 4.5: Solving Data Problems with UNIX

Continuing from the Hands-On Example 4.1, try changing "-k2" to "-k1". How is the data being sorted now? Repeat these steps for number of bedrooms. In other words, extract and sort the data in descending order of number of bedrooms, displaying house value, total number of rooms, and, of course, number of bedrooms.

Hopefully, now you have got a hang of how these things work. Go ahead and play around some more with this data, trying to answer some questions or satisfying your curiosity about this housing market data. You now know how to wield the awesome power of UNIX!

FYI: When Should You Consider UNIX?

If you know more than one programming languages or have familiarity with multiple programming environments, you know that you tend to develop preferences of which to use when. It is also not uncommon for people to use their favorite programming tool for solving a problem that it is not most suitable for. So, if you have not practiced on UNIX or Linux before, it would be hard to consider it as an option for a problem-solving need. Given that, it might help you if I describe when and how I personally consider UNIX.

Most times I work on a Mac system, which makes it easy to bring up Terminal app. Mac, as you may know, is built on UNIX, and Terminal app can execute most commonplace UNIX commands. One need with textual data that I often have is counting tokens – characters, words, lines. As you can imagine, writing a program just to do that is just too much. What I have seen most people doing is opening up that text document in a word processing software, such as Microsoft Word, and using the in-built document statistics functionality to come up with the answer. This can easily take a minute or two. But with "wc" command, I can get the answer in two seconds. But that is not all. There are documents or files that are so large that I would not dare to open them in a software just so that I can get a line count. It may take a long time just to load it, and the program may even crash. But once again, a simple use of "wc" would yield the desired results in seconds without any side effects.

Another common use I have for UNIX commands is when I am dealing with CSV files and need column extraction, sorting, or filtering done. Sure, I could use Excel, but that could take longer, especially if my data is large.

And these are just a couple of simple cases of frequent uses of UNIX utilities; I have many other uses – some are more occasional than others. I admit that it all comes down to what you know and what you are willing to pay. But I hope this chapter has at least taken care of the former, that is, knowing enough UNIX. For the latter (amount of time and effort), give it some time. The more you practice, the better it gets. And before you know, you would be saving precious time and getting more productive with your data processing needs!

Summary

UNIX is one of the most powerful platforms around, and the more you know about it and how to use it, the more amazing things you can do with your data, without even writing any code. People do not often think about using UNIX for data science, but as you can see in this chapter, we could get so much done with so little work. And we have only scratched the surface.

We learned about how to have a UNIX-like environment on your machine or to connect to a UNIX server, as well as how to transfer files to/from that server. We tried a few basic and a few not-so-basic commands. But it is really the use of pipes and redirections that make these things pop out; this is where UNIX outshines anything else. Finally, we applied these basic skills to solve a couple of small data problems. It should be clear by now that those commands or programs on UNIX are highly efficient and effective. They could crunch through a large amount of data without ever choking!

Earlier in this chapter I told you that UNIX can also help with data visualization. We avoided that topic here because creating visualizations (plots, etc.) will require a few installations and configurations on the UNIX server. Since that is a tall order and I cannot expect everyone to have access to such a server (and very friendly IT staff!), I decided to leave that part out of this chapter. Besides, soon we will see much better and easier ways to do data visualizations.

Going further, I recommend learning about shell scripting or programming. This is UNIX's own programming language that allows you to leverage the full potential of UNIX. Most shell scripts are small and yet very powerful. You will be amazed by the kinds of things you can have your operating system do for you!

Key Terms

- **File:** A file is collection of related data that appears to the user as a single, contiguous block of information, has a name, and is retained in storage.
- **Directory:** A directory in an operating system (e.g., UNIX) is a special type of file that contains a list of objects (i.e., other files, directories, and links) and their corresponding details (e.g., when the file was created, last modified, file type, etc.) except the actual content of those objects.
- **Protocols:** The system of rules governing affairs of a process, for example, the FTP protocol defines the rules of file transfer process.
- **SSH (Secure Shell):** This is an application or interface that allows one to either run UNIX commands or connect with a UNIX server.
- **FTP (File Transfer Protocol):** This is an Internet protocol that allows one to connect two remote machines and transfer files between them.

Conceptual Questions

1. What is a shell in the context of UNIX?
2. Name at least two operating systems that are based on UNIX.
3. What is the difference between a pipe and a redirection?

Hands-On Problems

Problem 4.1

You are given a portion of the data from NYC about causes of death for some people in 2010 (available for download from OA 4.2). The data is in CSV format with the following fields: Year, Ethnicity, Sex, Cause of Death, Count, Percent.

Answer the following questions using this data. Use UNIX commands or utilities. Show your work. Note that the answers to each of these questions should be the direct result of running appropriate commands/utilities and not involve any further processing, including manual work. Answers without the method to achieve them will not get any grade.

a. How many male record groups and how many female record groups does the data have?
b. How many white female groups are there? Copy entire records of them to a new file where the records are organized by death count in descending order.
c. List causes of death by their frequencies in descending order. What are the three most frequent causes of death for males and females?

Problem 4.2

Over the years, UNICEF has supported countries in collecting data related to children and women through an international household survey program. The survey responses on sanitation and hygiene from 70 countries in 2015 are constructed into a dataset on handwashing. You can download the CSV file from OA 4.3. Use the dataset to answer the following questions using UNIX commands or utilities:

a. Which region has the lowest percentage of urban population?
b. List the region(s) where the number of urban population in thousands are more than a million and yet they comprise less than half of the population.

Problem 4.3

For the following exercise, use the data on availability of essential medicines in 38 countries from the World Health Organization (WHO). You can find the dataset in OA 4.4. Download the filtered data as a CSV table and use it to answer the following questions.

1. Between 2007 and 2013, which country had the lowest percentage median availability of selected generic medicines in private.
2. List the top five countries which have the highest percentage of public and private median availability of selected medicines in 2007–2013.
3. List the top three countries where it is best to rely on the private availability of selected generic medicines than public. Explain your answer with valid reasons.

Further Reading and Resources

As noted earlier in this chapter, UNIX is often ignored as a tool/system/platform for solving data problems. That being said, there are a few good options for educating yourself about the potential of UNIX for data science that do a reasonable job of helping a beginner wield at least part of the awesome power that UNIX has.

Data Science at the Command Line[10] provides a nice list of basic commands and command-line utilities that one could use while working on data science tasks. The author, Jerosen Janssens, also has a book *Data Science at Command Line*, published by O'Reilly, which is worth consideration if you want to go further in UNIX.

Similarly, Dr. Bunsen has a nice blog on explorations in UNIX available from http://www.drbunsen.org/explorations-in-unix/.

There are several cheat sheets that one could find on the Web containing UNIX commands and shortcuts. Some of them are here:

- http://cheatsheetworld.com/programming/unix-linux-cheat-sheet/
- http://www.cheat-sheets.org/saved-copy/ubunturef.pdf
- https://www.cheatography.com/davechild/cheat-sheets/regular-expressions/

Notes

1. Picture of console window on a Linux KDE console: https://www.flickr.com/photos/okubax/29814358851
2. Cygwin project: http://www.cygwin.com
3. Cygwin running on a Windows desktop: https://commons.wikimedia.org/wiki/File:Cygwin_X11_rootless_WinXP.png
4. Free UNIX: http://sdf.lonestar.org/index.cgi
5. WinSCP: http://winscp.net/eng/index.php

6. Download PuTTY: http://www.chiark.greenend.org.uk/~sgtatham/putty/download.html
7. Using PuTTY in Windows: https://mediatemple.net/community/products/dv/204404604/using-ssh-in-putty-
8. It is not uncommon for students to literally type the instructions rather than interpreting it and substituting correct values. I have done a lot of "debugging" for such cases. So, do not literally type "ssh username@hostname". You will substitute "username" with your actual username on that server, and "hostname" with the full address of the server. Save your instructor the debugging hassle! And be sure to make a note of these details where you can find them again later!
9. Arguments to a command or a program are the options or inputs it takes. No, that command is not trying to fight with you!
10. Data Science at the Command Line: http://datascienceatthecommandline.com/

5 Python

"Most good programmers do programming not because they expect to get paid or get adulation by the public, but because it is fun to program."

— Linus Torvalds

What do you need?

- Computational thinking (refer to Chapter 1).
- Ability to install and configure software.
- Knowledge of basic statistics, including correlation and regression.
- (Ideally) Prior exposure to any programming language.

What will you learn?

- Basic programming skills with Python.
- Using Python to do statistical analysis, including producing models and visualizations.
- Applying introductory machine learning techniques such as classification and clustering with Python to various data problems.

5.1 Introduction

Python is a simple-to-use yet powerful scripting language that allows one to solve data problems of varying scale and complexity. It is also the most used tool in data science and most frequently listed in data science job postings as the requirement. Python is a very friendly and easy-to-learn language, making it ideal for the beginner. At the same time, it is very powerful and extensible, making it suitable for advanced data science needs.

This chapter will start with an introduction to Python and then dive into using the language for addressing various data problems using statistical processing and machine learning.

5.2 Getting Access to Python

One of the appeals of Python is that it is available for almost every platform you can imagine, and for free. In fact, in many cases – such as working on a UNIX or Linux machine – it is likely to be already installed for you. If not, it is very easy to obtain and install.

5.2.1 Download and Install Python

For the purpose of this book, I will assume that you have access to Python. Not sure where it is? Try logging on to the server (using SSH) and run the command "python -version" at the terminal. This should print the version of Python installed on the server.

It is also possible that you have Python installed on your machine. If you are on a Mac or a Linux, open a terminal or a console and run the same command as above to see if you have Python installed, and, if you do, what version.

Finally, if you would like, you can install an appropriate version of Python for your system by downloading it directly from Python[1] and following the installation and configuration instructions. See this chapter's further reading and resources for a link, and Appendices C and D for more help and details.

5.2.2 Running Python through Console

Assuming you have access to Python – either on your own machine or on the server – let us now try something. On the console, first enter "python" to enter the Python environment. You should see a message and a prompt like this:

```
Python 3.5.2 |Anaconda 4.2.0 (x86_64)| (default, Jul 2 2016,
17:52:12)
[GCC 4.2.1 Compatible Apple LLVM 4.2 (clang-425.0.28)] on darwin
Type "help", "copyright", "credits" or "license" for more infor-
mation.
>>>
```

Now, at this prompt (the three "greater than" signs), write 'print ("Hello, World!")' (without the single quotation marks) and hit enter. If things go right, you should see "Hello, World!" printed on the screen like the following:

```
>>> print ("Hello, World!")
Hello, World!
```

Let us now try a simple expression: 2+2. You see 4? Great!

Finally, let us exit this prompt by entering exit(). If it is more convenient, you could also do Ctrl+d to exit the Python prompt.

5.2.3 Using Python through Integrated Development Environment (IDE)

While running Python commands and small scripts are fine on the console, there are times when you need something more sophisticated. That is when an **Integrated Development Environment** (IDE) comes in. An IDE can let you not only write and run programs, but it can also provide help and documentation, as well as tools to debug, test, and deploy your programs – *all in one place* (thus, "integrated").

There are several decent options for Python IDE, including using the Python plug-in for a general-purpose IDE, such as Eclipse. If you are familiar with and invested in Eclipse, you might get the Python plug-in for Eclipse and continue using Eclipse for your Python programming. Look at the footnote for PyDev.[2]

If you want to try something new, then look up Anaconda, Spyder, and IPython (more in Appendix D). Note that most beginners waste a lot of time trying to install and configure packages needed for running various Python programs. So, to make your life easier, I recommend using Anaconda as the platform and Spyder on top of it.

There are three parts to getting this going. The good news is – you will have to do this only once.

First, make sure you have Python installed on your machine. Download and install an appropriate version for your operating system from the Python[3] link in the footnote. Next, download and install Anaconda Navigator[4] from the link in the footnote. Once ready, go ahead and launch it. You will see something like Figure 5.1. Here, find a panel for "spyder." In the screenshot, you can see a "Launch" button because I already have Spyder installed. For you, it may show "Install." Go ahead and install Spyder through Anaconda Navigator.

Once installed, that "Install" button in the Spyder panel should become "Launch." Go ahead and launch Spyder. Figure 5.2 shows how it may look. Well, it is probably not going to have all the stuff that I have showing here, but you should see three distinct panes: one occupying the left half of the window and two on the right side. The left panel is where you

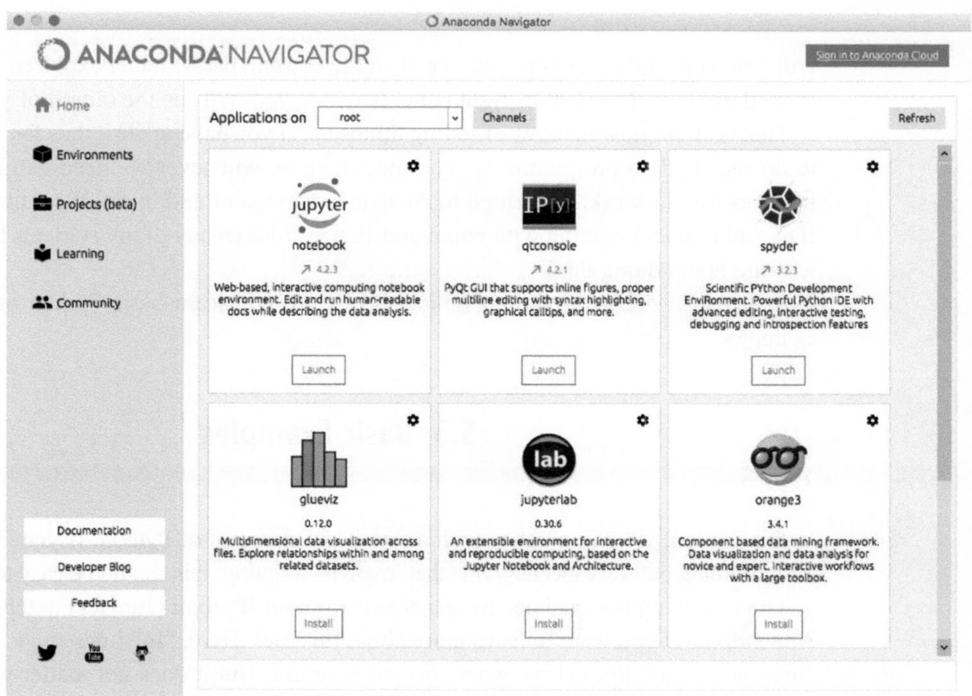

Figure 5.1 A screenshot of Anaconda Navigator.

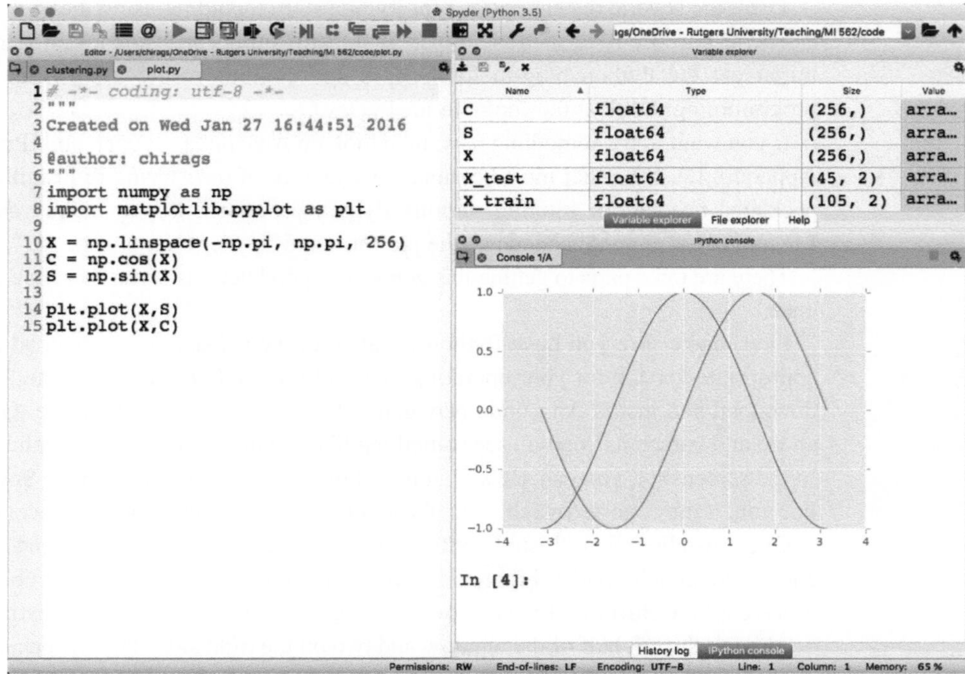

Figure 5.2 A screenshot of Spyder IDE.

will type your code. The top-right panel, at the bottom, has Variable explorer, File explorer, as well as Help. The bottom-right panel is where you will see the output of your code.

That is all for now in terms of setting things up. If you have made it thus far, you are ready to do *real* Python programming. The nice thing is, whenever we need extra packages or libraries for our work, we can go to Anaconda Navigator and install them through its nice IDE, rather than fidgeting with command-line utilities (many of my students have reported wasting hours doing that).

Rather than doing any programming theory, we will learn basic Python using hands-on examples.

5.3 Basic Examples

In this section, we will practice with a few basic elements of Python. If you have done any programming before, especially one that involves scripting, this should be easy to understand.

The following screenshots are generated from an IPython (Jupyter) notebook. Refer to Appendix D if you want to learn more about this tool. Here, "In" lines show you what you enter, and "Out" lines show what you get in return. But it does not matter where you are typing your Python code – directly at the Python console, in Spyder console, or in some other Python tool – you should see the same outputs.

```
In [8]: print ("Hello, World!")
        Hello, World!
```

Simple math operations and variable assignments

```
In [9]: 2+2
Out[9]: 4

In [10]: x = 2

In [11]: y = 2

In [12]: z = x + y

In [13]: z
Out[13]: 4
```

In the above segment, we began with a couple of commands that we tried when we first started up Python earlier in this chapter. Then, we did variable assignments. Entering "x = 2" defines variable "x" and assigns value "2" to it. In many traditional programming languages, doing this much could take up two to three steps as you have to declare what kind of variable you want to define (in this case, an integer – one that could hold whole numbers) before you could use it to assign values to it. Python makes it much simpler. Most times you would not have to worry about declaring **data types** for a variable.

After assigning values to variables "x" and "y", we performed a mathematical operation when we entered "z = x + y". But we do not see the outcome of that operation until we enter "z". This also should convey one more thing to you – generally speaking, when you want to know the value stored in a variable, you can simply enter that variable's name on the Python prompt.

Continuing on, let us see how we can use different **arithmetic operators**, followed by the use of **logical operators**, for comparing numerical quantities.

Practicing arithmetic operators

```
In [16]: 2 + 3, 2 - 3, 2 * 3, 2 / 3, 2**3
Out[16]: (5, -1, 6, 0.6666666666666666, 8)
```

Logical operators for comparing quantities

```
In [17]: 2 > 3, 3 > 2
Out[17]: (False, True)

In [18]: 3 >= 3, 3 <= 3
Out[18]: (True, True)

In [19]: # Checking for equality
         2 == 2
Out[19]: True

In [20]: # Checking for equality
         [2, 3] == [2, 3]
Out[20]: True
```

Here, first we entered a series of mathematical operations. As you can see, Python does not care if you put them all on a single line, separated by commas. It understands that each of them is a separate operation and provides you answers for each of them.

Most programming languages use logical operators such as ">," "<," ">=," and "<=." Each of these should make sense, as they are exact representations of what we would use in regular math or logic studies. Where you may find a little surprise is how we represent comparison of two quantities (using "==") and negation (using "!="). Use of logical operations results in **Boolean** values – "true" or "false," or 1 or 0. You can see that in the above output: "2 > 3" is false and "3 >= 3" is true. Go ahead and try other operations like these.

Python, like most other programming languages, offers a variety of data types. What is a data type? It is a format for storing data, including numbers and text. But to make things easier for you, often these data types are hidden. In other words, most times, we do not have to explicitly state what kind of data type a variable is going to store.

Data types

```
In [3]: x=1

In [4]: type(x)
Out[4]: int

In [5]: y=2

In [6]: z=x/y

In [7]: z
Out[7]: 0.5

In [8]: type(z)
Out[8]: float

In [9]: test = (z>1)

In [10]: test
Out[10]: False

In [11]: type(test)
Out[11]: bool

In [ ]:
```

As you can see above, we could use "type" operation or function around a variable name (e.g., "type(x)") to find out its data type. Given that Python does not require you to explicitly define a variable's data type, it will make an appropriate decision based on what is being stored in a variable. So, when we tried storing the result of a division operation – x/y – into variable "z," Python automatically decided to set z's data type to be "float," which is for storing real numbers such as 1.1, −3.5, and 22/7.

Try It Yourself 5.1: Basic Operations

Work on the following exercises using Python with any method you like (directly on the console, using Spyder, or using IPython notebook).

1. Perform the arithmetic operation, 182 modulo 13 and store the result in a variable, named "output."
2. Print the value and data type of "output."
3. Check if the value stored in "output" is equal to zero.
4. Repeat steps 1–3 with the arithmetic operation of 182 divided by 13.
5. Report if the data type of "output" is the same in both cases.

5.4 Control Structures

To make decisions based on meeting a condition (or two), we can use "if" statements. Let us say we want to find out if 2020 is a leap year. Here is the code:

```
year = 2020
if (year%4 == 0):
    print ("Leap year")
else:
    print ("Not a leap year")
```

Here, the modulus operator (%) divides 2020 by 4 and gives us the remainder. If that remainder is 0, the script prints "Leap year," otherwise we get "Not a leap year."

Now what if we have multiple conditions to check? Easy. Use a sequence of "if" and "elif" (short for "else if"). Here is the code that checks one variable (collegeYear), and, based on its value, declares the corresponding label for that year:

```
collegeYear = 3
if (collegeYear == 1):
    print ("Freshman")
elif (collegeYear == 2):
    print ("Sophomore")
elif (collegeYear == 3):
    print ("Junior")
elif (collegeYear == 4):
    print ("Senior")
```

```
else:
    print ("Super-senior or not in college!")
```

Another form of control structure is a loop. There are two primary kinds of loops: "while" and "for". The "while" loop allows us to do something until a condition is met. Take a simple case of printing the first five numbers:

```
a, b = 1, 5
while (a<=b):
    print (a)
    a += 1
```

And here is how we could do the same with a "for" loop:

```
for x in range(1, 6):
   print (x)
```

Let us take another set of examples and see how these control structures work. As always, let us start with if–else. You probably have guessed the overall structure of the if–else block by now from the previous example. In case you have not, here it is:

```
if condition1:
   statement(s)
elif condition2:
   statement(s)
else:
   statement(s)
```

In the previous example, you saw a condition that involves numeric variables. Let us try one that involves character variables. Imagine in a multiple-choice questionnaire you are given four choices: A, B, C, and D. Among them, A and D are the correct choices and the rest are wrong. So, if you want to check if the answer chosen is the correct answer, the code can be as follows:

```
if ans == 'A' or ans == 'D':
   print ("Correct answer")
else
   print ("Wrong answer")
```

Next, let us see if the same problem can be solved with the while loop:

```
ans = input('Guess the right answer: ')
while (ans != 'A') and (ans != 'D'):
     print ("Wrong answer")
     ans = input('Guess the right answer: ')
```

The above code, will prompt the user to provide a new choice until the correct answer is provided. As evidenced from the two examples, the structure of the while loop can be viewed as:

```
while condition:
      statement(s)
```

The statement(s) within the while loop are going to be executed repeatedly as long as the condition remains true. The same programming goal can be accomplished with the for loop as well:

```
correctAns = ["A", "D"]
for ans in  correctAns:
      print(ans)
```

The above lines of code will print the correct choices for the question.

Try It Yourself 5.2: Control Structures

Pick any number within the range of 99 and 199 and check if the number is divisible by 7 using Python code. If the number is divisible, print the following: "the number is divisible by 7"; otherwise, print the number closest to the number you picked that is divisible by 7. Using a while loop, print all the numbers that are divisible by 7 within the same range.

5.5 Statistics Essentials

In this section, we will see how some statistical elements can be measured and manifested in Python. You are encouraged to learn basic statistics or brush up on those concepts using external resources (see Chapter 3 and Appendix C for some pointers).

Let us start with a distribution of numbers. We can represent this distribution using an array, which is a collection of elements (in this case, numbers).

For example, we are creating our family tree, and having put some data on the branches and leaves of this tree, we want to do some statistical analysis. Let us look at everyone's age. Before doing any processing, we need to represent it as follows:

```
data1=[85,62,78,64,25,12,74,96,63,45,78,20,5,30,45,78,45,
96,65,45,74,12,78,23,8]
```

If you like, you can call this a dataset. We will use a very popular Python package or library called "numpy" to run our analyses. So, let us import and define this library:

```
import numpy as np
```

What did we just do? We asked Python to import a library called "numpy" and we said, internally (for the current session or program), that we will refer to that library as "np". This particular library or package is extremely useful for us, as you will see. (Do not be surprised if many of your Python sessions or programs have this line somewhere in the beginning.)

Now, let us start asking (and answering) questions.

1. What is the largest (**max**) and the smallest (**min**) of these values?

```
max=np.max(data1)
print("Max:{0:d}".format(max))
min=np.min(data1)
print("Min:{0:d}".format(min))
```

2. What is the average age? This can be measured using **mean**.

```
mean=np.mean(data1)
print("Mean:{0:8.4f}".format(mean))
```

3. How are age values spread across this distribution? We can use **variance** and **standard deviation** for this.

```
variance=np.var(data1)
print("Variance:{0:8.4f}".format(variance))
standarddev=np.std(data1)
print("STD:{0:8.4f}".format(standarddev))
```

4. What is the middle value of the age range? This is answered by finding the **median**.

```
median=np.median(data1)
print("Median:{0:8.4f}".format(median))
```

Finally, we can also plot the whole distribution (a **histogram**) using an appropriate library. Let us import it first:

```
import matplotlib.pyplot as plt
```

Once again, we are importing a package called "matplotlib.pyplot" and assigning a shortcut "plt" for the purpose of our current session. Now we run the following commands on our dataset:

```
plt.figure()
hist1, edges1 = np.histogram(data1)
plt.bar(edges1[:-1], hist1, width=edges1[1:]-edges1[:-1])
```

Here, plt.figure() creates an environment for plotting a figure. Then, we get the data for creating a histogram using the second line. This data is passed to plt.bar() function, along with some parameters for the axes to produce the histogram we see in Figure 5.3.

Note that if you get an error for plt.figure(), just ignore it and continue with the rest of the commands. It just might work!

If we are too lazy to type in a whole bunch of values to create a dataset to play with, we could use the random number initialization function of numpy, like this:

```
data2 = np.random.randn(1000)
```

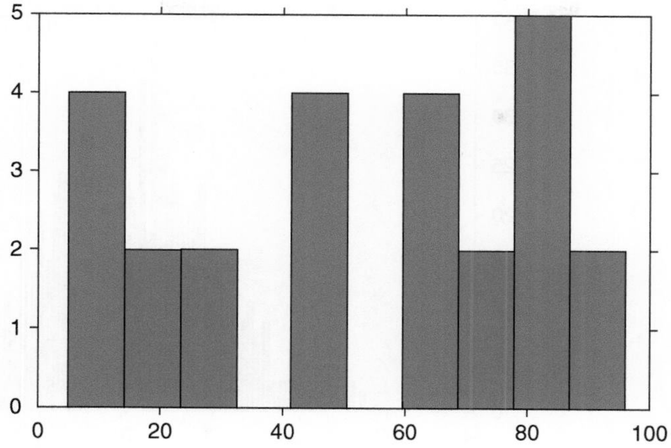

Figure 5.3 Bar graph showing age distribution.

Try It Yourself 5.3: Basic Statistics 1

Create an artificial dataset with 1000 random numbers. Run all of the analyses we did before with the new dataset. That means finding ranges, mean, and variance, as well as creating a visualization.

If you did this exercise, you would notice that you get bars. But what if you wanted a different number of bars? This may be useful to control the resolution of the figure. Here, we have 1000 data points. So, on one extreme, we could ask for 1000 bars, but that may be too much. At the same time, we may not want to let Python decide for us. There is a quick fix. We can specify how many of these bars, also called "bins," we would like. For instance, if we wanted 100 bins or bars, we can write the following code.

```
plt.figure()
hist2, edges2 = np.histogram(data2, bins=100)
plt.bar(edges2[:-1], hist2, width=edges2[1:]-edges2[:-1])
```

And the result is shown in Figure 5.4. Note that your plot may look a little different because your dataset may be different than mine. Why? Because we are getting these data points using a random number generator. In fact, you may see different plots every time you run your code starting with initializing data2!

Try It Yourself 5.4: Basic Statistics 2

For this hands-on problem, you will need the Daily Demand Forecasting Orders dataset from the UCI machine learning repository,[5] comprising 60 days of data from a Brazilian company of large logistics. The dataset has 13 attributes including 12 predictors and the target attribute, total of orders per day. Use this

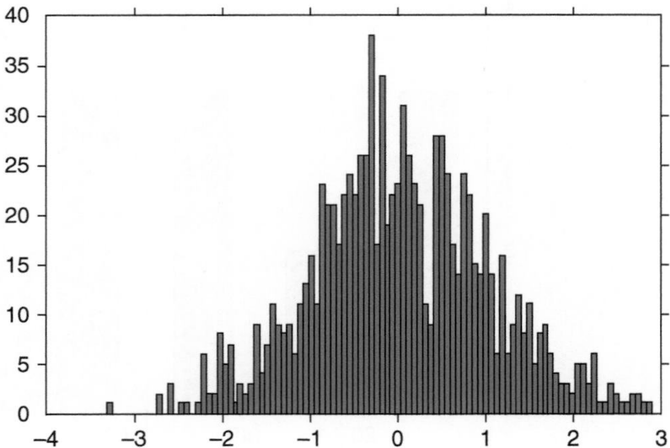

Figure 5.4 Bar graph showing distribution of 1000 random numbers.

dataset to practice calculating the minimum, maximum, range, and average for all the attributes. Plot the data per attribute in a bar graph to visualize the distribution.

We have gathered a few useful tools and techniques in the previous section. Let us apply them to a data problem, while also extending our reach with these tools. For this exercise, we will work with a small dataset available from github[6] (see link in footnote). This is a macroscopic dataset with seven economic variables observed from the years 1947 to 1962 ($n = 16$).

5.5.1 Importing Data

First, we need to import that data into our Python environment. For this, we will use Pandas library. Pandas is an important component of the Python scientific stack. The Pandas **DataFrame** is quite handy since it provides useful information, such as column names read from the data source so that the user can understand and manipulate the imported data more easily. Let us say that the data is in a file "data.csv" in the current directory. The following line loads that data in a variable "CSV_data."

```
from pandas import read_csv CSV_data = read_csv('data.csv')
```

Another way to use Pandas functionalities is the way we have worked with numpy. First, we import Pandas library and then call its appropriate functions like this:

```
import pandas as pd
df = pd.read_csv('data.csv')
```

This is especially useful if we need to use Pandas functionalities multiple times in the code.

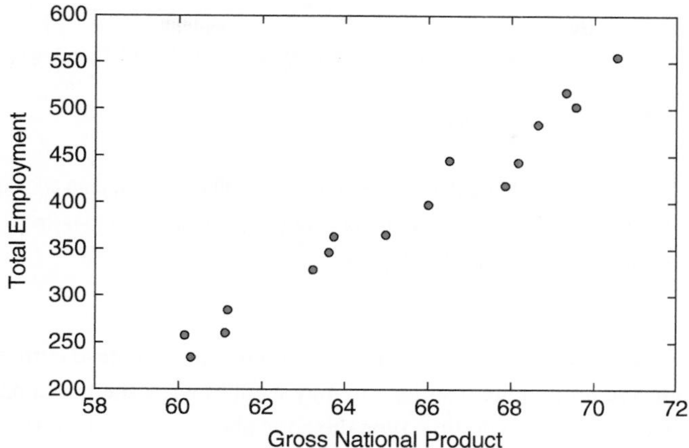

Figure 5.5 Scatterplot to visualize the relationship between GNP and Employment.

5.5.2 Plotting the Data

One of the nice things about Python, with the help of its libraries, is that it has very easy-to-use functionalities when it comes to visualizing the data. All we have to do is to import matplotlib.pyplot and use an appropriate function. Let us say we want to produce a **scatterplot** of "Employed" and "GNP" variables. Here is the code:

```
import matplotlib.pyplot as plt
plt.scatter(df.Employed, df.GNP)
```

Figure 5.5 shows the result. It seems these two variables are somehow related. Let us explore it further by first finding the strength of their relation using a correlation function, and then performing a regression.

FYI: Dataframes

If you have used arrays in a programming language before, you should feel well at home with the idea of a dataframe in Python. A very popular way to implement a dataframe in Python is using Pandas library.

We saw above how to use Pandas to import structured data in CSV format into a DataFrame kind of object. Once imported, you could visualize the DataFrame object in Spyder by double-clicking its name in Variable explorer. You will see that a dataframe is essentially a table or a matrix with rows and columns. And that is how you can access each of its data points.

For instance, in a dataframe "df", if you want the first row, first column element, you can ask for df.iat [0,0]. Alternatively, if the rows are labeled as "row-1", "row-2", . . . and the columns are labeled as "col-1", "col-2", . . ., you can also ask for the same with df.at['row-1','col-1']. You see how such addressing makes it more readable?

Do you ever need to save your dataframe to a CSV file? That is easy with

```
df.to_csv('mydata.csv')
```

There is a lot more that you can do with dataframes, including adding rows and columns, and applying functions. But those are out of scope for us. If you are still interested, I suggest you consult some of the pointers at the end of this chapter.

Before proceeding, note that while you can run these commands on your Spyder console and see immediate results, you may want to write them as a part of a program/script and run that program. To do this, type the code above in the editor (left panel) in Spyder, save it as a .py file, and click "Run file" (the "play" button) on the toolbar.

5.5.3 Correlation

One of the most common tests we often need to do while solving data-driven problems is to see if two variables are related. For this, we can do a statistical test for correlation.

Let us assume we have the previous data ready in dataframe df. And we want to find if the "Employed" field and "GNP" field are correlated. We could use the "corrcoef" function of numpy to find the **correlation** coefficient, which gives us an idea of the strength of correlation between these two variables. Here is that line of code:

```
np.corrcoef(df.Employed,df.GNP)[0,1]
```

The output of this statement tells us that there is very high correlation between these two variables as represented by the correlation coefficient = 0.9835. Also note that this number is positive, which means both variables move together in the same direction. If this correlation coefficient were negative, we would still have a strong correlation, but just in the opposite direction.

In other words, in this case knowing one variable should give us enough knowledge about the other. Let us ask: If we know the value of one variable (independent variable or predictor), can we predict the value of the other variable (dependent variable or response)? For that, we need to perform regression analysis.

5.5.4 Linear Regression

So, we can learn about two variables relating in some way, but if there is a relationship of some kind, can we figure out if and how one variable could predict the other? **Linear regression** allows us to do that. Specifically, we want to see how a variable X affects a variable y.[7] Here, X is called the **independent variable** or **predictor**; and y is called the **dependent variable** or **outcome**.

Figuring out this relationship between *X* and *y* can be seen as building or fitting a model with linear regression. There are many methods for doing so, but perhaps the most common is ordinary least squares (OLS).

For doing linear regression with Python, we can use statsmodels library's API functions, as follows:

```
import statsmodels.api as sm
lr_model = sm.OLS(y, X).fit()
```

Here, lr_model is the model built using linear regression with the OLS fitting approach.

How do we know this worked? Let us check the results of the model by running the following command:

```
print(lr_model.summary())
```

Somewhere in the output here, we can find values of coefficients – one for const (constant) and the other for GNP. And here is our regression equation:

```
Employed = coeff*GNP + const
```

Now just substitute a value for GNP, its coefficient (found from the output above), and constant. See if the corresponding value in Employed matches with the data. There might be some difference, but hopefully not much! Let us look at an example. We know from the dataset that in 1960, GNP value was 502.601. We will use our regression equation to calculate the value of Employed. Plugging in the values GNP = 502.601, coeff = 0.0348, and const = 51.8436 in the above equation, we get:

```
Employed = 0.0348*502.601 + 51.8436 = 69.334
```

Now let us look up the actual value of "Employed" for 1960. It is 69.564. That means we were off by only 0.23. That is not bad for our prediction. And, more important, we now have a model (the line equation) that could allow us also to interpolate and extrapolate. In other words, we could even plug in some unknown GNP value and find out what the approximate value for Employed would be.

Well, why do not we do this more systematically? Specifically, let us come up with all kinds of values for our independent variable, find the corresponding values for the dependent variable using the above equation, and plot it on the scatterplot. We will see this as a part of a full example below.

Hands-On Example 5.1: Linear Regression

Here is the full code that shows all the things we have talked about in this section: from importing data to doing various statistical analysis and plotting. Note that anything that starts with "#" in Python is considered a comment and ignored (not run). At the end of the code is one of the plots with a regression line (Figure 5.6). The dataset (Longley.csv) is available for download from OA 5.1.

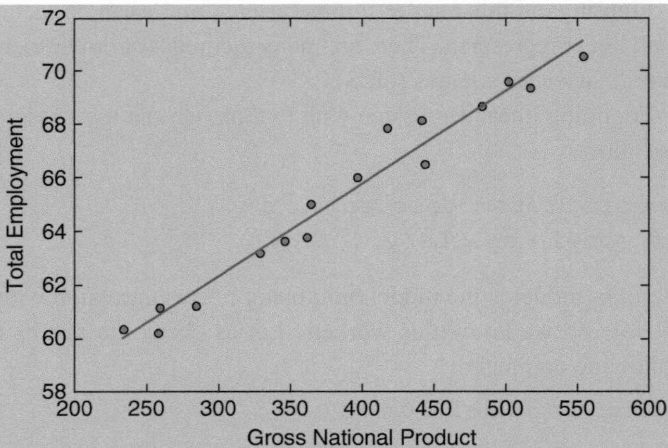

Figure 5.6 Scatterplot of GNP vs. Employed overlaid with a regression line.

```
# Load the libraries we need - numpy, pandas, pyplot, and
statsmodels.api
import numpy as np
import pandas as pd
import matplotlib.pyplot as plt
import statsmodels.api as sm

# Load the Longley dataset into a Pandas DataFrame - first
column (year) used as row labels
df = pd.read_csv('longley.csv', index_col=0)

# Find the correlation between Employed and GNP
print("Correlation coefficient = ", np.corrcoef(df.
Employed,df.GNP)[0,1])

# Prepare X and y for the regression model: y =
y = df.Employed # response (dependent variable)
X = df.GNP # predictor (independent variable)
X = sm.add_constant(X) # Adds a constant term to the predictor

# Build the regression model using OLS (ordinary least
squares)
lr_model = sm.OLS(y, X).fit()
print(lr_model.summary())

# We pick 100 points equally spaced from the min to the max
X_prime = np.linspace(X.GNP.min(), X.GNP.max(), 100)
X_prime = sm.add_constant(X_prime) # Add a constant as we did
before
```

```
# Now we calculate the predicted values
y_hat = lr_model.predict(X_prime)

plt.scatter(X.GNP, y) # Plot the raw data
plt.xlabel("Gross National Product")
plt.ylabel("Total Employment")
# Add the regression line, colored in red
plt.plot(X_prime[:, 1], y_hat, 'red', alpha=0.9)
```

If you see something strange in your plots from the above code, chances are your plotting environments are getting messed up. To address that, change the code for your plotting as shown below:

```
plt.figure(1)

plt.subplot(211)
plt.scatter(df.Employed, df.GNP)

plt.subplot(212)
plt.scatter(X.GNP, y) # Plot the raw data
plt.xlabel("Gross National Product")
plt.ylabel("Total Employment")
# Add the regression line, colored in red
plt.plot(X_prime[:, 1], y_hat, 'red', alpha=0.9)
```

Essentially, we are creating separate spaces to display the original scatterplot, and the new scatterplot with the regression line.

5.5.5 Multiple Linear Regression

What we have seen so far is one variable (predictor) helping to predict another (response or dependent variable). But there are many situations in life when there is not a single factor that contributes to an outcome. And so, we need to look at multiple factors or variables. That is when we use **multiple linear regression**.

As the name suggests, this is a method that takes into account multiple predictors in order to predict one response or outcome variable. Let us take an example.

Hands-On Example 5.2: Multiple Linear Regression

We will start by getting a small dataset from OA 5.2. This dataset contains information about advertising budgets for TV and radio and corresponding sales numbers. What we want to learn here is how much those budgets influence product sales.

Let us first load it up in our Python environment.

```
# Load the libraries we need - numpy, pandas, pyplot, and
statsmodels.api
```

```
import numpy as np
import pandas as pd
import matplotlib.pyplot as plt
import statsmodels.api as sm

# Load the advertising dataset into a pandas dataframe
df = pd.read_csv('Advertising.csv', index_col=0)
```

We start our analysis by doing linear regression, as we did before, to see how well we could use the "TV" variable to predict "Sales".

```
y = df.Sales
X = df.TV
X = sm.add_constant(X)

lr_model = sm.OLS(y,X).fit()

print(lr_model.summary())
print(lr_model.params)
```

In this output, what we are looking for is the R-squared value. It is around 0.61, which means that about 61% of the variance in this TV–sales relationship can be explained using the model we built. Well, that is not too bad, but before we move on, let us plot this relationship:

```
plt.figure()
plt.scatter(df.TV,df.Sales)
plt.xlabel('TV')
plt.ylabel('Sales')
```

The outcome is shown in Figure 5.7.

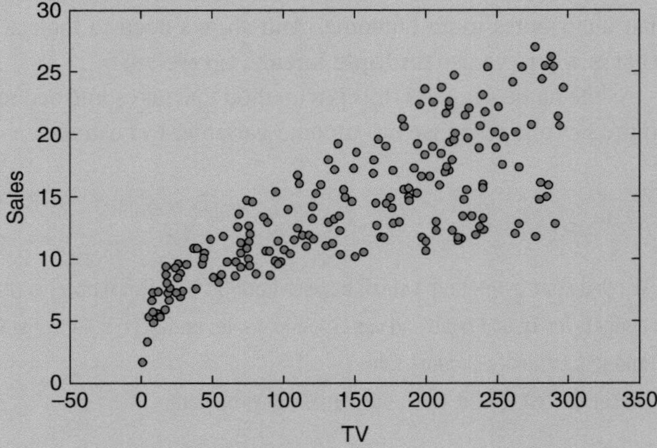

Figure 5.7 Scatterplot of TV vs. Sales from the advertising data.

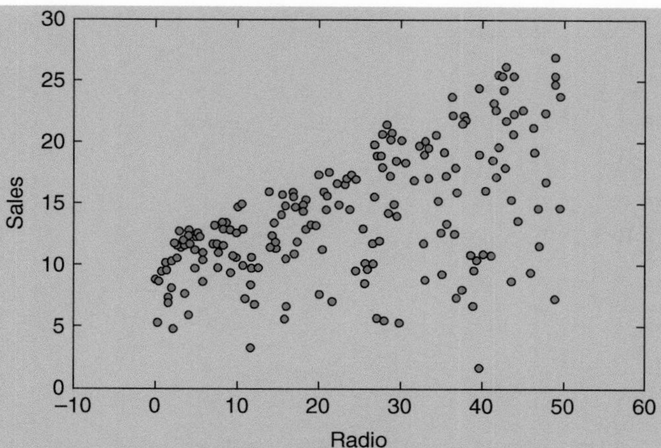

Figure 5.8 Scatterplot of Radio vs. Sales from the advertising data.

Let us repeat the process for radio.

```
y = df.Sales
X = df.Radio
X = sm.add_constant(X)

lr_model = sm.OLS(y,X).fit()

print(lr_model.summary())
print(lr_model.params)

plt.figure()
plt.scatter(df.Radio,df.Sales)
plt.xlabel('Radio')
plt.ylabel('Sales')
```

And Figure 5.8 is what we get as the result.

This model gives us R-squared value around 0.33, which is even worse than what we got with TV. Now, let us see what happens if we put both of these independent variables (TV and radio) together to predict sales:

```
y = df['Sales']
X = df[['TV','Radio']]
X = sm.add_constant(X)

lr_model = sm.OLS(y,X).fit()

print(lr_model.summary())
print(lr_model.params)
```

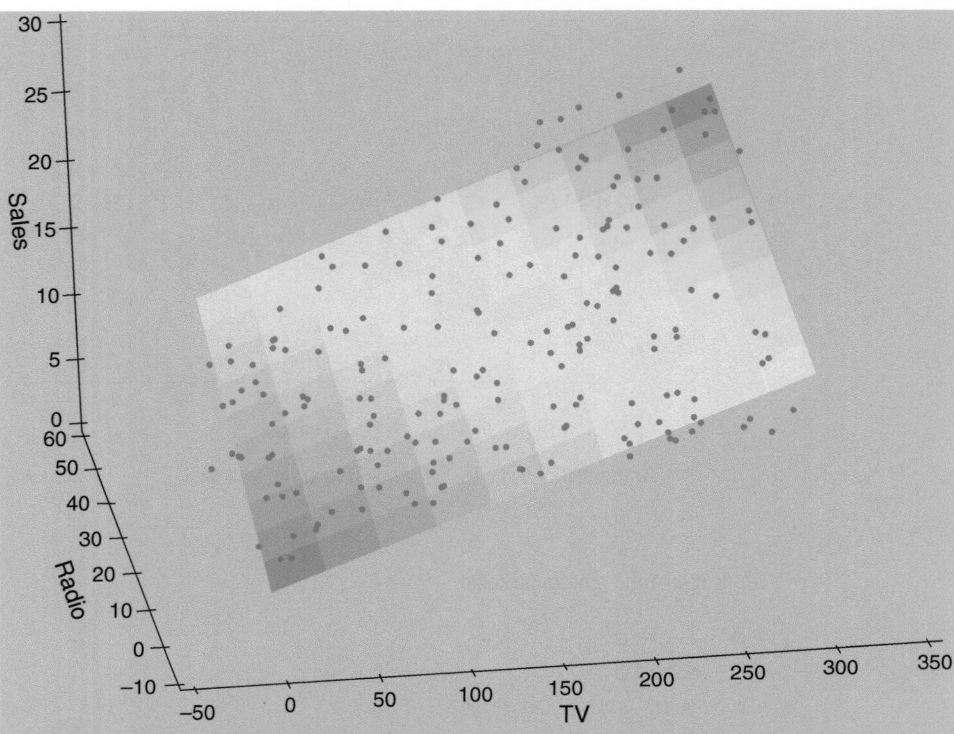

Figure 5.9 Three-dimensional scatterplot showing TV, Radio, and Sales variables.

This comes up with R-squared close to 90%. That is much better. Seems like two are better than one, and that is our multiple linear regression!

And here is the code for plotting this regression in three dimensions (3D), with the result shown in Figure 5.9. Consider this as optional or extra stuff.

```
from mpl_toolkits.mplot3d import Axes3D

# Figure out X and Y axis using ranges from TV and Radio
X_axis, Y_axis = np.meshgrid(np.linspace(X.TV.min(), X.TV.
max(), 100), np.linspace(X.Radio.min(), X.Radio.max(), 100))

# Plot the hyperplane by calculating corresponding Z axis
(Sales)
Z_axis = lr_model.params[0] + lr_model.params[1] * X_axis +
lr_model.params[2] * Y_axis

# Create matplotlib 3D axes
fig = plt.figure(figsize=(12, 8)) # figsize refers to width and
height of the figure
ax = Axes3D(fig, azim=-100)
```

```
# Plot hyperplane
ax.plot_surface(X_axis, Y_axis, Z_axis, cmap=plt.cm.cool-
warm, alpha=0.5, linewidth=0)

# Plot data points
ax.scatter(X.TV, X.Radio, y)

# set axis labels
ax.set_xlabel('TV')
ax.set_ylabel('Radio')
ax.set_zlabel('Sales')
```

Try It Yourself 5.5: Regression

Let us practice what you have learned about correlation, regression, and visualization so far with a small dataset that you can obtain from OA 5.3. The All Greens Franchise dataset contains 30 observations about All Greens sales that has five predictor variables apart from the annual net sales figure. Use this dataset to:

1. determine the correlation of annual net sales with money spent on advertising and number of competitors in the area;
2. visualize the above correlation in a scatterplot; and
3. build a regression model to predict the annual net sales figure using the other five columns in the dataset.

5.6 Introduction to Machine Learning

In a couple of chapters, we are going to see machine learning at its full glory (or at least the glory that we could achieve in this book!). But while we are on a roll with Python, it would be worthwhile to dip our toes in the waters of machine learning and see what sorts of data problems we could solve.

We will start in the following subsection with a little introduction to machine learning, and then quickly move to recognizing some of the basic problems, techniques, and solutions. We will revisit most of these with more details and examples in Part III of this book.

5.6.1 What Is Machine Learning?

Machine learning (ML) is a field of inquiry, an application area, and one of the most important skills that a data scientist can list on their résumé. It sits at the intersections of

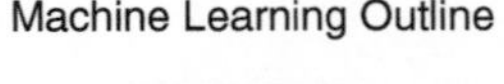

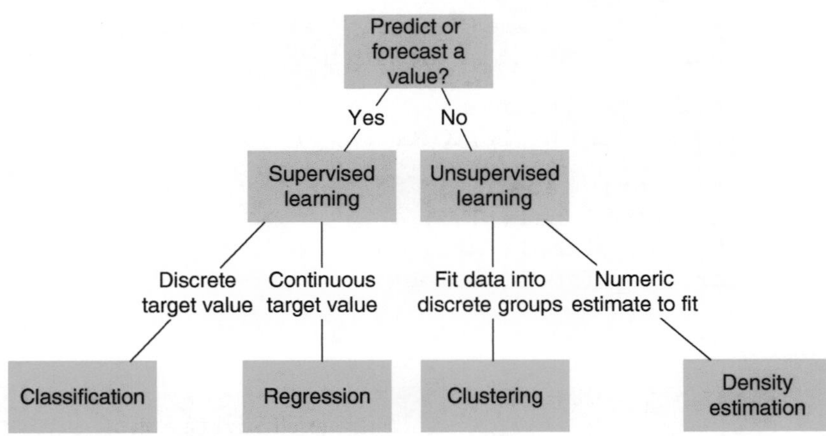

Figure 5.10 An outline of core machine learning problems.

computer science and statistics, among other related areas like engineering. It is used in pretty much every area that deals with data processing, including business, bioinformatics, weather forecasting, and intelligence (the NSA and CIA kind!).

Machine learning is about enabling computers and other artificial systems to *learn* without explicitly programming them. This is where we want such systems to see some data, *learn* from it, and then use that *knowledge* to infer things from other data.

Why machine learning? Because machine learning can help you turn your data into information; it can allow you to translate a seemingly *boring* bunch of data points into meaningful patterns that could help in critical decision-making; it lets you harness the true power of having a lot of data.

We have already seen and done a form of machine learning when we tried predicting values based on learned relationship between a **predictor** and an **outcome**. The core of machine learning can be explained using the decision tree (which also happens to be the name of one of the ML algorithms!) shown in Figure 5.10.

If we are trying to predict a value by learning (from data) how various predictors and the response variables relate, we are looking at **supervised learning**. Within that branch, if the response variable is continuous, the problem becomes that of **regression**, which we have already seen. Think about knowing someone's age and occupation and predicting their income. If, on the other hand, the response variable is discrete (having a few possible values or labels), this becomes a **classification** problem. For instance, if you are using someone's age and occupation to try to learn if they are a high-earner, medium-earner, or low-earner (three classes), you are doing classification.

These learning problems require us to know the truth first. For example, in order to learn how age and occupation could tell us about one's earning class, we need to know the true value of someone's class – do they belong to high-earner, medium-earner, or low-earner. But there are times when the data given to us do not have clear labels or true values. And yet, we are tasked with exploring and explaining that data. In this case, we are dealing with **unsupervised learning** problems. Within that, if we want to organize data into various groups, we encounter a **clustering** problem. This is similar to classification, but, unlike classification, we do not know how many classes there are and what they are called. On the other hand, if we are trying to explain the data by estimating underlying processes that may be responsible for how the data is distributed, this becomes a **density estimation** problem. In the following subsections, we will learn more about these branches, with, of course, hands-on exercises.

Since we have already worked with regression, in this section we will focus on classification, clustering, and density estimation branches.

5.6.2 Classification (Supervised Learning)

The task of classification is this: Given a set of data points and their corresponding labels, learn how they are classified, so when a new data point comes, we can put it in the correct class. There are many methods and algorithms for building classifiers, one of which is *k-nearest neighbor* (kNN).

Here is how kNN works:

1. As in the general problem of classification, we have a set of data points for which we know the correct class labels.
2. When we get a new data point, we compare it to each of our existing data points and find similarity.
3. Take the most similar k data points (k nearest neighbors).
4. From these k data points, take the majority vote of their labels. The winning label is the label or class of the new data point.

Usually k is a small number between 2 and 20. As you can imagine, the more the number of nearest neighbors (value of k), the longer it takes us to do the processing.

Finding similarity between data points is also something that is very important, but we are not going to discuss it here. For the time being, it is easier to visualize our data points on a plane (in two or three dimensions) and think about distance between them using our knowledge from linear algebra.

Hands-On Example 5.3: Classification

Let us take an example. We will use a wine dataset available from OA 5.4. This data contains information about various attributes of different wines and their corresponding quality. Specifically, the wine is classified as high quality or not. We will consider these as class labels and build a classifier that learns (based on other attributes) how a wine is classified in one of these two classes.

We will start by importing different libraries we will need. Notice a new library sklearn, which comes from *scikit-learn* (http://scikit-learn.org/stable/index.html), a popular library for doing machine learning applications in Python. This example loads the data, trains a classifier on 70% of the total data, tests that classifier on the remaining 30% of the data, and calculates the accuracy of the classifier:

```
import numpy as np
import pandas as pd
import matplotlib.pyplot as plt
from sklearn.neighbors import KNeighborsClassifier
from sklearn.cross_validation import train_test_split

df = pd.read_csv("wine.csv")

# Mark about 70% of the data for training and use the rest for
testing
# We will use 'density', 'sulfates', and 'residual_sugar'
features
# for training a classifier on 'high_quality'
X_train, X_test, y_train, y_test = train_test_split(df
[['density','sulfates','residual_sugar']], df['high_qu-
ality'], test_size=.3)
classifier = KNeighborsClassifier(n_neighbors=3)
classifier.fit(X_train, y_train)

# Test the classifier by giving it test instances
prediction = classifier.predict(X_test)

# Count how many were correctly classified
correct = np.where(prediction==y_test, 1, 0).sum()
print (correct)

# Calculate the accuracy of this classifier
accuracy = correct/len(y_test)
print (accuracy)
```

Note that the above example uses $k = 3$ (checking on three nearest neighbors when doing comparison). The accuracy is around 76% (you will get a different number every time because a different set of data is used for training and testing every time you run the program). But what would happen if the value of k were different? Let us try building and testing the classifier using a range of values for k and plot the accuracy corresponding to each k.

```
# Start with an array where the results (k and corresponding
# accuracy) will be stored
results = []

for k in range(1, 51, 2):
    classifier = KNeighborsClassifier(n_neighbors=k)
    classifier.fit(X_train, y_train)
    prediction = classifier.predict(X_test)
    accuracy = np.where(prediction==y_test, 1, 0).sum() /
    (len(y_test))
    print ("k=",k,"Accuracy=", accuracy)
```

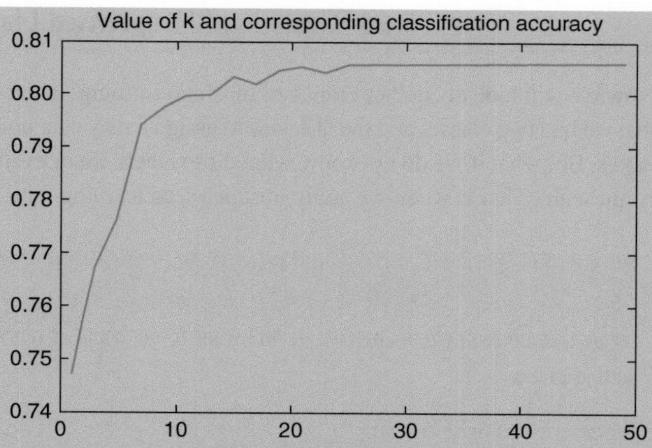

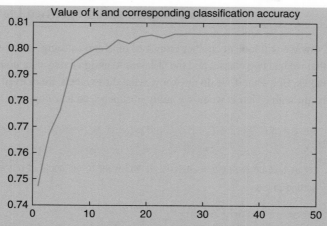

Figure 5.11 Plot showing how different values of *k* affect the accuracy of the kNN model built here.

```
results.append([k, accuracy]) # Storing the k,accuracy
tuple in results
array

# Convert that series of tuples in a dataframe for easy
plotting
results = pd.DataFrame(results, columns=["k", "accu-
racy"])

plt.plot(results.k, results.accuracy)
plt.title("Value of k and corresponding classification
accuracy")
plt.show()
```

The plotting result is shown in Figure 5.11. Note that, again, every time you run this program, you will see slightly different results (and plot). In the output, you will also notice that after a certain value of *k* (typically 15), the improvements in accuracy are hardly noticeable. In other words, we reach the saturation point.

Try It Yourself 5.6: Classification

Let us try what you just learned about classification with another dataset. The wheat dataset in UCI's repository (get it from OA 5.5) comprises data about kernels belonging to three different varieties of wheat: Kama, Rosa and Canadian. For each wheat variety, with a random sample of 70 elements, high-quality visualization of the internal kernel structure was detected using a soft X-ray technique. Seven geometric parameters of wheat kernels were measured. Use these measures to classify the wheat variety.

5.6.3 Clustering (Unsupervised Learning)

Now we will look at another branch of machine learning. In the example we just saw, we knew that we had two classes and the task was to assign a new data point to one of those existing class labels. But what if we do not know what those labels are or even how many classes there are to begin with? That is when we apply unsupervised learning with the help of clustering.

Hands-On Example 5.4: Clustering

Let us take an example. As before, we will want to get some of our required libraries imported before getting to work:

```
import numpy as np
import matplotlib.pyplot as plt

# Import style class from matplotlib and use that to apply
ggplot styling
from matplotlib import style
style.use("ggplot")
```

Now, we will take a bunch of data points and cluster them. How, you ask? Using a fantastic algorithm called *k-means*. In addition to being fantastic, *k-means* is a simple algorithm. Here is how it works.

1. First, we guess or determine the number of clusters (k) we want. If our data points are in n dimensions, the centers of these clusters, or centroids, will also be n-dimensional points. In other words, we will have a total of k n-dimensional points that we will call the centroids. Yes, these are essentially just some random points in that n-dimensional space.
2. Now, we assign each of the actual data points to one of these k centroids based on their distances to these centroids. After this step, each data point will be assigned to one of the k clusters.
3. Now, we recompute each cluster's centroid. So, we end up with k centroids again, but these are now adjusted to reflect how the data points are distributed.

We keep repeating steps 2 and 3 until we converge. In other words, we cease this iterative process when the centroids of the k clusters are no longer changing. And at that point we have "real" k clusters, with each data point belonging to one of them.

Fortunately, with the right package in Python, we do not need to implement all of this from scratch. That right package is sklearn.cluster, which contains implementations for various clustering algorithms, including k-means. Let us import it:

```
# Get KMeans class from clustering library available within
scikit-learn
from sklearn.cluster import KMeans
```

For this exercise, we are just going to make up some data points in two-dimensional (2D) space (so we can visualize them easily):

```
# Define data points on 2D plane using Cartesian coordinates
X = np.array([[1, 2],
              [5, 8],
              [1.5, 1.8],
              [8, 8],
              [1, 0.6],
              [9, 11]])
```

Now, we will proceed with clustering as well as visualizing the clusters that *k-means* algorithm generates:

```
# Perform clustering using k-means algorithm
kmeans = KMeans(n_clusters=2)
kmeans.fit(X)

# 'kmeans' holds the model; extract information about
clusters
# as represented by their centroids, along with their
labels
centroids = kmeans.cluster_centers
labels = kmeans.labels

print(centroids)
print(labels)

# Define a colors array
colors = ["g.", "r.", "c.", "y."]

# Loop to go through each data point, plotting it on the
plane
# with a color picked from the above list - one color per
cluster
for i in range(len(X)):
   print("Coordinate:",X[i], "Label:", labels[i])
   plt.plot(X[i][0], X[i][1], colors[labels[i]],
  markersize = 10)

# Plot the centroids using "x"
plt.scatter(centroids[:, 0],centroids[:, 1],
marker="x", s=150, linewidths=2, zorder=10)
plt.show()
```

Figure 5.12 has the output. As you can see, there are six points plotted. It is easy to imagine that if we were to look for two clusters, we can have one group at the bottom-left (represented in red) and another group in top-right (represented in green). Here we have used the *k-means* algorithm, which aims to find *k* unique clusters where the center of each cluster (centroid) is the mean of the values in that cluster. These clusters are represented using blue "X" symbols.

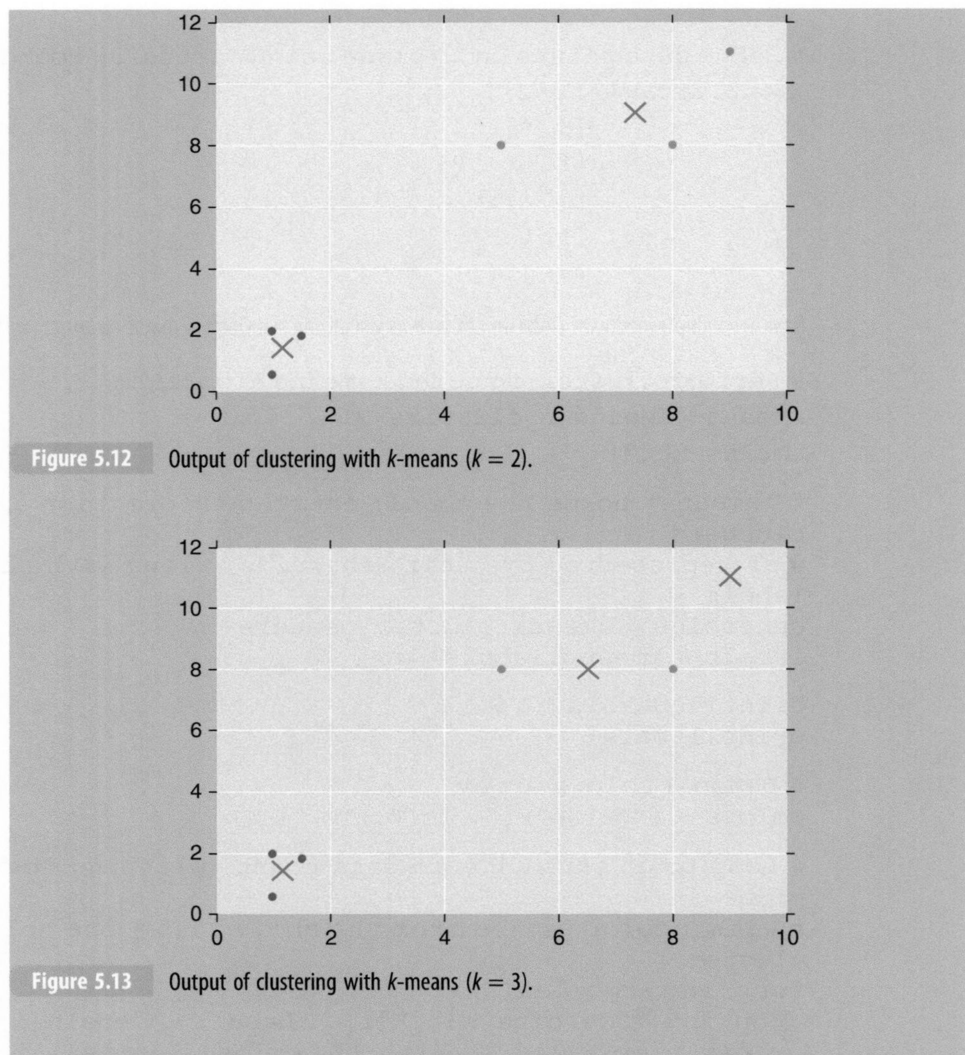

Figure 5.12 Output of clustering with *k*-means ($k = 2$).

Figure 5.13 Output of clustering with *k*-means ($k = 3$).

Now let us see what happens if we want three clusters. Change the n_clusters argument (input or parameter) in KMeans function to be 3. And voilà! Figure 5.13 shows how this algorithm can give us three clusters with the same six data points.

You can even try `n_clusters=4`. So, you see, this is unsupervised learning because the labels or colors of the data points are not known to be able to put them in classes. In fact, we do not even know how many labels or classes there should be, and so we could impose almost as many of those as we like.

But things are not always this simple. Because we were dealing with two dimensions and so few data points, we could even visually identify how many clusters could be appropriate. Nonetheless, the example above demonstrates how unsupervised clustering typically works.

Try It Yourself 5.7: Clustering

For this homework, you are going to use the travel reviews dataset (see OA 5.6) in UCI's repository, which was created by crawling the travelers' reviews from TripAdvisor.com. Reviews on destinations across East Asia are considered in 10 categories. Each traveler's rating is categorized as Terrible (0), Poor (1), Average (2), Very Good (3), or Excellent (4), and average rating is used against each category per user. Use the clustering method you just learned to group the destinations that have similar ratings.

5.6.4 Density Estimation (Unsupervised Learning)

One way to think about clustering when we do not know how many clusters we should have is to let a process look for data points that are dense together and use that density information to form a cluster. One such technique is *MeanShift*.

Let us first understand what density information or function is. Imagine you are trying to represent the likelihood of finding a Starbucks in an area. You know that if it is a mall or a shopping district, there is a good probability that there is a Starbucks (or two or three!), as opposed to a less populated rural area. In other words, Starbucks has higher density in cities and shopping areas than in less populated or less visited areas. A density function is a function (think about a curve on a graph) that represents a relative likelihood of a variable (e.g., existence of Starbucks) to taking on a given value.

Now let us get back to *MeanShift*. This is an algorithm that locates the maxima (maximum values) of a density function given a set of data points that fit that function. So, roughly speaking, if we have data points corresponding to the locations of Starbucks, *MeanShift* allows us to figure out where we are likely to find Starbucks; or on the other hand, given a location, how likely are we to find a Starbucks.

Hands-On Example 5.5: Density Estimation

To see this in action, we will define a density function, have it generate a bunch of data points that fit that function, and then try to locate centroids of these data points using density estimation. This almost seems like a self-fulfilling prophecy! But it allows us to practice and see how unsupervised clustering works when we do not even know how many clusters there should be.

Here is the code for this whole example, along with inline comments. The visual output as a 3D plot is also shown in Figure 5.14.

```
import numpy as np
from sklearn.cluster import MeanShift
from sklearn.datasets.samples_generator import make_blobs
import matplotlib.pyplot as plt
from mpl_toolkits.mplot3d import Axes3D

# Import style class from matplotlib and use that to apply
```

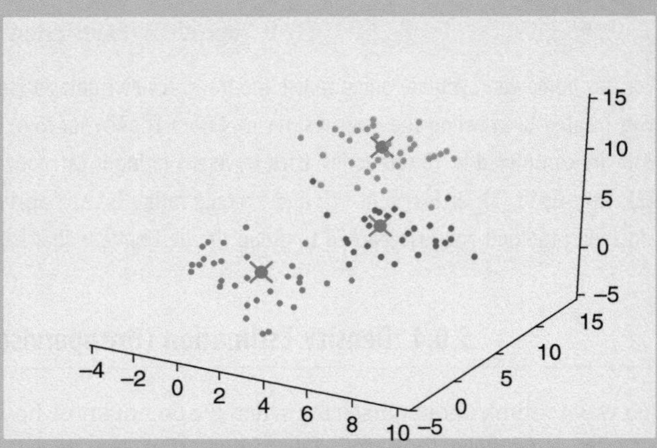

Figure 5.14 Density estimation plot with three clusters identified.

```
ggplot styling
from matplotlib import style
style.use(“ggplot”)

# Let’s create a bunch of points around three centers in a 3D
# space X has those points and we can ignore y
centers = [[1,1,1],[5,5,5],[3,10,10]]
X, y = make_blobs(n_samples = 100, centers = centers, clus-
ter_std = 2)

# Perform clustering using MeanShift algorithm
ms = MeanShift()
ms.fit(X)

# “ms” holds the model; extract information about clusters as
# represented by their centroids, along with their labels
centroids = ms.cluster_centers
labels = ms.labels

print(centroids)
print(labels)

# Find out how many clusters we created
n_clusters_ = len(np.unique(labels))
print(“Number of estimated clusters:”, n_clusters_)

# Define a colors array
colors = [‘r’,‘g’,‘b’,‘c’,‘k’,‘y’,‘m’]

# Let’s do a 3D plot
fig = plt.figure()
ax = fig.add_subplot(111, projection=‘3d’)
```

```
# Loop to go through each data point, plotting it on the 3D
space
# with a color picked from the above list - one color per
cluster
for i in range(len(X)):
   print("Coordinate:",X[i], "Label:", labels[i])
   ax.scatter(X[i][0], X[i][1], X[i][2], c=colors[labels
[i]], marker='o')

ax.scatter(centroids[:,0],centroids[:,1],centroids
[:,2], marker="x", s=150, linewidths=5, zorder=10)
plt.show()
```

This plot shows three clusters, but try running the program multiple times and you may find a different number of clusters. And you guessed it – that is because the data points may be slightly different, and how and where we start applying the *MeanShift* algorithm may differ.

And this is where we are going to stop our exploration of applying machine learning to various data problems using Python. If you are interested in more, go to Part III of this book. But if you do not know enough about the R statistical tool, you should go through the next chapter first, because later, when we do machine learning, we are going to exclusively use R.

Summary

Python has recently taken the number one spot for programming languages, according to the IEEE.[8] And that is not a surprise. It is an easy-to-learn, yet very powerful, language. It is ideal for data scientists because it offers straightforward ways to load and plot data, provides a ton of packages for doing data visualization to parallel processing, and allows easy integration to other tools and platforms. Want to do network programming? Python has got it. Care about object-oriented programming? Python has you covered. What about GUI? You bet!

It is hard to imagine any data science book without coverage of Python, but one of the reasons it makes even more sense for us here is that, unlike some other programming languages (e.g., Java), Python has a very low barrier. One can start seeing results of various expressions and programming structures almost immediately without having to worry about a whole lot of syntax or compilation. There are very few programming environments that are easier than this.[9] Not to mention, Python is free, open-source, and easily available. This may not mean much in the beginning, but it has implications for its sustainability and support. Python continues to flourish, be supported, and further enhanced due to a large community of developers who have created outstanding packages that allow a Python programmer to do all sorts of data processing with very little work. And such development continues to grow.

Often students ask for a recommendation for a programming language to learn. It is hard to give a good answer without knowing the context (why do you want to learn programming, where would you use it, how long, etc.). But Python is an easy recommendation for all the reasons above.

Having said that, I recommend not being obsessed with any programming tools or languages. Remember what they are – just tools. Our goal, at least in this book, is not to master these tools, but to use them to solve data problems. In this chapter, we looked at Python. In the next, we will explore R. In the end, you may develop a preference for one over the other, but as long as you understand how these tools can be used in solving problems, that is all that matters.

Key Terms

- **Integrated Development Environment (IDE):** This is an application that contains various tools for writing, compiling, debugging, and running a program. Examples include Eclipse, Spyder, and Visual Studio.
- **Correlation:** This indicates how closely two variables are related and ranges from −1 (negatively related) to +1 (positively related). A correlation of 0 indicates no relation between the variables.
- **Linear regression:** Linear regression is an approach to model the relationship between the outcome variable and predictor variable(s) by fitting a linear equation to observed data.
- **Machine learning:** This is a field that explores the use of algorithms that can learn from the data and use that knowledge to make predictions on data they have not seen before.
- **Supervised learning:** This is a branch of machine learning that includes problems where a model could be built using the data and true labels or values.
- **Unsupervised learning:** This is a branch of machine learning that includes problems where we do not have true labels for the data to train with. Instead, the goal is to somehow organize the data into some meaningful clusters or densities.
- **Predictor variable:** A predictor variable is a variable that is being used to measure some other variable or outcome. In an experiment, predictor variables are often independent variables, which are manipulated by the researcher rather than just measured.
- **Outcome or response variable:** An outcome or response variable is in most cases the dependent variable, which is observed and measured by changing the independent variable(s).
- **Classification:** In our context, a classification task represents the systematic arrangement of data points in groups or categories according to some shared qualities or characteristics. These groups or categories have predefined labels, called class labels.
- **Clustering:** Clustering involves the grouping of similar objects into a set, called a cluster. The clustering task is similar to classification without the predefined class labels.

- **Density estimation:** This is a machine learning (typically, unsupervised learning) example where we try to explain the data by estimating underlying processes that may be responsible for how the data is distributed.

Conceptual Questions

1. List arithmetic operators that you can use with Python.
2. List three different data types.
3. How do you get user input in Python?

Hands-On Problems

Problem 5.1

Write a Python script that assigns a value to variable "age" and uses that information about a person to determine if he/she is in high school. Assume that for a person to be in high school, their age should be between 14 and 18. You do not have to write a complicated code – simple and logical code is enough.

Problem 5.2

The following are weight values (in pounds) for 20 people:
164, 158, 172, 153, 144, 156, 189, 163, 134, 159, 143, 176, 177, 162, 141, 151, 182, 185, 171, 152.
Using Python, find the mean, median, and standard deviation; and then plot a histogram.

Problem 5.3

You are given a dataset named **boston** (OA 5.7). This dataset contains information collected by the US Census Service concerning housing in the area of Boston, Mass. The dataset is small in size, with only 506 cases. The data was originally published by Harrison, D., & Rubinfeld, D.L. (1978). Hedonic prices and the demand for clean air. *Journal of Environmental Economics and Management*, 5, 81–102.

Here are the variables captured in this dataset:

```
CRIM - per capita crime rate by town
ZN - proportion of residential land zoned for lots over 25,000 sq.ft.
INDUS - proportion of non-retail business acres per town.
CHAS - Charles River dummy variable (1 if tract bounds river; 0
otherwise)
```

```
NOX – nitric oxides concentration (parts per 10 million)
RM – average number of rooms per dwelling
AGE – proportion of owner-occupied units built prior to 1940
DIS – weighted distances to five Boston employment centres
RAD – index of accessibility to radial highways
TAX – full-value property-tax rate per $10,000
PTRATIO – pupil-teacher ratio by town
B – 1000(Bk – 0.63)^2 where Bk is the proportion of blacks by town
LSTAT – % lower status of the population
MEDV – median value of owner-occupied homes in $1000's
```

Using appropriate correlation and regression tests, find which of the variables is the best predictor of NOX (nitric oxides concentration). For that model, provide the regression plot and equation.

Using appropriate correlation and regression tests, find which of the variables is the best predictor of MEDV (median home value). For that model, provide the regression plot and equation.

Problem 5.4

You have experienced a classification method, kNN classifier, in the class. A classification method or algorithm is developed aiming to address different types of problems. As a result, different classifiers show different classification results, or accuracy. The goal of this assignment is to compare the different accuracy over the classifiers.

The dataset to use for this assignment is Iris, which is a classic and very easy multiclass classification dataset. This dataset consists of three different types of irises' (setosa, versicolor, and virginica) petal and sepal length, stored in a 150 × 4 numpy.ndarray. The rows are the samples and the columns are: Sepal length, Sepal width, Petal length, and Petal width.

You can load the iris dataset through the Python code below:

Classes	3
Samples per class	50
Samples total	150
Dimensionality	4
Features	Real, positive

```
from sklearn import datasets
iris = datasets.load_iris()
```

You already know how to use kNN. Let's try another classifier: Support Vector Machine (SVM). To use SVM as a classifier, you can use the following code.

```
from sklearn.svm import SVC # importing the package
SVC(kernel="linear") # building the classifier
```

The second line will give you a classifier that you can store and process further just like you do with a kNN-built classifier. Here we are saying that we want to use a linear kernel for our SVM. Other options are "rbf" (radial basis function) and "poly" (polynomial). Try each of these and see what accuracies you get. Note that every time you run your program, you may get slightly different numbers, so try running it a few times:

For the classification, take only the first two columns from the dataset.

Split the dataset into 70% for training and 30% for test.

Show the resulting accuracies from kNN and three variations of SVM.

Problem 5.5

Let us work with Iris data again. For the previous question, we used it for doing classification. Now we will do clustering.

First, load the data and extract the first two features.

Now, do flat clustering using *k*-means. You can decide how many clusters are appropriate. For this, you may like to plot the data first and see how it is scattered. Show the plot with clusters marked.

Having done both classification and clustering on the same dataset, what can you say about this data and/or the techniques you used? Write your thoughts in one or two paragraphs.

Problem 5.6

For this exercise, you need to work with the breast cancer Coimbra dataset. First download the dataset from OA 5.8 and load the data. The dataset has 10 features including the class labels (1 or 2). Next, you need to round off the Leptin feature values to two decimal places. Having done that, use the first nine attributes (dataset minus the class label) to group the data points into two clusters. You can use any clustering algorithm of your choice, but the number of clusters should remain the same. Once the clustering is complete, use the class labels to evaluate the accuracy of the clustering algorithm that you chose.

Further Reading and Resources

If you want to learn more about Python and its versatile applications, here are some useful resources.

Python tutorials:

- https://www.w3schools.in/python-tutorial/
- https://www.learnpython.org/
- https://www.tutorialspoint.com/python/index.htm
- https://www.coursera.org/learn/python-programming
- https://developers.google.com/edu/python/
- https://wiki.python.org/moin/WebProgramming

Hidden features of Python:

- https://stackoverflow.com/questions/101268/hidden-features-of-python

DataCamp tutorial on Pandas DataFrames:

- https://www.datacamp.com/community/tutorials/pandas-tutorial-dataframe-python

Notes

1. Python download: https://www.python.org/downloads/
2. PyDev: http://www.pydev.org
3. Python: https://www.python.org/downloads/
4. Anaconda Navigator: https://anaconda.org/anaconda/anaconda-navigator
5. Daily Demand Forecasting Orders dataset: https://archive.ics.uci.edu/ml/machine-learning-databases/00409/Daily_Demand_Forecasting_Orders.csv
6. GitHub: http://vincentarelbundock.github.io/Rdatasets/csv/datasets/longley.csv
7. Notice that the predictor variable X is in uppercase and the outcome y is in lowercase. This is on purpose. Often, there are multiple predictor variables, making X a vector (or a matrix), whereas most times (and perhaps for us, all the time), there will be a single outcome variable.
8. IEEE (Python #1): http://spectrum.ieee.org/computing/software/the-2017-top-programming-languages
9. Yes, there are easier and/or more fun ways to learn/do programming. One popular example is Scratch: https://scratch.mit.edu/.

6 R

"Not everything that can be counted counts, and not everything that counts can be counted."

— *Albert Einstein*

What do you need?

- Computational thinking (refer to Chapter 1).
- Ability to install and configure software.
- Knowledge of basic statistics, including correlation and regression.
- (Ideally) Prior exposure to any programming language.

What will you learn?

- Loading structured data into R.
- Using R to do statistical analysis, including producing models and visualizations.
- Applying introductory machine learning techniques such as classification and clustering with R to various data problems.

6.1 Introduction

While a versatile programming language such as Python can provide a framework to work with data and logic effectively, often we want to stay focused on data analysis. In other words, we could use a programming environment that is designed for handling data and is not concerned with programming so much. There are several such environments or packages available – SPSS, Stata, and Matlab. But nothing can beat R for a free, open-source, and yet a very powerful data analytics platform.

And just because R is free, do not think even for a second that it is somehow inferior. R can do it all – from simple math manipulations to advanced visualization. In fact, R has become one of the most-used tools in data science and not just because of its price.

This chapter provides an introduction to the R language with its syntax, a few examples, and how it can be integrated with Python. Together, Python and R are, perhaps, the two most important tools in data science.

6.2 Getting Access to R

R is an open-source software for statistical computing, and it is available on all the major platforms for free. If you have ever used or heard about Matlab, SPSS, SAS, etc., well, R can do those kinds of things: statistics, data manipulation, visualization, and running data mining and machine learning algorithms. But it costs you nothing and you have an amazing set of tools at your disposal that is constantly expanding. There is also an active community building and supporting these tools. R offers you all the power of statistics and graphics that you can handle. No wonder it is becoming an industry standard for scientific computing.

You can download R from the R site.[1] There you can also read up on R and related projects, join mailing lists, and find all the help you need to get started and do amazing things. Appendix D has more details for downloading and installing, if you like.

Once downloaded and installed, start the R program. You will be presented with the R console (Figure 6.1). Here, you can run R commands and programs that we will see in the next sections of this chapter. To leave the program, enter q().

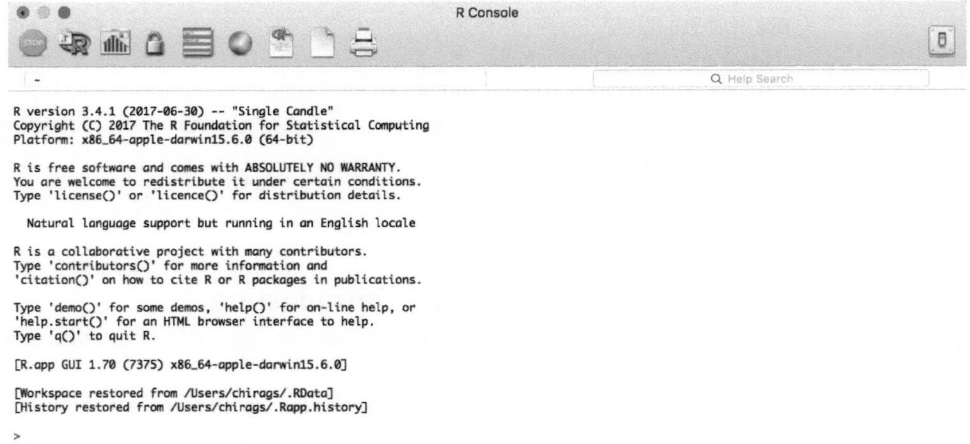

Figure 6.1 A screenshot of the R console.

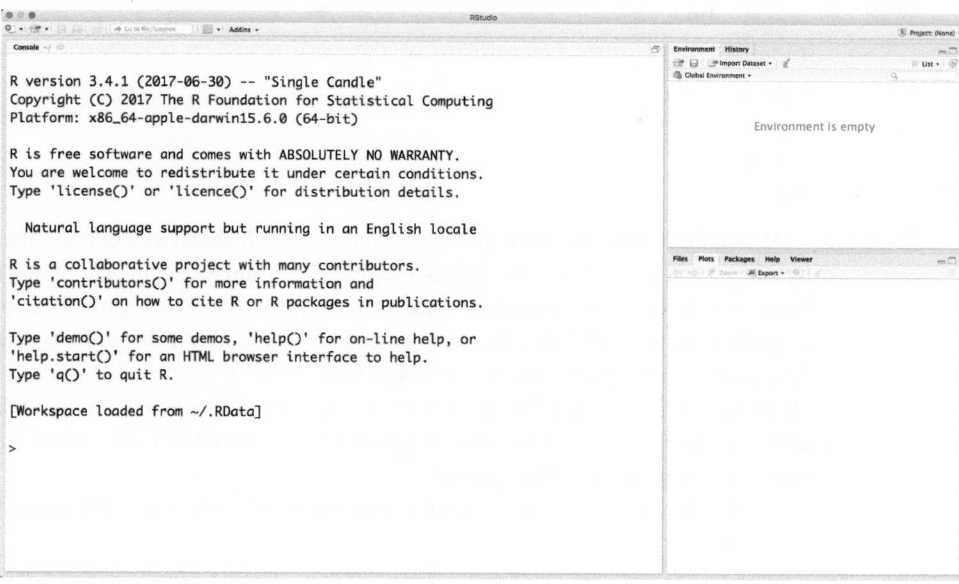

Figure 6.2 A screenshot of RStudio.

But, as before, instead of using this program directly, we will take advantage of an **Integrated Development Environment** (IDE). In this case, it is RStudio. So, go to RStudio[2] and pick the version that matches your operating system.

Again, once you have downloaded and installed RStudio, go ahead and start it up. You should see multiple windows or panes (see Figure 6.2), including the familiar R console where you can run R commands. As with the regular R, you can enter q() on the RStudio console and exit.

6.3 Getting Started with R

Let us get started with actually using R now, and we will do it the way we have been learning in this book – using hands-on exercises.

6.3.1 Basics

Let us start with things that are similar to what we did on the Python console. Everything below that you see with ">" is what you would enter at the command prompt (">") in R (or RStudio). The lines with bracketed numbers (e.g., "[1]") show outputs from running those commands.

```
> 2+2
[1] 4
> x=2
> y=2
> z=x+y
> z [1] 4
```

While these may be self-explanatory, let us still go ahead and explain them. We started by simply entering a mathematical expression (2+2) and R executes it, giving us the answer. Next, we defined and assigned values to variables x and y. Similar to other scripting languages such as Python, we do not need to worry about the **data type** of a variable. Just as we can assign a value to a variable (e.g., "x=2"), we can also assign a mathematical expression to a variable (above, "z=x+y") and, in that case, R will compute that expression and store the result in that variable. If you want to see what is in a variable, simply enter the name of that variable on the prompt.

We should note here that you could also assign values to a variable using "<-" like this:

```
> a<-7
```

In this book, you will see me using both of these notations for assigning values and writing expressions.

Next, let us work with logical operations. The most common logical operators should sound quite familiar: ">", "<", ">=", and "<=". What may not be so apparent, especially if you have not done much or any programming before, are operators for comparison ("==") and for negation ("!="). Let us go ahead and practice some of these:

```
> 2>3
[1] FALSE
> 2==2
[1] TRUE
```

As you can see, the result of a logical operation is a **Boolean** value – "TRUE" or "FALSE."

Hands-On Example 6.1: Basics

Now, let us write a small program on the R console:

```
> year = 2020
> if (year%%4==0)
+ print ("Leap year")
[1] "Leap year"
```

Here, we assigned a value to variable "year" and checked if it is divisible by 4 using the modulus operator (%%). If it is, then declare the year to be a leap year. We have done this before, but now we see how the same problem can be solved using R.

Now let us put this code in a file. In RStudio, select "File > New File > R Script." This should open an editor where you can type your code. There, write the following:

```
year = 2020
if (year%%4==0) {
    print ("Leap year")
} else {
   print ("Not a leap year")
}
```

Save the file. Typically, R scripts have an ".r" extension. You can run one line at a time by putting your cursor on that line and hitting the "Run" button in the toolbar of the editor. If you want to run the whole script, just select it all ("Ctrl+A" on a PC or "Cmd+A" on a Mac) and click "Run." The output will be in the console. Now that you know how to put R code in a file and run it, you can start taking advantage of existing R scripts and even creating your own.

Try It Yourself 6.1: Basics

1. Use R to calculate the value of the following equation:
   $((2 \times 7) + 12)^2$
2. Use the if–else structure to check if the value from the last question is divisible by 3. If the number is divisible by 3, check if the same number is also divisible by 4. If the number is not divisible by either 3 or 4, print the immediate larger number that is divisible by both 3 and 4.

6.3.2 Control Structures

Just like Python, R supports some basic control structures. In general, the control structures are of two types: decision control structure and loop control structure. As the name suggests, if you want to decide if a statement or a set of statements can be executed or not, based on some condition, you need a decision control structure, for example, an "if–else" block. But if you need the same set of statements to be executed iteratively as long as the decision condition remains true, you would want loop control structures, for example, a "for loop," "do–while" loop, etc.

Let us look at a few examples. Say you would like to decide if the weather is OK for a bicycle trip based on the percentage of humidity present, and you want to write code for this. It may look something like:

```
humidity = 45

if (humidity<40) {
   print ("Perfect for a trip")
} else if (humidity>70) {
  print ("Not suitable for a trip")
} else {
  print ("May or may not be suitable for a trip")
}
```

As shown in the above lines of code, the three conditions based on which decision to be made is defined here as "humidity less than 40%," or "more than 70%," or the rest.

Hands-On Example 6.2: Control Structures

We will now work on an extended example to practice loop control structures. What if you have accurate predictions of humidity for the next seven days. Wouldn't it be good if you could make some decisions for all seven days? Here is how to do it:

```
# This is to store the humidity percentages in a vector
humidity <- c(20, 30, 60, 70, 65, 40, 35)

count <- 1
while (count <= 7) {
cat ("Weather for day ", count, ":")
if (humidity[count] < 40) {
print ("Perfect for a trip")
} else if (humidity[count] > 70) {
        print ("Not suitable for a trip!")
} else {
print ("May or may not be suitable for trip")
}
count = count + 1
}
```

The same objective can be achieved with a "for loop" as well. Here is a demonstration:

```
# This is to store the humidity percentages in a vector
humidity <- c(20, 30, 60, 70, 65, 40, 35)

for (count in 1:7) {
cat ("Weather for day ", count, ":")
if (humidity[count] < 40) {
print ("Perfect for a trip")
} else if (humidity[count] > 70) {
        print ("Not suitable for a trip!")
} else {
print ("May or may not be suitable for trip")
}
}
```

Stop here for a moment and make sure all of the code above makes sense to you. Of course, the best way to ensure this is to actually try it all by yourself and make some changes to see if your logic works out the right way. Recall our discussion on computational thinking from the first chapter in this book. This will be a good place to practice it.

Try It Yourself 6.2: Control Structures

1. Use a "for loop" to print all the years that are leap years between 2008 and 2020.
2. Use a "while loop" to calculate the number of characters in the following line: "Today is a good day."

6.3.3 Functions

As you know, functions allow us to store a procedure, or a computational or a logical block that can be reused. It is like a chef pre-making broth that she can then keep using in different dishes throughout the day without having to make it every time a recipe calls for it.

Hands-On Example 6.3: Functions

Let us start by creating a function that can be reused. Here is a function named "Square" that takes a value (often called parameter or input) and returns its square.

```
Square = function(x) {
    return (x*x)
}
```

Write this code in a file and save it. Now run the whole script. Nothing will happen. But now when you go to the console and run a command like "Square(4)", you should see an appropriate answer. What is happening? You have guessed it! We just created a function called "Square" and it is ready to be used anytime we need that kind of functionality. In fact, you can see in the "Environment" pane of RStudio that we have this particular function available to us.

Try It Yourself 6.3: Functions

Write a function that takes two values as inputs and returns the one that is the smaller of those two. Show how you could use this function by writing some code that calls the function and outputs the result.

6.3.4 Importing Data

Now we come to the most useful parts of R for data science. Almost none of our actual problem-solving will work without first having some data available to us in R. Let us see how to import data into R. For now, we will work with CSV data, as we have done before. R has a function "file.choose()" that allows you to pick out a file from your computer and a "read.table()" function to read that file as a table, which works great for csv-formatted data.

For this example, we will use the IQ data file (iqsize.csv), available from OA 6.7. Type the following code line by line, or save it as an R script and run one line at a time:

```
df = read.table(file.choose(),header=TRUE,sep=",")
brain = df["Brain"]
print(summary(brain))
```

Running the first line brings up a file selection box. Navigate to the directory where iqsize.csv is stored and select it. This is the result of the "file.choose()" function, which is the first argument (parameter, input) in the "read.table()" function on that first line. Alternatively, you can put the file name (with full path) in quotes for that first argument. The second argument means we are expecting to see column labels in the first row (header), and the third argument indicates how the columns are separated.

Once we have the data loaded in our dataframe (df) variable, we can process it. In the second line, we are selecting the data stored in "Brain" column. And then in the third line we are using the function "summary()" so we can obtain some basic statistical characteristics of this **dataframe** and print them, as seen below:

```
    Brain
Min.   : 79.06
1st Qu.: 85.48
Median : 90.54
Mean   : 90.68
3rd Qu.: 94.95
Max.   :107.95
```

Do these quantities look familiar? They should if you know your basic statistics or have reviewed descriptive statistics covered earlier in this book!

6.4 Graphics and Data Visualization

One of the core benefits of R is its ability to provide data visualizations with very little effort, thanks to its built-in support, as well as numerous libraries or packages and functions available from many developers around the world. Let us explore this.

6.4.1 Installing ggplot2

Before working with graphics and plotting, let us make sure we have the appropriate libraries. Open RStudio and select Tools > Install Packages. In the dialog box that pops up, make sure CRAN repository is selected for the installation source. Now, type "ggplot2" in the packages box. Make sure "Install dependencies" is checked. Hit "Install" and the ggplot2 package should be downloaded and installed.

FYI: Dataframes

We saw the idea of a dataframe in the Python chapter. In a way, it is the same for R, that is, a dataframe is like an array or a matrix that contains rows and columns. There are a couple of key differences, however.

First, in R, a dataframe is inherently available without having to load any external packages like we did for Python with Pandas. The second big difference is how elements in a dataframe are addressed. Let us see this using an example.

We will use one of the in-built dataframes called "mtcars". This dataframe has car models as rows and various attributes about a car as columns. If you want to find the mpg for a Fiat 128 model, you can enter

```
> mtcars['Fiat 128', 'mpg']
```

If you want the whole record for that car, you can enter

```
> mtcars['Fiat 128',]
```

In other words, you are referring to a specific row and all corresponding columns with the above addressing. Of course, you can also address an element in a dataframe using an index such as mtcars[12,1], but, as you can see, addressing rows, columns, or a specific element by name make things a lot more readable.

If you are interested in exploring dataframes in R, you may want to look at some of the pointers for further reading at the end of this chapter.

6.4.2 Loading the Data

For the examples in this section, we will work with customer data regarding health insurance. It is available from OA 6.1. The data is in a file named custdata.tsv. Here, "tsv" stands for tab-separated values. That means, instead of commas, the fields are separated using tabs. Therefore, our loading command will become:

```
custdata = read.table('custdata.tsv',header=T,sep='\t')
```

Here, '\t' indicates the tab character. The above command assumes that the custdata.tsv file is in the current directory. If you do not want to take chances with that, you can replace the file name with the "file.choose()" function, so when the "read.table()" function is run, a file navigation box will pop up, allowing you to pick out the data file from your computer. That line will look like:

```
custdata = read.table(file.choose(),header=T,sep='\t')
```

6.4.3 Plotting the Data

Let us start with a simple histogram of our customers' ages. First, we need to load the "ggplot2" library and use its histogram function, like this:

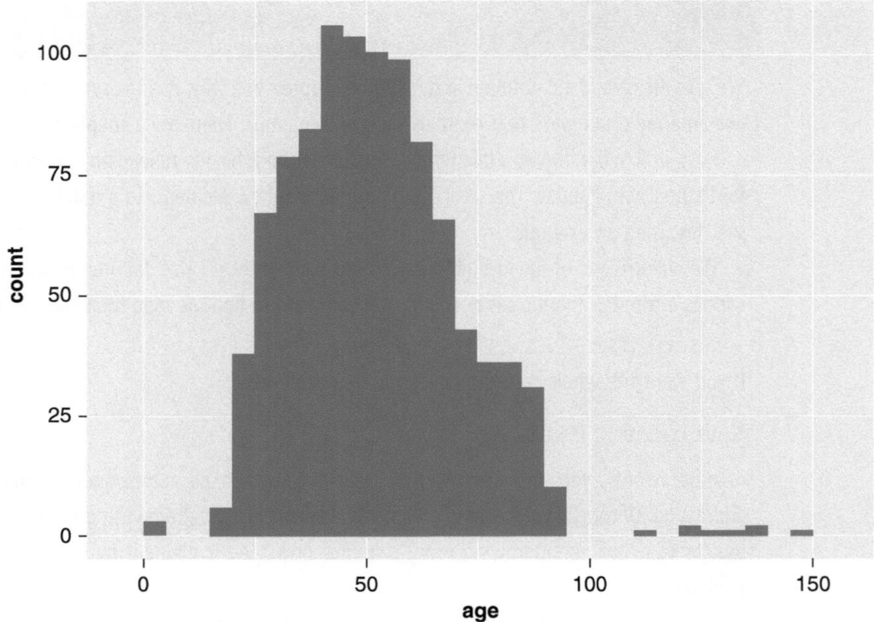

Figure 6.3 Histogram showing customer age distribution.

```
library(ggplot2)
ggplot(custdata) +geom_histogram(aes(x=age), binwidth=5,
fill="blue")
```

This generates a nice **histogram** (Figure 6.3). In the code, "binwidth" indicates the range that each bar covers on the *x*-axis. Here, we set it to 5, which means it would look at ranges such as 0–5, 6–10, and so on. Each bar on the plot then represents how many items or members fall within a given range. So, as you can imagine, if we increase the range, we get more items per bar and the overall plot gets "flatter." If we reduce the range, fewer items fit in one bar and the plot looks more "jagged."

But did you see how easy creating such a plot was? We typed only one line. Now, if you have never used such a statistical package before and relied on spreadsheet programs to create graphs, you might have thought it was easy to create a graph with those programs using point and click. But was it difficult to type that one line here? Besides, with this one line, we can more easily control how the graph looks than how you could with that point and click. And, maybe it is just me, but I think the result looks a lot more "professional" than what one could get from those spreadsheet programs!

Here, you can see that the histogram function has an argument for what the *x*-axis will show, and how many data points to fit in each bin.

Let us now look at a field with categorical values. The data, "marital.stat," is like that. We can use a bar chart to plot the data (Figure 6.4).

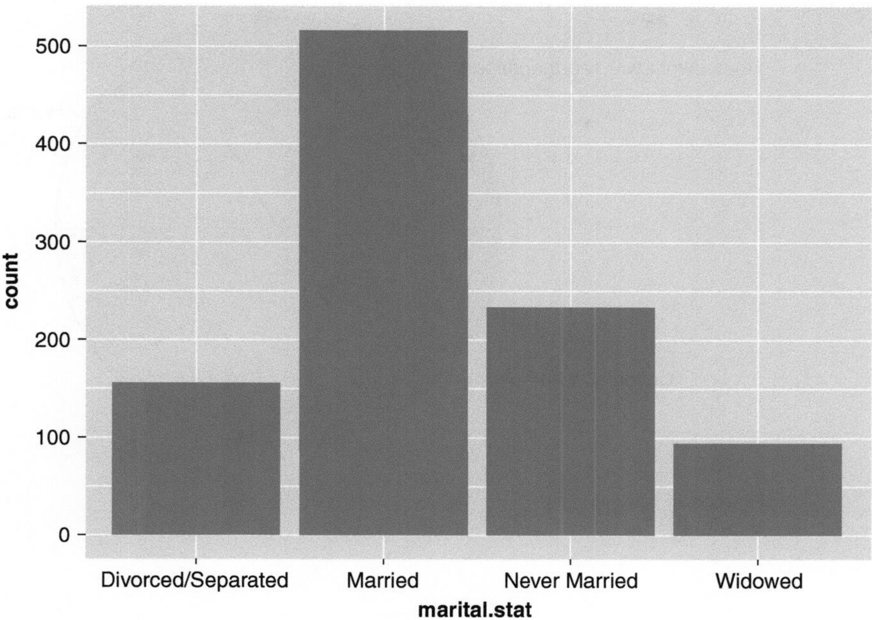

Figure 6.4 Bar plot showing distribution of marital status in the customer data.

```
ggplot(custdata) + geom_bar(aes(x=marital.stat), fill="blue")
```

So, is histogram the only type of chart available in R? Of course not. There are many other types of charts one could draw. For example, you can draw a pie chart to plot the distribution of the housing types, even though pie charts are not recommended in the standard R documentation, and the features available are somewhat limited. Here is how to do it. First, you need to build a contingency table of the counts at each factor level.

```
contigencyTable <- table(custdata$housing.type)
```

Now, you can use the pie() function in R to draw the pie chart of housing types (Figure 6.5).

```
pie(contigencyTable, main="Pie Chart of Housing Types")
```

If you do not like the default color scheme of pie() in R, you can select different color variations from the available, but you may need to specify the numbers of colors you need according to the number of pie slices in your chart. Here is how to do it.

```
  pie(contigencyTable, main="Pie Chart of Housing Types", col =
rainbow(length(contigencyTable)))
```

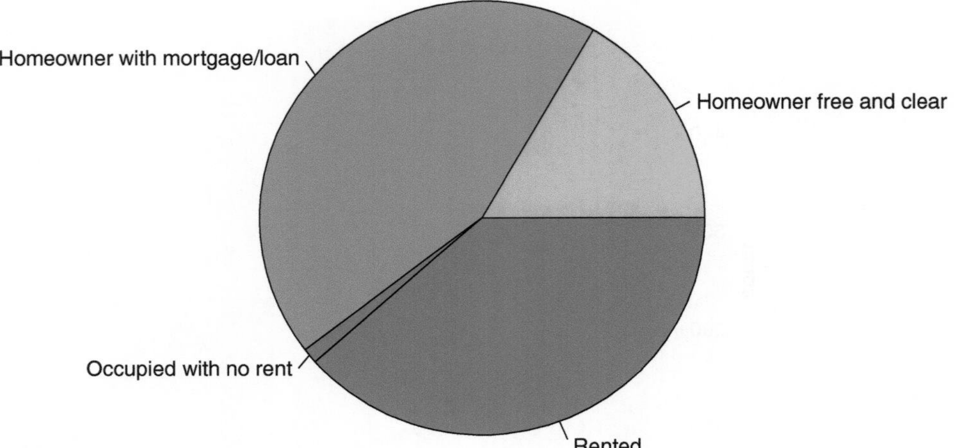

Figure 6.5 Pie chart of housing types.

Hands-On Example 6.4: Plotting

In the last two visualizations, one similarity that stands out is the discreteness of the data points. But what if all the data points belong to a sequence, and you want to preserve the sequential nature of the data in your visualization? One possible solution is a line graph. Let us take an example.

Table 6.1 contains a dataset on average stock price of a company, X, in the first five hours of trading in the stock exchange. You can obtain it from OA 6.2.

If you are interested in the progress of the stock price of the company, you can use a line graph to visualize the situation. The following lines of code should do the job.

Table 6.1 Average stock price (in USD) of company X in first five hours of trading.

Hour of operation	Average stock price in USD
1	12.04
2	12.80
3	13.39
4	13.20
5	13.23

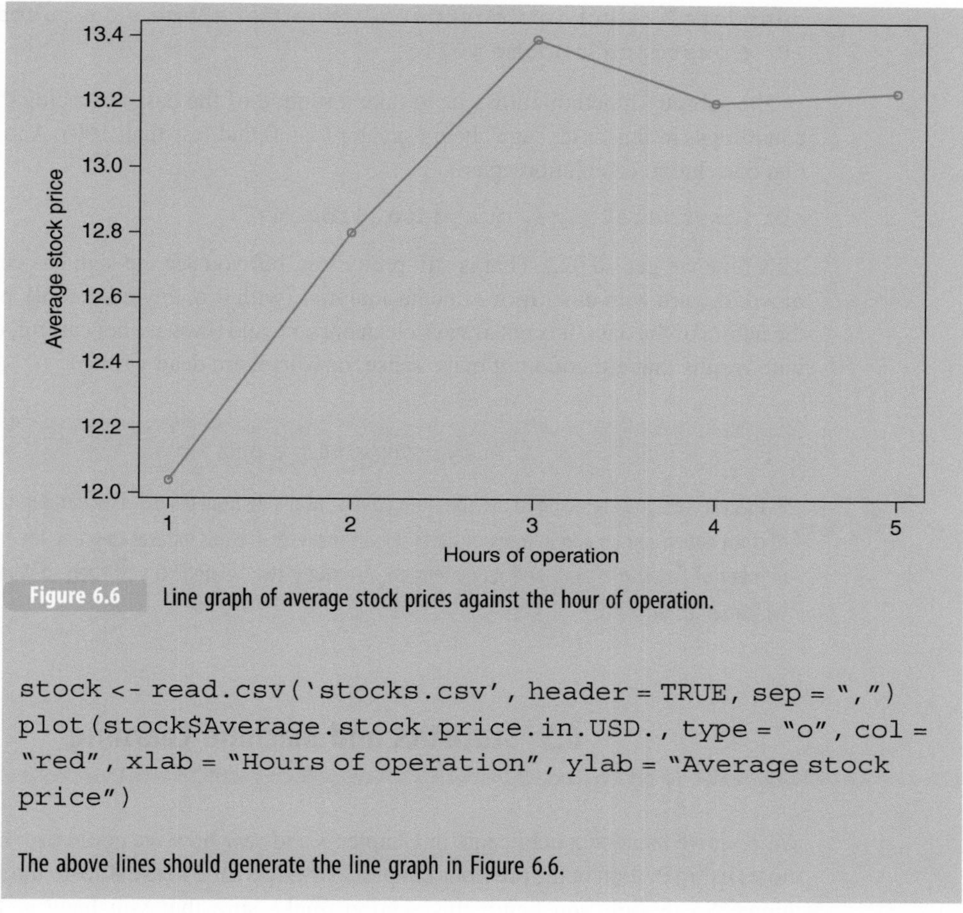

Figure 6.6 Line graph of average stock prices against the hour of operation.

```
stock <- read.csv('stocks.csv', header = TRUE, sep = ",")
plot(stock$Average.stock.price.in.USD., type = "o", col =
"red", xlab = "Hours of operation", ylab = "Average stock
price")
```

The above lines should generate the line graph in Figure 6.6.

There are many other types of charts and different variations of the same chart that one can draw in R. But we will stop at these four here and look at some other things we could do and plot with the data we have.

We will start by first loading a dataset about customer age and income:

```
custdata <- read.csv('custdata.tsv', header = TRUE, sep = "\t")
```

Let us find a **correlation** between age and income, which will tell us how much and in which ways age and income are related. It is done using a simple command:

```
cor(custdata$age, custdata$income)
```

This gives a low correlation of 0.027. That means these two variables do not relate to one another in any meaningful way. But wait a minute. A careful examination of the data tells us that there are some null values, meaning some of the ages and incomes are reported to be 0. That cannot be true, and perhaps this is a reflection of missing values. So, let us redo the correlation, this time picking the values that are non-zero. Here is how we could create such a subset:

```
custdata2 <- subset(custdata, (custdata$age > 0 & custdata$age <
100 & custdata$income >0))
```

The subset() function allows us to take a sample of the data according to the specified conditions (in this case, "age" being greater than 0 and less than 100). And now let us do that correlation calculation again:

```
cor(custdata2$age, custdata2$income)
```

This time we get −0.022. That is still pretty low, but you see the sign has changed? As we move forward with other forms of data analytics (with R or any other tool), pay attention to the nature of the data. It is not always clean or right, and if we are not careful, we may end up with results that either do not make sense, or worse, are dead wrong.

Try It Yourself 6.4: Correlation

In this exercise you are going to use the cloth dataset available from OA 6.3. This dataset has measurement of cloth dimension (*x*) and number of flaws (*y*) in the piece. Use this dataset to probe the relation between number of flaws in a cloth and its dimension. Are these two related? If yes, then to what extent and in which direction?

6.5 Statistics and Machine Learning

We reviewed statistical concepts in Chapter 3 and saw how we could use them (and some more) using Python in the previous chapter. Now, it is time to use R to do the same or similar things. So, before you begin this section, make sure that you have at least reviewed statistical concepts. In addition, we will see how some of the basic **machine learning** techniques using R could help us solve data problems. Regarding machine learning, I would suggest reviewing the introductory part of the previous chapter.

6.5.1 Basic Statistics

We will start with getting some descriptive statistics. Let us work with "size.csv" data, which you can download from OA 6.4. This data contains 38 records of different people's sizes in terms of height and weight. Here is how we load it:

```
size = read.table('size.csv',header=T,sep=',')
```

Once again, this assumes that the data is in the current directory. Alternatively, you can replace "size.csv" with "file.choose()" to let you pick the file from your hard drive when you run this line. Also, while you can run one line at a time on your console, you could type them and save as an ".r" file, so that not only can you run line-by-line, but you can also store the script for future runs.

Either way, I am assuming at this point that you have the data loaded. Now, we can ask R to give us some basic statistics about it by running the summary command:

```
summary(size)
     Height           Weight
Min.    :62.00  Min.    :106.0
1st Qu.:66.00  1st Qu.:135.2
Median :68.00  Median :146.5
Mean    :68.42  Mean    :151.1
3rd Qu.:70.38  3rd Qu.:172.0
Max.    :77.00  Max.    :192.0
```

The output, as shown above, shows descriptive statistics for the two variables or columns we have here: "Height" and "Weight." We have seen such output before, so I will not bother with the details.

Let us visualize this data on a scatterplot. In the following line, "ylim" is for specifying minimum and maximum values for the *y*-axis:

```
library(ggplot2)
ggplot(size, aes(x=Height,y=Weight)) + geom_point() + ylim
(100,200)
```

The outcome is shown in Figure 6.7. Once again, you have got to appreciate how easy it is with R to produce such professional-looking visualizations.

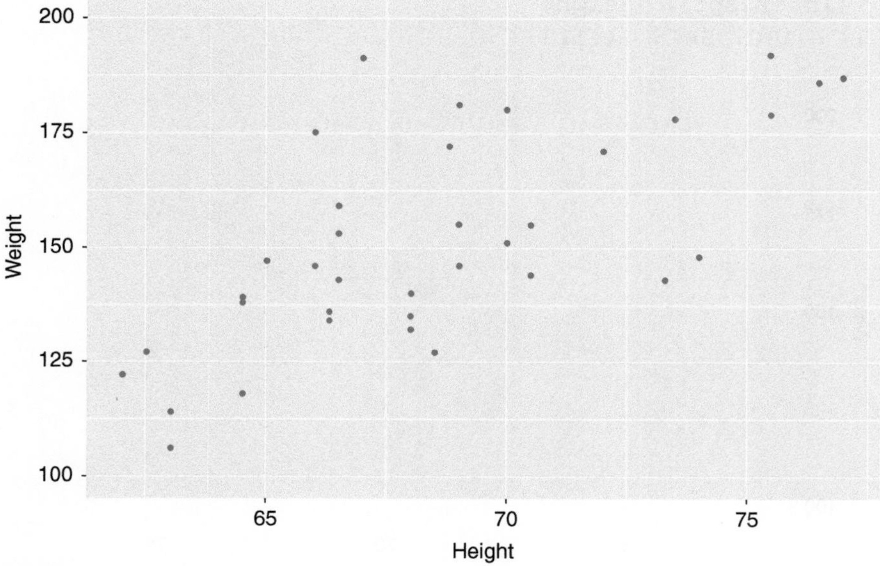

Figure 6.7 Scatterplot of Height vs. Weight.

6.5.2 Regression

Now that we have a scatterplot, we can start asking some questions. One straightforward question is: What is the relationship between the two variables we just plotted? That is easy. With R, you can keep the existing plotting information and just add a function to find a line that captures the relationship:

```
ggplot(size, aes(x=Height,y=Weight)) + geom_point()+
stat_smooth(method="lm") + ylim(100,200)
```

Compare this command to the one we used above for creating the plot in Figure 6.7. You will notice that we kept all of it and simply added a segment that overlaid a line on top of the scatterplot. And that is how easy it is to do basic **linear regression** in R, a form of **supervised learning**. Here, "lm" method refers to linear model. The output is in Figure 6.8.

You see that blue line? That is the regression line. It is also a model that shows the connection between "Height" and "Weight" variables. What it means is that if we know the value of "Height," we could figure out the value of "Weight" anywhere on this line.

Want to see the line equation? Use the "lm" command to extract the coefficients:

```
lm(Weight ~ Height, size)
```

And here is the output.

```
Call:
lm(formula = Weight ~ Height, data = size)
Coefficients:
(Intercept)   Height
   -130.354    4.113
```

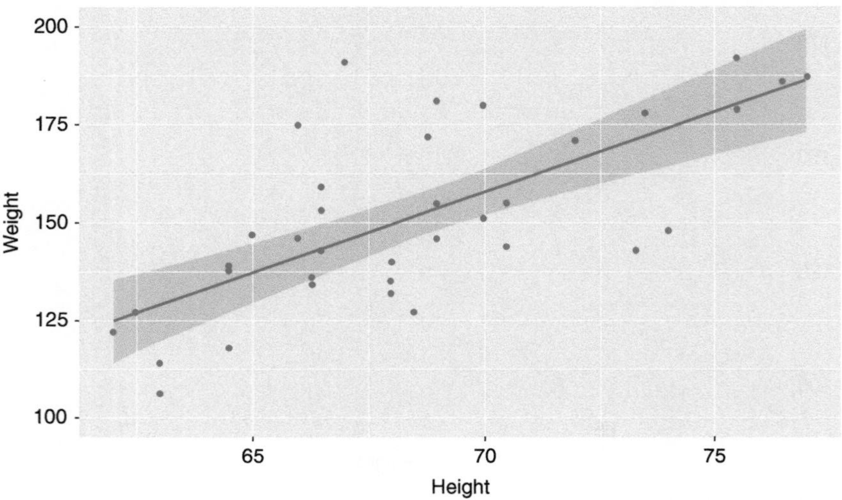

Figure 6.8 Linear regression connecting Height to Weight.

You can see that the output contains coefficients for the independent or **predictor** variable (Height) and the constant or intercept. The line equation becomes:

```
Weight = -130.354 + 4.113*Height
```

Try plugging in different values of "Height" in this equation and see what values of "Weight" you get and how close your predicted or estimated values are to reality.

With linear regression, we managed to fit a straight line through the data. But perhaps the relationship between "Height" and "Weight" is not all that straight. So, let us remove that restriction of linear model:

```
ggplot(size, aes(x=Height,y=Weight)) + geom_point() + geom_
smooth() + ylim(100,200)
```

And here is the output (Figure 6.9). As you can see, our data fits a curved line better than a straight line.

Yes, the curved line fits the data better, and it may seem like a better idea than trying to draw a straight line through this data. However, we may end up with the curse of *overfitting* and *overlearning* with a curved shape for doing regression. It means we were able to model the existing data really well, but in the process, we compromised so much that we may not do so well for new data. Do not worry about this problem for now. We will come back to these concepts in the machine learning chapters. For now, just accept that a line is a good idea for doing regression, and whenever we talk about regression, we would implicitly mean linear regression.

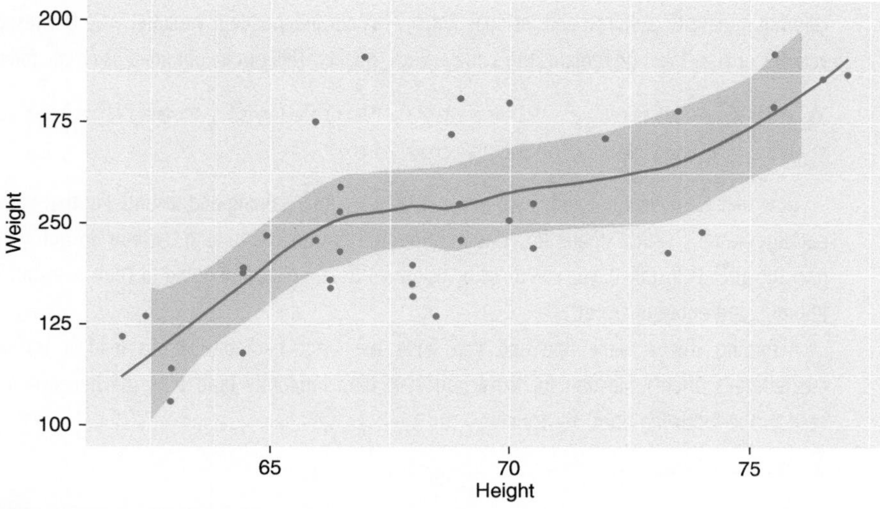

Figure 6.9 Regression without requiring linear requirement.

Try It Yourself 6.5: Regression

In this exercise, use the cloth data available from OA 6.3 and build a regression model to predict the number of flaws in the cloth from the cloth's dimension. What is the accuracy of the model?

6.5.3 Classification

We will now see how we could do some of the same things we did using Python. Let us start with **classification** using the kNN method. As you may recall, classification with kNN is an example of **supervised learning**, where we have some training data with true labels, and we build a model (classifier) that could then help us classify unseen data.

Before we use classification in R, let us make sure we have a library or package named "class" available to us. You can find available packages in the "Packages" tab in RStudio (typically in the bottom-right window where you also see the plots). If you see "class" there, make sure it is checked. If it is not there, you need to install that package using the same method you did for the ggplot2 package.

Hands-On Example 6.5: Classification

Let us begin our work by first loading some data. We worked with wine data for classification before, and that is what we will use here again. Running the following statement in R should bring up a file navigation box that you can use to select "wine.csv" file from your computer.

```
wine = read.table(file.choose(), header=T, sep=",")
```

Think of "wine" as a dataframe here. From this dataframe or table, we want to take all rows and specific columns – density, sulfates, and residual_sugar – as our independent variable, or *X*. Our response/target variable or class label (*y*) remains the same – high_quality. This can be obtained using the following lines:

```
X_wine <- wine[,c("density","sulfates","residual_sugar")]
y_wine <- wine[,c("high_quality")]
```

Now that we have our *X* and *y*, we can split the data into training and testing. For that we will use the package "caret," which stands for "classification and regression training." If you do not have the caret package already installed, you can do so by using our usual method of going to Tools > Install Packages in RStudio, and entering "caret".

Assuming things went fine and you have the caret package, let us load it up and use its createDataPartition() function for extracting 70% data randomly (and thus the generation of random seed in the following lines) for training:

```
library(caret)
set.seed(123)
inTrain <- createDataPartition(y = y_wine, p = 0.7, list =
FALSE)
```

Now let us extract training and testing sets for *X* and *y*:

```
X_train <- X_wine[inTrain,]
X_test <- X_wine[-inTrain,]
y_train <- y_wine[inTrain]
y_test <- y_wine[-inTrain]
```

Here, X_wine contains all the rows, but only some of the columns. It is a table or a matrix with [rows, columns], and when we enter X_wine[inTrain,], we are picking only the rows that are marked in "inTrain," with all the columns of X_wine. In other words, we are generating our training data. The remaining data is in X_wine[-inTrain,], giving us the test data.

On the other hand, y_wine is a vector (many rows, but one column). We can similarly split that vector into training and testing using y_wine[inTrain] and y_wine[-inTrain].

We are now ready to run kNN on this data. For that, we will need to load the "class" library. Then use X_train and y_train to build a model, and use X_test to find our predicted values for *y*:

```
library(class)
wine_pred <- knn(train=X_train, test=X_test, cl=y_train,k=3)
```

Finally, we want to see how well we were able to fit the model and how good our predictions were. For this, let us load "gmodels" library[3] and use its "CrossTable()" function:

```
library (gmodels)
CrossTable(x = y_test, y = wine_pred, prop.chisq=FALSE)
```

You should see output that looks something like:

```
Total Observations in Table: 1949
             | wine_pred
      y_test |         0 |         1 | Row Total |
-------------|-----------|-----------|-----------|
           0 |      1363 |       198 |      1561 |
             |     0.873 |     0.127 |     0.801 |
             |     0.836 |     0.623 |           |
             |     0.699 |     0.102 |           |
-------------|-----------|-----------|-----------|
           1 |       268 |       120 |       388 |
             |     0.691 |     0.309 |     0.199 |
             |     0.164 |     0.377 |           |
             |     0.138 |     0.062 |           |
-------------|-----------|-----------|-----------|
Column Total |      1631 |       318 |      1949 |
             |     0.837 |     0.163 |           |
-------------|-----------|-----------|-----------|
```

Here, you can see out of 1949 instances (that is, 30% of data) for testing, how many times we predicted 0 and it was 0, or we predicted 1 and it was 1 (success), and how often we predicted 0 for 1 or 1 for 0 (true negative or false positive).

Note that the last argument "prop.chisq" indicates whether or not the chi-square contribution of each cell is included. The chi-square statistic is the sum of the contributions from each of the individual cells and is used to decide whether the difference between the observed and the expected values is significant.

Try It Yourself 6.6: Classification

Reynolds[4] described a part of a study which measured the long-term temperature dynamics of beaver *Castor canadensis* in north-central Wisconsin. Body temperature was recorded by telemetry every 10 minutes. The dataset, which you can download from OA 6.5, has four attributes that include days of observation, time, temperature as recorded by the telemetry, and activity indicator outside the retreat. Use this dataset to build a classifier that will predict the activity from the first three attributes. Report the accuracy of the classifier.

6.5.4 Clustering

Now we will switch to the **unsupervised learning** branch of machine learning. Recall from Chapter 5 that this covers a class of problems where we do not have labels on our training data. In other words, we do not have a way to know which data point should go to which class. Instead, we are interested in somehow characterizing and explaining the data we encounter. Perhaps there are some classes or patterns in them. Can we identify and explain these? Such a process is often exploratory in nature. Clustering is the most widely used method for such exploration and we will learn about it using a hands-on example.

Hands-On Example 6.6: Clustering

Previously we tried clustering with Iris data, and so that is what we will use here with R. Let us start by loading the "datasets" library and see a portion of the "iris" data:

```
library(datasets)
head(iris)
```

Let us see what this data looks like. First, we will load the "ggplot2" library and then do a scatterplot where the color of a data point indicates the species:

```
library(ggplot2)
ggplot(iris, aes(Petal.Length, Petal.Width, color =
Species)) + geom_point()
```

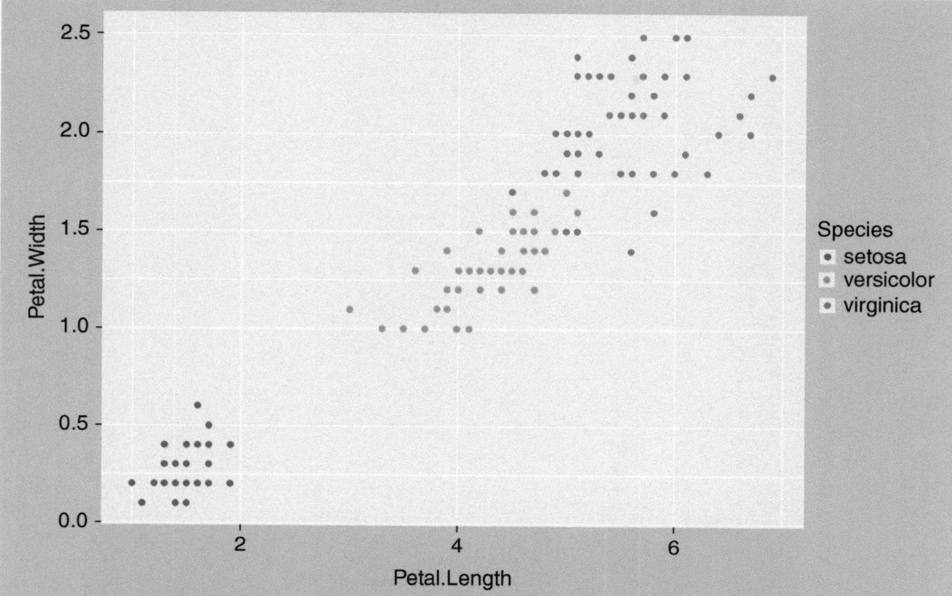

Figure 6.10 Visualization of Iris data according to the species.

The outcome is shown in Figure 6.10.

Now we are ready to start doing clustering. For this, we will generate a random number seed and then use the "kmeans" function. Note that in the following code we are asking for three clusters:

```
set.seed(20)
irisCluster <- kmeans(iris[, 3:4], 3, nstart = 20)
irisCluster
```

The last line of the code above should provide an output that gives a nice summary of the clusters generated. We can see how well we were able to cluster data points corresponding to different species by creating a table like this:

```
table(irisCluster$cluster, iris$Species)
```

Finally, let us recreate the scatterplot using the clustering information:

```
ggplot(iris, aes(Petal.Length, Petal.Width, color =
irisCluster$cluster)) + geom_point()
```

In Figure 6.11 you can see that the clustering information almost matches the actual classes for the data points, but not quite. There are a few points that you can see are in the wrong class. See if this information corresponds to the table we generated before.

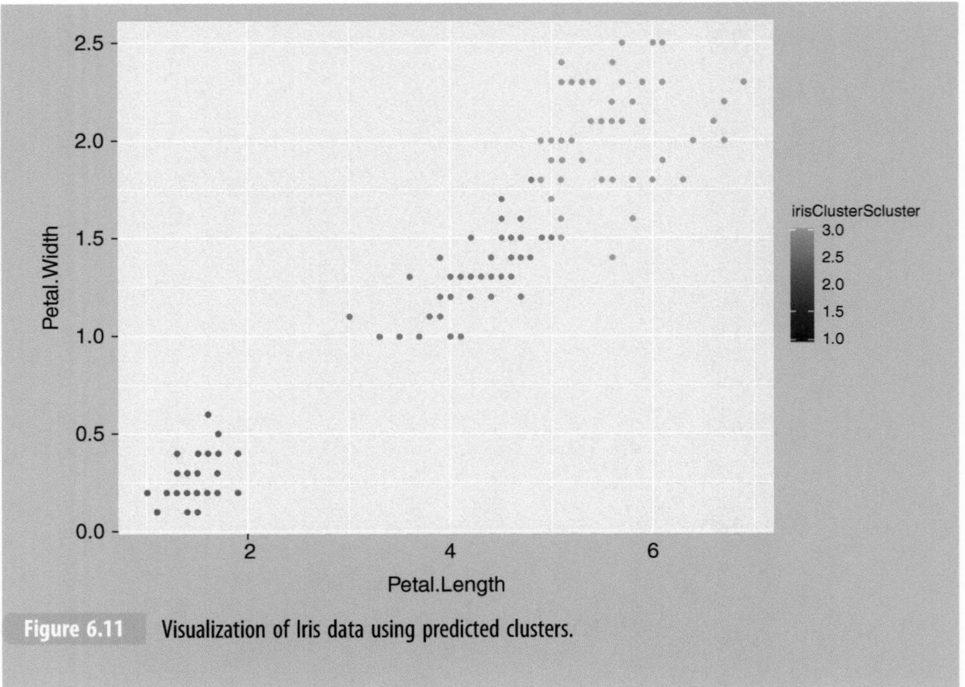

Figure 6.11 Visualization of Iris data using predicted clusters.

Try It Yourself 6.7: Clustering

Use the beavers dataset available from OA 6.5 and build a clustering model (with two clusters) instead that will consider the temperature recorded and the day and timing of recording. Evaluate if the clustering model is a better approach to predict the beavers' activity than the classifier you built in the last homework.

Summary

R is a fantastic programming environment. More important for us, it is an easy and surprisingly powerful platform for solving data problems. Under the hood, R has specific provisions to handle large amounts of data that is only restricted by the size of the RAM in your computer. This feature will not become apparent when you are working with just a few dozen or a few hundred records, but when you start dealing with "big data," you would be pleased that you picked the right platform.

Like Python, R also boasts a number of packages specifically developed for handling various data processing problems. They provide enhanced features on top of the basic R environment. In this chapter, we saw a few of those packages, but we did not go into a lot of detail. As you learn more about these packages (more functions in them and more parameters for each of those functions), as well as explore other packages, you will realize how easy and amazing it is to work with R. No wonder many data scientists start (and often finish) with R for their needs.

It may be tempting to ask at this point which one is better – Python or R? I will not answer that; I will leave it up to you. Sure, there are structural differences between them, and at some level it is like comparing apples and oranges. But in the end, the choice often comes down to personal preference, because you will discover that you could use either of these tools to solve the problem at hand.

Key Terms

- **Dataframe:** Dataframe generally refers to "tabular" data, a data structure that represents cases (represented by the rows), each of which consists of a number of observations or measurements (represented by the columns). In R it is a special case of list where each component is of equal length.
- **Package:** In R, packages are collections of functions and compiled code in a well-defined format.
- **Library:** The directory where the packages are stored is R called the library. Often, "package" and "library" are used interchangeably.
- **Integrated Development Environment (IDE):** This is an application that contains various tools for writing, compiling, debugging, and running a program. Examples include Eclipse, Spyder, and Visual Studio.
- **Correlation:** This indicates how closely two variables are related and ranges from −1 (negatively related) to +1 (positively related). A correlation of 0 indicates no relation between the variables.
- **Linear regression:** Linear regression is an approach to model the relationship between the outcome variable and predictor variable(s) by fitting a linear equation to observed data.
- **Machine learning:** This is a field that explores the use of algorithms that can learn from the data and use that knowledge to make predictions on data they have not seen before.
- **Supervised learning:** This is a branch of machine learning that includes problems where a model could be built using the data and true labels or values.
- **Unsupervised learning:** This is a branch of machine learning that includes problems where we do not have true labels for the data to train with. Instead, the goal is to somehow organize the data into some meaningful clusters or densities.
- **Predictor:** A predictor variable is a variable that is being used to measure some other variable or outcome. In an experiment, predictor variables are often independent variables, which are manipulated by the researcher rather than just measured.
- **Outcome or response:** Outcome or response variables are in most cases the dependent variables which are observed and measured by changing the independent variables.

- **Classification:** In our context, a classification task represents the systematic arrangement of data points in groups or categories according to some shared qualities or characteristics. These groups or categories have predefined labels, called class labels.
- **Clustering:** Clustering involves the grouping of similar objects into a set, called a cluster. The clustering task is similar to classification without the predefined class labels.

Conceptual Questions

1. What is the difference between R and RStudio?
2. Two variables – income and tax refund – have correlation value of −0.73. How would you explain this result?
3. List three kinds of plots/charts you can create with R and give an example of what kind of variables/quantities you would plot for each of them.
4. What does "binwidth" in a histogram indicate? How would you adjust it to get more or less "resolution" of your data in terms of visualizing it?

Hands-On Problems

Problem 6.1

Write a multiplication script using either a "for" loop or a "while" loop. Show your script.

Problem 6.2

Like histogram, you can also plot the density of a variable. We have not seen this in this chapter, but it is easy to do. Figure out how to plot density of income. Provide a couple of sentences of description along with the plot.

Problem 6.3

Create a bar chart for housing type using the customers data (custdata.tsv, available from OA 6.1). Make sure to remove the "NA" type. [Hint: You can use subset function with an appropriate condition on housing type field.] Provide your commands and the plot.

Problem 6.4

Using the customers data (custdata.tsv, available from OA 6.1), extract a subset of customers that are married and have an income more than $50,000. What percentage of these customers have health insurance? How does this percentage differ from that for the whole dataset?

Problem 6.5

In the customers data (custdata.tsv, available from OA 6.1), do you think there is any correlation between age, income, and number of vehicles? Report your correlation numbers and interpretations. [Hint: Make sure to remove invalid data points, otherwise you may get incorrect answers!]

Problem 6.6

You are given a data file containing observations for dating (see OA 6.6). Someone who dated 1000 people (!) recorded data about how much that person travels (Miles), plays games (Games), and eats ice cream (Icecream). With this, the decision about that person (Like) is also noted. Use this data to answer the following questions using R:

a. Is there a relationship between eating ice cream and playing games? What about traveling and playing games? Report correlation values for these and comment on them.
b. Let us use Miles to predict Games. Perform regression using Miles as the predictor and Games as the response variable. Show the regression graph with the regression line. Write the line equation.
c. Now let us see how well we can cluster the data based on the outcome (Like). Use Miles and Games to plot the data and color the points using Like. Now cluster the data using *k*-means and plot the same data using clustering information. Show the plot and compare it with the previous plot. Provide your thoughts about how well your clustering worked in two to four sentences.

Further Reading and Resources

If you are interested in learning more about programming in R, or the platform RStudio, following are a few links that might be useful:

- https://www.r-bloggers.com/how-to-learn-r-2/
- https://www.rstudio.com/online-learning/
- https://cran.r-project.org/doc/manuals/R-intro.pdf
- https://www.tutorialspoint.com/r/
- http://www.cyclismo.org/tutorial/R/

R Tutorial on dataframes:

- http://www.r-tutor.com/r-introduction/data-frame

Notes

1. Site for downloading R: https://www.r-project.org
2. RStudio: https://www.rstudio.com/products/rstudio/download/
3. I hope you are now comfortable with installing and using libraries/packages. If at any time you get an error regarding a package not found, go ahead and install it first.
4. Reynolds, P. S. (1994). Time-series analyses of beaver body temperatures. In *Case Studies in Biometry* (eds. Lange, N., Ryan, L., Billard, L., Brillinger, D., Conquest, L., & Greenhouse, J.). John Wiley & Sons, New York, ch. 11.

7 MySQL

"If we have data, let us look at data. If all we have are opinions, let us go with mine."
— Jim Barksdale, former Netscape CEO

What do you need?

- A general understanding of client–server configuration in a networked environment (refer to Chapter 4).
- A basic understanding of structured data (spreadsheets, CSV files).
- (Ideally) Introductory experience with UNIX – specifically, being able to run commands on a console.

What will you learn?

- Connecting to a MySQL server using a client software.
- Running SQL queries to retrieve data from a MySQL database.
- Connecting to MySQL using Python and R.

7.1 Introduction

So far, we have seen data that comes in a file – whether it is in a table, a CSV, or an XML format. But text files (including CSV) are not the best way to store or transfer data when we are dealing with a large amount of them. We need something better – something that allows us not only to store data more effectively and efficiently, but also provides additional tools to process that data. That is where databases come in. There are several databases in use today, but MySQL tops them all in the free, open-source category. It is widely available and used, and thanks to its powerful **Structured Query Language** (SQL), it is also a comprehensive solution for data storage and processing.

This chapter will introduce MySQL, the most popular open-source database platform in the world. We will learn how to create and access structured data using MySQL. And by now, since we already know some Python and R, we will see how we can integrate them with MySQL. I should emphasize this last part – our goal is not to study SQL for the sake of studying databases; instead, we are still interested in using Python or R as our main tool of choice and simply replacing text files with SQL databases. And because of that, we will not cover certain basic elements of SQL that are otherwise covered in an introduction to MySQL, including creating databases and records, as well as defining keys and pointers to indicate relationships among various entities. Instead, we will assume that the data is already stored in the correct format, with appropriate relationships among different fields and tables defined, and we will see how to retrieve and process data from such databases.

7.2 Getting Started with MySQL

MySQL is a popular open-source database system, available for free. Most UNIX-based systems come pre-installed with the server component, but one can install it on almost any system.

7.2.1 Obtaining MySQL

There are two primary components of MySQL: server and client. In case you are wondering, both of these are software. If you are on a UNIX or a Linux system (but not a Mac), chances are you already have the MySQL server installed. If not, or if you are on a non-UNIX system like Windows or a Mac without a pre-existing installation, you can download the community version of the MySQL server from the MySQL community server.[1] I will not go into the details, but if you have ever done installation on your system this should be no different. My suggestion would be to find an existing MySQL server – perhaps provided by your school, your organization, or by a third-party website host – rather than trying to install and configure it by yourself.

What is more important for us is the client software. Once again, on most UNIX or Linux systems (but not a Mac), you should already have the client, which comes as a program or utility that you can run straight from your terminal. So, if you are on a UNIX system, just type "mysql" (later we will see the exact command). If you are on a Mac or a Windows, you have two options: you can log in to a UNIX server using SSH and use the MySQL client there, or you can install this client on your machine. In fact, you can download and install Graphical User Interface (GUI)-based MySQL clients. An example of such clients is MySQL Workbench[2] that is available for almost all platforms. If you are on a Mac, I suggest Sequel Pro.[3] Both of these are available for free, and on their websites you can see instructions for installing and using them.

7.2.2 Logging in to MySQL

Once you have access to a MySQL server, you are ready to log in to it. Depending on the kind of MySQL client you have, the way you log in to a MySQL server will vary. But no matter what method you follow, you will need at least the following information: your MySQL username, your MySQL password, and the server name or its IP address. This is similar to connecting using SSH as we saw in Chapter 4.

Method 1: Using Command Line

Run the following command on the command line where you have your MySQL client installed:

```
mysql -h <servername> -u <username> -p
```

Here, `<servername>` is the full address (e.g., example.organization.com) or the IP address of the server. If you are already logged in to the server where the MySQL server is installed, you can use "localhost" or "127.0.0.1" as your `<servername>`.

Once you run that command, you will be asked to enter your MySQL password. Remember – at the password prompt, you may not see what you are typing, not even "********". Just type your password and hit "enter." Once you do that successfully, you will be at the MySQL prompt, where you can run your MySQL commands.

For example, you can run the following command to see what databases you have available:

```
show databases;
```

Remember to put a semicolon at the end of each command.

To exit the MySQL prompt, enter:

```
exit;
```

Method 2: Using a GUI Client

If you are using one of those GUI-based MySQL clients mentioned earlier, you will see a different interface in which to enter the same details. Here, you have two possibilities depending on the security setting on your server.

If no special security settings are enabled for the MySQL server, you can connect to it using the standard approach, where you provide the same three details you did with the command-line approach. See the screenshot in Figure 7.1.

Here, "Name" is just for your reference. Enter some string that makes sense for you as this connection will be saved for future use. "Host" is the same as <servername>, "Username" is the same as <username> and "Password" indicates your MySQL password. Other parameters are optional.

If, on the other hand, your MySQL server does not let you directly connect to its database server, you need to do what is called SSH tunneling. This means that you need to first log in to the server using SSH and then connect to its MySQL server. Most GUI-based MySQL clients let you do these two steps on one single screen. See the screenshot in Figure 7.2.

Once again, "Name" is just for your reference, so you should save this connection information for the future. "SSH Host" is the full address of the server, "SSH User" is your username for that server, and "SSH Password" is the password you need to connect to that server. "MySQL Host" is the same as `<servername>`, "Username" is the same as `<username>`, and "Password" is your MySQL password. Note that this screenshot is from Sequel Pro. If you are using MySQL Workbench or some other client, these names may be slightly different. But the idea remains the same – you need to enter two sets of credentials: one for connecting to the server through SSH, and the other for connecting to the MySQL database server.

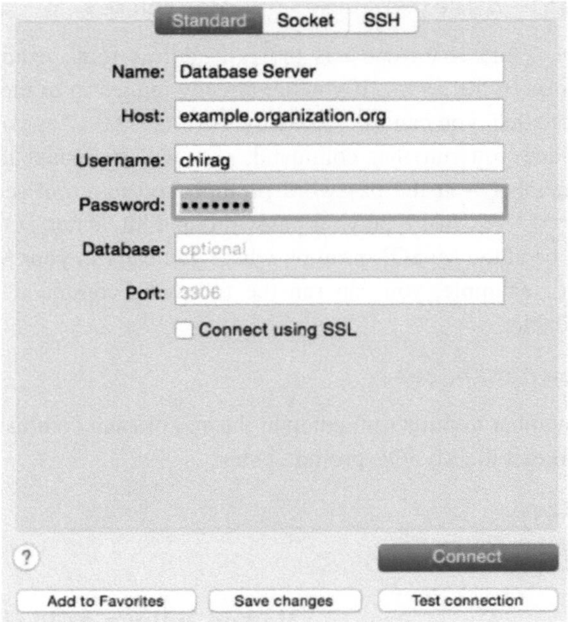

Figure 7.1 Connecting to a MySQL server with a standard security measure using a client.

Figure 7.2 Connecting to a MySQL server with the SSH tunneling approach using a client.

Once connected, you can see tabs or a dropdown box that lists your databases. Once you select a database you want to work with, you should see the tables within that database.

7.3 Creating and Inserting Records

Since our focus here is using MySQL as a storage format that we could query from and process data, we will not worry about constructing tables or datasets. Instead, we will start with existing datasets or import some data directly into a MySQL database, and proceed with retrieving and analyzing that data.

7.3.1 Importing Data

Before we could do any retrieval, let us import some data into our database. If you have rights to create a database on the server, you could run the following command on the MySQL prompt:

```
create database world;
```

This will create a database named “world”.

If you cannot create the database, then work with the one already assigned to you (perhaps this happened through your school’s IT department or your instructor). It is OK if that database is named differently, but unless you have at least one database available to you, you will not be able to proceed further in this chapter.

Now, let us get some data. MySQL provides several example datasets. The one that we are interested in getting here is called the world dataset and it can be downloaded from MySQL downloads.[4] Once downloaded, unzip the file to get world.sql. This is a text file with SQL commands. You can, in fact, open it in a text editor to view its content.

We need this file on our server. Use your favorite FTP software (see Chapter 4 for details) to connect to the server and transfer world.sql from your machine to the server.

Let us assume you copied this file to your home directory. Now, let us log in to the server using SSH. Once logged in, run the “mysql” command (see the first section of this chapter) to log into and start MySQL. Once you are at your MySQL prompt, let us first open the database. Assuming your database is called “world”, issue the following command:

```
use world;
```

Alternatively, if you are using a GUI-based client, simply select that database by clicking on its name in the dropdown box or wherever/however you see the existing databases. Now you are working within the “world” database. Let us go ahead and import that world.sql file in this database. Run:

```
source world.sql;
```

You will see lots of statements flying by on your console. Hopefully everything runs smoothly and you get your MySQL prompt back. That’s it. You have just imported a whole lot of data into your database.

If you are using a GUI-based MySQL client, you could import this data with a few clicks. First, make sure the correct database is opened or selected in your client. Then find an option from the File menu that says "Import . . .". Once you click that, you will be able to browse your local directories to find world.sql. Once selected, your MySQL client should be able to import that file.

7.3.2 Creating a Table

Just in case you are wondering how to create the same data manually, here are some instructions. If you were able to do the previous section successfully, you should simply skip this section (otherwise you would encounter many errors and duplicate data!).

First, make sure you have the right database open. To do so, once you are at your MySQL prompt, enter:

```
use world;
```

If we want to create a table "City" that stores information about cities, here is the full command:

```
CREATE TABLE 'City' (
  'ID' int(11) NOT NULL auto_increment,
  'Name' char(35) NOT NULL default '',
  'CountryCode' char(3) NOT NULL default '',
  'District' char(20) NOT NULL default '',
  'Population' int(11) NOT NULL default '0',
  PRIMARY KEY ('ID')
);
```

Here, we are saying that we want to create a table named "City" with five fields: ID, Name, CountryCode, District, and Population. Each of these fields has different characteristics, which include the type of data that will be stored in that field and default value. For instance, ID field will store numbers (int), will not have a null (non-existence) value, and will have value automatically incremented as new records are added. We are also declaring that "ID" is our primary key, which means whenever we want to refer to a record, we could use the "ID" value; it will be unique and non-empty.

7.3.3 Inserting Records

Now let us go ahead and add a record to this table. Run the following:

```
INSERT INTO City VALUES ('', 'New York', 'USA', 'New
York', '10000000');
```

Here, we are saying that we want to insert a new record in table "City" and specify values in different fields. Note that the first value, which corresponds to the first field, ID, is empty (''). That is because we have set ID field to automatically get its value (1, 2, 3, . . .). Seems like too much to remember? Well, here is something to put your mind at ease: for most work in data science, you will be reading the records from a database rather than inserting them. Even if you want to insert a record or two at times, or edit them, you are better off using a GUI-based MySQL client. With such a client, you could enter a record or edit an existing record very much like how you would in a spreadsheet program.

7.4 Retrieving Records

As noted above, fetching or reading the records from a database is what you would be doing most times, and that is what we are going to see in detail now. For the examples here, we will assume you are using a terminal-based MySQL client. If you are using a GUI, well, things will be easier and more straightforward, and I will leave it to you to play around and see if you can do the same kind of things as described below.

7.4.1 Reading Details about Tables

To see what tables you have available within a database, you can enter the following at the MySQL prompt:

```
show tables;
```

How do you do the same in a GUI-based MySQL client? By simply selecting the database. Yes, the client should show you the tables a database has once you select it.

To find out the structure of a table, you can use the "describe" command on your MySQL command prompt. For instance, to know the structure of the "Country" table in our "world" database, you can enter:

```
describe Country;
```

7.4.2 Retrieving Information from Tables

To extract information from MySQL tables, the primary command you have is "select". It is a very versatile and useful command. Let us see some examples.

To retrieve all the records from table "City":

```
SELECT * FROM City;
```

To see how many records "City" has:

```
SELECT count(*) FROM City;
```

To get a set of records matching some criteria:

```
SELECT * FROM City WHERE population>7000000;
```

This will fetch us records from "City" where the value of "Population" is greater than 7,000,000.

```
SELECT Name, Population FROM Country WHERE Region="Caribbean"
ORDER BY Population;
```

This command will list Name and Population fields of the records from the "Country" table that are from Caribbean regions. These records will also be ordered by their populations. By default, it is in ascending order. To reverse the order, add "desc" at the end:

```
SELECT Name, Population FROM Country WHERE Region="Caribbean"
ORDER BY Population desc;
```

If you run into a problem, try different enclosures for your strings. These include ` (back tick, usually found at the left of your number "1" key), ' (single quote), and " (double quotes). The validity of these enclosures depends on your OS platform and the version of MySQL you are using.

While all these examples were done on a terminal-based MySQL client, what if you are using a GUI-based client? Sure, you can do simple sorting and filtering, but can you run more sophisticated queries? You bet! Each GUI-based client will also provide a query console where you can run free-form SQL queries. See Figure 7.3 for an example of how Sequel Pro does this.

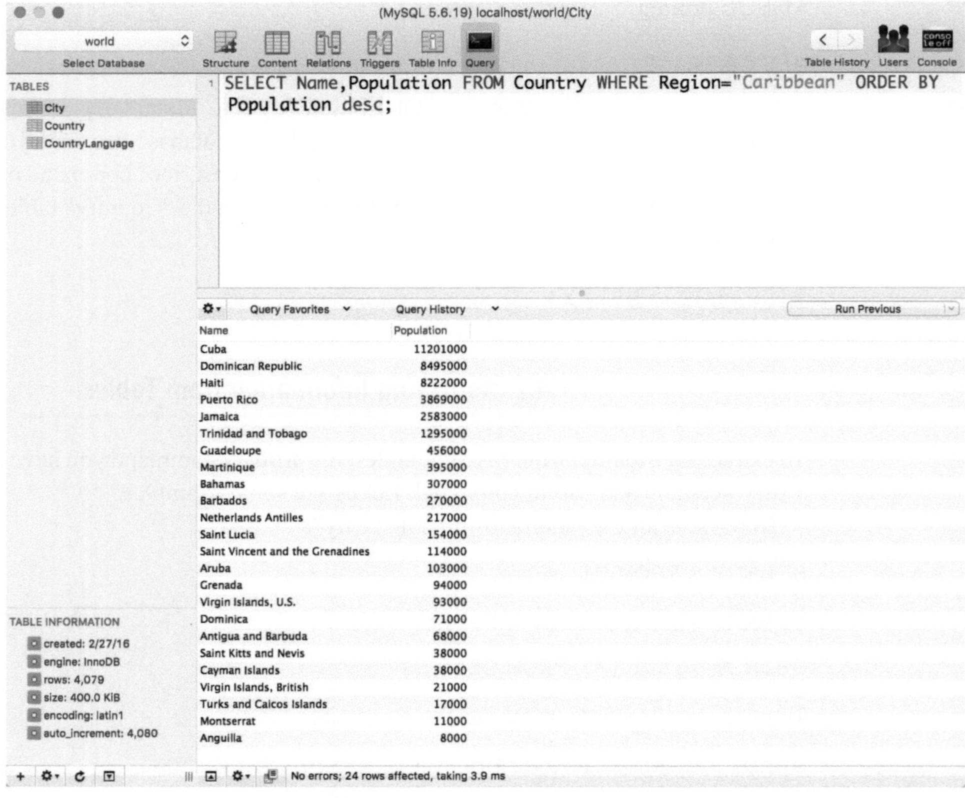

Figure 7.3 Example of running an SQL query in a GUI-based MySQL client (here, Sequel Pro).

Try It Yourself 7.1: Retrieval

Let us do some more practice exercises.

1. Use the above dataset to retrieve the name of the place which has the third largest population in the Caribbean region.
2. List the name of two places which are least populated among the places which have at least 400,000 people.

7.5 Searching in MySQL

In this section, we will see how to do searching within MySQL. There are two primary ways: using the "LIKE" expression and using the "MATCH..AGAINST" expression. The former can be used without doing any extra work but has limitations in terms of the kinds of fields it works on and the way searching is done. The latter requires us to build a full text index. If you have a lot of textual data, it is a good idea to go with the latter option.

7.5.1 Searching within Field Values

Even without doing anything extra, our MySQL database is ready to give us text-search functionalities. Let us give it a spin with our "world" database. Try the queries below, and similar ones, and see what you get:

```
SELECT * FROM Country WHERE HeadOfState LIKE '%bush%';
SELECT * FROM Country WHERE HeadOfState LIKE '%elisa%';
SELECT * FROM Country WHERE HeadOfState LIKE '%II%';
```

You might notice that in the above expressions, "%" acts as a **wildcard**. Thus, looking for %elisa% gives all the records that have "elisa" as a substring.

7.5.2 Full-Text Searching with Indexing

Now let us take this a step further and see how MySQL supports more sophisticated full-text searching. Add an index to the "Country" table by issuing the following command:

```
ALTER TABLE 'Country' ADD FULLTEXT 'HeadOfState'
('HeadOfState');
```

This should create an **index** (an efficient representation of the field that has been indexed) inside the "Country" table. Once this index is created, we can issue queries, such as:

```
SELECT * FROM Country WHERE MATCH(HeadOfState) AGAINST('elisa');
```

Table 7.1 Comparison of LIKE and MATCH approaches for database searching.

LIKE	MATCH
No need to create an index	Need to create an index
Serial scanning while searching	Efficient searching with sophisticated data structures
No change in write operation	Write operation becomes slightly costlier
No change in reading operation	Reading (searching) becomes significantly costlier
Consider all the terms	Disregards stop words

Since the above query does not contain any wildcards, you should get the results with records where head of state has "elisa" as a full word. Can you obtain the same set of results using the LIKE expression?

The real question is: Why would we want to create an index if we could do searches using the LIKE expression? A comparison between the above two approaches is given in Table 7.1.

Now, to answer the above question, while usage of MATCH requires you to create an index and induces a slight overhead (in terms of processing power and memory needs) while writing a record, it helps significantly during searches. Without an index, MySQL goes record-by-record looking for an expression (serial scanning approach). This is inefficient and impractical for large datasets. Indexing allows MySQL to organize the information in a better data structure that can reduce the search time significantly. On top of that, MySQL also removes stop words from the text while indexing. **Stop words** are words that are not useful for storage or matching. Typically, these words include the most frequent words used in a language (e.g., in English, articles and forms of "to be," such as *a*, *an*, *the*, *is*, *are*, etc.). In addition to these words, MySQL also discounts all the words that occur in more than 50% of the records or are shorter than three characters. Note that the MySQL stop words list is available at MySQL Full-Text Stopwords.[5]

Try It Yourself 7.2: Searching

1. Search for population in the last table where Name contains "US."
2. Search for records in the Country table where the head of state's name ends with "i" and the country name starts with a "U."

7.6 Accessing MySQL with Python

We will now incorporate MySQL into other data science programming tools or environments we know. This way, instead of retrieving and separately analyzing the data from

MySQL, we could create a workflow or a pipeline that integrates data connection to MySQL and data analysis using Python or R.

To access the MySQL database with Python, we will need PyMySQL. You can download it from GitHub.[6] The installation instructions can also be found on that page.

Now that you have PyMySQL installed, let us proceed. We will first import that package, along with our familiar Pandas package:

```
import pymysql.cursors
import pandas as pd
```

Now, let us provide the MySQL connection parameters to connect to the database:

```
# Connect to the database
connection = pymysql.connect(host='localhost',
                             user='bugs',
                             password='bunny',
                             db='world',
                             charset='utf8mb4',
        cursorclass=pymysql.cursors.DictCursor)
```

Note that we are assuming that your MySQL server is on your local machine (localhost), but if it is somewhere else, make sure to change the "host" parameter value in the code below accordingly. And yes, change the values of the "user," "password," and "db" as well. Once connected, we can try running a query, and once it is finished, close the database connection:

```
# Try running a query
try:
    with connection.cursor() as cursor:
        sql = "SELECT * FROM City WHERE population>7000000"
        cursor.execute(sql)
        # Extract the data in a dataframe
        df = pd.DataFrame(cursor.fetchall())
finally:
    connection.close()
```

The resulting dataframe (a table or a matrix containing multiple rows and columns) can be found in the "df" variable. And now that you have the dataframe, you can do all kinds of things with the data that we did before using Python.

Hands-On Example 7.1: MySQL with Python

Let us take another database and see how it can be accessed from Python. For this exercise, we will use a database available from OA 7.1. Once you unzip the file, you will see "mysqlsampledatabase.sql". Yes, this is an SQL file with the instructions to create data records in your database.

First, we will create a new database:

```
create database classicmodels;
```

Of course, this was using the SQL query console, but you could also do it using your GUI client. Now, you will need to extract the database file and import it into your MySQL Workbench, SQL Pro, of whichever GUI client you are using. Once the dataset is loaded, you should be able to see a list of tables (e.g., customers, employees, offices, order details, to name a few) in your database.

Now, let us try to access some of the tables from Python. Imagine you want to find all the employees who work at the Boston office, retrieve their IDs, and first and last names. Below is the code showing how to do it. For the purpose of this exercise, we will assume that your MySQL server is on your local machine (localhost), but if it is somewhere else, make sure to change the "host" parameter value in the code below accordingly.

```
import pymysql
# Connect to the database
connection = pymysql.connect(host='localhost',
                             user='root',
                             password='*******',
                             db='classicmodels',
                             charset='utf8mb4')
# Initiate cursor
conn = connection.cursor()

# Write the SQL query to be executed
sql = "select e.employeeNumber, e.firstName, e.lastName from
employees e
inner join offices o on e.officeCode = o.officeCode
and o.city like '%Boston%';"

output = conn.execute(sql)
while True:
    row = conn.fetchone()
    if row == None:
        break
    print(row)

# Close the connection
connection.close()
```

Try It Yourself 7.3: MySQL with Python

Using the database "classicmodels" created in Hands-On Example 7.1, write a Python code snippet that will retrieve the phone number (office phone number, followed by the extension) of the president of the company.

7.7 Accessing MySQL with R

We will now see how to access MySQL using R. As you might have guessed, to use MySQL through R, we need a package. This time, it is "RMySQL." First install the package if you do not already have it, and then load it in the environment:

```
> install.packages("RMySQL")
> library(RMySQL)
```

Now, let us connect to our database server and select the database. This is equivalent to specifying the parameters in your MySQL client:

```
> mydb = dbConnect(MySQL(), user='bugs', password='bunny',
dbname='world', host='server.com')
```

In this command, we are connecting to a MySQL server "server.com" with user "bugs" and password "bunny." We are also opening "world" database.

If we want to see the tables available in the database we just opened, we can run the following:

```
> dbListTables(mydb)
```

Now, let us run a query to retrieve some results.

```
> rs = dbSendQuery(mydb, "SELECT * FROM City WHERE
population>7000000")
```

Here, we are working with "mydb" – the database we just opened. We sent it a query that we had tried before and the resulting set is captured in "rs." To extract the data from this result set, we can use the "fetch()" function:

```
> data = fetch(rs,n=-1)
```

Here, n specifies how many records we want to extract; $n = -1$ means we want to extract everything.

That is it. Now you have the data in "data" that you asked for. And once you have the data, you can do all that you did with your R skills before. So, we will just leave it there.

Hands-On Example 7.2: MySQL with R

Need more practice? Let us take a similar example to the one used in the previous section for Python. The same "classicmodels" database is going to be used for this exercise. Say you are interested in retrieving the records of employees – their names, employee IDs and their roles – who report directly to the president in the office. The following lines of code should do the job:

```
# Load the package
library(RMySQL)
```

```
# Set the connection parameters
connection = dbConnect(MySQL(), user='root',
password='*******', dbname='classicmodels',
host='localhost')

# Check the connection
dbListTables(connection)

# Write the SQL query
query = dbSendQuery(connection, "SELECT e1.employeeNumber,
e1.firstName, e1.lastName, e1.jobTitle from employees e1
where e1.reportsTo = (select e2.employeeNumber from
employees e2 where e2.jobTitle like '%President');")

# Store the result
result = fetch(query, n= -1)

# View the result
View(result)

# Close the connection
dbDisconnect(connection)
```

Try It Yourself 7.4: MySQL with R

Using the database from the Hands-On Example 7.2, write an R script that will retrieve the address of all the customers whose first name is "Alexander."

7.8 Introduction to Other Popular Databases

As we noted earlier in this chapter, there is a good reason we devoted this chapter to MySQL; it is the most popular open-source, free database. But there are many other choices, and it may be possible that you end up working at an organization where one of these other choices is used. So, let us cover a few of them before we finish this chapter.

7.8.1 NoSQL

NoSQL, which stands for "not only SQL," is a new approach to database design that goes beyond the relational database like MySQL and can accommodate a wide variety of data models, such as key-value, document, columnar, and graph formats. NoSQL databases are most useful for working with large datasets that are distributed.

The name "NoSQL" sometimes is associated with early database designs that predate the relational database management system (RDBMS). However, in general NoSQL refers to the databases built in the early twenty-first century that were purposely designed to create large-scale database clusters for cloud and Web applications, where performance and scalability requirements surpassed the need for the rigid data consistency that the RDBMS provided for transactional applications.

The basic NoSQL database classifications (key-value, document, wide columns, graph) only serve as guidelines. Vendors, over time, have mixed and matched elements from different NoSQL database families to create more useful systems. Popular implementations of NoSQL include MongoDB, Redis, Google Bigtable, etc.

7.8.2 MongoDB

MongoDB is a cross-platform NoSQL database program that supports storage and retrieval of unstructured data such as documents. To support document-oriented database programs, MongoDB relies on JSON-like structure of documents with schemata. Data records stored in MongoDB are called BSON files, which are, in fact, a little-modified version of JSON files and hence support all JavaScript functionalities. MongoDB documents are composed of field-and-value pairs and have the following structure:

```
{
 field1: value1 [e.g., name: "Marie"]
 field2: value2 [e.g., sex: "Female"]
 ...
 fieldN: valueN [e.g., email: marie@abc.com]
}
```

One of the significant advantages of MongoDB over MySQL is that, unlike the latter, in MongoDB there are no restrictions on schema design. The schema-free implementation of a database in MongoDB eliminates the need for prerequisites of defining a fixed structure like tables and columns in MySQL. However, schema-less documents in MongoDB, where it is possible to store any information, may cause problems with data consistency.

7.8.3 Google BigQuery

BigQuery (https://cloud.google.com/bigquery/) is a cloud-based Web service offered by Google that enables interactive analysis of massively large datasets that can be used complementary with MapReduce. It is a serverless Platform as a Service (PaaS) solution, which has two significant advantages over most of the other database management systems.

- It is a serverless implementation that works in conjunction with Google storage. Since there is no server to manage, the user can focus more on the data analysis part. BigQuery has the in-built BI Engine (business intelligence engine) to support the user's data analysis requirement.

- The other advantage of having a serverless solution is that such implementation enables the data storage to be separated from the computation part, which in turn offers seamless scaling of the data storage possible.

While MySQL has obvious benefits of large userbase, compatibility with all major platforms, and cost-effectiveness as an open-source platform, it simply cannot support real-time analytics at scale the way BigQuery can, or at least for now. And the reason behind this lies in how these two store data internally. Relational databases like MySQL store data in row form, meaning that all data rows are stored together and the primary key acts as an index which makes the data easily accessible, whereas BigQuery uses a columnar structure, meaning the data is stored in columns instead of rows. The row form is great for transactional purposes – like reading rows by ID – but it is inefficient if you wish to get analytical insights from your data, as the row-form storage requires that you read through the entire database, along with unused columns, to produce results.

Summary

Databases allow us to store, retrieve, and process data in an effective and efficient manner. Of all the databases out there, MySQL is the most popular open-source database. It is free, it is open, and it is widely available on all kinds of platforms. There are two parts to it – server and client. While it is possible to have the server part installed on your machine, usually you are going to use an actual server (one that your organization provides) and have the client installed on your computer to access that server. In this chapter, we saw how to do that.

We also saw how easy it is to take a database file (with .sql extension) and import into a MySQL database, and to insert records using either the SQL or the client software. However, our focus here is on retrieving and processing the data, so we spent most of this chapter doing that.

Once again, we have only scratched the surface with MySQL. The more you learn about the SQL and the more data problems you practice with, the more skilled you will become. Having said that, what we practiced here should allow you to address many kinds of data problems. Make sure to do the exercises that follow here to hone your SQL skills.

Key Terms

- **Database:** A database is an organized collection of information that can be easily accessed, managed, and updated.
- **Structured Query Language (SQL):** SQL is a standard computer language for relational database management and data manipulation.

- **Client–server model:** In a distributed application structure, the client–server model is the partition of tasks or workloads between the service or resource providers, called servers, and service requesters, clients.
- **Wildcard:** In a programming or scripting language, a wildcard character (often represented using a character such as "*" or "%") is used to look for a substring in a string while ignoring the rest of that string.
- **Index:** This is an efficient representation of information that allows one to (typically) access that information in a more effective and efficient manner. A phonebook is indexed using alphabets, which allows one to easily look up a name in a more direct way without having to go through the entire phonebook.
- **Stop words:** They are words that are not useful for storage or matching. Typically, these words include the most frequent words used in a language (e.g., in English, articles and forms of "to be," such as *a, an, the, is, are,* etc.).

Conceptual Questions

1. The "world" database example we saw in this chapter is said to contain structured data. Why?
2. What is SSH tunneling? When is it needed?
3. What are the three pieces of information one needs to connect to a MySQL server? What additional pieces of information are needed if that connection requires SSH tunneling?
4. How do "LIKE" and "MATCH" expressions for database searching differ?
5. "IP" is not a stop word, and yet you are not able to search for it in a MySQL database because MySQL does not index it. Why is MySQL not indexing it?

Hands-On Problems

Problem 7.1

Answer the following questions using the "world" database, available for download from OA 7.2. Present your SQL queries and/or processes that you used to derive the answers.

a. How many countries became independent in the twentieth century?
b. How many people in the world are expected to live for 75 years or more?
c. List the 10 most populated countries in the world with their population as percentage of the world population. [Hint: You can first find the population of the world and then use it for percentage for countries, so something like: select Population/5000000000 from Country . . ..]

d. List the top 10 countries with the highest population density. [Hint: For population density, you can try something like: select Population/SurfaceArea from Country where . . ..]

Problem 7.2

Answer the following questions using the “auto” database, available for download from OA 7.3.

a. Let us use Python to explore the relationship of different variables to miles per gallon (mpg). Find out which of the variables have high correlation with mpg. Report those values. Build a regression model using one of those variables to predict mpg. Do the same using two of those variables. Report your models along with the regression line equations.
b. Let us use R to understand how horsepower and weights are related to each other. Plot them using a scatterplot and color the data points using mpg. Do you see anything interesting/useful here? Report your observations with this plot. Now let us cluster the data on this plane in a “reasonable” number of groups. Show your plot where the data points are now colored with the cluster information and provide your interpretations.

Problem 7.3

For the following exercise, first download the AIS Dynamic Data available from OA 7.4. This data is collected by a Naval Academy receiver and is available from “Heterogeneous integrated dataset for maritime intelligence, surveillance, and reconnaissance.” Using the dataset, answer the following questions:

a. How many unique vessels are available in the dataset?
b. List the number of records available for each vessel in the dataset.
c. Find out the spatial (latitude and longitude) and temporal coverage of each vessel in the dataset.
d. Let us use R to understand the relation between speed over the ground and spatial coverage of the vessels that have multiple records.

Further Reading and Resources

Following are a few resources that may be useful if you are interested in learning more about MySQL in general:

1. https://www.w3schools.com/sql/default.asp
2. https://dev.mysql.com/doc/mysql-shell-excerpt/5.7/en/
3. https://dev.mysql.com/doc/refman/5.7/en/tutorial.html

4. https://www.tutorialspoint.com/mysql/
5. https://www.javatpoint.com/mysql-tutorial

Notes

1. MySQL community server: http://dev.mysql.com/downloads/mysql/
2. MySQL Workbench: http://www.mysql.com/products/workbench/
3. Sequel Pro download: http://sequelpro.com/
4. MySQL downloads: http://downloads.mysql.com/docs/world.sql.zip
5. MySQL Full-Text Stopwords: http://dev.mysql.com/doc/refman/5.7/en/fulltext-stopwords.html
6. GitHub for PyMySQL download: https://github.com/PyMySQL/PyMySQL

PART III

MACHINE LEARNING FOR DATA SCIENCE

Machine learning is a very important part of doing data science, providing several crucial tools for working on data problems. For instance, many data-intensive problems require us to do regression or classification to develop decision-making insights. This falls squarely within the machine learning realm. Then there are problems related to data mining and data organization that call for various exploration techniques, such as clustering and density estimation. Recognizing this need, we have a whole part of this book dedicated to machine learning. There are three chapters in this part.

Chapter 8 provides a more formal introduction to machine learning and includes a few techniques that are basic and broadly applicable at the same time. Chapter 9 describes in some depth supervised learning methods, and Chapter 10 presents unsupervised learning.

It should be noted that, since this book is focused on data science and not core computer science or mathematics, we skip much of the underlying math and formal structuring while discussing and applying machine learning techniques. The chapters in this part, however, do present machine learning methods and techniques using adequate math in order to discuss the theories and intuitions behind them in detail.

Before beginning this part, make sure you are very comfortable with computational thinking (Chapter 1), the basics of statistics (Chapter 3), partial derivatives (Appendix A), probability theory (Appendix B), and R (Chapter 6). You should also be at ease with installing and configuring software and packages, especially related to R.

Finally, since we are not approaching machine learning in a typical computer science way, where we do a deep dive on theoretical aspects, to really grasp the concepts presented here, plan on doing a lot of practice. Each of these chapters is filled with many in-chapter exercises, homework exercises, and end-of-chapter hands-on problems, often with real-life data. So make sure to take advantage of these and practice as much as possible.

8 Machine Learning Introduction and Regression

"People worry that computers will get too smart and take over the world, but the real problem is that they're too stupid and they've already taken over the world."

— Pedro Domingos

What do you need?

- A good understanding of statistical concepts, including measures of central tendency, distributions, correlation, and regression (refer to Chapter 3).
- Basics of differential calculus (see Appendix A for a few handy formulas).
- Introductory to intermediate-level experience with R (refer to Chapter 6).

What will you learn?

- Definitions and example applications of machine learning.
- Solving linear regression using linear modeling and gradient descent approaches.

8.1 Introduction

So far, our work on data science problems has primarily involved applying statistical techniques to analyze the data and derive some conclusions or insights. But there are times when it is not as simple as that. Sometimes we want to learn something from that data and use that learning or knowledge to solve not only the current problem but also future data problems. We might want to look at shopping data at a grocery chain, combined with farming and poultry data, and learn how supply and demand are related. This would enable us to make recommendations for investments in both the grocery store and the food industries. In addition, we want to keep updating the knowledge – often called a model – derived from analyzing the data so far. Fortunately, there is a systematic way for tackling such data problems. In fact, we have already seen this in the previous chapters: machine learning.

In this chapter, we will introduce machine learning with a few definitions and examples. Then, we will look at a large class of problems in machine learning called regression. This is not the first time we have encountered regression. The first time we covered it was in Chapter 3 while discussing various statistical techniques. And then, if you went through either the Python or R chapter earlier, you would have seen regression in action. Here, we will approach regression as a learning problem and study linear regression by way of applying a linear model as well as gradient descent.

In subsequent chapters (Chapters 9 and 10) we will see specific kinds of learning – supervised and unsupervised. But first, let us start by introducing machine learning.

8.2 What Is Machine Learning?

Machine learning is a spin-off or a subset of artificial intelligence (AI), and in this book it is an application of data science skills. Here, the goal, according to Arthur Samuel,[1] is to give "computers the ability to learn without being explicitly programmed." Tom Mitchell[2] puts it more formally: "A computer program is said to learn from experience *E* with respect to some class of tasks *T* and performance measure *P* if its performance at tasks in *T*, as measured by *P*, improves with experience *E*."

Now that we know what machine learning is, in principle, let us see what it does and why. First, we must consider the following questions:[3] What is *learning*, anyway? What is it that the machine is trying to learn here?

These are deep philosophical questions. But we will not be too concerned with philosophy, as our emphasis is firmly on the practical side of machine learning. However, it is worth spending a few moments at the outset on fundamental issues, just to see how tricky they are, before rolling up our sleeves and looking at machine learning in practice.

For a moment, let us forget about the machine and think about learning in general. The *New Oxford American Dictionary* (third edition)[4] defines "to learn" as: "To get knowledge of something by study, experience, or being taught; to become aware by information or from observation; to commit to memory; to be informed of or to ascertain; to receive instruction."

All of these meanings have limitations when they are associated with computers or machines. With the first two meanings, it is virtually impossible to test whether learning has been achieved or not. How can you check whether a machine has obtained knowledge of something? You probably cannot ask it questions; and even if you could, you would not be testing its ability to learn but its ability to answer questions. How can you tell whether it has become aware of something? The whole question of whether computers can be aware, or conscious, is a burning philosophical issue.

As for the last three meanings, although we can see what they denote in human terms, merely committing to memory and receiving instruction seems to fall short of what we might mean by machine learning. These are too passive, and we know that these tasks are trivial for today's computers. Instead, we are interested in improvements in performance, or at least in the potential for performance, in new situations. You can commit something to memory or be informed of something by rote learning without being able to apply the new knowledge to new situations. In other words, you can receive instruction without benefitting from it at all.

Therefore, it is important to come up with a new operational definition of *learning* in the context of the machine, which we can formulate as:

> Things learn when they change their behavior in a way that makes them perform better in the future.

This ties learning to performance rather than knowledge. You can test learning by observing present behavior and comparing it with past behavior. This is a more objective kind of definition and is more satisfactory for our purposes. Of course, the more comprehensive and formal definition based on this idea is what we saw before by Tom Mitchell.

In the context of this definition, machine learning explores the use of algorithms that can learn from the data and use that knowledge to make predictions on data they have not seen before – such algorithms are designed to overcome strictly static program instructions by making data-driven predictions or decisions through building a model from sample inputs. While quite a few machine learning algorithms have been around for a long time, the ability to automatically apply complex mathematical calculations to big data in an efficient manner is a recent development. Following are a few widely publicized examples of machine learning applications you may be familiar with.

The first is the heavily hyped, self-driving Google car (now rebranded as WAYMO). As shown in Figure 8.1, this car is taking a real view of the road to recognize objects and patterns such as sky, road signs, and moving vehicles in a different lane. This process itself is quite complicated for a machine to do. A lot of things may look like a car (that blue blob in the bottom image is a car), and it may not be easy to identify where a street sign is. The self-driving car needs not only to carry out such object recognition, but also to make decisions about navigation. There is just so much unknown involved here that it is impossible to come up with an algorithm (a set of instructions) for a car to execute. Instead, the car needs to know the rules of driving, have the ability to do object and pattern

Figure 8.1 Machine learning technology behind self-driving car. (Source: YouTube: Deep Learning: Technology behind self-driving car.[5])

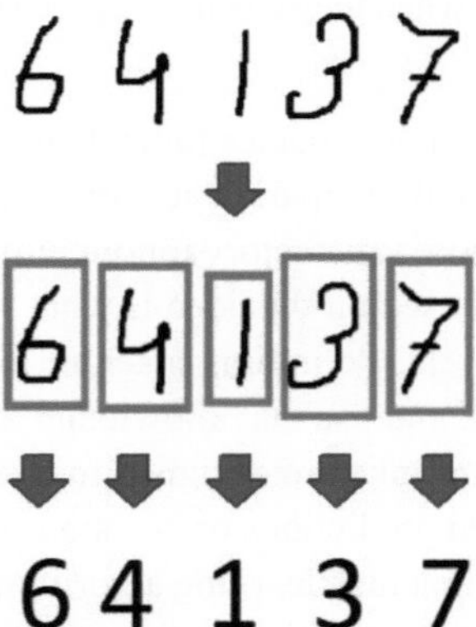

Figure 8.2 Problem of optical character recognition.

recognition, and apply these to making decisions in real time. In addition, it needs to keep improving. That is where machine learning comes into play.

Another classic example of machine learning is optical character recognition (OCR). Humans are good with recognizing hand-written characters, but computers are not. Why? Because there are too many variations in any one character that can be written, and there is no way we could teach a computer all those variations. And then, of course, there may be noise – an unfinished character, joining with another character, some unrelated stuff in the background, an angle at which the character is being read, etc. So, once again, what we need is a basic set of rules that tells the computer what "A," "a," "5," etc., look like, and then have it make a decision based on pattern recognition. The way this happens is by showing several versions of a character to the computer so it *learns* that character, just like a child will do through repetitions, and then have it go through the recognition process (Figure 8.2).

Let us take an example that is perhaps more relevant to everyday life. If you have used any online services, chances are you have come across recommendations. Take, for instance, services such as Amazon and Netflix. How do they know what products to recommend? We understand that they are *monitoring* our activities, that they have our past records, and that is how they are able to give us suggestions. But how exactly? They use something called collaborative filtering (CF). This is a method that uses your past behavior and compares its similarities with the behaviors of other users in that community to figure out what you may like in the future.

Take a look at Table 8.1. Here, there are data about four people's ratings for different movies. And the objective for a system here is to figure out if Person 5 will like a movie or not based on that data as well as her own movie likings from the past. In other words, it is trying to *learn* what kinds of things Person 5 likes (and dislikes), what others similar to Person 5 like, and uses that *knowledge* to make new recommendations. On top of that, as Person 5 accepts or rejects its recommendations, the system extends its learning to include knowledge about how Person 5 responds to its suggestions, and further corrects its models.

Table 8.1 Machine learning-based collaborative filtering for movie recommendation.

		Movie Name				
		Sherlock	Avengers	Titanic	La La Land	Wall-E
Rating	Person 1	4	5	3	4	2
	Person 2	3	2	3	4	4
	Person 3	4	3	4	5	3
	Person 4	3	4	4	5	2
	Person 5	4	?	4	?	4

Here are a couple more examples. Facebook uses machine learning to personalize each member's news feed. Most financial institutions use machine learning algorithms to detect fraud. Intelligence agencies use machine learning to sift through mounds of information to look for credible threats of terrorism.

There are many other applications that we encounter in daily life when machine learning is working one way or another. In fact, it is almost impossible to finish our day without having used something that is driven by machine learning. Did you do any online browsing or searching today? Did you go to a grocery store? Did you use a social media app on your phone? Then you have used machine learning applications.

So, are you convinced that machine learning is a very important field of study? If the answer is "yes" and you are wondering what it takes to create a good machine learning system, then the following list of criteria from SAS[6] may help:

a. Data preparation capabilities.
b. Algorithms – basic and advanced.
c. Automation and iterative processes.
d. Scalability.
e. Ensemble modeling.

In this chapter, we will primarily focus on the second criterion: algorithms. More specifically, we will see some of the most important techniques and algorithms for developing machine learning applications.

We will note here that, in most cases, the application of machine learning is entwined with the application of statistical analysis. Therefore, it is important to remember the differences in the nomenclature of these two fields.

- In machine learning, a target is called a *label*.
- In statistics, a target is called a dependent variable.
- A variable in statistics is called a *feature* in machine learning.
- A transformation in statistics is called *feature creation* in machine learning.

Machine learning algorithms are organized into a taxonomy, based on the desired outcome of the algorithm. Common algorithm types include:

a. Supervised learning. When we know the labels on the training examples we are using to learn.
b. Unsupervised learning. When we do not know the labels (or even the number of labels or classes) from the training examples we are using for learning.
c. Reinforcement learning. When we want to provide feedback to the system based on how it performs with training examples.

Let us go through these systematically in the following sections, working with examples and applying our data science tools and techniques.

FYI: Data Mining

One phrase you often hear with machine learning is data mining. That is because machine learning and data mining overlap quite significantly in many places. Depending on who you talk to, one is seen as a precursor or entry point for the other. In the end, it does not matter as long as we keep our focus on understanding the context and deriving some meaning out of the data.

Data mining is about understanding the nature of the data to gain insight into the problem that generated the dataset in the first place, or some unidentified issues that may arise in the future. Take the case of customers' brand loyalty in the highly competitive e-commerce market. All of the e-commerce platforms store a database of customers' previous purchases and return history along with customer profiles. This kind of dataset not only helps the business owners to understand existing customers' purchasing patterns, such as the products they may be interested in, or to measure brand loyalty, but also provides in-depth knowledge about potential new customers.

In today's highly competitive, customer-centered, service-oriented economy, data is the raw material that fuels business growth – if only it can be mined properly. Data mining is defined as the process of discovering patterns in data. Data mining uses sophisticated mathematical algorithms to segment the data and evaluate the probability of future events. Data mining is also known as Knowledge Discovery in Data (KDD).[7] In fact, there is a KDD community that holds its annual conference with research presentations as well as the well-known KDD Cup Challenge (http://www.kdd.org/kdd-cup).

The key properties of data mining are:

- Automatic discovery of patterns
- Prediction of likely outcomes
- Creation of actionable information
- Focus on large datasets and databases

From these properties, it is evident that machine learning algorithms, which we will discuss starting in this chapter, can be used for data mining. At this point, I must also mention artificial intelligence (AI), the other term often used synonymously with machine learning. Theoretically, AI is much broader than either machine learning or data mining. AI is the study of building intelligent agents that act like humans. However, in practice, it has been limited to programming a system to perform a task *intelligently*. This may involve learning or induction, but it is not a necessary precondition for developing an AI agent. Thus, AI can include any activity that a machine does, so long as it does not do it *stupidly*.

However, it has been our experience that most intelligent tasks require some ability to induce new knowledge from past experience.

This inducing knowledge is achieved through an explicit set of rules or using machine learning that can extract some form of information automatically (i.e., without any constant human moderation). Recently, we have seen machine learning becoming so successful that when we see AI mentioned, it almost invariably refers to some form of machine learning.

In comparison, data mining as a field has taken much of its inspiration and techniques from machine learning and some from statistics, but with a different goal. Data mining can be performed by a human expert on a specific dataset, often with a clear end goal in mind. Typically, the goal is to leverage the power of various algorithms from machine learning and statistics to discover insights to a problem where knowledge is limited. Thus, data mining can use other techniques besides or on top of machine learning.

Let us take an example to disentangle these two closely related concepts. Whenever you go to Yelp, a popular platform for reviewing local businesses, you see a list of recommendations based on your location, past reviews, time, weather, and other factors. Any such review platform employs machine learning algorithms in its back end, where the goal is to provide an effective list of recommendations to cater to the needs of different users. However, at a lower level, the platform is running a set of data mining applications on the huge dataset it has accumulated from your past interaction with the platform and leveraging that to predict what might be of interest to you. So, for a game day, it might recommend a nearby wings and beer place, whereas on a rainy day it might suggest a place where you can get hot soup delivered.

8.3 Regression

Our first stop is regression. Think about it as a much more sophisticated version of extrapolation. For example, if you know the relationship between education and income (the more someone is educated, the more money they make), we could predict someone's income based on their education. Simply speaking, learning such a relationship is regression.

In more technical terms, regression is concerned with modeling the relationship between variables of interest. These relationships use some measures of error in the predictions to refine the models iteratively. In other words, regression is a process.[8]

We can learn about two variables relating in some way (e.g., correlation), but if there is a relationship of some kind, can we figure out if or how one variable could predict the other? Linear regression allows us to do that. Specifically, we want to see how a variable X affects a variable y. Here, X is called the independent variable or predictor; y is called the dependent variable or response. Take a note of the notation here. The X is in uppercase because it could have multiple feature vectors, making it a feature matrix. If we are dealing with only a

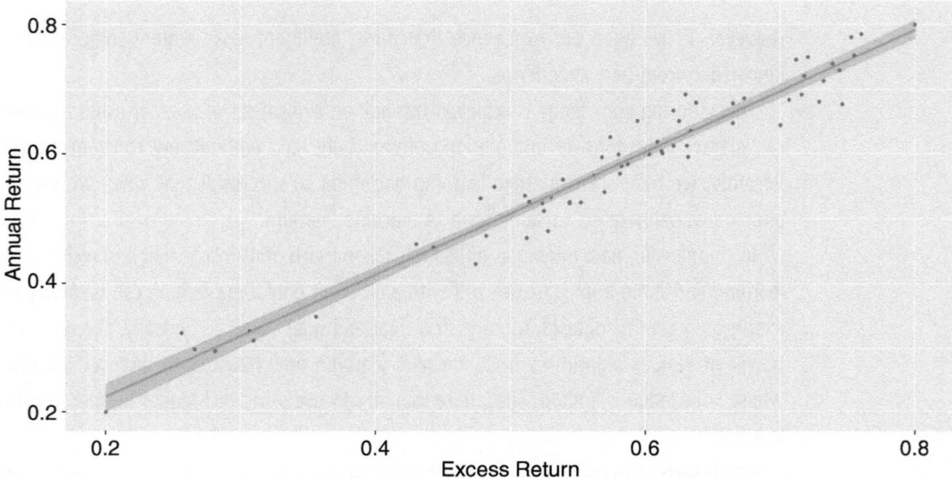

Figure 8.3 An example showing a relationship between annual return and excess return of stock using linear regression from the stock portfolio dataset.[9]

single feature for X, we may decide to use the lowercase x. On the other hand, y is in lowercase because it is a single value or feature being predicted.

As mentioned previously, linear regression fits a line (or plane, or hyperplane) to the dataset. For example, in Figure 8.3, we want to predict the annual return using excess return of stock in a stock portfolio. The line represents the relation between these two variables. Here, it happens to be quite linear (see most of the data points close to the line), but such is not always the case.

Some of the most popular regression algorithms are:

- Ordinary least squares regression (OLSR)
- Linear regression
- Logistic regression
- Stepwise regression
- Multivariate adaptive regression splines (MARS)
- Locally estimated scatterplot smoothing (LOESS)

Since linear regression is covered in an earlier chapter, here we will move to something more general and a lot more useful in machine learning. For this, we need to take a step back and think about how linear regression is solved. Take a look at Figure 8.3. Imagine we only have those dots (data points) and no line. We can draw a random line and see how well it fits the data. For this, we can find the distance of each data point from that line and add it all up. That gives a number, often called cost or error. Now, let us draw another line and repeat the process. We get another number for cost. If this is lower than the previous one, the new line is better. If we keep repeating this until we find a line that gives us the lowest cost or error, we have found our most fitting line, solving the problem of regression.

How about generalizing this process? Imagine we have some function or procedure for finding the cost, given our data, and then the objective is to keep adjusting how the function operates by picking different values for its input or parameters and see if we could lower the cost. Whenever we find the lowest cost, we stop and note the values of the parameters to that function. And those parameter values construe the most fitting model for the data. This model could be a line, a plane, or in general a function. This is the essence of a technique called gradient descent.

Hands-On Example 8.1: Linear Regression

Before we move on to the gradient descent technique, let us see how we could solve linear regression in a way described above. Below, in Table 8.2, is *regression.csv*, a completely made up dataset (you can download it from OA 8.1). The attribute *x* is the input variable and *y* is the output variable that we are trying to predict.

If we get more data (test set), we will only have *x* values and we would be interested in predicting *y* values. To solve the problem of predicting *y* from *x*, we will start with a simple scatterplot of *x* versus *y* as shown in Figure 8.4.

How did we create this plot? Think about your R training. First, we load the data using the following command.

Table 8.2 Data for regression.

x	y
1	3
2	4
3	8
4	4
5	6
6	9
7	8
8	12
9	15
10	26
11	35
12	40
13	45
14	54
15	49
16	59
17	60
18	62
19	63
20	68

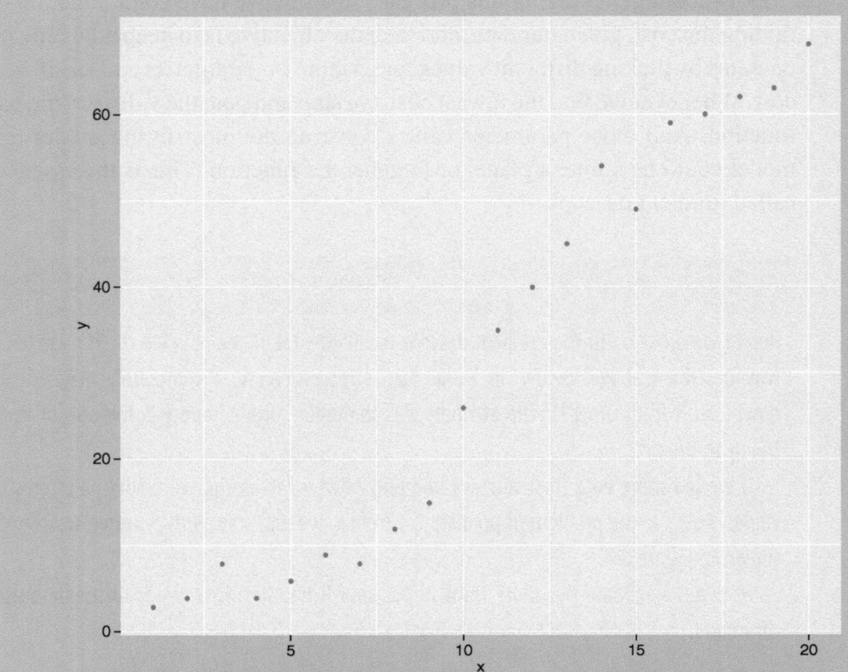

Figure 8.4 Scatterplot of regression.csv data (x vs. y).

```
> regressionData = read.table(file.choose(),
header=TRUE,sep=",")
```

Note that this will open up a dialog box that you can use to navigate to your regression.csv file. After loading it, you can run the following to generate the plot. The first command is for loading the ggplot library, and the second one is for creating a scatterplot.

```
> library(ggplot2)
> ggplot(regressionData, aes(x=x, y=y)) + geom_point()
```

As we can see in Figure 8.4, the data is more or less linear (something that can be represented using a line), going from bottom-left to top-right. So, by using linear regression, we can fit a line to represent the data. Let us assume the equation of the line is

$$y = mx + b$$

where m is the line's slope and b is the line's y-intercept. To solve this using linear regression in R, we can use the "lm" (linear model) function:

```
> lm (y~x, regressionData)
Call:
lm(formula = y ~ x, data = regressionData)
Coefficients:
```

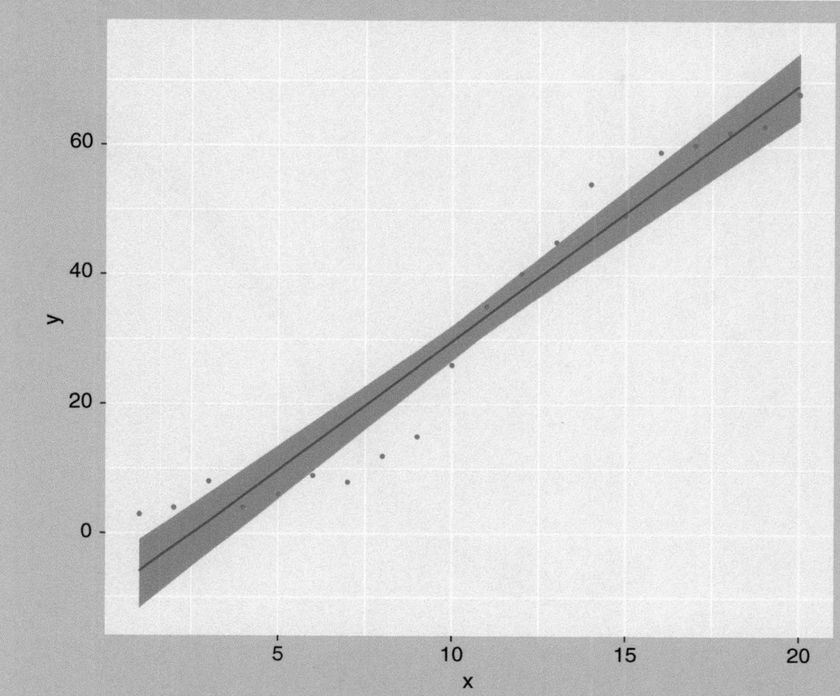

Figure 8.5 Regression line plotted on the scatterplot of x vs. y.

```
(Intercept)      x
    -10.263   3.977
```

What follows the "lm" command is the output, where we can see the values of *b* (intercept) and *m* (coefficient of *x*). Well, that was easy. But how did R come up with this solution? Let us dig deeper. Before we move forward, though, let us see how this model looks. In this case, the model is a line. Let us plot it on our data:

```
> ggplot(regressionData, aes(x=x, y=y)) + geom_point() +
stat_smooth(method="lm")
```

What we see is shown in Figure 8.5.

That blue line is the representation of the line equation we found by doing regression. Keep in mind that we asked for a linear model (thus, "lm" command). In other words, we are doing linear regression. But if we were not so picky about being linear, we could ask for any curve that fits the data best. For this, we could use the following command:

```
> ggplot(regressionData, aes(x=x, y=y)) + geom_point() +
geom_smooth()
```

And that gives us the visualization shown in Figure 8.6.

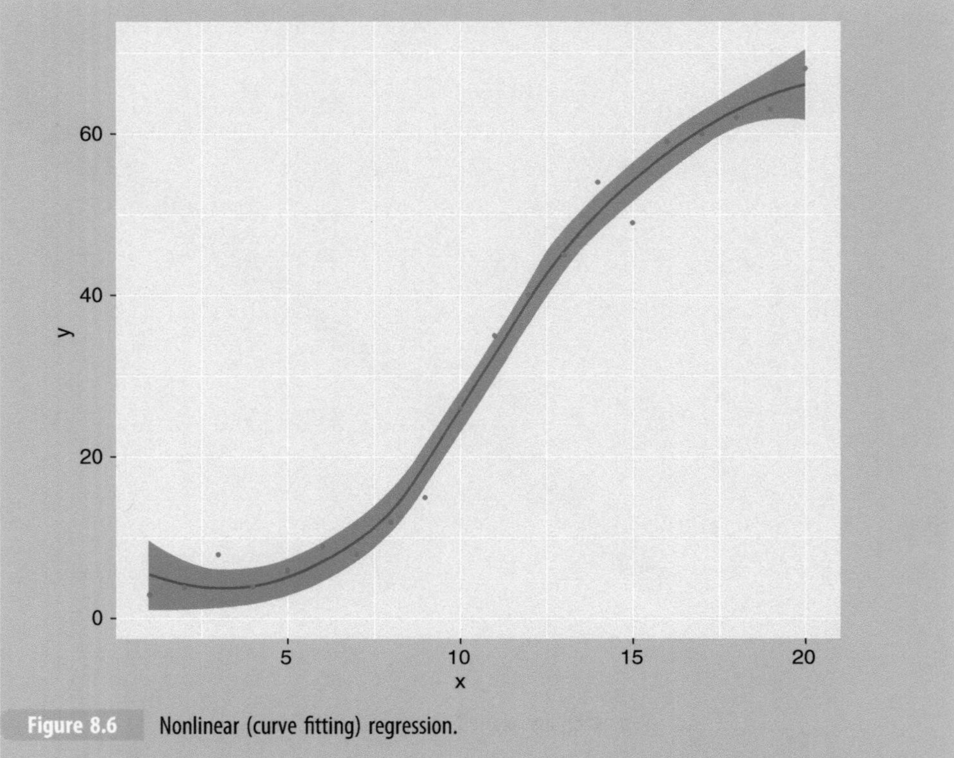

Figure 8.6 Nonlinear (curve fitting) regression.

Obviously, this is a better fit, but it could also be an *overfit*. That means the model has learned the existing data so well that it has very little error in explaining that data, but, on the flip side, it may be difficult for it to adapt to a new kind of data. Do you know what stereotyping is? Well, that is us overfitting the data or observation so far, and while we may have reasons for developing that stereotypical view of a given phenomenon, it prevents us from easily accepting data that do not fit our preconceived notions. Think about it.

8.4 Gradient Descent

Now, let us get back to that line. It is possible to fit multiple lines to the same dataset, each represented by the same equation but with different m and b values. Our job is to find the best one, which will represent the dataset better than the other lines. In other words, we need to find the best set of m and b values.

A standard approach to solving this problem is to define an *error function* (sometimes also known as a *cost function*) that measures how *good* a given line is. This function will take in a (m, b) pair and return an error value based on how well the line fits our data. To compute this error for a given line, we will iterate through each (x, y) point in our dataset and sum the square distances between each point's y value and the candidate line's y value (computed at $mx + b$).

Formally, this error function looks like:

$$\epsilon = \frac{1}{n}\sum_{i=1}^{n}((mx_i + b) - y_i)^2. \tag{8.1}$$

We have squared the distance to ensure that it is positive and to make our error function differentiable. Note that normally we will use m to indicate number of data points, but here we are using that letter to indicate the slope, so we have made an exception and used n. Also note that often the intercept for a line equation is represented using c instead of b, as we have done.

The error function is defined in such a way that the lines that fit our data better will result in lower error values. If we minimize this function, we will get the best line for our data. Since our error function consists of two parameters (m and b), we can visualize it as a 3D surface. Figure 8.7 depicts what it looks like for our dataset.

Each point in this 3D space represents a line. Let that sink in for a bit. Each point in this 3D figure represents a line. Can you see how? We have three dimensions: slope (m), y-intercept (b), and error. Each point has values for these three, and that is what gives us the line (technically, just the m and the b). In other words, this 3D figure presents a whole bunch of possible lines we could have to fit the data shown in Table 8.2, allowing us to see which line is the best.

The height of the function at each point is the error value for that line. You can see that some lines yield smaller error values than others (i.e., fit our data better). The darker blue

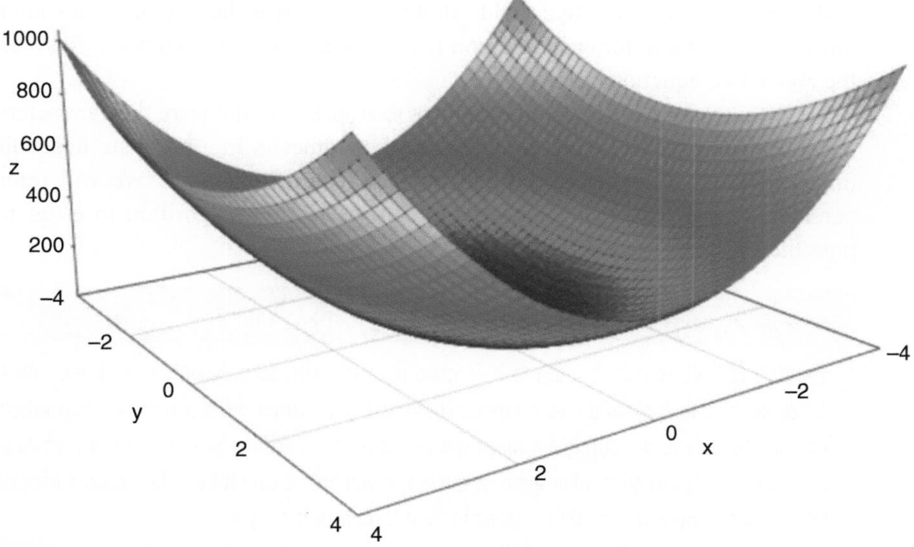

Figure 8.7 Error surface for various lines created using linear regression (x represents slope, y represents intercept and z is the error value).

color indicates the lower the error function value and the better it fits our data. We can find the best m and b set that will minimize the cost function using gradient descent.

Gradient descent is an approach for looking for minima – points where the error is at its lowest. When we run a gradient descent search, we start from some location on this surface and move downhill to find the line with the lowest error.

To run gradient descent on this error function, we first need to compute its gradient or slope. The gradient will act like a compass and always point us downhill. To compute it, we will need to differentiate our error function. Since our function is defined by two parameters (m and b), we will need to compute a partial derivative for each. These derivatives work out to be:

$$\begin{aligned}\frac{\partial \epsilon}{\partial m} &= \frac{2}{n}\sum_{i=1}^{n}((mx_i + b) - y_i)\frac{\partial}{\partial m}((mx_i + b) - y_i)\\ &= \frac{2}{n}\sum_{i=1}^{n}((mx_i + b) - y_i)x_i\end{aligned} \tag{8.2}$$

and

$$\begin{aligned}\frac{\partial \epsilon}{\partial b} &= \frac{2}{n}\sum_{i=1}^{n}((mx_i + b) - y_i)\frac{\partial}{\partial b}((mx_i + b) - y_i)\\ &= \frac{2}{n}\sum_{i=1}^{n}((mx_i + b) - y_i).\end{aligned} \tag{8.3}$$

Now we know how to run gradient descent and get the smallest error. We can initialize our search to start at any pair of m and b values (i.e., any line) and let the gradient descent algorithm march downhill on our error function toward the best line. Each iteration will update m and b to a line that yields slightly lower error than the previous iteration. The direction to move in for each iteration is calculated using the two partial derivatives from the above two equations.

Let us now generalize this. In the above example, m and b were the parameters we were trying to estimate. But there could be many parameters in a problem, depending on the dimensionality of the data or the number of features available. We will refer to these parameters as θ values, and it is the job of the learning algorithm to estimate the best possible values of the θ.

FYI: Math for Data Science and Machine Learning

You do not have to master math to be a good data scientist. Sure, having a good grasp on statistical concepts, probabilities, and linear algebra could take you further down a direction that otherwise you may not be able to go. But, given that there are so many directions one could go in with data science, and that nobody can go to all or many of them, you will not be cut off from data science because of your fear of math; there would still be many more directions left for you.

That being said, I offer you a middle ground: do not worry about doing math derivations yourself, but also do not just ignore them. Walk through them with me (or your instructors, or other sites you may use) – step by step. I have often found students to be concerned about such derivations because they think, since they will not be able to come up with such things on their own, somehow, they would not be so good at doing data science, or, specifically here, machine learning. And I am telling you (and them) that it is a big misunderstanding.

Unless I am teaching machine learning to those who are focused on the algorithms themselves (as opposed to their applications), I present these derivations as a way to convey intuition behind those algorithms. The actual math is not that important; it is simply a way to present an idea in a compact form.

So, there – think of all this math as just a shorthand writing to communicate complex, but still intuitive, ideas. Was there a time in your life when you did not know what "LOL," "ICYMI," and "IMHO" stood for? But now these are standard abbreviations that people use all the time – not intimidating at all. Think about all this math the same way – you do not have to invent it; you just have to accept this special language of abbreviations and understand the underlying concepts, ideas, and intuitions.

Earlier we defined an error function using a model built with two parameters ($mx_i + b$). Now, let us generalize it. Imagine that we have a model that could have any number of parameters. Since this model is built using training examples, we would call it a hypothesis function and represent it using h. It can be defined as

$$h(x) = \sum_{i=0}^{n} \theta_i x_i. \tag{8.4}$$

If we consider $\theta_0 = b$, $\theta_1 = m$, and assign $x_0 = 1$, we can derive our line equation using the above hypothesis function. In other words, a line equation is a special case of this function.

Now, just as we defined the error function using the line equation, we could define a cost function using the above hypothesis function as in the following:

$$J(\theta) = \frac{1}{2m} \sum_{i=1}^{m} (h(x^i) - y^i)^2. \tag{8.5}$$

Compare this to the error function defined earlier. Yes, we are now back to using m to represent number of samples or data points. And we have also added a scaling factor of ½ in the mix, which is purely out of convenience, as you will see soon.

And just as we did before, finding the best values for our parameters means chasing the slope for each of them and trying to reach as low cost as possible. In other words, we are trying to minimize $J(\theta)$ and we will do that by following its slope along each parameter. Let us say we are doing this for parameter θ_j. That means we will take the partial derivative of $J(\theta)$ with respect to θ_j:

$$\begin{aligned}\frac{\partial}{\partial\theta_j}J(\theta) &= \frac{1}{2m}\frac{\partial}{\partial\theta_j}\sum_{i=1}^{m}(h(x^i)-y^i)^2\\ &= \frac{2}{2m}\sum_{i=1}^{m}(h(x^i)-y^i)\frac{\partial}{\partial\theta_j}(h(x^i)-y^i)\\ &= (h(x^i)-y^i)\frac{1}{m}\sum_{i=1}^{m}\frac{\partial}{\partial\theta_j}(\theta_0x_0^i+\theta_1x_1^i+\ldots+\theta_jx_j^i+\ldots+\theta_nx_n^i-y)\\ &= \frac{1}{m}\sum_{i=1}^{m}(h(x^i)-y^i)x_j^i.\end{aligned} \tag{8.6}$$

This gives us our learning algorithm or rule, called gradient descent, as in the following:

$$\theta_j := \theta_j - \alpha\frac{1}{m}\sum_{i=1}^{m}(h(x^i)-y^i)x_j^i. \tag{8.7}$$

This means we update θ_j (override its existing value) by subtracting a weighted slope or gradient from it. In other words, we take a step in the direction of the slope. Here, α is the learning rate, with value between 0 and 1, which controls how large a step we take downhill during each iteration. If we take too large a step, we may step over the minimum. However, if we take small steps, it will require many iterations to arrive at the minimum.

The above algorithm considers all the training examples while calculating the slope, and therefore it is also called batch gradient descent. At times when the sample size is too large and computing the cost function is too expensive, we could take one sample at a time to rule the above algorithm. That method is called stochastic or incremental gradient descent.

Hands-On Example 8.2: Gradient Descent

Now, let us practice gradient descent with R. First, import the regression dataset (see OA 8.1) into a dataframe and build a model:

```
regressionData <- read.csv(file.choose(), header = TRUE,
sep = ",")
```

This is a very simple, very small dataset with only 20 rows and two columns. You can see it in Table 8.2.

What we want to do here is to learn or model the relationship between *x* and *y*. And here is how we can build that model using R:

```
# Build a linear model
model <- lm(y~x, data = regressionData)
summary(model)

# Visualize the model
attach(regressionData)
plot(x, y, col = rgb(0.2,0.4,0.6,0.4), main = "Linear
regression")
abline(model, col = "red")
```

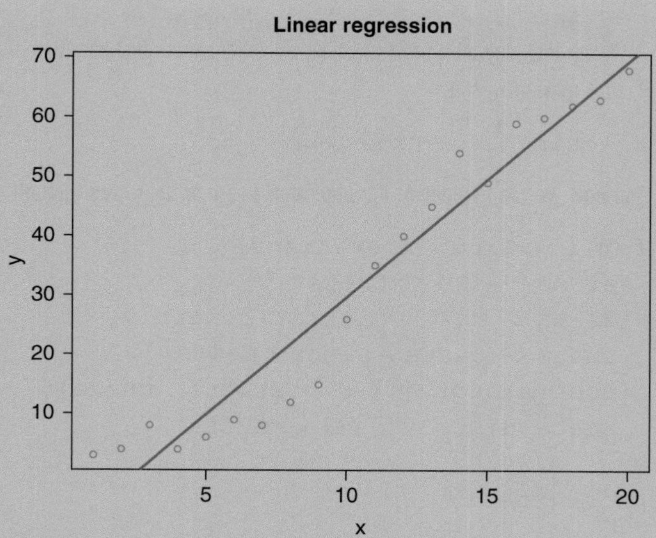

Figure 8.8 Linear regression plot for the data in Table 8.2.

The above lines should generate the output shown in Figure 8.8.

In other words, we got the answer (the red regression line). But let us do this systematically. After all, we are all about learning this process and not just getting the answer. For this, we will implement the gradient descent algorithm using R. Let us first define our cost function.

```
#cost function
cost <- function(X, y, theta){
  sum(X%*% theta - y)^2/(2*length(y))
}
```

We will recall this function later as we go through various possibilities for the parameters. For now, let us go ahead and initialize that parameter vector or matrix with zeros. Here, we have two parameters, m and b, so we need a 2D vector called θ (theta):

```
theta <- matrix(c(0,0), nrow = 2)
num_iterations <- 300
alpha <- 0.01
```

Here, α (alpha) indicates the learning rate, and we have decided to go with a very small value for it. We got all our initial values to start the gradient descent. But before we run the algorithm, let us create storage spaces to store values of cost or error and the parameters at every iteration:

```
cost_history <- double(num_iterations)
theta_history <- list(num_iterations)
```

To use the generalized cost function, we will want our first parameter θ_0 to be without any feature with it, thus making $x_0 = 1$:

```
X<-cbind(1, matrix(x))
```

And now we can implement our algorithm as a loop that goes through a certain number of iterations:

```
for(i in 1:num_iterations){
  error <- (X %*% theta - y)
  delta <- t(X) %*% error/length(y)
  theta <- theta - alpha * delta
  cost_history[i] <- cost(X, y, theta)
  theta_history[[i]] <- theta
}
print(theta)
```

This will print out the final values of the parameters. If you are interested in the values of these parameters as well as the cost that we calculated at every step, you could look into the theta-history and cost-history variables. For now, let us go ahead and visualize how some of those interactions would look:

```
plot(x,y, main = "Gradient descent")
abline(coef = theta_history[[1]])
abline(coef = theta_history[[2]])
abline(coef = theta_history[[3]])
abline(coef = theta_history[[4]])
abline(coef = theta_history[[5]])
```

Figure 8.9 shows how the output looks.

We could put this line drawing part in a loop to see how the whole process evolved with all those iterations (see Figure 8.10):

```
plot(x,y, main = "Gradient descent")
# Draw the first few lines and then draw every 10th line
for(i in c(1,2,3,4,5,seq(6,num_iterations, by = 10))){
  abline(coef = theta_history[[i]], col=rgb(0.8,0,0,0.3))
}
```

We can also visualize how the cost function changes in each iteration by doing the following steps:

```
plot(cost_history, type = 'line', col = 'blue', lwd=2, main =
'Cost function', ylab='cost', xlab = 'Iterations')
```

The output is shown in Figure 8.11.

As we can see, the cost quickly jumps down in just a few iterations, thus giving us a very fast convergence. Of course, that is to be expected because we have only a couple of parameters and a very

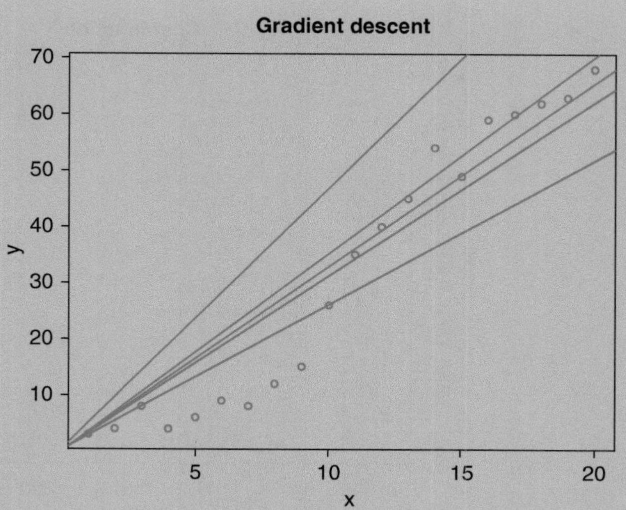

Figure 8.9 Regression lines produced using the gradient descent algorithm.

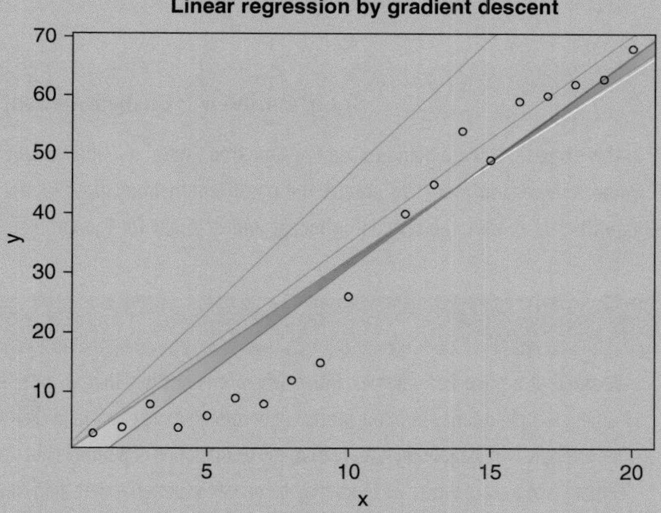

Figure 8.10 Finding the best regression line using gradient descent.

small sample size here. Try practicing this with another dataset (see a homework exercise below). Play around with things like number of iterations and learning rate. If you want to have more fun and try your coding skills, see if you could modify the algorithm to consider the change in the cost function to decide when to stop rather than running it for a fixed number of steps as we did here.

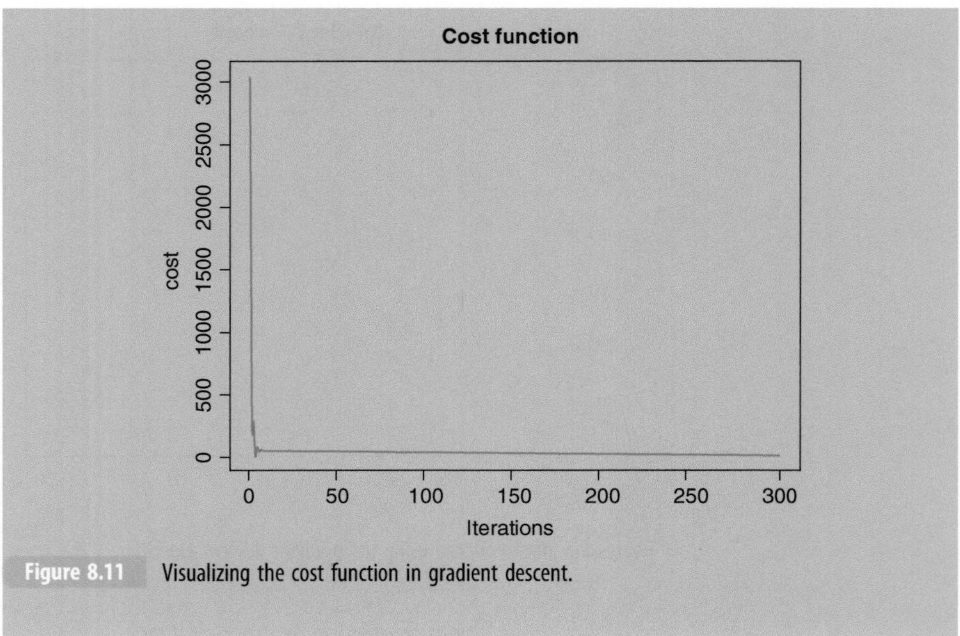

Figure 8.11 Visualizing the cost function in gradient descent.

Try It Yourself 8.1: Gradient Descent

In this exercise, you are going to use the kangaroo's nasal dimension data (download from OA 8.2) to build a linear regression model to predict the nasal length from nasal width. Next, use the gradient descent algorithm to predict the optimal intercept and gradient for this problem.

FYI: Machine Learning Bias, Ethics, and Healthcare

We stand at a point in human evolution where it is possible that in some fields, such as medicine, machine learning techniques may be in the process of becoming more efficient in clinical settings than the human doctor. One example is in diagnosing disease from the examination of a sample obtained from a single patient. Machine learning is at a place where accuracy may be on par or better at detecting cancer than the degreed human. But in a macro sense, the overall healthcare system has a subtle systemic racial bias, so machine learning may not be where it needs to be yet in predicting an overall cancer trend. It would be great if someday IBM's Watson could outsmart human doctors in this realm. A philosophical question is: Is that what we want or need?

You may want to check out the following reading if you are interested in the role of machine learning in health, with implications on ethics.

Char, D. S., Shah, N. H., & Magnus, D. (2018). Implementing machine learning in health care – addressing ethical challenges. *New England Journal of Medicine*, 378(11), March 15.

Summary

In this chapter, we started exploring a host of new tools and techniques collectively parked under the umbrella of machine learning, which we could use to solve various data science problems. While it is easy to understand individual tools and methods, it is not always clear how to pick the best one(s) given a problem. There are multiple factors that need to be considered before choosing the right algorithm for a problem. Some of these factors are discussed below.

Accuracy

Most of the time, beginners in machine learning incorrectly assume that for each problem the best algorithm is the most accurate one. However, getting the most accurate answer possible is not always necessary. Sometimes an approximation is adequate, depending on the problem. If so, you may be able to cut your processing time dramatically by sticking with more approximate methods. Another advantage of more approximate methods is that they naturally tend to avoid overfitting. We will revisit the notion of accuracy and other metrics for measuring how good a model is in Chapter 12.

Training Time

The number of minutes or hours necessary to train a model varies between algorithms. Training time is often closely tied to accuracy – one typically accompanies the other. In addition, some algorithms are more sensitive to the number of data points than others. A limit on time can drive the choice of algorithm, especially when the dataset is large.

Linearity

Lots of machine learning algorithms make use of linearity. Linear classification algorithms assume that classes can be separated by a straight line (or its higher-dimensional analog). These include logistic regression and support vector machines. Linear regression algorithms assume that data trends follow a straight line. These assumptions are not bad for some problems, but on others they bring accuracy down.

Number of Parameters

Parameters are the knobs a data scientist gets to turn when setting up an algorithm. They are numbers that affect the algorithm's behavior, such as error tolerance, number of iterations, or options between variants of how the algorithm behaves. The training time and accuracy of the algorithm can sometimes be quite sensitive to getting just the right settings. Typically, algorithms with a large number of parameters require the most trial and error to find a good combination.

Some off-the-shelf applications or service providers may include extra functionalities for parameter tuning. For example, Microsoft Azure (see Appendix F) provides a parameter sweeping module block that automatically tries all parameter combinations at whatever granularity the user may decide. While this is a great way to make sure you have tried every possible combination in the parameter space, the time required to train a model increases exponentially with number of parameters.

The upside is that having many parameters typically indicates that an algorithm has greater flexibility. It can often achieve high accuracy, provided you find the right combination of parameter settings.

Number of Features

For certain types of data, the number of features can be very large compared to the number of data points. This is often the case with genetics or textual data. The large number of features can bog down some learning algorithms, making training time unfeasibly long. Support vector machines are particularly well suited to this case (see Chapter 9).

Choosing the Right Estimator

Often the hardest part of solving a machine learning problem can be finding the right estimator for the job. Different estimators are better suited for different types of data and different problems. How do we learn about when to use which estimator or technique? There are two primary ways that I can think of: (1) developing a comprehensive theoretical understanding of different ways we could develop estimators or build models; and (2) through lots of hands-on experience. As you may have guessed, in this book, we are going with the latter.

If you are looking for a comprehensive and theoretical treatment of various machine learning algorithms, you will have to use other textbooks and resources. You can find some of those pointers at the end of this chapter. But if you are open to working with different data problems and try different techniques in a hands-on manner in order to develop a practical understanding of this matter, you are holding the right book. In the next two chapters, we will go through many of the machine learning techniques by applying them to various data problems.

Key Terms

- **Machine learning:** This is a field that explores the use of algorithms that can learn from the data and use that knowledge to make predictions on data they have not seen before.
- **Supervised learning:** This is a branch of machine learning that includes problems where a model could be built using the data and true labels or values.
- **Unsupervised learning:** This is a branch of machine learning that includes problems where we do not have true labels for the data to train with. Instead, the goal is to somehow organize the data into some meaningful clusters or densities.

- **Collaborative filtering (CF):** This is a technique for recommender systems that uses data from other people's past behaviors to estimate what to recommend to a given user.
- **Model:** In machine learning a model refers to an artifact that is created by the training process on a dataset that is representative of the population, often called a training set.
- **Linear model:** Linear model describes the relation between a continuous response variable and one or more predictor variable(s).
- **Parameter:** A parameter is any numerical quantity that characterizes a given population or some aspect of it.
- **Feature:** In machine learning, a feature is an individual measurable property or characteristic of a phenomenon or object being observed.
- **Independent /predictor variable:** A variable that is thought to be controlled or not affected by other variables.
- **Dependent /outcome /response variable:** A variable that depends on other variables (most often other independent variables).
- **Gradient descent:** This is a machine learning algorithm that computes a slope down an error surface in order to find a model that provides the best fit for the given data.
- **Batch gradient descent:** This is a gradient descent algorithm that considers all the training examples while calculating the gradient.
- **Stochastic or incremental gradient descent:** This is a gradient descent algorithm that considers one data point at a time while calculating the gradient.

Conceptual Questions

1. There is a lot around us that is driven by some form of machine learning (ML), but not everything is. Give an example of a system or a service that does not use ML, and one that does. Use this contrast to explain ML in your own words.
2. Many of the ML models are represented using parameters. Use this idea to define ML.
3. How do supervised learning and unsupervised learning differ? Give an example for each.
4. Compare batch gradient descent and stochastic gradient descent using their definitions, and pros and cons.

Hands-On Problems

Problem 8.1 (Linear regression)

A popular restaurant review website has released the dataset you can download from OA 8.3. Here each row represents an average rating of a restaurant's different aspects as provided by previous customers. The dataset contains records for the restaurants using the following attributes: ambience, food, service, and overall rating. The first three attributes are predictor variables and the remaining one is the outcome. Use a linear regression model to predict how the predictor attributes impact the overall rating of the restaurant.

First, express the linear regression in mathematical form. Then, try solving it by hand as we did in class. Here, you will have four parameters (the constant, and the three attributes), with one predictor. You do not have to actually solve this with all possible values for these parameters. Rather, show a couple of possible sets of values for the parameters with the predictor value calculated. Finally, use R to find the linear regression model and report it in appropriate terms (do not just dump the output from R).

Problem 8.2 (Linear regression)

For the next exercise, you are going to use the Airline Costs dataset available to download from OA 8.4. The dataset has the following attributes, among others:

i. Airline name
ii. Length of flight in miles
iii. Speed of plane in miles per hour
iv. Daily flight time per plane in hours
v. Customers served in 1000s
vi. Total operating cost in cents per revenue ton-mile
vii. Total assets in $100,000s
viii. Investments and special funds in $100,000s

Use a linear regression model to predict the number of customers each airline serves from its length of flight and daily flight time per plane. Next, build another regression model to predict the total assets of an airline from the customers served by the airline. Do you have any insight about the data from the last two regression models?

Problem 8.3 (Gradient descent)

Download data from OA 8.5, which was obtained from BP Research (image analysis by Ronit Katz, University of Oxford). This dataset contains measurements on 48 rock samples from a petroleum reservoir. Here 12 core samples from petroleum reservoirs were sampled in four cross-sections. Each core sample was measured for permeability, and each cross-section has total area of pores, total perimeter of pores, and shape. As a result, each row in the dataset has the following four columns:

i. Area: area of pore space, in pixels out of 256 by 256
ii. Peri: perimeter in pixels
iii. Shape: perimeter/square-root(area)
iv. Perm: permeability in milli-darcies

First, create a linear model and check if the perm has linear relationship with the remaining three attributes. Next, use the gradient descent algorithm to find the optimal intercept and gradient for the dataset.

Problem 8.4 (Gradient descent)

For this exercise, you are going to work again with a movie review dataset. In this dataset, conventional and social media movies, the ratings, budgets, and other information of popular movies released in 2014 and 2015 were collected from social media websites, such as YouTube, Twitter, and IMDB, etc.; the aggregated dataset can be downloaded from OA 8.6. Use this dataset to complete the following objectives:

a. What can you tell us about the rating of a movie from its budget and aggregated number of followers in social media channels?
b. If you incorporate the type of interaction the movie has received (number of likes, dislikes, and comments) in social media channels, does it improve your prediction?
c. Among all the factors you considered in the last two models, which one is the best predictor of movie rating? With the best predictor feature, use the gradient descent algorithm to find the optimal intercept and gradient for the dataset. Often the hardest part of solving a machine learning problem can be finding the right estimator for the job. Different estimators are better suited for different types of data and different problems.

Further Reading and Resources

If you are interested in learning more about the topics discussed in this chapter, following are a few links that might be useful:

1. http://rstatistics.net/linear-regression-advanced-modelling-algorithm-example-with-r/
2. https://www.analyticsvidhya.com/blog/2017/06/a-comprehensive-guide-for-linear-ridge-and-lasso-regression/
3. https://www.kdnuggets.com/2017/04/simple-understand-gradient-descent-algorithm.html
4. https://machinelearningmastery.com/gradient-descent-for-machine-learning/
5. http://ruder.io/optimizing-gradient-descent/

Notes

1. Samuel, A. L. (1959). Some studies in machine learning using the game of checkers. *IBM Journal of Research and Development*, 44, 206–226.
2. Mitchell, T. M. (1997). *Machine Learning*. WCB/McGraw-Hill, Burr Ridge, IL.
3. Witten, I. H., Frank, E., Hall, M. A., & Pal, C. J. (2016). *Data Mining: Practical Machine Learning Tools and Techniques*. Morgan Kaufmann.
4. The *New Oxford American Dictionary*, defined on Wikipedia: https://en.wikipedia.org/wiki/New_Oxford_American_Dictionary
5. YouTube: Deep Learning: Technology behind self-driving car: https://www.youtube.com/watch?v=kMMbW96nMW8

6. SAS® list of machine learning insights: https://www.sas.com/en_us/insights/analytics/machine-learning.html
7. Knowledge Discovery in Data: https://docs.oracle.com/cd/B28359_01/datamine.111/b28129/process.htm#CHDFGCIJ
8. http://machinelearningmastery.com/a-tour-of-machine-learning-algorithms/
9. Stock portfolio dataset: https://archive.ics.uci.edu/ml/machine-learning-databases/00390/stock%20portfolio%20performance%20data%20set.xlsx

9 Supervised Learning

"Artificial Intelligence, deep learning, machine learning – whatever you're doing if you do not understand it – learn it. Because otherwise you're going to be a dinosaur within 3 years."

— *Mark Cuban*

What do you need?

- A good understanding of statistical concepts, probability theory (see Appendix B), and functions.
- Basics of differential calculus (see Appendix A for a few handy formulas).
- Introductory to intermediate-level experience with R, including installing packages or libraries (refer to Chapter 6).
- Everything covered in Chapter 8.

What will you learn?

- Solving data problems when truth values for training are available.
- Performing classification using various machine learning techniques.

9.1 Introduction

In the previous chapter we were introduced to the concept of learning – both for humans and for machines. In either case, a primary way one learns is first knowing what is a correct outcome or label of a given data point or a behavior. As it happens, there are many situations when we have training examples with correct labels. In other words, we have data for which we know the correct outcome value. This set of data problems collectively fall under supervised learning.

Supervised learning algorithms use a set of examples from previous records to make predictions about the future. For instance, existing car prices can be used to make guesses about the future models. Each example used to train such an algorithm is labeled with the value of interest – in this case, the car's price. A supervised learning algorithm looks for patterns in a training set. It may use any information that might be relevant – the season, the car's current sales records, similar offerings from competitors, the manufacturer's brand perception owned by the consumers – and each algorithm may look for a different set of information and find different types of patterns. Once the algorithm has found the best pattern it can, it uses that pattern to make predictions for unlabeled testing data – tomorrow's values.

There are several types of supervised learning that exist within machine learning. Among them, the three most commonly used algorithm types are regression, classification, and anomaly detection. In this chapter, we will focus on regression and classification. Yes, we covered linear regression in the previous chapter, but that was for predicting a continuous variable such as age and income. When it comes to predicting discrete values, we need to use another form of regression – logistic regression or softmax regression. These are essentially forms of classification. And then we will see several of the most popular and useful techniques for classification. You will also find a quick introduction to anomaly detection in an FYI box later in the chapter.

9.2 Logistic Regression

One thing you should have noticed by now about linear regression is that the outcome variable is numerical. So, the question is: What happens when the outcome variable is not numerical? For example, if you have a weather dataset with the attributes humidity, temperature, and wind speed, each is describing one aspect of the weather for a day. And based on these attributes, you want to predict if the weather for the day is suitable for playing golf. In this case, the outcome variable that you want to predict is categorical ("yes" or "no"). Fortunately, to deal with this kind of classification problem, we have logistic regression.

Let us think of this in a formal way. Before, our outcome variable y was continuous. Now, it can have only two possible values (labels). For simplicity, let us call these labels "1" and "0" ("yes" and "no"). In other words,

$$y \in \{0, 1\}.$$

We are still going to have continuous value(s) for the input, but now we need to have only two possible values for the output. How do we do this? There is an amazing function called sigmoid, which is defined as

$$g(z) = \frac{1}{1 + e^{-z}} \tag{9.1}$$

and it looks like Figure 9.1.

As you can see in Figure 9.1, for any input, the output of this function is bound between 0 and 1. In other words, if used as the hypothesis function, we get the output in 0 to 1 range, with 0 and 1 included:

$$h_\theta(x) \in \lfloor 0, 1 \rfloor. \tag{9.2}$$

The nice thing about this is that it follows the constraints of a probability distribution that it should be contained between 0 and 1. And if we could compute a probability that ranges

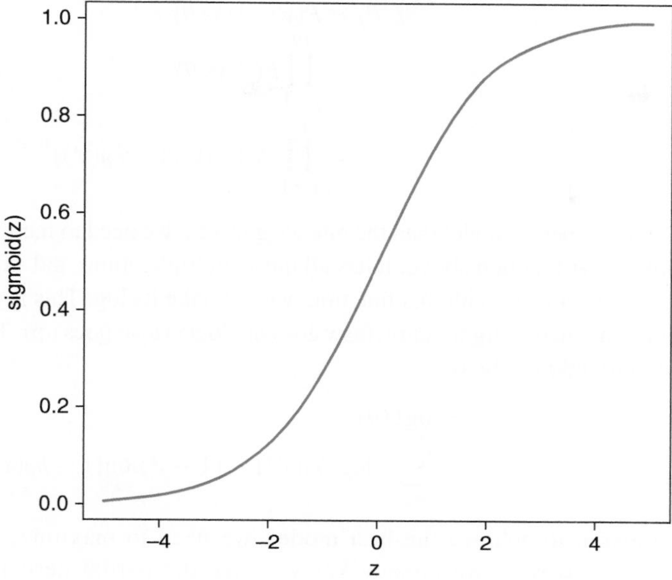

Figure 9.1 Sigmoid function.

from 0 to 1, it would be easy to draw a threshold at 0.5 and say that any time we get an outcome value from a hypothesis function h greater than that, we put it in class "1," otherwise it goes in class "0." Formally:

$$\begin{aligned} P(y = 1|x; \theta) &= h_\theta(x), \\ P(y = 0|x; \theta) &= 1 - h_\theta(x), \\ P(y|x; \theta) &= (h_\theta(x))^y(1 - h_\theta(x))^{1-y}. \end{aligned} \tag{9.3}$$

The last formulation is the result of combining the first two lines to form one expression. See if that makes sense. Try putting $y = 1$ and $y = 0$ in that expression and see if you get the previous two lines.

Now, how do we use this for classification? In essence, we want to input whatever features from the data we have into the hypothesis function (here, a sigmoid) and find out the value that comes out between 0 and 1. Based on which side of 0.5 it is, we can declare an appropriate label or class. But before we can do that (called testing), we need to train a model. For this we need some data. One way we could build a model from such data is to assume a model and ask if that model could explain or classify the training data and how well. In other words, we are asking how *good* our model is, given the data.

To understand the *goodness* of a model (as represented by the parameter vector θ), we can ask how likely it is that the data we have is generated by the given model. This is called the **likelihood** of the model and is represented as $L(\theta)$. Let us expand this likelihood function:

$$\begin{aligned} L(\theta) &= P(y = 1|X; \theta) \\ &= \prod_{i=1}^{m} P(y^i|x^i; \theta) \\ &= \prod_{i=1}^{m} (h_\theta(x^i))^{y^i}(1 - h_\theta(x^i))^{1-y^i}. \end{aligned} \tag{9.4}$$

To achieve a better model than the one we guessed, we need to increase the value of $L(\theta)$. But, look at that function above. It has all those multiplications and exponents. So, to make it easier for us to work with this function, we will take its log. This is using the property of log that it is an increasing function (as x goes up, $\log(x)$ also goes up). This will give us a log likelihood function as below:

$$\begin{aligned} l(\theta) &= \log L(\theta) \\ &= \sum_{i=1}^{m} [y^i \log(h_\theta(x^i)) + (1 - y^i)\log(1 - h_\theta(x^i))]. \end{aligned} \tag{9.5}$$

Once again, to achieve the best model, we need to maximize this log likelihood. For that, we do what we already know – take the partial derivative, one parameter at a time. In fact, for simplicity, we will even consider just one sample data at a time:

$$\begin{aligned} \frac{\partial}{\partial \theta_j} l(\theta) &= \left(y \frac{1}{h_\theta(x)} - (1 - y) \frac{1}{1 - h_\theta(X)} \right) \frac{\partial}{\partial \theta_j} h_\theta(x) \\ &= [y(1 - h_\theta(x)) - (1 - y) h_\theta(x)] x_j \\ &= (y - h_\theta(x)) x_j. \end{aligned} \tag{9.6}$$

The second line above follows the fact that, for a sigmoid function $g(z)$, the derivative can be expressed as: $g'(z) = g(z)(1 - g(z))$.

Considering all training samples, we get:

$$\frac{\partial}{\partial \theta_j} l(\theta) = \sum_{i=1}^{m} (y^i - h_\theta(x^i)) x_j^i. \tag{9.7}$$

This gives us our learning algorithm:

$$\theta_j = \theta_j + \alpha \sum_{i=1}^{m} (y^i - h_\theta(x^i)) x_j^i. \tag{9.8}$$

Notice how we are updating the θ this time. We are moving up on the gradient instead of moving down. And that is why this is called gradient ascent. It does look similar to gradient descent, but the difference is the nature of the hypothesis function. Before, it was a linear function. Now it is sigmoid or logit function. And because of that, this regression is called **logistic regression**.

Hands-On Example 9.1: Logistic Regression

Let us practice logistic regression with an example. We are going to use the *Titanic dataset*, different versions of which are freely available online; however, I suggest using the one from OA 9.1, since it is almost ready to be used and requires minimum pre-processing. In this exercise, we are trying to predict the survival chances of the passengers on the *Titanic*.

After obtaining the datasets, first import the training dataset into a dataframe in R:

```
> titanic.data <- read.csv("train.csv", header = TRUE,
sep = ",")
> View(titanic.data)
```

Figure 9.2 shows a snapshot from RStudio with a sample of the data.

Before we go ahead and build the model, we need to check for missing values and find how many unique values there are for each variable using the sapply() function, which applies the function passed as argument to each column of the dataframe. Here is how to do it:

```
> sapply(titanic.data,function(x) sum(is.na(x)))
PassengerId Survived Pclass Name        Sex   Age  SibSp
          0        0      0    0          0   177      0
      Parch   Ticket   Fare Cabin   Embarked
          0        0      0     0          0

> sapply(titanic.data,function(x)length(unique(x)))
PassengerId Survived Pclass  Name       Sex   Age  SibSp
        891        2      3   891         2    89      7
      Parch   Ticket   Fare Cabin  Embarked
          7      681    248   148         4
```

Another way to estimate the missing values is to use a visualization package: the "Amelia" package has a plotting function missmap() that serves the purpose. It will plot your dataset and highlight missing values:

```
> library(Amelia)
Loading required package: Rcpp
##
## Amelia II: Multiple Imputation
## (Version 1.7.4, built: 2015-12-05)
## Copyright (C) 2005-2017 James Honaker, Gary King and
Matthew Blackwell
## Refer to http://gking.harvard.edu/amelia/for more
information
##
  >missmap(titanic.data, main = "Missing values vs observed")
```

	PassengerId	Survived	Pclass	Name	Sex	Age	SibSp	Parch	Ticket	Fare	Cabin	Embarked
1	1	0	3	Braund, Mr. Owen Harris	male	22.00	1	0	A/5 21171	7.2500		S
2	2	1	1	Cumings, Mrs. John Bradley (Florence Briggs Thayer)	female	38.00	1	0	PC 17599	71.2833	C85	C
3	3	1	3	Heikkinen, Miss. Laina	female	26.00	0	0	STON/o2. 3101282	7.9250		S
4	4	1	1	Futrelle, Mrs. Jacques Heath (Lily May Peel)	female	35.00	1	0	113803	53.1000	C123	S
5	5	0	3	Allen, Mr. William Henry	male	35.00	0	0	373450	8.0500		S
6	6	0	3	Moran, Mr. James	male	*NA*	0	0	330877	8.4583		Q
7	7	0	1	McCarthy, Mr. Timothy J	male	54.00	0	0	17463	51.8625	E46	S
8	8	0	3	Palsson, Master. Gosta Leonard	male	2.00	3	1	349909	21.0750		S
9	9	1	3	Johnson, Mrs. Oscar W (Elisabeth Vilhelmina Berg)	female	27.00	0	2	347742	11.1333		S
10	10	1	2	Nasser, Mrs. Nicholas (Adele Achem)	female	14.00	1	0	237736	30.0708		C
11	11	1	3	Sandstrom, Miss. Marguerite Rut	female	4.00	1	1	PP 9549	16.7000	G6	S
12	12	1	1	Bonnell, Miss. Elizabeth	female	58.00	0	0	113783	26.5500	C103	S
13	13	0	3	Saundercock, Mr. William Henry	male	20.00	0	0	A/5. 2151	8.0500		S
14	14	0	3	Andersson, Mr. Anders Johan	male	39.00	1	5	347082	31.2750		S
15	15	0	3	Vestrom, Miss. Hulda Amanda Adolfina	female	14.00	0	0	350406	7.8542		S

Figure 9.2 Sample of the *Titanic* data.

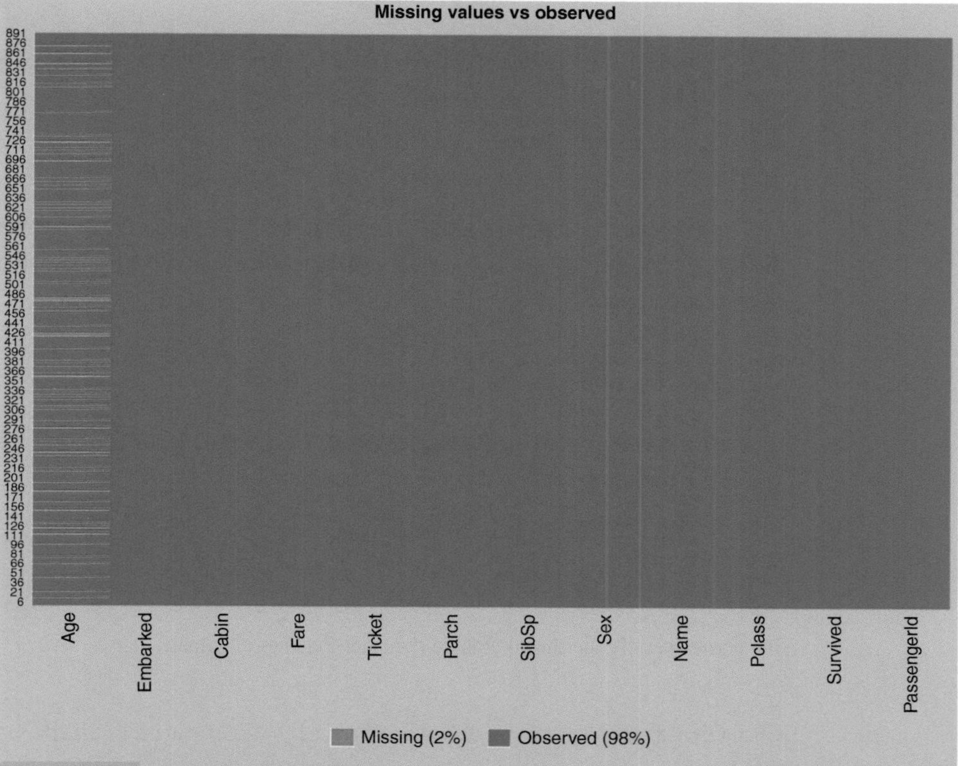

Figure 9.3 Visualizing missing values.

As Figure 9.3 suggests, the Age column has multiple missing values. So, we must clean up the missing values before proceeding further. In Chapter 2, we saw multiple methods for doing such data cleanup. In this case, we will go with replacing those missing values with the mean age value. This is how to do that:

```
> titanic.data$Age[is.na(titanic.data$Age)] <- mean
(titanic.data$Age,na.rm=T)
```

Here we have replaced the missing values with the mean age of the rest of the population. If any column has a significant number of missing values, you may want to consider removing the column altogether. For the purpose of this exercise, we will use only the Age, Embarked, Fare, Ticket, Parch, SibSp, Sex, Pclass, and Survived columns to simplify our model:

```
> titanic.data <- subset(titanic.data,select=c
(2,3,5,6,7,8,10,12))
```

For the categorical variables in the dataset, using the read.table() or read.csv() by default will encode the categorical variables as factors. A factor is how R deals with categorical variables.

We can check the encoding using the is.factor() function, which should return "true" for all the categorical variables:

```
> is.factor(titanic.data$Sex)
[1] TRUE
```

Now, before building the model you need to separate the dataset into training and test sets. I have used the first 800 instances for training and the remaining 91 as test instances. You can opt for different separation strategies:

```
> train <- titanic.data[1:800,]
> test <- titanic.data[801:891,]
```

Now our dataset is ready for building the model. We are going to use parameter `family=binomial` (two classes or labels) in the glm() function:

```
> model <- glm(Survived ~.,family=binomial(link='logit'),
data=train)
> summary(model)
```

The above lines of code should produce the following lines of output:

```
Call:
glm(formula = Survived ~ ., family = binomial(link = "logit"),
   data = train)
Deviance Residuals:
   Min       1Q   Median      3Q      Max
-2.6059  -0.5933  -0.4250  0.6215  2.4148
Coefficients:
             Estimate  Std. Error  z value    Pr(>|z|)
(Intercept) 15.947761  535.411378    0.030   0.9762
Pclass      -1.087576    0.151088   -7.198   6.10e-13***
Sexmale     -2.754348    0.212018  -12.991     <2e-16***
Age         -0.037244    0.008192   -4.547   5.45e-06***
SibSp       -0.293478    0.114660   -2.560   0.0105*
Parch       -0.116828    0.128113   -0.912   0.3618
Fare         0.001515    0.002352    0.644   0.5196
EmbarkedC  -10.810682  535.411254   -0.020   0.9839
EmbarkedQ  -10.812679  535.411320   -0.020   0.9839
EmbarkedS  -11.126837  535.411235   -0.021   0.9834
---
Signif. codes: ***, 0; **,0.001; *, 0.01.

Dispersion parameter for binomial family taken to be 1
  Null deviance: 1066.33 on 799 degrees of freedom.
Residual deviance: 708.93 on 790 degrees of freedom.
```

```
AIC: 728.93.
Number of Fisher scoring iterations: 12.
```

From the result, it is clear that Fare and Embarked are not statistically significant. That means we do not have enough confidence that these factors contribute all that much to the overall model. As for the statistically significant variables, Sex has the lowest *p*-value, suggesting a strong association of the sex of the passenger with the probability of having survived. The negative coefficient for this predictor suggests that, all other variables being equal, the male passenger is less likely to have survived. At this time, we should pause and think about this insight. As *Titanic* started sinking and the lifeboats were being filled with rescued passengers, priority was given to women and children. And thus, it makes sense that a male passenger, especially a male adult, would have had less chance of survival.

Now, we will see how good our model is in predicting values for test instances. By setting the parameter `type='response'`, R will output probabilities in the form of $P(y = 1 \mid X)$. Our decision boundary will be 0.5. If $P(y = 1 \mid X) > 0.5$ then $y = 1$, otherwise $y = 0$.

```
> fitted.results <-
predict(model,newdata=subset(test,select=c
(2,3,4,5,6,7,8)), type='response')
> fitted.results <- ifelse(fitted.results > 0.5,1,0)
>
> misClasificError <- mean(fitted.results != test$Survived)
> print(paste('Accuracy',1-misClasificError))
[1] "Accuracy 0.842696629213483"
```

As we can see from the above result, the accuracy of our model in predicting the labels of the test instances is at 0.84, which suggests that the model performed decently.

At the final step, we are going to plot the receiver operating curve (ROC) and calculate the area under curve (AUC), which are typical performance measurements for a binary classifier (see Figure 9.4). For the details of these measures, refer to Chapter 12.

```
> library(ROCR)
Loading required package: gplots
Attaching package: 'gplots'
The following object is masked from 'package:stats': lowess
> p <- predict(model, newdata=subset(test,select=c
(2,3,4,5,6,7,8)), type="response")
> pr <- prediction(p, test$Survived)
> prf <- performance(pr, measure = "tpr", x.measure = "fpr")
> plot(prf)
> auc <- performance(pr, measure = "auc")
```

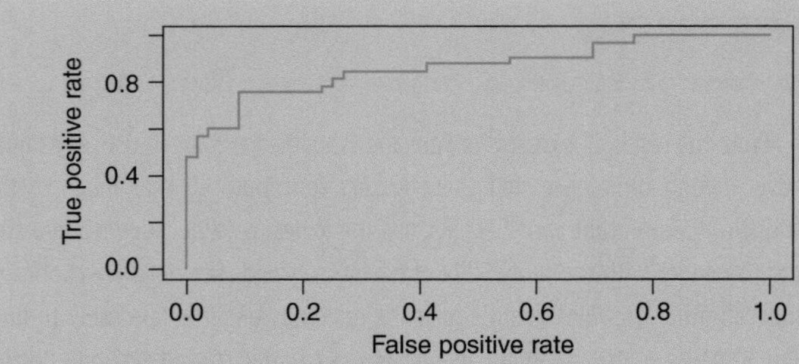

Figure 9.4 Receiver operating curve (ROC) for the classifier built on *Titanic* data.

```
> auc <- auc@y.values[[1]] > auc
[1] 0.866342
```

The ROC curve is generated by plotting the **true positive rate** (TPR) against the **false positive rate** (FPR) at various threshold settings, while the AUC is the area under the ROC curve. TPR indicates how much of what we detected as "1" was indeed "1," and FPR indicates how much of what we detected as "1" was actually "0." Typically, as one goes up, the other goes up too. Think about it – if you declare everything "1," you will have a high TPR, but you would have also wrongly labeled everything that was supposed to be "0," leading to high FPR.

As a rule of thumb, a model with good predictive ability should have an AUC closer to 1 than to 0.5. In Figure 9.4, we can see that the area under the curve is quite large – covering about 87% of the rectangle. That is quite a good number, indicating a good and balanced classifier.

Try It Yourself 9.1: Logistic Regression

First, obtain the social media ads data from OA 9.2. Using this data, build a logistic regression-based classifier to determine if the social media user's demographics can be used to predict the user buying the product being advertised. Report your model's classification accuracy as well as ROC value.

9.3 Softmax Regression

So far, we have seen regression for numerical outcome variable as well as regression for binomial ("yes" or "no", "1" or "0") categorical outcome. But what happens if we have more than two categories. For example, you want to rate a student's performance based on the numbers he got in individual subjects as "excellent," "good," "average," or "below average." We need to have multinomial logistic regression for this. In this sense multinomial logistic regression or softmax regression is a generalization of regular logistic regression to handle multiple (more than two) classes.

In softmax regression, we replace the sigmoid function from the logistic regression by the so-called softmax function. This function takes a vector of n real numbers as input and normalizes the vector into a distribution of n probabilities. That is, the function transforms all the n components from any real values (positive or negative) to values in the interval (0, 1). How it does that is a discussion beyond this book; however, if you are interested, you can check the further reading and resources at the end of this chapter.

Hands-On Example 9.2: Softmax Regression

We will see softmax regression through an example in R. In this example, we will use the "hsbdemo" dataset available from OA 9.3. The dataset is about entering high-school students who make program choices among general programs, vocational programs, and academic programs. Their choices might be modeled using their writing scores and their social economic status. The dataset contains attribute values on 200 students. The outcome variable is "prog," which is the program type chosen by the student. The predictor variables are social economic status, "ses," a three-level categorical variable, and writing score, "write," a continuous variable.

Let us start with getting some descriptive statistics of the variables of interest.

```
> hsbdemo <- read.csv("hsbdemo.csv", header = TRUE, sep = ",")
> View(hsbdemo)
> with(hsbdemo, table(ses, prog))
        prog
ses    academic general vocation
 high        42       9        7
 low         19      16       12
 middle      44      20       31
> with(hsbdemo, do.call(rbind, tapply(write, prog, function
(x) c(M = mean(x), SD = sd(x)))))
                  M       SD
academic  56.257147.943343
general   51.333339.397775
vocation  46.760009.318754
```

There are multiple ways and packages available in R capable of performing multinomial logistic regression. For example, you can use the mlogit package to do multinomial logistic regression. However, for this example, if we want to use the mlogit package, we must reshape the dataset first. A possible work-around of this pre-processing step is to use the multinom function from the nnet package to estimate a multinomial logistic regression model, which does not require any reshaping of the data.

Before running the multinomial regression, we need to remember our outcome variable is not ordinal (e.g., "good," "better," and "best"). So, to create our model, we need to choose the level of the outcome that we wish to use as the baseline and specify this in the relevel function. Here is how to do that:

```
> hsbdemo$prog2 <- relevel(hsbdemo$prog, ref = "academic")
```

Here, instead of transforming the original variable "prog," we have declared another variable "prog2" using the relevel function, where the level "academic" is declared as baseline:

```
> library(nnet)
> model1 <- multinom(prog2 ~ ses + write, data = hsbdemo)
# weights: 15 (8 variable)
initial value 219.722458
iter 10 value 179.983731
final value 179.981726
Converged
```

Ignore all the warning messages. As we can see, we have built a model where the outcome variable is "prog2." For demonstration purposes, we used only "ses" and "write" as our predictors and ignored the remaining variables. As we can see, the model has generated some output itself even though we are assigning the model to a new R object. This model-running output includes some iteration history and includes the final negative log-likelihood value, 179.981726.

Next, to explore more details about the model we have built so far, we can issue a summary command on our model:

```
> summary(model1)
Call:
multinom(formula = prog2 ~ ses + write, data = hsbdemo)
Coefficients:
         (Intercept)    seslow  sesmiddle       write
general     1.689478 1.1628411  0.6295638 -0.05793086
vocation    4.235574 0.9827182  1.2740985 -0.11360389
Std. Errors:
         (Intercept)     seslow  sesmiddle       write
general     1.226939  0.5142211  0.4650289  0.02141101
vocation    1.204690  0.5955688  0.5111119  0.02222000

Residual Deviance: 359.9635
AIC: 375.9635
```

The output summary generated by the model has a block of coefficients and a block of standard errors. Each of these blocks has one row of values corresponding to a model equation. We are going to focus on the block of coefficients first. As we can see, the first row is comparing `prog=general` to our baseline `prog=academic`. Similarly, the second row represents a comparison between `prog=vocation` and the baseline.

Let us declare the coefficients from the first row to be "b_1" (b_{10} for the intercept, b_{11} for "seslow," b_{12} for "sesmiddle," and b_{13} for "write") and our coefficients from the second row to be "b_2" (b_{20} for the intercept, b_{21} for "seslow," b_{22} for "sesmiddle," and b_{23} for "write"). Using these, we can compute something called log odds, which compares a given model to the baseline and informs us how a one-unit change in an independent variable would change a dependent variable in the model compared to how it would change the same variable for the baseline. These model equations as can be written as follows:

$$\ln\left(\frac{P(\text{prog2} = \text{general})}{P(\text{prog2} = \text{academic})}\right) = b_{10} + b_{11}(\text{ses} = 2) + b_{12}(\text{ses} = 3) + b_{13}(\text{write}) \tag{9.9}$$

and

$$\ln\left(\frac{P(\text{prog2} = \text{vocation})}{P(\text{prog2} = \text{academic})}\right) = b_{20} + b_{21}(\text{ses} = 2) + b_{22}(\text{ses} = 3) + b_{23}(\text{write}). \tag{9.10}$$

Using these equations, we can find out that a one-unit increase in the variable "write" is associated with the decrease in the log odds of being in "general" program vs. "academic" program in the amount of 0.058. You can derive similar insights using the results from the summary of our model.

You will often come across a term – **relative risk** – in this kind of analysis, which is the ratio of the probability of choosing any outcome category ("vocation", "general") other than baseline over that of the baseline category. To find relative risk, we can exponentiate the coefficients from our model:

```
> exp(coef(model1))
         (Intercept)     seslow sesmiddle     write
general    5.416653  3.199009  1.876792 0.9437152
vocation  69.101326  2.671709  3.575477 0.8926115
```

As we can see, the relative risk ratio for a one-unit increase in the variable write is 0.9437 for being in "general" program vs. "academic" program.

You have seen before the need to have some test instances to examine the accuracy of your model. We saw how we could divide the entire dataset into training and test instances in cases where we do not have any pre-supplied test instances. I am not going to repeat the same here; instead, I will leave it to you to process the data and analyze the accuracy of the model.

Try It Yourself 9.2: Softmax Regression

Download the Car evaluation dataset from OA 9.4. Then, build a softmax regression model to classify the car acceptability class from other attributes of the class.

9.4 Classification with kNN

Sections 9.1 and 9.2 covered two forms of regression that accomplished one task: classification. We will continue with this now and look at other techniques for performing classification. The task of classification is: given a set of data points and their corresponding labels, to learn how they are classified so, when a new data point comes, we can put it in the correct class.

Classification can be supervised or unsupervised. The former is the case when assigning a label to a picture as, for example, either "cat" or "dog." Here the number of possible choices is predetermined. When there are only two choices, it is called two-class or binomial classification. When there are more categories, such as when predicting the winner of the NCAA March Madness tournament, it is known as multiclass or multinomial classification. There are many methods and algorithms for building classifiers, with *k* nearest neighbor (kNN) being one of the most popular ones.

Let us look at how kNN works by listing the major steps of the algorithm.

1. As in the general problem of classification, we have a set of data points for which we know the correct class labels.
2. When we get a new data point, we compare it to each of our existing data points and find similarity.
3. Take the most similar *k* data points *(k* nearest neighbors).
4. From these *k* data points, take the majority vote of their labels. The winning label is the label/class of the new data point.

The number *k* is usually small between 2 and 20. As you can imagine, the more the number of nearest neighbors (value of *k*), the longer it takes us to do the processing.

Hands-On Example 9.3: kNN

Let us take an example and try to visualize how to do the classification with kNN in R. For this example, we will use the "Iris" dataset. A brief description as well as the dataset itself are available from OA 9.5.

The dataset includes a sample of 50 flowers from three species of iris (*Iris setosa*, *Iris virginica* and *Iris versicolor*). Each sample was measured for four features: the length and the width of the sepals and petals, in centimeters. Based on the combination of these four attributes, we need to distinguish the species of iris.

The Iris dataset is built into R, so we can take a look at this dataset by typing "iris" into your R (or RStudio) console.

Before we proceed into classification, let us look into the distribution of values in the dataset. For this visualization, we will use the package *ggvis* in R. Here is how:

```
# Load the library "ggvis"
library(ggvis)
```

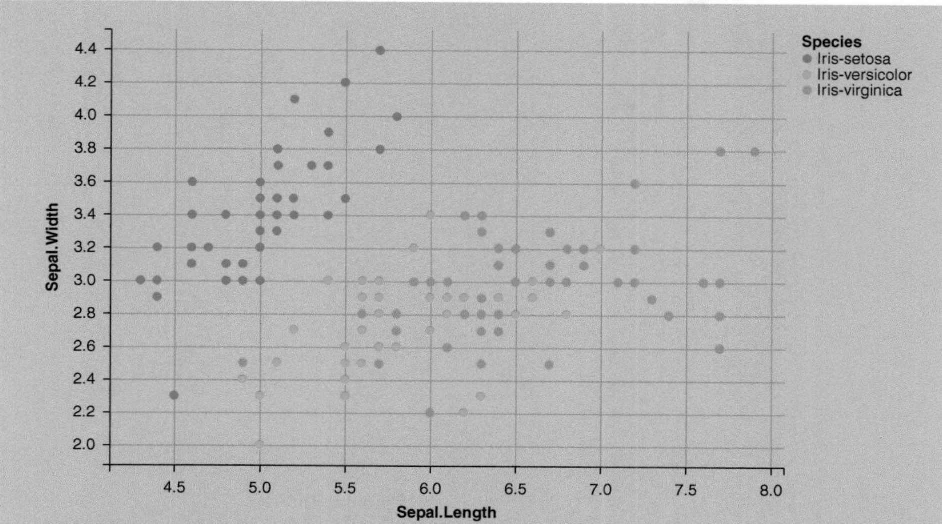

Figure 9.5 Plotting of IRIS data based on various flowers' sepal lengths and widths.

```
# Iris scatterplot
iris %>% ggvis(~Sepal.Length, ~Sepal.Width, fill = ~Species)
```

From Figure 9.5, we can see that there is a high correlation between the sepal length and the sepal width of the *Iris setosa* flowers, whereas the correlation is somewhat less for the *I. virginica* and *I. versicolor* flowers.

If we map the relation between petal length and the petal width, it tells a similar story, as shown in Figure 9.6.

```
iris %>% ggvis(~Petal.Length, ~Petal.Width, fill = ~Species)
```

The graph indicates a positive correlation between the *petal length* and the *petal width* for all different species that are included in the Iris dataset.

Once we have at least some idea of the nature of the dataset, we will see how to do kNN classification in R.

But before we proceed into the classification task, we need to have a test set to assess the model's performance later. Since we do not have that yet, we will need to divide the dataset into two parts: a training set and a test set. We will split the entire dataset into two-thirds and one-third. The first part, the larger chunk of the dataset, will be reserved for training, whereas the rest of the dataset is going to be used for testing. We can split them any way we want, but we need to remember that the training set must be sufficiently large to produce a good model. Also, we must make sure that all three classes of species are present in the training model. Even more important, the amounts of instances of all three species needs to be more or less equal, so that you do not favor one or the other class in your predictions.

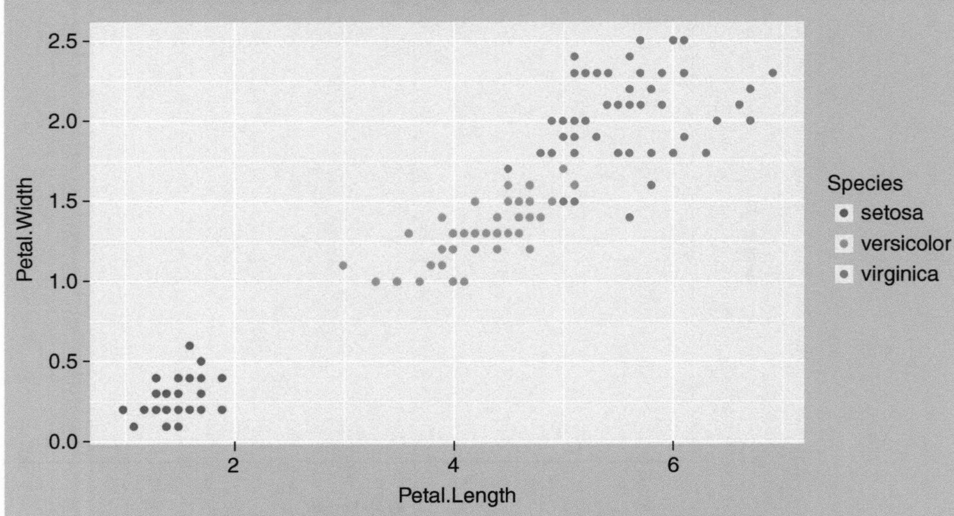

Figure 9.6 Plotting of Iris data based on various flowers' petal lengths and widths.

To divide the dataset into training and test sets, we should first set a seed. This is a number of R's random number generator. The major advantage of setting a seed is that we can get the same sequence of random numbers whenever you supply the same seed in the random number generator. Here is how to do that:

```
set.seed(1234)
```

You can pick any number other than 1234 in the above line. Next, we want to make sure that our Iris dataset is shuffled and that we have an equal amount of each species in our training and test sets. One way to ensure that is to use the *sample()* function to take a sample with a size that is set as the number of rows of the Iris dataset (here, 150). We sample with replacement: we choose from a vector of two elements and assign either "1" or "2" to the 150 rows of the Iris dataset. The assignment of the elements is subject to probability weights of 0.67 and 0.33. This results in getting about two-thirds of the data labeled as "1" (training) and the rest as "2" (testing).

```
ind <- sample(2, nrow(iris), replace=TRUE, prob=c
(0.67, 0.33))
```

We can then use the sample that is stored in the variable "ind" to define our training and test sets, only taking the first four columns or attributes from the data.

```
iris.training <- iris[ind==1, 1:4]
iris.test <- iris[ind==2, 1:4]
```

Also, we need to remember that "Species," which is the class label, is our target variable, and the remaining attributes are predictor attributes. Therefore, we need to store the class label in factor vectors and divide them over the training and test sets, which can be done by following steps:

```
iris.trainLabels <- iris[ind==1,5]
iris.testLabels <- iris[ind==2,5]
```

It is alright if you do not understand the above steps, as those have nothing to do with kNN, but are to do with how to prepare the dataset into training and test sets. What is more important is coming next.

Once all these preparatory steps are complete, we are ready to use the kNN in our training dataset. To do that, we need to use the knn() function as available in R. The knn() function uses the Euclidean distance to find the similarities between the *k*-training instances and your test instance. The value of *k* has to be supplied by the user, which is you in this case.

We can build the kNN-based model by executing the following steps:

```
library(class)
iris_pred <- knn(train = iris.training, test = iris.test, cl =
iris.trainLabels, k=3)
```

At this point, entering "iris_pred" prints the entire vector of our predictions. Or, we can ask for a summary by issuing "summary(iris_pred)" and get the following output:

```
setosa  versicolor  virginica
    12          13         15
```

Since we have built a model and predicted the class labels for our test attributes, let us evaluate how accurate those predictions are. For this, we will use cross-tabulation. A function for this can be found in the "gmodels" library. If you do not already have it installed, go ahead and install that package, and then run the following:

```
library(gmodels)
CrossTable(x=iris_pred, y=iris.testLabels, prop.chisq =
FALSE)
```

This gives us the cross-tabulation table as shown below. From this table, we can see how our predictions (iris_pred) matched up with the truth (iris.testLabels). There seems to be only one case when we were wrong – predicting "versicolor" for something that was "virginica." That is not bad at all.

```
Cell Contents
|-------------------|
|                  N|
|       N/Row Total|
|       N/Col Total|
|     N/Table Total|
|-------------------|

Total Observations in Table: 40
```

```
            |iris.testLabels
  iris_pred|     setosa| versicolor| virginica| Row Total|
-----------|-----------|-----------|----------|----------|
     setosa|         12|          0|         0|        12|
           |      1.000|      0.000|     0.000|     0.300|
           |      1.000|      0.000|     0.000|          |
           |      0.300|      0.000|     0.000|          |
-----------|-----------|-----------|----------|----------|
 versicolor|          0|         12|         1|        13|
           |      0.000|      0.923|     0.077|     0.325|
           |      0.000|      1.000|     0.062|          |
           |      0.000|      0.300|     0.025|          |
-----------|-----------|-----------|----------|----------|
  virginica|          0|          0|        15|        15|
           |      0.000|      0.000|     1.000|     0.375|
           |      0.000|      0.000|     0.938|          |
           |      0.000|      0.000|     0.375|          |
-----------|-----------|-----------|----------|----------|
Column Total|        12|         12|        16|        40|
           |      0.300|      0.300|     0.400|          |
-----------|-----------|-----------|----------|----------|
```

Using this table, you can easily calculate our accuracy. Out of 40 predictions, we were wrong one time. So that gives us 39/40 = 97.5% accuracy.

Try It Yourself 9.3: kNN

Obtain the "hsbdemo" dataset from OA 9.3. Create a kNN-based classifier from the reading, writing, mathematics, and science scores of the high-school students. Evaluate the classifier's accuracy in predicting which academic program the student will be joining.

9.5 Decision Tree

In machine learning, a decision tree is used for classification problems. In such problems, the goal is to create a model that predicts the value of a target variable based on several input variables. A decision tree builds classification or regression models in the form of a tree structure. It breaks down a dataset into smaller and smaller subsets while at the same time an associated

Table 9.1 Balloons dataset.

Color	Size	Act	Age	Inflated
Yellow	Small	Stretch	Adult	T
Yellow	Small	Stretch	Adult	T
Yellow	Small	Stretch	Child	F
Yellow	Small	Dip	Adult	F
Yellow	Small	Dip	Child	F
Yellow	Large	Stretch	Adult	T
Yellow	Large	Stretch	Adult	T
Yellow	Large	Stretch	Child	F
Yellow	Large	Dip	Adult	F
Yellow	Large	Dip	Child	F
Purple	Small	Stretch	Adult	T
Purple	Small	Stretch	Adult	T
Purple	Small	Stretch	Child	F
Purple	Small	Dip	Adult	F
Purple	Small	Dip	Child	F
Purple	Large	Stretch	Adult	T
Purple	Large	Stretch	Adult	T
Purple	Large	Stretch	Child	F
Purple	Large	Dip	Adult	F
Purple	Large	Dip	Child	F

decision tree is incrementally developed. The final result is a tree with decision nodes and leaf nodes.

Consider the balloons dataset (download from OA 9.6) presented in Table 9.1. The dataset has four attributes: color, size, act, and age, and one class label, inflated (T = true or F = false). We will use this dataset to understand how a decision tree algorithm works.

Several algorithms exist that generate decision trees, such as ID3/4/5, CART, CLS, etc. Of these, the most popular one is ID3, developed by J. R. Quinlan, which uses a top-down, greedy search through the space of possible branches with no backtracking. ID3 employs *Entropy* and *Information Gain* to construct a decision tree. Before we go through the algorithm, let us understand these two terms.

Entropy: Entropy (E) is a measure of disorder, uncertainty, or randomness. If I toss a fair coin, there is an equal chance of getting a head as well as a tail. In other words, we would be most uncertain about the outcome, or we would have a high entropy. The formula of this measurement is:

$$\text{Entropy}(E) = -\sum_{i=1}^{k} p_i \log_2(p_i). \tag{9.11}$$

Here, k is the number of possible class values, and p_i is the number of occurrences of the class i=1 in the dataset. So, in the "balloons" dataset the number of possible class values is 2

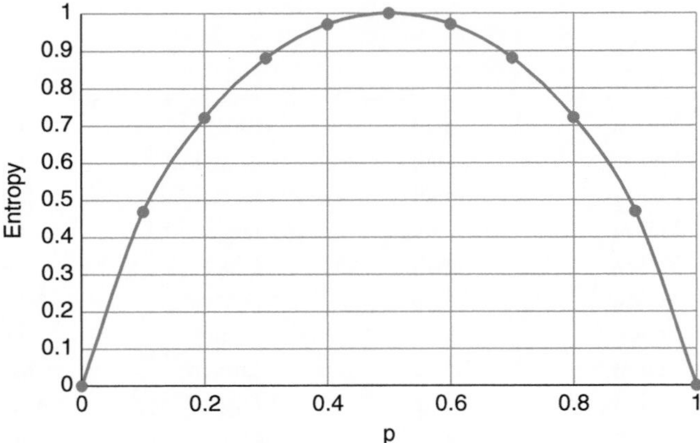

Figure 9.7 Depiction of entropy.

(T or F). The reason for the minus signs is that the logarithms of fractions $p_1, p_2, \ldots, p_n$ are negative, so the entropy is actually positive. Usually the logarithms are expressed in base 2, and then the entropy is in units called bits – just the usual kind of bits used with computers.

Figure 9.7 shows the entropy curve with respect to probability values for an event. As you can see, it is at its highest (1) when the probability of a two-outcome event is 0.5. If we are holding a fair coin, the probability of getting a head or a tail is 0.5. Entropy for this coin is the highest at this point, which reflects the highest amount of uncertainty we will have with this coin's outcome. If, on the other hand, our coin is completely unfair and flips to "heads" every time, the probability of a getting heads with this coin will be 1 and the corresponding entropy will be 0, indicating that there is no uncertainty about the outcome of this event.

Information Gain: If you thought it was not going to rain today and I tell you it will indeed rain, would you not say that you gained some information? On the other hand, if you already knew it was going to rain, then my prediction will not really impact your existing knowledge much. There is a mathematical way to measure such **information gain**:

$$\mathrm{IG}(A, B) = \mathrm{Entropy}(A) - \mathrm{Entropy}(A, B). \tag{9.12}$$

Here, information gain achieved by knowing B along with A is the difference between the entropy (uncertainty) of A and both A and B. Keep this in the back of your mind and we will revisit it as we work through an example next.

But first, let us get back to that decision tree algorithm. A decision tree is a hierarchical, top-down tree, built from a root node to leaves, and involves partitioning the data into smaller subsets that contain instances with similar values (homogeneous). The ID3 algorithm uses entropy to calculate the homogeneity of a sample. If the sample is completely homogeneous, the entropy is zero, and if the sample is equally divided, it has entropy of one. In other words, entropy is a measurement of disorder in the data.

Now, to build the decision tree, we need to calculate two types of entropy using frequency tables, as follows:

a. Entropy using the frequency table of one attribute:

Inflated	
True	False
8	12

Therefore,

$$
\begin{aligned}
E(\text{Inflated}) &= E(12, 8) \\
&= E(0.6, 0.4) \\
&= -(0.6\log_2 0.6) - (0.4\log_2 0.4) \\
&= 0.4422 + 0.5288 \\
&= 0.9710.
\end{aligned}
$$

b. Similarly, entropy using the frequency table of two attributes:

$$E(A, B) = \sum_{k \in B} P(k)E(k). \tag{9.13}$$

Following is the explanation. Let us take a look at Table 9.2.
Therefore,

$$
\begin{aligned}
E(\text{Inflated}, \text{Act}) &= P(\text{Dip}) \times E(8, 0) + P(\text{Stretch}) \times E(4, 8) \\
&= \left(\frac{8}{20}\right) \times 0.0 + \left(\frac{12}{20}\right) \times \{-(0.3\log_2 0.3) - (0.7\log_2 0.7)\} \\
&= \left(\frac{12}{20}\right) \times (0.5278 + 0.3813) \\
&= \left(\frac{12}{20}\right) \times 0.9090 \\
&= 0.5454.
\end{aligned}
$$

As the above value suggests, there is a reduction of entropy from the first case. This decrease of entropy is called information gain. Here, information gain (IG) is:

$$
\begin{aligned}
\text{IG} &= \text{E(Inflated)} - \text{E(Inflated, Act)} \\
&= 0.9710 - 0.5454 \\
&= 0.4256.
\end{aligned}
$$

Table 9.2 Frequency table of act and inflated.

		Inflated		
		True	False	
Act	Dip	0	8	8
	Stretch	8	4	12
Total				20

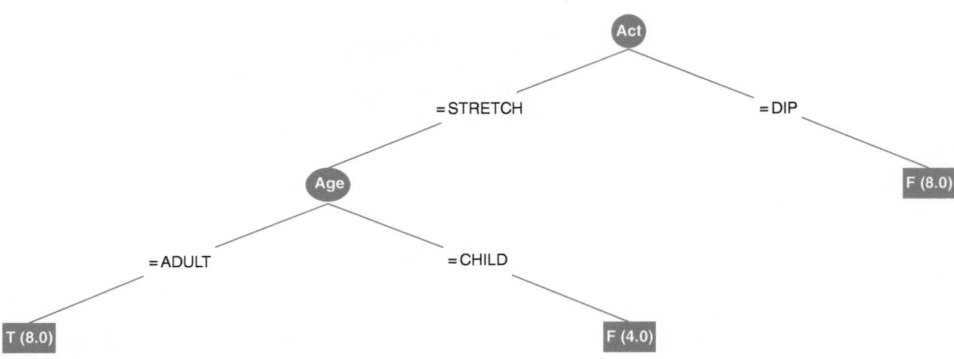

Figure 9.8 Final decision tree for the "balloons" dataset.

If entropy is disorder, then information gain is a measurement of reduction in that disorder achieved by partitioning the original dataset. Constructing a decision tree is all about finding an attribute that returns the highest information gain (i.e., the most homogeneous branches). Following are the steps to create a decision tree based on *entropy* and *information gain:*

Step 1: Calculate entropy of the target or class variable, which is 0.9710, in our case.

Step 2: The dataset is then split on the different attributes into smaller subtables, for example, Inflated and Act, Inflated and Age, Inflated and Size, and Inflated and Color. The entropy for each subtable is calculated. Then it is added proportionally, to get total entropy for the split. The resulting entropy is subtracted from the entropy before the split. The result is the information gain or decrease in entropy.

Step 3: Choose the attribute with the largest information gain as the decision node, divide the dataset by its branches, and repeat the same process on every branch.

If you follow the above guidelines step-by-step, you should end up with the decision tree shown in Figure 9.8.

9.5.1 Decision Rule

Rules are a popular alternative to decision trees. Rules typically take the form of an {IF: THEN} expression (e.g., {IF "condition" THEN "result"}). Typically for any dataset, an individual rule in itself is not a model, as this rule can be applied when the associated condition is satisfied. Therefore, rule-based machine learning methods typically identify a set of rules that collectively comprise the prediction model, or the knowledge base.

To fit any dataset, a set of rules can easily be derived from a decision tree by following the paths from the root node to the leaf nodes, one at a time. For the above decision tree in Figure 9.8, the corresponding decision rules are shown on the left-hand side of Figure 9.9.

Decision rules yield orthogonal hyperplanes in n-dimensional space. What that means is that, for each of the decision rules, we are looking at a line or a plane perpendicular to the axis for the corresponding dimension. This hyperplane (fancy word for a line or a plane in higher dimension) separates data points around that dimension. You can think about it as a

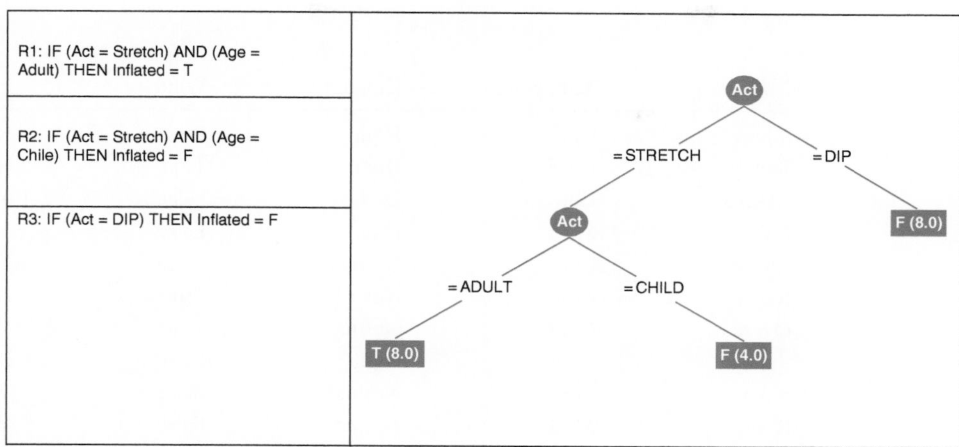

Figure 9.9 Deriving decision rules using a decision tree.

decision boundary. Anything on one side of it belongs to one class, and those data points on the other side belong to another class.

9.5.2 Classification Rule

It is easy to read a set of classification rules directly off a decision tree. One rule is generated for each leaf. The antecedent of the rule includes a condition for every node on the path from the root to that leaf, and the consequent of the rule is the class assigned by the leaf. This procedure produces rules that are unambiguous in that the order in which they are executed is irrelevant. However, in general, rules that are read directly off a decision tree are far more complex than necessary, and rules derived from trees are usually pruned to remove redundant tests. Because decision trees cannot easily express the disjunction implied among the different rules in a set, transforming a general set of rules into a tree is not quite so straightforward. A good illustration of this occurs when the rules have the same structure but different attributes, such as:

If a and b then x
If c and d then x

Then it is necessary to break the symmetry and choose a single test for the root node. If, for example, "if a" is chosen, the second rule must, in effect, be repeated twice in the tree. This is known as the replicated subtree problem.

9.5.3 Association Rule

Association rules are no different from classification rules except that they can predict any attribute, not just the class, and this gives them the freedom to predict combinations of attributes, too. Also, association rules are not intended to be used together as a set, as classification rules are. Different association rules express different regularities that underlie the dataset, and they generally predict different things.

Table 9.3 Weather data.				
Outlook	Temperature	Humidity	Windy	Play
Sunny	Hot	High	False	No
Sunny	Hot	High	True	No
Overcast	Hot	High	False	Yes
Rainy	Mild	High	False	Yes
Rainy	Cool	Normal	False	Yes
Rainy	Cool	Normal	True	No
Overcast	Cool	Normal	True	Yes
Sunny	Mild	High	False	No
Sunny	Cool	Normal	False	Yes
Rainy	Mild	Normal	False	Yes
Sunny	Mild	Normal	True	Yes
Overcast	Mild	High	True	Yes
Overcast	Hot	Normal	False	Yes
Rainy	Mild	High	True	No

Because so many different association rules can be derived from even a very small dataset, interest is restricted to those that apply to a reasonably large number of instances and have a reasonably high accuracy on the instances to which they apply. The coverage of an association rule is the number of instances for which it predicts correctly; this is often called its support. Its accuracy – often called confidence – is the number of instances that it predicts correctly, expressed as a proportion of all instances to which it applies.

For example, consider the weather data in Table 9.3, a training dataset of weather and corresponding target variable "Play" (suggesting possibilities of playing). The decision tree and the derived decision rules for this dataset are given in Figure 9.10.

Let us consider this rule:

If *temperature* = *cool* then *humidity* = *normal*.

The coverage is the number of days that are both cool and have normal humidity (four in the data of Table 9.3), and the accuracy is the proportion of cool days that have normal humidity (100% in this case). Some other good quality association rules for Figure 9.10 are:

If *humidity* = *normal* and *windy* = *false* then *play* = *yes*.
If *outlook* = *sunny* and *play* = *no* then *windy* = *true*.
If *windy* = *false* and *play* = *no* then *outlook* = *sunny* and *humidity* = *high*.

See if these rules make sense by going through the tree in Figure 9.10 as well as logically questioning them (e.g., if it is sunny but very windy outside, will we play?). Also try deriving some new rules.

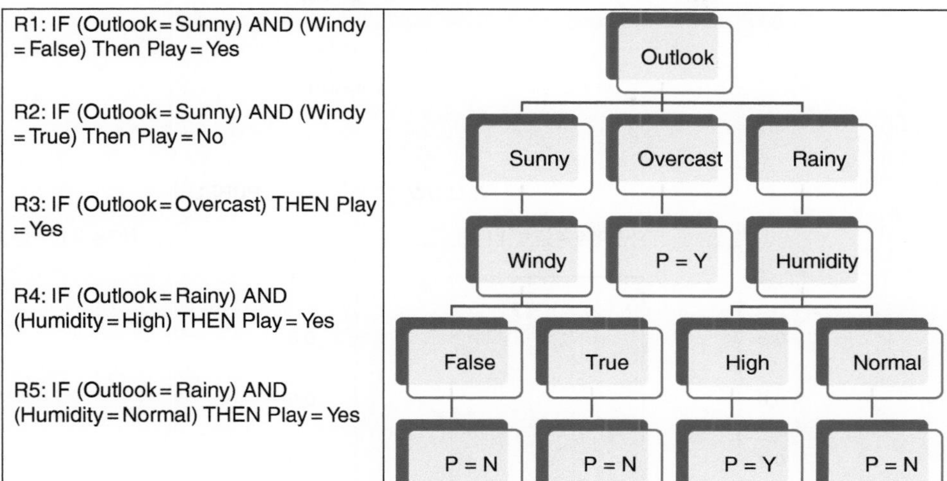
R1: IF (Outlook = Sunny) AND (Windy = False) Then Play = Yes
R2: IF (Outlook = Sunny) AND (Windy = True) Then Play = No
R3: IF (Outlook = Overcast) THEN Play = Yes
R4: IF (Outlook = Rainy) AND (Humidity = High) THEN Play = Yes
R5: IF (Outlook = Rainy) AND (Humidity = Normal) THEN Play = Yes
Outlook
Sunny
Overcast
Rainy
Windy
P = Y
Humidity
False
True
High
Normal
P = N
P = N
P = Y
P = N

Figure 9.10 Decision rules (left) and decision tree (right) for the weather data.

Hands-On Example 9.4: Decision Tree

Let us see how a decision tree-based classifier can be implemented with R. For this demonstration we are going to use the other balloons dataset that you can download from OA 9.7. This is from the repository that we have used in the example earlier (see Table 9.1).

The first step is to import the data into RStudio. It is always recommended that, before performing any operation, the data types of all the attributes are checked first (one shown here).

```
> balloon <- read.csv("yellow-small.csv", sep = ',',
header = TRUE)
> View(balloon)
> is.factor(balloon$Size)
```

We are going to use the "party" package here. You have to install this package before you proceed to the next step.

```
> install.packages("party")
> library(party)
```

In the next step we are going to create the decision tree:

```
> View(balloon)
> inflated.Tree<- ctree(Inflated~., data = balloon)
```

To plot the tree, execute the following line:

```
> plot(inflated.Tree)
```

If you have correctly followed the steps, you should see a tree like the one in Figure 9.11. From the tree, it can be concluded that color is a good predictor if the balloon is inflated or not.

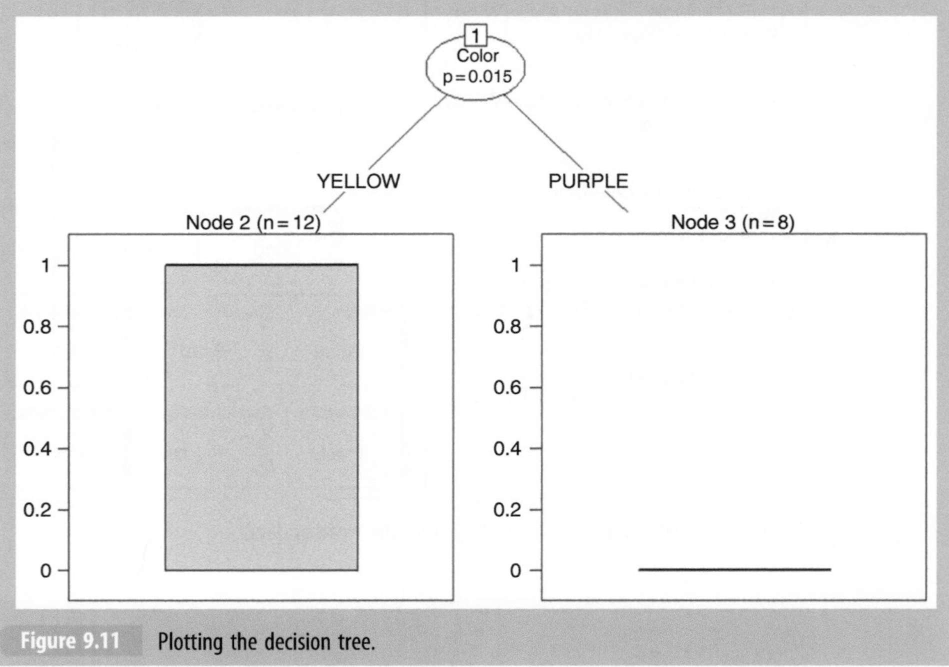

Figure 9.11 Plotting the decision tree.

Try It Yourself 9.4: Decision Tree

Let us test your understanding of a decision tree algorithm with all categorical variables. The dataset you are going to use is about contact lenses (download from OA 9.8), which has three class labels:

1. The patient should be prescribed hard contact lenses.
2. The patient should be prescribed soft contact lenses.
3. The patient should not be fitted with contact lenses.

Build a decision tree-based classifier that would recommend the class label based on the other attributes from the dataset.

9.6 Random Forest

A decision tree seems like a nice method for doing classification – it typically has a good accuracy, and, more importantly, it provides human-understandable insights. But one big problem the decision tree algorithm has is that it could overfit the data. What does that mean? It means it could try to model the given data so well that, while the classification accuracy on that dataset would be wonderful, the model may find itself crippled when looking at any new data; it learned *too much* from the data!

One way to address this problem is to use not just one, not just two, but many decision trees, each one created slightly differently. And then take some kind of average from what these trees decide and predict. Such an approach is so useful and desirable in many situations where there is a whole set of algorithms that apply them. They are called **ensemble methods**.

In machine learning, ensemble methods rely on multiple learning algorithms to obtain better prediction accuracy than what any of the constituent learning algorithms can achieve. In general, an ensemble algorithm consists of a concrete and finite set of alternative models but incorporates a much more flexible structure among those alternatives. One example of an ensemble method is random forest, which can be used for both regression and classification tasks.

Random forest operates by constructing a multitude of decision trees at training time and selecting the mode of the class as the final class label for classification or mean prediction of the individual trees when used for regression tasks. The advantage of using random forest over decision tree is that the former tries to correct the decision tree's habit of overfitting the data to their training set. Here is how it works.

For a training set of N, each decision tree is created in the following manner:

1. A sample of the N training cases is taken at random but with replacement from the original training set. This sample will be used as a training set to grow the tree.
2. If the dataset has M input variables, a number m (m being a lot smaller than M) is specified such that, at each node, m variables are selected at random out of M. Among this m, the best split is used to split the node. The value of m is held constant while we grow the forest.
3. Following the above steps, each tree is grown to its largest possible extent and there is no pruning.
4. Predict new data by aggregating the predictions of the n trees (i.e., majority votes for classification, average for regression).

Let us say a training dataset, N, has four observations on three predictor variables, namely A, B, and C. The training data is provided in Table 9.4.

We will now work through the random forest algorithm on this small dataset.

Step 1: Sample the N training cases at random. So these subsets of N, for example, n_1, n_2, n_3, . . ., n_n (as depicted in Figure 9.12) are used for growing (training) the n number of decision trees. These samples are drawn as randomly as possible, with or without

Table 9.4 Training dataset.

	Independent variables		
	A	B	C
Training instances	A_1	B_1	C_1
	A_2	B_2	C_2
	A_3	B_3	C_3
	A_4	B_4	C_4

Table 9.5 Selection of attributes for the tree.

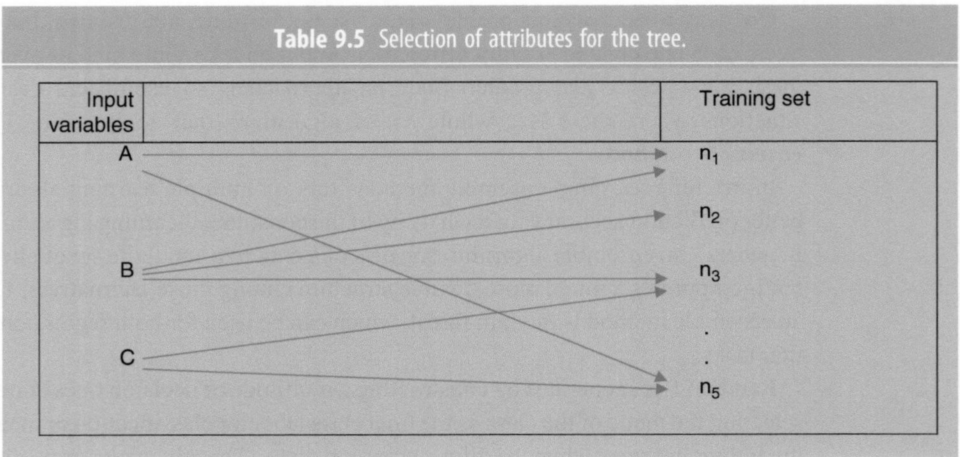

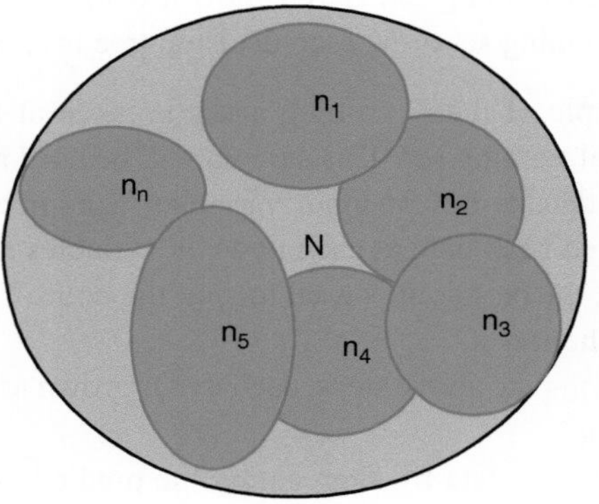

Figure 9.12 Sampling the training set.

overlap between them. For example, n_1 may consist of the training instances 1, 1, 1, and 4. Similarly, n_2 may consist of 2, 3, 3, and 4, and so on.

Step 2: Out of the three predictor variables, a number $m \ll 3$ is specified such that, at each node, m variables are selected at random out of the M. Let us say here m is 2. So, n_1 can be trained on A, B; n_2 can be trained on B, C; and so on (see Table 9.5).

So, the resultant decision trees may look something like what is shown in Figure 9.13.

Random forest uses a bootstrap sampling technique, which involves sampling of the input data with replacement. Before using the algorithm, a portion of the data (typically one-third) that is not used for training is set aside for testing. These are sometimes known as out-of-bag samples. An error estimation on this sample, known as out-of-bag error, provides evidence that the out-of-bag estimate can be as accurate as having a test set of equal size as the training set. Thus, use of an out-of-bag error estimate removes the need for a set-aside test set here.

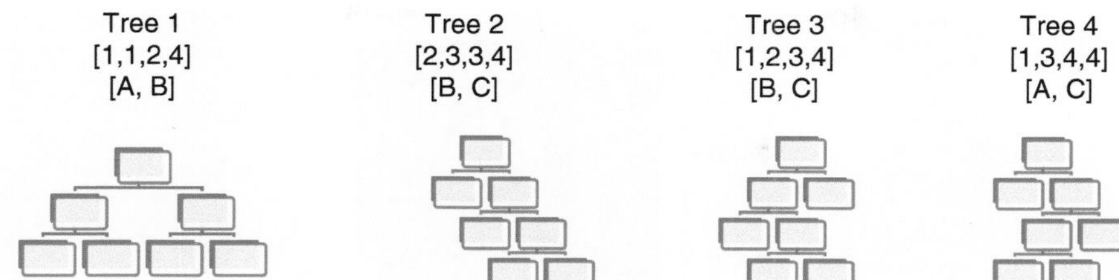

Figure 9.13 Various decision trees for the random forest data.

So, the big question is why does the random forest as a whole do a better job than the individual decision trees? Although there is no clear consensus among researchers, there are two major beliefs behind this:

1. As the saying goes, "Nobody knows everything, but everybody knows something." When it comes to a forest of trees, not all of them are perfect or most accurate. Most of the trees provide correct predictions of class labels for most of the data. So, even if some of the individual decision trees generate wrong predictions, the majority predict correctly. And since we are using the mode of output predictions to determine the class, it is unaffected by those wrong instances. Intuitively, validating this belief depends on the randomness in the sampling method. The more random the samples, the more decorrelated the trees will be, and the less likely are the chances of other trees being affected by wrong predictions from the other trees.
2. More importantly, different trees are making mistakes at different places and not all of them are making errors at the same location. Again, intuitively, this belief depends on how randomly the attributes are selected. The more random they are, the less likely the trees will make mistakes at the same location.

Hands-On Example 9.5: Random Forest

We will now take an example and see how to use random forest in R. For this, we are going to use the *Bank Marketing* dataset from the University of California, Irvine, machine learning dataset, which you can download from OA 9.9. Given the dataset, the goal is to predict if the client will subscribe (yes/no) a term deposit (variable *y*).

Let us import the dataset to RStudio first. Note that in the original dataset the columns are separated by semicolons. If you are not familiar with how to handle semicolon-delimited data, you may want to convert it into .csv or .tsv, or the format you are familiar with the most.

```
> bank <- read.csv(file.choose(), header = TRUE, sep = ",")
> View(bank)
> barplot(table(bank$y))
```

The above line of code generates the barplot shown in Figure 9.14.

As the barplot depicts, the majority of the data points in this dataset have class label "no." Now, before we build our model, let us separate the dataset into training and test instances:

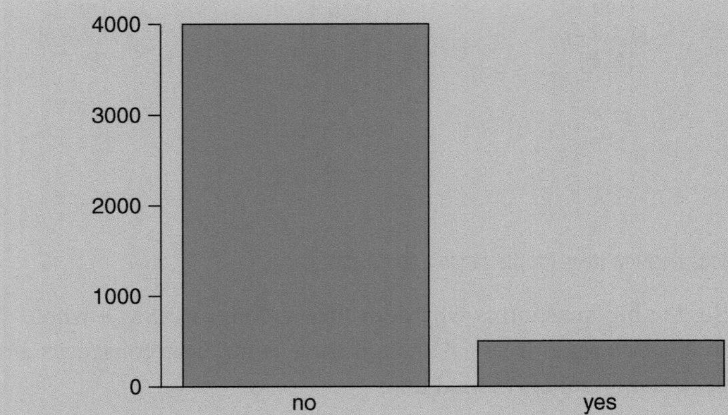

Figure 9.14 Bar plot depicting data points with "No" and "Yes" labels.

```
> set.seed(1234)
> population <- sample(nrow(bank), 0.75 * nrow(bank))
> train <- bank[population, ]
> test <- bank[-population, ]
```

As shown, the dataset is split into two parts: 75% for training purposes and the remaining to evaluate our model. To build the model, the *randomForest* library is used. In case your system does not have this package, make sure to install it first. Next, use the training instances to build the model:

```
> install.packages("randomForest")
> library(randomForest)
> model <- randomForest(y ~ ., data = train)
> model
```

We can use ntree and mtry to specify the total number of trees to build (default = 500), and the number of predictors to randomly sample at each split, respectively. The above lines of code should generate the following result:

```
Call:
 randomForest(formula = y ~ ., data = train)
               Type of random forest: classification
                     Number of trees: 500
No. of variables tried at each split: 4
        OOB estimate of error rate: 9.94%
Confusion matrix:
      no yes class.error
no  2901  97   0.0323549
yes  240 152   0.6122449
```

We can see that 500 trees were built, and the model randomly sampled four predictors at each split. It also shows a confusion matrix containing prediction vs. actual, as well as classification error for each class. Let us test the model to see how it performs on the test dataset:

```
> prediction <- predict(model, newdata = test)
> table(prediction, test$y)
```

The following output is produced:

```
prediction  no   yes
       no  964    84
       yes  38    45
```

We can further evaluate the accuracy as follows:

```
> (964 + 45)/nrow(test)
[1] 0.8921309
```

There you have it. We achieved about 89% accuracy with a very simple model. We can try to improve the accuracy by feature selection, and also by trying different values of ntree and mtry.

Random forest is considered a *panacea* of all data science problems among most of its practitioners. There is a belief that when you cannot think of any algorithm irrespective of situation, use random forest. It is a bit irrational, since no algorithm strictly dominates in all applications (one size does not fit all). Nonetheless, people have their favorite algorithms. And there are reasons why, for many data scientists, random forest is the favorite:

1. It can solve both types of problems, that is, classification and regression, and does a decent estimation for both.
2. Random forest requires almost no input preparation. It can handle binary features, categorical features, and numerical features without any need for scaling.
3. Random forest is not very sensitive to the specific set of parameters used. As a result, it does not require a lot of tweaking and fiddling to get a decent model; just use a large number of trees and things will not go terribly awry.
4. It is an effective method for estimating missing data and maintains accuracy when a large proportion of the data are missing.

So, is random forest a *silver bullet*? Absolutely not. First, it does a good job at classification but not as good as for regression problems, since it does not give precise continuous nature predictions. Second, random forest can feel like a black-box approach for statistical modelers, as you have very little control on what the model does. At best, you can try different parameters and random seeds and hope that will change the output.

Try It Yourself 9.5: Random Forest

Get the balloons dataset presented in Table 9.1 and downloadable from OA 9.6. Use this dataset and create a random forest model to classify if the balloons are inflated or not from the available attributes. Compare the performance (e.g., accuracy) of this model against that of one created using a decision tree.

9.7 Naïve Bayes

We now move on to a very popular and robust approach for classification that uses Bayes' theorem. The Bayesian classification represents a supervised learning method as well as a statistical method for classification. In a nutshell, it is a classification technique based on Bayes' theorem with an assumption of independence among predictors. Here, all attributes contribute equally and independently to the decision.

In simple terms, a Naïve Bayes classifier assumes that the presence of a particular feature in a class is unrelated to the presence of any other feature. For example, a fruit may be considered to be an apple if it is red, round, and about three inches in diameter. Even if these features depend on each other or upon the existence of other features, all of these properties independently contribute to the probability that this fruit is an apple, and that is why it is known as *naïve*. It turns out that in most cases, while such a naïve assumption is found to be not true, the resulting classification models do amazingly well.

Let us first take a look at Bayes' theorem, which provides a way of calculating posterior probability $P(c|x)$ from $P(c)$, $P(x)$, and $P(x|c)$. Look at the equation below:

$$P(c|x) = \frac{P(x|c)P(c)}{P(x)}. \tag{9.14}$$

Here:

- $P(c|x)$ is the posterior probability of *class* (*c*, *target*) given *predictor* (*x*, *attributes*).
- $P(c)$ is the prior probability of *class*.
- $P(x|c)$ is the likelihood, which is the probability of *predictor* given *class*.
- $P(x)$ is the prior probability of *predictor*.

And here is that naïve assumption: we believe that evidence can be split into parts that are independent,

$$P(c|x) = \frac{P(x_1|c)P(x_2|c)P(x_3|c)P(x_4|c)\ldots P(x_n|c)P(c)}{P(x)}, \tag{9.15}$$

where $x_1, x_2, x_3, \ldots, x_n$ are independent priors.

To understand Naïve Bayes in action, let us revisit the golf dataset from earlier in this chapter to see how this algorithm works step-by-step. This dataset is repeated in reordered form in Table 9.6, and can be downloaded from OA 9.10.

Table 9.6 Weather dataset.

Outlook	Temperature	Humidity	Windy	Play
Overcast	Hot	High	False	Yes
Overcast	Cool	Normal	True	Yes
Overcast	Mild	High	True	Yes
Overcast	Hot	Normal	False	Yes
Rainy	Mild	High	False	Yes
Rainy	Cool	Normal	False	Yes
Rainy	Cool	Normal	True	No
Rainy	Mild	Normal	False	Yes
Rainy	Mild	High	True	No
Sunny	Hot	High	False	No
Sunny	Hot	High	True	No
Sunny	Mild	High	False	No
Sunny	Cool	Normal	False	Yes
Sunny	Mild	Normal	True	Yes

(The source of this dataset is http://storm.cis.fordham.edu/~gweiss/data-mining/weka-data/weather.arff)

As shown in Table 9.6, the dataset has four attributes, namely *Outlook*, *Temperature*, *Humidity*, and *Windy*, which are all different aspects of weather conditions. Based on these four attributes, the goal is to predict the value of the outcome variable, *Play* (yes or no) – whether the weather is suitable to play golf. Following are the steps of the algorithm through which we could accomplish that goal.

- Step 1: First convert the dataset into a frequency table (see Figure 9.15).
- Step 2: Create a likelihood table by finding the probabilities, like probability of being hot is 0.29 and probability of playing is 0.64 as shown in Figure 9.15.
- Step 3: Now, use the Naïve Bayesian equation to calculate the posterior probability for each class. The class with the highest posterior probability is the outcome of the prediction.

To see this in action, let us say that we need to decide if one should go out to play when the weather is mild based on the dataset. We can solve it using the above discussed method of posterior probability. Using Bayes' theorem:

$$P(\text{Yes}|\text{Mild}) = \frac{P(\text{Mild}|\text{Yes}) \times P(\text{Yes})}{P(\text{Mild})}$$

Here we have:

$$P(\text{Mild}|\text{Yes}) = 4/9 = 0.44,$$
$$P(\text{Mild}) = 6/14 = 0.43,$$

Temperature	Play	Frequency Table			Likelihood Table				
Hot	no	Temperature	No	Yes	Temperature	No	Yes		
Hot	no	Hot	2	2	Hot	2	2	4/14	0.29
Hot	yes	Mild	2	4	Mild	2	4	6/14	0.43
Mild	yes	Cool	1	3	Cool	1	3	4/14	0.29
Cool	yes	Total	5	9	All	5	9		
Cool	no					5/14	9/14		
Cool	yes					0.36	0.64		
Mild	no								
Cool	yes								
Mild	yes								
Mild	yes								
Mild	yes								
Hot	yes								
mild	no								

Figure 9.15 Conversion of the dataset to a frequency table and to a likelihood table.

Now,

$$P(\text{Yes}|\text{Mild}) = (0.44 \times 0.64)/0.43 = 0.65.$$

In other words, we have derived that the probability of playing when the weather is mild is 65%, and if we wanted to turn that into a Yes–No decision, we can see that this probability is higher than the mid-point, that is, 50%. Thus, we can declare "Yes" for our answer.

Naïve Bayes uses a similar method to predict the probability of different classes based on various attributes. This algorithm is mostly used in text classification and with problems having two or more classes. One prominent example is spam detection. Spam filtering with Naïve Bayes is a two-classes problem, that is, to determine a message or an email as spam or not. Here is how it works.

Let us assume that there are certain words (e.g., "viagra," "rich," "friend") that indicate a given message as being spam. We can apply Bayes' theorem to calculate the probability that an email is spam given the email words as:

$$\begin{aligned} P(\text{spam}|\text{words}) &= \frac{P(\text{words}|\text{spam}) \times P(\text{spam})}{P(\text{words})} \\ &= \frac{P(\text{spam}) \times P(\text{viagra, rich, \ldots, friend}|\text{spam})}{P(\text{viagra, rich, \ldots, friend})} \\ &\propto P(\text{spam}) \times P(\text{viagra, rich, \ldots, friend}|\text{spam}). \end{aligned}$$

Here, $\propto$ is the proportion symbol.

According to Naïve Bayes, the word events are completely independent; therefore, simplifying the above formula using the Bayes formula would look like:

$$P(\text{spam}|\text{words}) \propto P(\text{viagra}|\text{spam}) \times P(\text{rich}|\text{spam}) \times \ldots \times P(\text{friend}|\text{spam})$$

Now, we can calculate *P*(viagra|spam), *P*(rich|spam), and *P*(friend|spam) each individually if we have a sizeable training dataset of previously categorized spam messages and the occurrences of these words ("viagra," "rich," "friend," etc.) in the training set. So, it is possible to determine the probability of an email from the test set as spam based on these values.

Naïve Bayes works surprisingly well even if the independence assumption is clearly violated because classification does not need accurate probability estimates so long as the greatest probability is assigned to the correct class. Naïve Bayes affords fast model building and scoring and can be used for both binary and multiclass classification problems.

Hands-On Example 9.6: Naïve Bayes

Let us use the golf data in Table 9.6 (available to download from OA 9.10) to explore how to perform Naïve Bayes classification in R.

First, you need to import the dataset into RStudio:

```
> golf <- read.csv(file = "golf.csv", header = TRUE, sep = ",")
> View(golf)
```

There are a bunch of packages in R that support Naïve Bayes classification. For this example, you are going to use the package "e1071." In case you do not have it in your system, make sure you install it first.

```
> install.packages("e1071")
> library(e1071)
```

Once you do that, building the Naïve Bayes model in R is simple and straightforward. However, when building a model, you will need test data to evaluate your model. Since you do not have that here, let us separate training and test data from your original dataset. Here is how to do that:

```
> set.seed(123)
> id <- sample(2, nrow(golf), prob = c(0.7, 0.3), replace = T)
> golfTrain <- golf[id ==1,]
> golfTest <- golf[id ==2,]
```

You check the training and test sets that you just built. From the original data, which have 14 data points, you reserved 70% for training; you should have nine data points in the training set and the remaining in the test set. Which individual data points will go into the training and which will go to the test depends on how you sample the data. You can explore more about both these datasets from the console.

```
> View(golfTest)
> View(golfTrain)
```

Next, let us build the model on the training data and evaluate it.

```
> golfModel <- naiveBayes(PlayGolf~., data = golfTrain)
> print(golfModel)
```

This should generate output similar to the following.

```
Naive Bayes Classifier for Discrete Predictors
Call:
naiveBayes.default(x = X, y = Y, laplace = laplace)
A-priori probabilities:
Y
      No       Yes
0.3333333 0.6666667
Conditional probabilities:
     Outlook
Y      Overcast     Rainy     Sunny
  No  0.0000000 0.3333333 0.6666667
  Yes 0.6666667 0.1666667 0.1666667

     Temp
Y          Cool       Hot      Mild
No    0.3333333 0.3333333 0.3333333
Yes   0.3333333 0.3333333 0.3333333

     Humidity
Y          High    Normal
No    0.6666667 0.3333333
Yes   0.3333333 0.6666667

     Windy
Y         FALSE      TRUE
No    0.3333333 0.6666667
Yes   0.6666667 0.3333333
```

The output contains a likelihood table as well as *a-priori* probabilities. The *a-priori* probabilities are equivalent to the prior probability in Bayes' theorem. That is, how frequently each level of class occurs in the training dataset. The rationale underlying the prior probability is that, if a level is rare in the training set, it is unlikely that such a level will occur in the test dataset. In other words, the prediction of an outcome is influenced not only by the predictors, but also by the prevalence of the outcome.

Let us move on to an evaluation of this model. You have to use the test set for this, the data which the algorithm did not see while training.

```
> prediction <- predict(golfModel, newdata = golfTest)
```

You can check what class labels your model has predicted for all the data points in the test data:

```
> print(prediction)
```

However, it will be easier if we can compare these predicted labels with actual labels side by side, or in a confusion matrix. Fortunately, in R there is a package for this functionality, named *caret*. Again, if you do not have it make sure you install it first. Keep in mind that installing *caret* requires some prerequisite packages such as *lattice* and *ggplot2*. Make sure you install them first. Once you have all of them, use the following command:

```
> confusionMatrix(prediction, golfTest$PlayGolf)
```

And you will have a nice confusion matrix along with *p*-values and all other evaluation matrices.

```
Confusion Matrix and Statistics

          Reference
Prediction  No  Yes
       No    2    2
       Yes   0    1

               Accuracy : 0.6
                 95% CI : (0.1466, 0.9473)
    No Information Rate : 0.6
    P-Value [Acc > NIR] : 0.6826

                  Kappa : 0.2857
 Mcnemar's Test P-Value : 0.4795

            Sensitivity : 1.0000
            Specificity : 0.3333
         Pos Pred Value : 0.5000
         Neg Pred Value : 1.0000
             Prevalence : 0.4000
         Detection Rate : 0.4000
   Detection Prevalence : 0.8000
      Balanced Accuracy : 0.6667

       'Positive' Class : No
```

As you can see, the accuracy is not great, 60%, which can be attributed to the fact that we had only nine examples in your training set. Still, by now, you should have some idea about how to build Naïve Bayes classifier in R.

Try It Yourself 9.6: Naïve Bayes

Use the contact lenses dataset (OA 9.8) from the decision tree problem under Try It Yourself 9.4 and build a Naïve Bayes classifier to predict the class label. Compare the accuracy between the Naïve Bayes algorithm and the decision tree.

9.8 Support Vector Machine (SVM)

Now we come to the last method for classification in this chapter. One thing that has been common in all the classifier models we have seen so far is that they assume linear separation of classes. In other words, they try to come up with a decision boundary that is a line (or a hyperplane in a higher dimension). But many problems do not have such linear characteristics. Support vector machine (SVM) is a method for the classification of both linear and nonlinear data. SVMs are considered by many to be the best stock classifier for doing machine learning tasks. By stock, here we mean in its basic form and not modified. This means you can take the basic form of the classifier and run it on the data, and the results will have low error rates. Support vector machines make good decisions for data points that are outside the training set. In a nutshell, an SVM is an algorithm that uses nonlinear mapping to transform the original training data into a higher dimension. Within this new dimension, it searches for the linear optimal separating hyperplane (i.e., a decision boundary separating the tuples of one class from another). With an appropriate nonlinear mapping to a sufficiently high dimension, data from two classes can always be separated by a hyperplane. The SVM finds this hyperplane using support vectors ("essential" training tuples) and margins (defined by the support vectors).

To understand what this means, let us look at an example. Let us start with a simple one, a two-class problem.

Let the dataset D be given as $(X_1, y_1), (X_2, y_2), \ldots, (X_{|D|}, y_{|D|})$, where X_i is the set of training tuples with associated class labels y_i. Each y_i can take one of two values, either +1 or −1 (i.e., $y_i \in \{+1, -1\}$), corresponding to the classes represented by the hollow red squares and blue circles (ignore the data points represented by the solid symbols for now), respectively, in Figure 9.16. From the graph, we see that the 2-D data are linearly separable (or "linear," for short), because a straight line can be drawn to separate all the tuples of class +1 from all the tuples of class −1.

Note that if our data had three attributes (two independent variables and one dependent), we would want to find the best separating plane (a demonstration is shown in Figure 9.17 for linearly non-separable data). Generalizing to n dimensions, if we had n number of attributes, we want to find the best (n−1)-dimensional plane, called a *hyperplane*. In general, we will use the term *hyperplane* to refer to the decision boundary that we are searching for, regardless of the number of input attributes. So, in other words, our problem is, how can we find the best hyperplane?

There are an infinite number of separating lines that could be drawn. We want to find the "best" one, that is, one that (we hope) will have the minimum classification error on previously unseen tuples. How can we find this best line?

An SVM approaches this problem by searching for the maximum marginal hyperplane. Consider Figure 9.18, which shows two possible separating hyperplanes and their associated margins. Before we get into the definition of margins, let us take an intuitive look at this Figure 9.18. Both hyperplanes can correctly classify all the given data tuples.

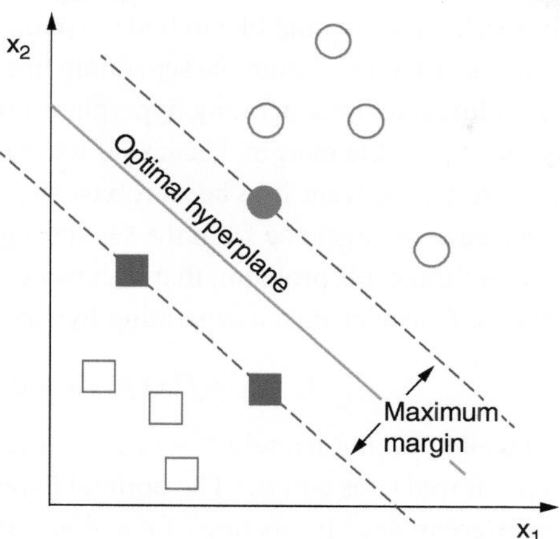

Figure 9.16 Linearly separable data.[1]

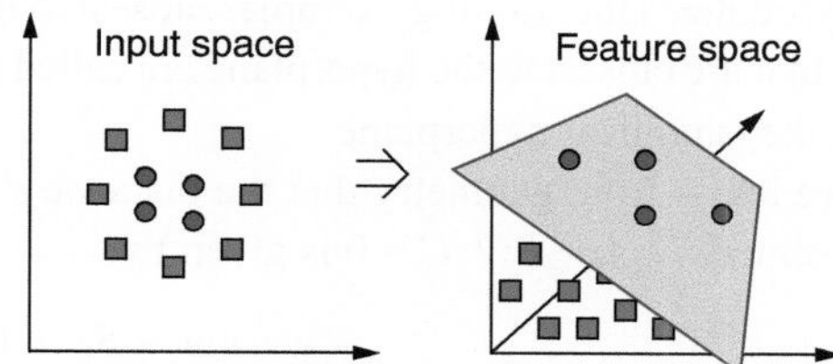

Figure 9.17 From line to hyperplane. (Source: Jiawei Han and Micheline Kamber. (2006). *Data Mining: Concepts and Techniques.* Morgan Kaufmann.)

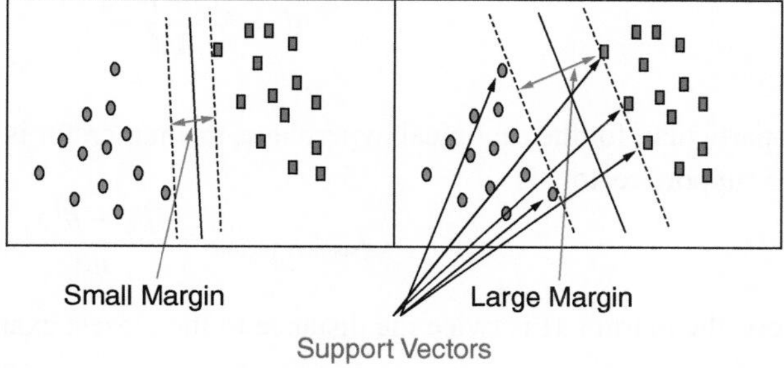

Figure 9.18 Possible hyperplanes and their margins. (Source: Jiawei Han and Micheline Kamber. (2006). *Data Mining: Concepts and Techniques.* Morgan Kaufmann.)

Intuitively, however, we expect the hyperplane with the larger margin to be more accurate at classifying future data tuples than the hyperplane with the smaller margin. This is why (during the learning or training phase) the SVM searches for the hyperplane with the largest margin, that is, the maximum marginal hyperplane (MMH). The associated margin gives the largest separation between classes.

Roughly speaking, we would like to find the point closest to the separating hyperplane and make sure this is as far away from the separating line as possible. This is known as "margin."

The points closest to the separating hyperplane are known as support vectors. We want to have the greatest possible margin, because if we made a mistake or trained our classifier on limited data, we would want it to be as robust as possible. Now that we know that we are trying to maximize the distance from the separating line to the support vectors, we need to find a way to optimize this problem; that is, how do we find an SVM with the MMH and the support vectors. Consider this: a separating hyperplane can be written as

$$f(x) = \beta_0 + \beta^T x, \tag{9.16}$$

where T is a weight vector, namely, $T = \{1,2,..., n\}$, n is the number of attributes, and β_0 is a scalar, often referred to as a bias.[2] The optimal hyperplane can be represented in an infinite number of different ways by scaling of β and β_0. As a matter of convention, among all the possible representations of the hyperplane, the one chosen is

$$\beta_0 + \beta^T x = 1, \tag{9.17}$$

where x symbolizes the training examples closest to the hyperplane. In general, the training examples that are closest to the hyperplane are called support vectors. This representation is known as the canonical hyperplane.

Now, we know from geometry that the distance d between a point (m, n) and a straight line represented by $Ax + By + C = 0$ is given by

$$d = \frac{|Am + Bn + C|}{\sqrt{A^2 + B^2}}. \tag{9.18}$$

Therefore, extending the same equation to a hyperplane gives the distance between a point x and a hyperplane:

$$d = \frac{|\beta_0 + \beta^T x|}{\|\beta\|}. \tag{9.19}$$

In particular, for the canonical hyperplane, the numerator is equal to one and the distance to the support vectors is

$$d_{\text{support vectors}} = \frac{|\beta_0 + \beta^T x|}{\|\beta\|}. \tag{9.20}$$

Now, the margin M is twice the distance to the closest examples. So

$$M = \frac{2}{\|\beta\|}. \tag{9.21}$$

Finally, the problem of maximizing M is equivalent to the problem of minimizing a function $L()$ subject to some constraints. The constraints model the requirement for the hyperplane to classify correctly all the training examples x_i. Formally,

$$\min_{\beta, \beta_0} L(\beta) = \frac{1}{2}\|\beta\|^2 \text{ subject to } y_i(\beta^T x_i + \beta_0) \geq 1 \ \forall i, \tag{9.22}$$

where y_i represents each of the labels of the training examples. This is a problem of Lagrangian optimization that can be solved using Lagrange multipliers to obtain the weight vector and the bias β_0 of the optimal hyperplane.

This was the SVM theory in a nutshell, which is given here with a primary purpose of developing intuition behind how SVMs and in general such maximum marginal classifiers work. But this is a book that covers hands-on data science, so let us see how we could use SVM for a classification or a regression problem.

Hands-On Example 9.7: SVM

Consider a simple classification problem using regression.csv data (Figure 9.19, downloaded from OA 9.11) with just two attributes *X* and *Y*.

We can now use R to display the data and fit a line:

```
# Load the data from the csv file
data <- read.csv('regression.csv', header = TRUE, sep=",")
# Plot the data
plot(data, pch=16)
# Create a linear regression model
```

```
X,Y
1,3
2,4
3,8
4,4
5,6
6,9
7,8
8,12
9,15
10,26
11,35
12,40
13,45
14,54
15,49
16,59
17,60
18,62
19,63
20,68
```

Figure 9.19 The regression.csv file.

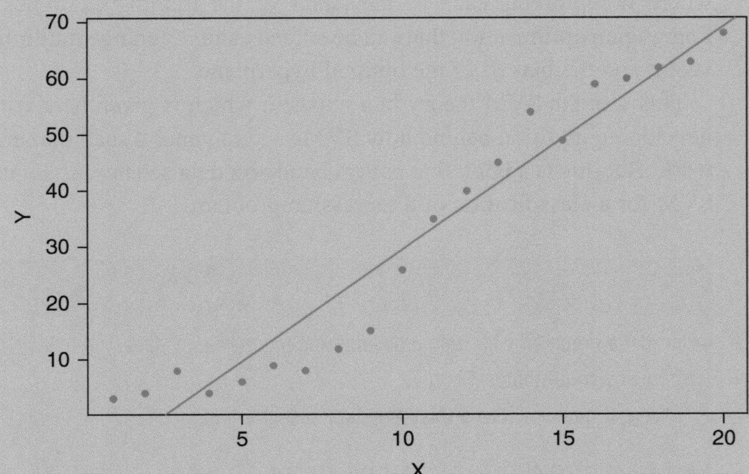

Figure 9.20 Regression line fitted onto the data.

```
model <- lm(y ~ x, data)
# Add the fitted line
abline(model)
```

Here, we have tried to use a linear regression model first to classify the data as shown in Figure 9.20. In order to be able to compare the linear regression with the support vector machine, first we need a way to measure how good it is.

To do that we will change our code just a little to visualize each prediction made by our model:

```
# re-plot the original data points
plot(data, pch=16)
# make a prediction for each X
predictedY <- predict(model, data)
# display the predictions
points(data$x, predictedY, col = "blue", pch=4)
```

This produces the graph shown in Figure 9.21.

For each data point x_i the model makes a prediction y_i displayed as a blue cross on the graph. The only difference with the previous graph is that the dots are not connected to each other.

In order to measure how good our model is, we will compute how many errors it makes, which we can accomplish by calculating the root mean square error (RMSE). The way to calculate RMSE in R is:

```
rmse <- function(error)
{
  sqrt(mean(error^2))
}
```

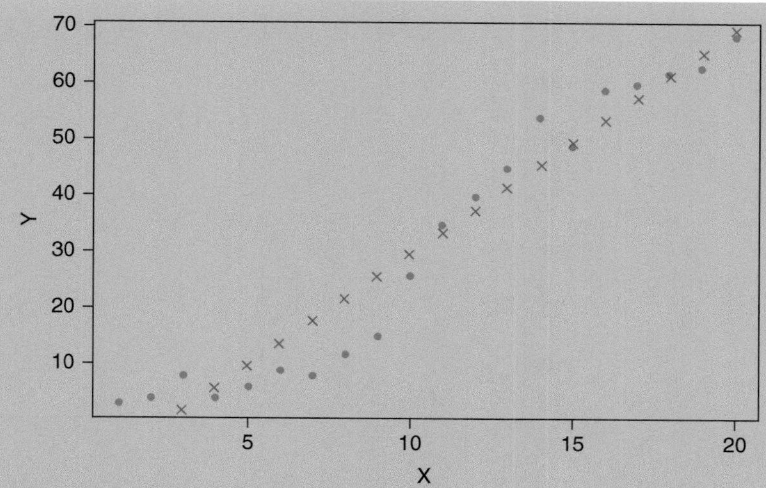

Figure 9.21 Predicted outcomes using linear regression plotted with the original data.

```
error <- model$residuals # same as data$Y - predictedY
lrPredictionRMSE <- rmse(error)
```

The RMSE value of our linear regression model that we have obtained from R is 5.70. Let us try to improve it with SVM.

Prerequisite: In order to create an SVM model with R, you will need the package "e1071." So before proceeding to the following steps, be sure to install it and add it to the library at the start of your file.[3]

Below is the code to create a model with SVM in R, once the "e1071" package is installed and loaded in the current session:

```
model2 <- svm(y ~ x, data)
predictedY <- predict(model2, data)
points(data$x, predictedY, col = "red", pch=4)
```

The code draws the graph shown in Figure 9.22.

This time the prediction is much closer to the real values. Let us compute the RMSE of our support vector regression model.

```
# /!\ this time svmModel$residuals is not the same as data$y -
predictedY in linear regression example, so we compute the
error like this:
error <- data$y - predictedY
svmPredictionRMSE <- rmse(error) # 3.157061
```

We can see that SVM gives better (lower) RMSE – 3.15 – compared to 5.70 with linear regression.

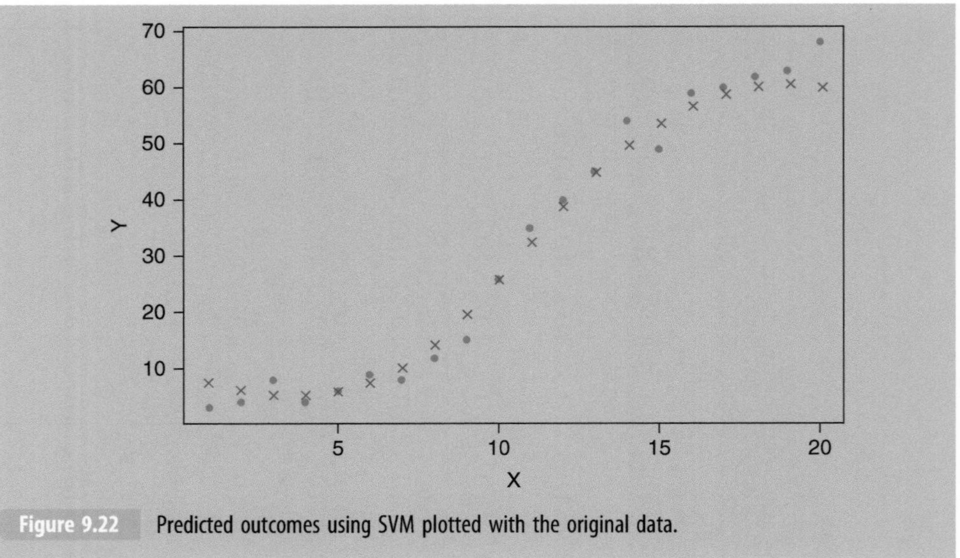

Figure 9.22 Predicted outcomes using SVM plotted with the original data.

Try It Yourself 9.7: SVM

The dataset you are going to use for this work comes from a Combined Cycle power plant and the measures were recorded for a period of six years (2006–2011). You can download it from OA 9.12. The features in this dataset consist of hourly average ambient variables and include

- Temperature (AT) in the range 1.81°C and 37.11°C
- Ambient pressure (AP) in the range 992.89–1033.30 millibar
- Relative humidity (RH) in the range 25.56% to 100.16%
- Exhaust vacuum (V) in the range 25.36–81.56 cm Hg
- Net hourly electrical energy output (PE) 420.26–495.76 MW

Create an SVM-based model that can be used to predict PE from the other four attributes. Note that none of the features are normalized in this dataset.

FYI: Anomaly Detection

In machine learning, anomaly detection (also outlier detection) is used to identify the items, events, or observations that do not conform to other similar items in a dataset. Typically, the anomalous items will not conform to some expected pattern from the dataset and therefore translate to some kind of problem. Such algorithms are used in a broad range of contexts, like identifying fraud in bank transactions, a structural defect in alloys, potential problems in medical records, or errors in a text. Anomalies in other subjects are also referred to as outliers, novelties, noise, deviations and exceptions.

Anomaly detection is applicable in a variety of domains, such as intrusion detection, fraud detection, fault detection, system health monitoring, event detection in sensor networks, and detecting ecosystem disturbances. For example, any highly unusual credit card spending patterns are suspect. Because the possible variations are so numerous and the training examples so few, it is not feasible to learn what fraudulent activity looks like. The approach that anomaly detection takes is to simply learn what normal activity looks like (using a history of non-fraudulent transactions) and identify anything that is significantly different.

Supervised approaches for anomaly detection include kNN, Bayesian network, decision tree, and support vector machine.

To illustrate anomaly detection, let us run through the process with the kNN clustering algorithm. To detect the outliers using kNN, first you have to train the kNN algorithm by supplying it with data clusters you know to be correct. Therefore, the dataset to be used to train the kNN has to be a different one from the data that will be used to identify the outliers. For example, you want to cluster the house listings that are similar in price range in your chosen locality. Now, all the current listings that you have collected from the Web may not reflect the correct price of the listings. This may happen for several reasons: some of the listings may be outdated, some may have unintentional mistakes in listing price, and some may even contain intentional lower prices for clickbait. Now, you want to do a kNN clustering to discriminate such anomalies from the correct listings. One way to do this would be to collect all the previous correct records of list prices of the current listings and train the kNN clustering algorithm on that dataset first. Since I have covered kNN clustering with examples before, I will leave this part to you. Once the trained model is generated, the same can be used to identify the data points in the current listings dataset that do not properly fit into any cluster and thus ought to be identified as anomalies.

Summary

This was the longest chapter in this book and there is a reason for it. Supervised learning, and classification in particular, covers a big portion of today's data problems. Many of the problems that we encounter in the real world require us to analyze the data to provide decision-making insights. Which set of features will be acceptable to our customers for the next version of our app? Is an incoming message spam or not? Should we trust that news story or is it fake? Where should we place this new wine we are going to start selling – "premium" (high quality), "great value" (medium quality), or "great deal" (low quality)?

In this chapter we started with logistic regression as a popular technique for doing binary decision-making; such two-class classification happens to cover a large range of possibilities. But, of course, there are situations that require us to consider more than two classes. For them, we saw several techniques: softmax regression to kNN and decision trees. Often, a problem with some of these techniques is that they could overfit the data, leading to biased models. To overcome this, we could use random forest, which uses a large set of decision trees, with each tree intentionally and randomly created imperfectly, and then combine their outputs to produce a single decision. This makes random forest an example of an ensemble model.

Then we saw Naïve Bayes – a very popular technique for binary decision-making problems. It is based on a very naïve assumption that the presence of a particular feature in a class is unrelated to the presence of any other feature. This is often not true. For example, think about the previous sentence. It has a structure. It has a logical flow, and a particular word is preceded by a certain word and followed by another. Naïve Bayes assumes that the order of these words is not important and the appearance of a word has nothing to do with the appearance of any other word in the sentence. Surprisingly, despite this simple and flawed assumption, the Naïve Bayes technique works really well. That independence assumption makes complex computations quite simple and feasible. And so, we find Naïve Bayes used in many commercial applications, especially information filtering (e.g., spam detection).

Finally, we dipped our toes into SVM. I say "dipped our toes" because SVM can be much more sophisticated and powerful than what we were able to afford in this chapter. The power and sophistication come from SVM's ability to use different kernels. Think about kernels as transformation functions that allow us to create nonlinear decision boundaries. There are situations where data seems hard to separate using a line or hyperplane, but we could perhaps draw a linear boundary in a higher dimension that looks like a curve in the current space. The full explanation of this process is beyond the scope of this book, but hopefully a few pointers provided at the end of this chapter will help you explore and learn more about this powerful technique.

Key Terms

- **Supervised learning:** Supervised learning algorithms use a set of examples from previous records that are labeled to make predictions about the future.
- **Gradient descent:** It is a machine learning algorithm that computes a slope down an error surface in order to find a model that provides the best fit for the given data.
- **Relative risk:** It is the ratio of the probability of choosing any outcome category other than baseline, over that of the baseline category.
- **Anomaly detection:** Anomaly detection refers to identification of data points, or observations that do not conform to the expected pattern of a given population.
- **Data overfitting:** When a model tries to create decision boundaries or curve fitting that connect or separate as many points as possible at the expense of simplicity. Such a process often leads to complex models that have very little error on the training data, but may not have an ability to generalize and do a good job on new data.
- **Training–validation–test data:** The training set consists of data points which are labeled and are to be used to learn the model. A validation set, often prepared separately from the training set, consists of observation that are used to tune the parameters of the model, for example, to test for overfitting, etc. The test set is used to evaluate the performance of the model.
- **Entropy:** It is a measure of disorder, uncertainty, or randomness. When the probability of each event in a given space happening is the same, entropy is the highest for that system. When there are imbalances in these probabilities, the absolute value of entropy goes down.
- **Information gain:** It is the decrease in entropy, and typically used to measure how much entropy (uncertainty) is reduced in a certain event, knowing the probability of another event.

- **Ensemble model:** It contains a combination of concrete and finite sets of alternative models, each perhaps with its own imperfections and biases, that are used together to produce a single decision.
- **True positive rate (TPR):** It indicates how much of what we detected as "1" was indeed "1."
- **False positive rate (FPR):** It indicates how much of what we detected as "1" was actually "0."

Conceptual Questions

1. What is supervised learning? Give two examples of data problems where you would use supervised learning.
2. Relate likelihood of a model given data, and probability of data given a model. Are these two the same? Different? How?
3. How does random forest address the issue of bias or overfitting?
4. Here are the past seven governors of the state of New Jersey based on their party affiliations (Democratic, Republican): R, D, D, D, D, R, D. Using Naïve Bayes formulation, calculate the probability of the next governor being a Republican. Show calculations.

Hands-On Problems

Problem 9.1 (Logistic regression)

The dataset crash.csv is an accident-survivors dataset portal for the USA (crash data for individual States can be searched) hosted by data.gov. The dataset, downloadable from OA 9.13, contains passengers' (not necessarily the driver's) age and the speed of the vehicle (mph) at the time of impact and the fate of the passengers (1 represents survived, 0 represents did not survive) after the crash. Now, use the logistic regression to decide if the age and speed can predict the survivability of the passengers.

Problem 9.2 (Logistic regression)

An automated answer-rating site marks each post in a community forum website as "good" or "bad" based on the quality of the post. The CSV file, which you can download from OA 9.14, contains the various types of quality as measured by the tool. Following are the type of qualities that the dataset contains:

i. num_words: number of words in the post
ii. num_characters: number of characters in the post
iii. num_misspelled: number of misspelled words
iv. bin_end_qmark: if the post ends with a question mark
v. num_interrogative: number of interrogative words in the post
vi. bin_start_small: if the answer starts with a lowercase letter ("1" means yes, otherwise no)
vii. num_sentences: number of sentences per post
viii. num_punctuations: number of punctuation symbols in the post
ix. label: the label of the post ("G" for good and "B" for bad) as determined by the tool.

Create a logistics regression model to predict the class label from the first eight attributes of the question set. Evaluate the accuracy of your model.

Problem 9.3 (Logistic regression)

In this exercise, you will use the Immunotherapy dataset, available from OA 9.15, which contains information about wart treatment results of 90 patients using immunotherapy. For each patient, the dataset has information about the patient's sex (either 1 or 0), age in years, number of warts, type, area, induration diameter, and result of treatment (a binary variable). Your objective in this exercise is to build a logistic regression model that will predict the result of treatment from the remaining features and to evaluate the accuracy of your model.

Problem 9.4 (Softmax regression)

The Iris flower dataset or Fisher's Iris dataset (built into R or downloadable from OA 9.16) is a multivariate dataset introduced by the British statistician and biologist Ronald Fisher in his 1936 paper.[4] The use of multiple measurements in taxonomic problems is an example of linear discriminant analysis. The dataset consists of 50 samples from each of three species of iris (*Iris sentosa*, *Iris virginica* and *Iris versicolor*). Four features were measured from each sample: the length and the width of the sepals and petals, in centimeters. Based on the combination of these four features, create a prediction model using softmax regression for the species of iris flower.

Problem 9.5 (Softmax regression)

For the softmax regression challenge you will work with horseshoe crab data, available from OA 9.17. This dataset has 173 observations of female crabs, including the following characteristics:

i. Satellites: number of male partners in addition to the female's primary partner.
ii. Yes: a binary factor indicating if the female has satellites.
iii. Width: width of the female crab in centimeters.
iv. Weight: weight of the female in grams.
v. Color: a categorical value having range of 1 to 4, where 1 = light color, and 4 = dark.
vi. Spine: a categorical variable, valued between 1 and 3, indicating the goodness of spine of the female.

Use Softmax regression to predict the condition of the spine of female crabs based on the remaining features in the dataset and report the accuracy of your predictions.

Problem 9.6 (kNN)

Download weather.csv from OA 9.18. Entirely fictitious, it supposedly concerns the weather conditions that are suitable for playing some unspecified game. There are four predictor variables: outlook, temperature, humidity, and wind. The outcome is whether to play ("yes," "no," "maybe"). Use kNN (or, if you prefer, a different classification algorithm) to build a classifier that learns how various predictor variables could relate to the outcome. Report the accuracy of your model.

Problem 9.7 (kNN)

The following dataset came from Project 16P5 in Mosteller, F., & Tukey, J. W. (1977). *Data Analysis and Regression: A Second Course in Statistics*. Addison-Wesley, Reading, MA, pp. 549–551 (indicating their source as "Data used by permission of Franice van de Walle").

You can download it from OA 9.19.

The dataset represents standardized fertility measures and socio-economic indicators for each of 47 French-speaking provinces of Switzerland, circa 1888. Switzerland, in 1888, was entering a period known as the *demographic transition*; that is, its fertility was beginning to fall from the high level typical of underdeveloped countries. The dataset has observations on six variables, *each* of which is in percent, that is, in [0,100].

Use the kNN algorithm to find the provinces that have similar fertility measures.

	Fertility	Agriculture	Examination	Education	Catholic	Infant. Mortality
Courtelary	80.2	17	15	12	9.96	22.2
Delemont	83.1	45.1	6	9	84.84	22.2
Franches-Mnt	92.5	39.7	5	5	93.4	20.2
Moutier	85.8	36.5	12	7	33.77	20.3
Neuveville	76.9	43.5	17	15	5.16	20.6
Porrentruy	76.1	35.3	9	7	90.57	26.6
Broye	83.8	70.2	16	7	92.85	23.6
Glane	92.4	67.8	14	8	97.16	24.9
Gruyere	82.4	53.3	12	7	97.67	21
Sarine	82.9	45.2	16	13	91.38	24.4
Veveyse	87.1	64.5	14	6	98.61	24.5
Aigle	64.1	62	21	12	8.52	16.5
Aubonne	66.9	67.5	14	7	2.27	19.1
Avenches	68.9	60.7	19	12	4.43	22.7
Cossonay	61.7	69.3	22	5	2.82	18.7
Echallens	68.3	72.6	18	2	24.2	21.2
Grandson	71.7	34	17	8	3.3	20

Lausanne	55.7	19.4	26	28	12.11	20.2
La Vallee	54.3	15.2	31	20	2.15	10.8
Lavaux	65.1	73	19	9	2.84	20
Morges	65.5	59.8	22	10	5.23	18
Moudon	65	55.1	14	3	4.52	22.4
Nyone	56.6	50.9	22	12	15.14	16.7
Orbe	57.4	54.1	20	6	4.2	15.3
Oron	72.5	71.2	12	1	2.4	21
Payerne	74.2	58.1	14	8	5.23	23.8
Paysd'enhaut	72	63.5	6	3	2.56	18
Rolle	60.5	60.8	16	10	7.72	16.3
Vevey	58.3	26.8	25	19	18.46	20.9
Yverdon	65.4	49.5	15	8	6.1	22.5
Conthey	75.5	85.9	3	2	99.71	15.1
Entremont	69.3	84.9	7	6	99.68	19.8
Herens	77.3	89.7	5	2	100	18.3
Martigwy	70.5	78.2	12	6	98.96	19.4
Monthey	79.4	64.9	7	3	98.22	20.2
St Maurice	65	75.9	9	9	99.06	17.8
Sierre	92.2	84.6	3	3	99.46	16.3
Sion	79.3	63.1	13	13	96.83	18.1
Boudry	70.4	38.4	26	12	5.62	20.3
La Chauxdfnd	65.7	7.7	29	11	13.79	20.5
Le Locle	72.7	16.7	22	13	11.22	18.9
Neuchatel	64.4	17.6	35	32	16.92	23
Val de Ruz	77.6	37.6	15	7	4.97	20
ValdeTravers	67.6	18.7	25	7	8.65	19.5
V. De Geneve	35	1.2	37	53	42.34	18
Rive Droite	44.7	46.6	16	29	50.43	18.2
Rive Gauche	42.8	27.7	22	29	58.33	19.3

Problem 9.8 (kNN)

For this exercise you will work with the NFL 2014 Combine Performance Results data available from OA 9.20, which contains performance statistics of college football players at NFL, February 2014, in Indianapolis. The dataset includes the following attributes among others:

i. Overall Grade: lowest 4.5, highest 7.5
ii. Height: in inches
iii. Arm Length: in inches
iv. Weight: in lbs
v. 40 Yard Time: in seconds
vi. Bench Press: reps @ 225 lbs
vii. Vertical Jump: in inches
viii. Broad Jump: in inches
ix. 3 Cone Drill: in seconds
x. 20-Yard Shuttle: in seconds

Use kNN on this dataset to find the players who have similar performance statistics.

Problem 9.9 (Decision trees)

Obtain the dataset from OA 9.21, which was collected from Worthy, S. L., Jonkman, J. N., & Blinn-Pike, L. (2010). Sensation-seeking, risk-taking, and problematic financial behaviors of college students. *Journal of Family and Economic Issues*, 31(2), 161–170.

For this dataset, the researchers conducted a survey of 450 undergraduates in large introductory courses at either Mississippi State University or the University of Mississippi. There were close to 150 questions on the survey, but only four of these variables are included in this dataset. (You can consult the paper to learn how the variables beyond these four affect the analysis.) The primary interest for the researchers was factors relating to whether or not a student has ever overdrawn a checking account.

The dataset contains the following variables:

Age	Age of the student (in years)
Sex	0 = male or 1 = female
DaysDrink	Number of days drinking alcohol (in past 30days)
Overdrawn	Has student overdrawn a checking account? 0 = no or 1 = yes

Create a decision tree-based model to predict the student overdrawing from the checking account based on Age, Sex, and DaysDrink. Since DaysDrink is a numeric variable; you may have to convert it into a categorical one. One suggestion for that would be:

if (no. of days of drinking alcohol > 7) = 0
(7 >= no. of days of drinking alcohol > 14) = 1
(no. of days of drinking alcohol >= 14) = 2

Problem 9.10 (Decision trees)

Download the dataset from OA 9.22 for this exercise, which is sourced from the study by Nicholas Gueaguen (2002). The effects of a joke on tipping when it is delivered at the same time as the bill. *Journal of Applied Social Psychology*, 32(9), 1955–1963.

Can telling a joke affect whether or not a waiter in a coffee bar receives a tip from a customer?

This study investigated this question at a coffee bar at a famous resort on the west coast of France. The waiter randomly assigned coffee-ordering customers to one of three groups: when receiving the bill, one group also received a card telling a joke, another group received a card containing an advertisement for a local restaurant, and a third group received no card at all. He recorded whether or not each customer left a tip.

The dataset contains the following variables:

Card	Type of card used: Ad, Joke, or None
Tip	1 = customer left a tip, or 0 = no tip
Ad	Indicator for Ad card
Joke	Indicator for Joke card
None	Indicator for No card

Use a decision tree to determine whether the waiter will receive a tip from the customer from the predictor variables.

Problem 9.11 (Random forests)

The following exercise is based on the abalone dataset, which can be downloaded from OA 9.23.

The job is to predict the age of abalone from physical measurements. The age of abalone is determined by cutting the shell through the cone, staining it, and counting the number of rings through a microscope – a boring and time-consuming task. Other measurements, which are easier to obtain, are used to predict the age.

Following are the list of attributes that are available in the current dataset:

The original data examples had a couple of missing values, which were removed (the majority having the predicted value missing), and the ranges of the continuous values have been scaled for use with an artificial neural network (by dividing by 200).

Name	Data type	Measurement unit	Description
Sex	Nominal	—	M, F, and I (infant)
Length	Continuous	millimeters	Longest shell measurement
Diameter	Continuous	millimeters	Perpendicular to length
Height	Continuous	millimeters	With meat in shell
Whole weight	Continuous	grams	Whole abalone
Shucked weight	Continuous	grams	Weight of meat
Viscera weight	Continuous	grams	Gut weight (after bleeding)
Shell weight	Continuous	grams	After being dried
Rings	Integer	—	+1.5 gives the age in years

Use this dataset to predict the age of abalone from the given attributes.

Problem 9.12 (Random forests)

In this exercise you will work with the Blues Guitarists Hand Posture and Thumbing Style by Region and Birth Period data, which you can download from OA 9.24. This dataset has 93 entries of various blues guitarists born between 1874 and 1940. Apart from the name of the guitarists, that dataset contains the following four features:

i. Regions: 1 means East, 2 means Delta, 3 means Texas
ii. Years: 0 for those born before 1906, 1 for the rest
iii. Hand postures: 1 = Extended, 2 = Stacked, 3 = Lutiform
iv. Thumb styles: between 1 and 3, 1 = Alternating, 2 = Utility, 3 = Dead

Using random forest on this dataset, how accurately can you tell their birth year from their hand postures and thumb styles? How does it affect the evaluation when you include the region while training the model?

Problem 9.13 (Naïve Bayes)

There is a YouTube spam collection dataset available from OA 9.25. It is a public set of comments collected for spam research. It has five datasets composed by 1956 real messages extracted from five videos. These five videos are popular pop songs that were among the 10 most viewed of the collection period.

All the five datasets have the following attributes:

COMMENT_ID: Unique ID representing the comment
AUTHOR: Author ID
DATE: Date the comment is posted
CONTENT: The comment
TAG: For spam 1, otherwise 0

For this exercise use any four of these five datasets to build a spam filter and use that filter to check the accuracy on the remaining dataset.

Problem 9.14 (Naïve Bayes)

The dataset for the following exercise on statistics of members and non-members of the Nazi party for teachers by religion, cohort, residence, and gender is sourced from Jarausch, K. H., & Arminger, G. (1989). The German teaching profession and Nazi party membership: A demographic logit model. *Journal of Interdisciplinary History*, 20(2), 197–225. It can be downloaded from OA 9.26. Following are the attribute values and their meaning:

i. Religion: 1 = Protestant, 2 = Catholic, 3 = None
ii. Cohort: 1 = Empire, 2 = Late Empire, 3 = Early Weimar, 4 = Late Weimar, 5 = Third Reich
iii. Residence: 1 = Rural, 2 = Urban
iv. Gender: 1 = Male, 2 = Female
v. Membership: 1 = Yes, 0 = No

vi. Count: in category

Use the Naïve Bayes algorithm on this dataset to determine the likelihood of the teachers being a member of the Nazi party from their religion, cohort, residence, and gender.

Problem 9.15 (SVM)

For this exercise, we have collected a sample of 198 cases from the NIST's AnthroKids dataset that is available for download from OA 9.27. The dataset comes from a 1977 anthropometric study of body measurements for children: Foster, T. A., Voors, A. W., Webber, L. S., Frerichs, R. R., & Berenson, G. S. (1977). Anthropometric and maturation measurements of children, ages 5 to 14 years, in a biracial community – the Bogalusa Heart Study. *American Journal of Clinical Nutrition*, 30(4), 582–591. Subjects in this sample are between the ages of 8 and 18 years old, selected at random from the much larger dataset of the original study.

Use the SVM to see if we can use Height, Weight, Age, and Sex (0 = male or 1 = female) to determine the Race (0 = white or 1 = other) of the child.

Problem 9.16 (SVM)

In this exercise you will use the Portuguese sea battles data from OA 9.28 that contains the outcomes of naval battles between Portuguese and Dutch/British ships between 1583 and 1663. The dataset has the following features:

i. Battle: Name of the battle place
ii. Year: Year of the battle
iii. Portuguese ships: Number of Portuguese ships
iv. Dutch ships: Number of Dutch ships
v. English ships: Number of ships from English side
vi. Ratio of Portuguese to Dutch/British ships
vii. Spanish Involvement: 1 = Yes, 0 = No
viii. Portuguese outcome: −1 = Defeat, 0 = Draw, +1 = Victory

Use an SVM based model to predict the Portuguese outcome of the battle from the number of ships involved in all sides and Spanish involvement.

Further Reading and Resources

If you are interested in learning more about supervised learning or any of the topics discussed above, following are a few links that might be useful:

1. Advanced regression models http://r-statistics.co/adv-regression-models.html
2. Further topics on logistic regression https://onlinecourses.science.psu.edu/stat504/node/217/
3. Common pitfalls in statistical analysis: logistic regression https://www.ncbi.nlm.nih.gov/pmc/articles/PMC5543767/

4. Decision trees in machine learning, simplified https://blogs.oracle.com/bigdata/decision-trees-machine-learning
5. A practical explanation of a Naïve Bayes classifier https://monkeylearn.com/blog/practical-explanation-naive-bayes-classifier/
6. Softmax regression http://deeplearning.stanford.edu/tutorial/supervised/SoftmaxRegression/
7. 6 Easy steps to learn the Naïve Bayes algorithm https://www.analyticsvidhya.com/blog/2015/09/naive-bayes-explained/

Notes

1. Linearly separable data source: https://docs.opencv.org/2.4/doc/tutorials/ml/introduction_to_svm/introduction_to_svm.html
2. Introduction to support vector machines: http://docs.opencv.org/2.4/doc/tutorials/ml/introduction_to_svm/introduction_to_svm.html
3. SVM tutorial: Support vector regression with R: https://www.svm-tutorial.com/2014/10/support-vector-regression-r/
4. Fisher, R. A. (1936). The use of multiple measurements in taxonomic problems. *Annals of Eugenics*, 7(2), 179–188. doi:10.1111/j.1469-1809.1936.tb02137.x

10 Unsupervised Learning

"If you mine the data hard enough, you can also find messages from God. [Dogbert]"
— Scott Adams, Dilbert

What do you need?

- A good understanding of statistical concepts, probability theory (see Appendix B), and functions.
- Introductory to intermediate-level experience with R (refer to Chapter 6).
- Everything covered in Chapters 8 and 9.

What will you learn?

- Solving data problems when truth-values for training are not available.
- Using unsupervised clustering methods to provide an explanation of data.
- Performing clustering using various machine learning techniques.

10.1 Introduction

In the previous chapter, we saw how to learn from data when the labels or true values associated with them are available. In other words, we knew what was right or wrong and we used that information to build a regression or classification model that could then make predictions for new data. Such a process fell under supervised learning. Now, we will consider the other big area of machine learning where we do not know true labels or values with the given data, and yet we will want to learn the underlying structure of that data and be able to explain it. This is called **unsupervised learning**.

In unsupervised learning, data points have no labels associated with them. Instead, the goal of an unsupervised learning algorithm is to organize the data in some way or to describe its structure. This can mean grouping it into clusters or finding different ways of looking at complex data so that it appears simpler or more organized.

Clustering is the assignment of a set of observations into subsets (called clusters) so that observations in the same cluster are similar in some sense. Clustering is a method of unsupervised learning, and a common technique for statistical data analysis used in many fields.

We will look at two types of clustering algorithms in this chapter: agglomerative (going bottom to top) and divisive (going top to bottom). In addition, we will also discuss a very important technique, called expectation maximization (EM), which is used in situations where we have too many unknowns and not enough guidance on how to explain or fit the data using a model. All of these are examples of unsupervised learning, as we do not have labels for data and yet we are trying to understand some potential underlying structure.

Let us begin by reviewing a couple of techniques for clustering the data as a way to explicate such a structure.

10.2 Agglomerative Clustering

This is a bottom-up approach of building clusters or groups of similar data points from individual data points. Following is a general outline of how an agglomerative clustering algorithm runs.

1. Use any computable cluster similarity measure, sim(C_i, C_j), for example, Euclidean distance, cosine similarity, etc.
2. For n objects $v_1, \ldots, v_n$, assign each to a singleton cluster $C_i = \{v_i\}$.
3. Repeat {
   - identify the two most similar clusters C_j and C_k (could be ties – chose one pair)
   - delete C_j and C_k and add ($C_j \cup C_k$) to the set of clusters

   } until just one cluster remains.

d. Use a dendrogram diagram to show the sequence of cluster mergers.

Hands-On Example 10.1: Agglomerative Clustering 1

Let us take an example and see how agglomerative clustering works. For this example, we will use five data points. The distances between every pair of data points is given in the distance matrix in Table 10.1. Do not worry about what the data means here. This table is simply to show you how the algorithm described above works.

As expected, the distance matrix is symmetric. This is because the distance between *x* and *y* is the same as the distance between *y* and *x*. It has zeros on the diagonal, as every item is a distance zero from itself. As the matrix is symmetric, only the lower triangle is shown in the table. The upper triangle will be a reflection of the lower one.

Table 10.1 Computation of distance matrix.

	1	2	3	4	5
1	0				
2	8	0			
3	3	6	0		
4	5	5	8	0	
5	13	10	<u>2</u>	7	0

Since we have distances for each pair of points, let us start clustering by grouping the smaller distances. As shown in Table 10.1, data points 3 and 5 are closer than any others, as their distance 2 (shown underlined) is the minimum between all the pairs. So, first we will merge this pair into a single cluster "35." So, at the end of this step, the cluster has four data points, for example, 1, 2, 4, and 35. Since the data points have changed, now we must recalculate the distance matrix. We need a procedure to determine the distance between 35 and every other data point. This can be done by assigning the maximum of the distance between an item and 3 and this item and 5. So the distance is calculated as

$$\text{dist}_{35,i} = \max(\text{dist}_{3,i}, \text{dist}_{5,i}). \tag{10.1}$$

Using the formula in Equation 10.1, the distance matrix is calculated as shown in Table 10.2.

If we continue this step using the above formula until all the data points are grouped into a single cluster, we will end up with the cluster shown in Figure 10.1. On this plot, the *y*-axis represents the cluster height, which is the distance between the objects at the time they were clustered.

Important note: The distance calculation formula for the matrix can vary from problem to problem, and, depending on the formula chosen, we may end up with completely different clustering. For example, for the same above dataset, if we calculate the distance as

$$\text{dist}_{35,i} = \min(\text{dist}_{3,i}, \text{dist}_{5,i}), \tag{10.2}$$

then the cluster we will end up with is shown in Figure 10.2.

Table 10.2 Next iteration of distance matrix.

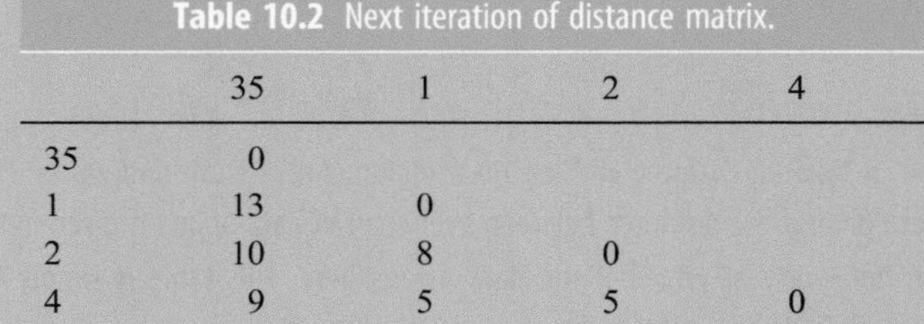

	35	1	2	4
35	0			
1	13	0		
2	10	8	0	
4	9	5	5	0

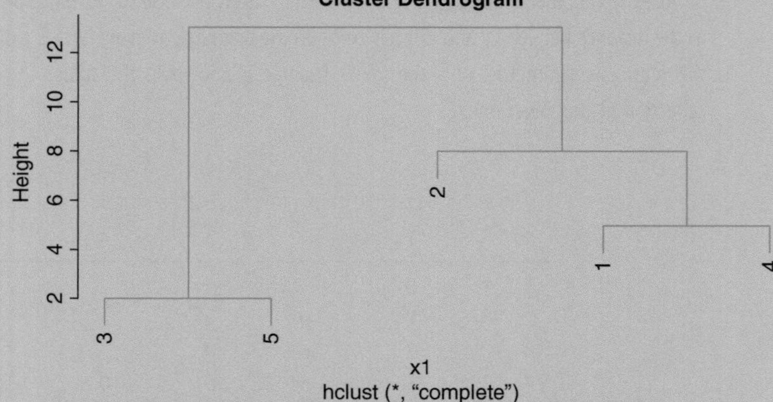

Figure 10.1 Cluster dendrogram from agglomerative clustering with maximum distance.

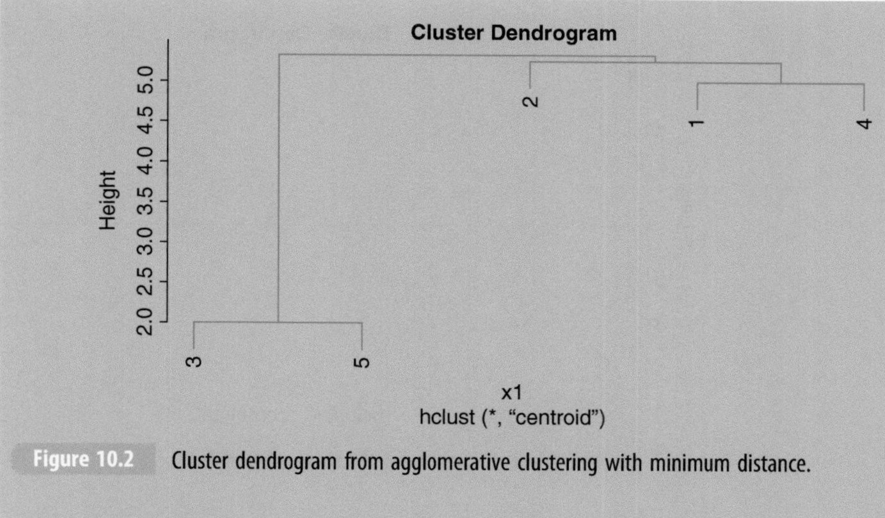

Figure 10.2 Cluster dendrogram from agglomerative clustering with minimum distance.

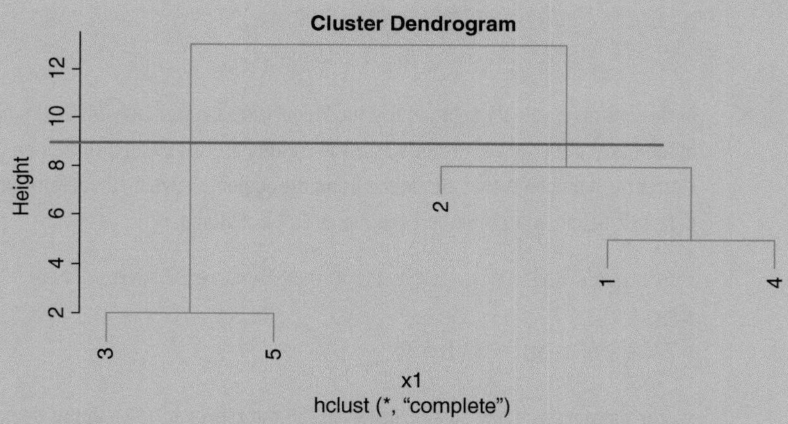

Figure 10.3 Number of clusters when the threshold is set at 9.

One of the common problems with hierarchical clustering (such as agglomerative) is that there is no universal way to say how many clusters there are. It depends on how we define the minimum threshold distance between two clusters. For example, in the first single linkage tree, if we set the threshold at 9, we will cut the tree into two clusters as shown by the red line in Figure 10.3, and we will end up with two clusters (1, 2, 4) and (3, 5).

Whereas, if we set the threshold at 6, the number of clusters will be three, as shown in Figure 10.4.

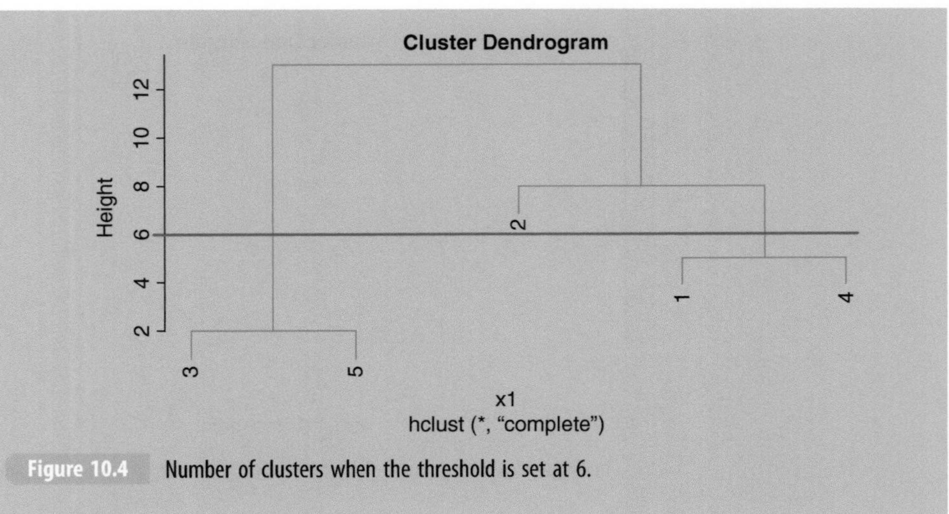

Figure 10.4 Number of clusters when the threshold is set at 6.

Hands-On Example 10.2: Agglomerative Clustering 2

In this example, you are going to use the StoneFlakes dataset (see OA 10.1) which contains measurement of the flakes from the waste products of the crafting process by prehistoric men. We will use this dataset to cluster the data points that are similar using the agglomerative method. Note, you may need to format the data first before you can import the file as CSV in RStudio.

```
> StoneFlakes <- read.csv('StoneFlakes.csv', header = TRUE,
sep = ',')
> View(StoneFlakes)
```

The dataset has a few missing instances (all the zeros and "?"s). In this demonstration we are going to remove the missing instances, remove the first attribute as it is non-numeric, and the output dataset would be standardized before proceeding for the clusters. Note, if the data values are non-numeric, you may need to convert them into numbers first before standardization, as the scale() function only works with numeric data.

```
> StoneFlakes[StoneFlakes == '?'] <- NA
> StoneFlakes <- na.omit(StoneFlakes)

# Converting the data entries into numbers
> StoneFlakes$LBI <- as.numeric(StoneFlakes$LBI)

# Standardizing the dataset
> StoneFlakes <- scale(StoneFlakes)
```

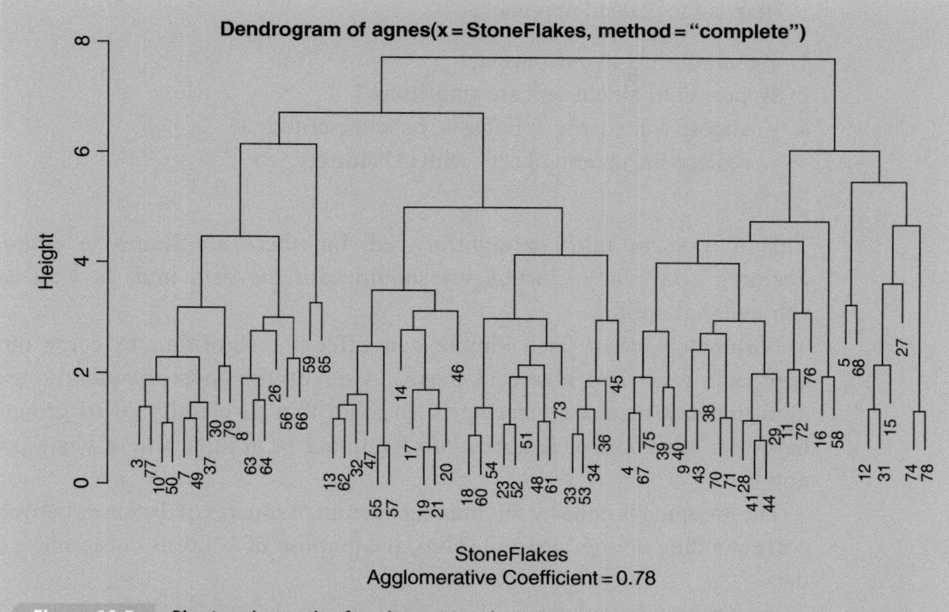

Figure 10.5 Plotting the result of agglomerative clustering.

In the next step, we are going to build the clusters in the agglomerative method using the agnes() function. Using the "agnes" function is as follows:

```
> library(cluster)
> aclusters <- agnes(StoneFlakes, method = "complete")
```

You can also check the agglomerative coefficient from the clusters:

```
> aclusters$ac
```

You can also visualize the clusters along with the agglomerative coefficient, and your visualization should look like Figure 10.5.

```
> plot(aclusters)
```

10.3 Divisive Clustering

The reverse of the agglomerative technique, divisive clustering works in a top-down mode, where the goal is to break up the cluster containing all objects into smaller clusters.

Here is the general approach:

1. Put all objects in one cluster.
2. Repeat until all clusters are singletons {
   - choose a cluster to split based on some criterion
   - replace the chosen cluster with subclusters.

   }

This may seem fairly straightforward, but there are issues to address, including deciding how many clusters we should split the data into, as well as how do we achieve that split.

Fortunately, there is a simple and effective algorithm to carry out the general approach described above: *k*-means. One of the most frequently used clustering algorithms, *k*-means clustering is an algorithm to classify or to group your objects based on attributes or features into *k* number of groups, where *k* is a positive integer number.

The grouping is done by minimizing the sum of squares of distances between data and the corresponding cluster centroid. Thus, the purpose of *k*-means clustering is to classify the data.

Here is how it works.

1. The basic step of *k*-means clustering is simple. In the beginning, we determine the number of clusters (k) that we want and we assume the centroid or center of these clusters. We can take any random objects as the initial centroids, or the first *k* objects in sequence can also serve as the initial centroids.
2. Then the *k*-means algorithm will do the three steps below until convergence.

   Step 1: Begin with a decision on the value of $k =$ number of clusters.

   Step 2: Put any initial partition that classifies the data into *k* clusters. You may assign the training samples randomly or systematically, as in the following:
   1. Take the first *k* training sample as single-element clusters.
   2. Assign each of the remaining $(N - K)$ training samples to the cluster with the nearest centroid. After each assignment, recompute the centroid of the gaining cluster.

   Step 3: Take each sample in sequence and compute its distance from the centroid of each of the clusters. If a sample is not currently in the cluster with the closest centroid, switch this sample to that cluster and update the centroid of the cluster gaining the new sample and the cluster losing the sample.

   Repeat the above three steps until convergence is achieved – that is, until a pass through the training sample causes no new assignments.

Seems more complicated than advertised? Let us do what we normally do in this book: take a hands-on approach and work through an example.

Hands-On Example 10.3: Divisive Clustering

Consider the dataset in Table 10.3, which represents the scores of two variables for each of seven individuals being studied.

At present, all seven individuals are grouped into a single cluster. Now let us divide the dataset into two clusters. A sensible approach for separation is parting the A and B values of the two individuals furthest apart into two groups. Let us plot these seven points on a 2D plane.

As we can see from Figure 10.6, the individuals 1 and 4 are the furthest apart, making them ideal candidates for partitioning. Therefore, we call them the centers of two different clusters, or centroids, as shown in Table 10.4.

At the next step, the remaining individuals are examined in sequence and allocated to the cluster to which they are closest, in terms of Euclidean distance to the cluster mean. The mean vector of the cluster

Table 10.3 Example dataset for *k*-means algorithm.

Individual	A	B
1	1.0	1.0
2	1.5	2.0
3	3.0	4.0
4	5.0	7.0
5	3.5	5.0
6	4.5	5.0
7	3.5	4.5

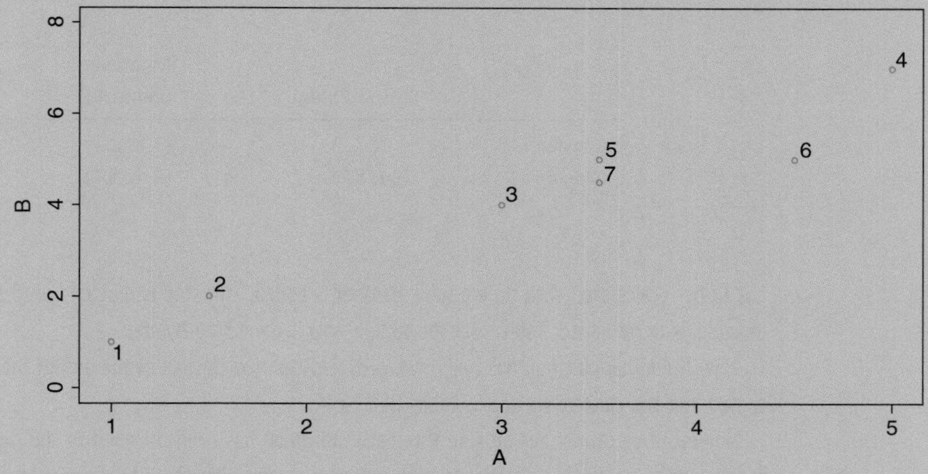

Figure 10.6 A against B plotted in 2D graph.

Table 10.4 Initialization of two clusters.

	Individual	Mean vector (centroid)
Cluster 1	1	(1.0, 1.0)
Cluster 2	4	(5.0, 7.0)

Table 10.5 First step-through with *k*-means algorithm.

	Cluster 1		Cluster 2	
Step	Individual	Mean vector (centroid)	Individual	Mean vector (centroid)
1	1	(1.0, 1.0)	4	(5.0, 7.0)
2	1, 2	(1.2, 1.5)	4	(5.0, 7.0)
3	1, 2, 3	(1.8, 2.3)	4	(5.0, 7.0)
4	1, 2, 3	(1.8, 2.3)	4, 5	(4.2, 6.0)
5	1, 2, 3	(1.8, 2.3)	4, 5, 6	(4.3, 5.7)
6	1, 2, 3	(1.8, 2.3)	4, 5, 6, 7	(4.1, 5.4)

Table 10.6 Result of the first step-through with *k*-means algorithm.

	Individual	Mean vector (centroid)
Cluster 1	1, 2, 3	(1.8, 2.3)
Cluster 2	4, 5, 6, 7	(4.1, 5.4)

has to be recalculated each time a new member is added. This step is repeated until there are no more individuals to be added. Table 10.5 shows how this is done step-by-step.

Now the initial partition has been changed, and the two clusters at the end of the previous step are turned into the clusters we see in Table 10.6.

However, we cannot yet be sure that each individual has been assigned to the right cluster. So, we compare each individual's distance to its own cluster mean and to that of the opposite cluster. The result is shown in Table 10.7.

As Table 10.7 shows, individual #3 is part of cluster 1, yet it is closest to cluster 2. Therefore, it makes sense to relocate #3 to cluster 2. The new partition is shown in Table 10.8.

Table 10.7 Second step-through with *k*-means algorithm.

Individual	Distance to mean (centroid) of cluster 1	Distance to mean (centroid) of cluster 2
1	1.5	5.4
2	0.4	4.3
3	2.1	1.8
4	5.7	1.8
5	3.2	0.7
6	3.8	0.6
7	2.8	1.1

Table 10.8 Result of the second step-through with *k*-means algorithm.

	Individual	Mean vector (centroid)
Cluster 1	1, 2	(1.3, 1.5)
Cluster 2	3, 4, 5, 6, 7	(3.9, 5.1)

This iterative relocation would continue from this new partition until no more relocations are required.

Try It Yourself 10.1: Clustering

To practice more on clustering, obtain the User knowledge modeling dataset (available from OA 10.2), which contains five numeric predictor attributes, and one categorical target attribute, which is the class label. Use both divisive and agglomerative clustering on this dataset and compare their accuracy in predicting the class label from the predictor attributes. How many clusters will you create? Why? Explain the various design decisions you make.

10.4 Expectation Maximization (EM)

So far, we have seen clustering, classification algorithms, and probabilistic models that are based on the existence of efficient and robust procedures for learning parameters from observations. Often, however, the only data available for training a model are incomplete. Missing values can occur, for example, in medical diagnoses, where patient histories generally include results from a limited battery of tests. Alternatively, in gene expression clustering, incomplete data arise from the intentional omission of gene-to-cluster assignments in the probabilistic model. The expectation maximization (EM) algorithm is a fantastic approach to addressing this problem. The EM algorithm enables parameter estimation in probabilistic models with incomplete data.

Consider an example of tossing coins. Assume that we are given a pair of coins, A and B, of unknown biases, θ_A and θ_B, respectively (that is, on any given flip, coin A will land on heads with probability θ_A and tails with probability $1 - \theta_A$. Similarly, for coin B, the probabilities are θ_B and $1 - \theta_B$. The goal of this experiment is to estimate $\theta = (\theta_A, \theta_B)$ by repeating the following steps five times: randomly choose one of the two coins (with equal probability), and perform 10 independent coin tosses with the selected coin. Thus, the entire procedure involves a total of 50 coin tosses.

During this experiment we count two vectors, for example, $\boldsymbol{x} = (x_1, x_2, \ldots, x_5)$, where $x_i \in \{0, 1, \ldots, 10\}$ is the number of heads observed during the ith round of tosses. Parameter estimation of this experiment is known as the complete data case in the instance that the values of all relevant random variables in our model (that is, the result of each coin flip and the type of coin used for each flip) are known.

A simple way to estimate θ_A and θ_B is to return the observed proportions of heads for each coin:

$$\theta_A = \frac{\text{number of heads using coin A}}{\text{total number of flips using coin A}} \tag{10.3}$$

and

$$\theta_B = \frac{\text{number of heads using coin B}}{\text{total number of flips using coin B}}. \tag{10.4}$$

This intuitive guess is, in fact, known in the statistical literature as **maximum likelihood estimation** (MLE). Roughly speaking, the MLE method assesses the quality of a statistical model based on the probability it assigns to the observed data. If $\log P(x, y)$ is the logarithm of the joint probability (or **log likelihood**) of obtaining any particular vector of observed head counts x and coin types y, then Equations 10.3 and 10.4 solve for the parameters (= A, B) that maximize $\log P(x, y)$.

The expectation maximization (EM) algorithm is used to find (locally) MLE parameters of a statistical model in cases where the equations cannot be solved directly. Often these models involve latent variables in addition to unknown parameters and known data observations. That is, either missing values exist among the data, or the model can be formulated more simply by assuming the existence of further unobserved data points.

Hands-On Example 10.4: EM

Now, let us take an example and see how this works in R. For this experiment, we will use the diabetes dataset that is available as part of the package "mclust" (MCLUST, version 5.3; type 'citation("mclust")' to cite this R package in publications).

```
> library(mclust)
> data("diabetes")
> summary(diabetes)
      class        glucose         insulin          sspg
Chemical:36   Min.   : 70    Min.   :  45.0   Min.   : 10.0
Normal  :76   1st Qu.: 90    1st Qu.: 352.0   1st Qu.:118.0
Overt   :33   Median : 97    Median : 403.0   Median :156.0
              Mean   :122    Mean   : 540.8   Mean   :186.1
              3rd Qu.:112    3rd Qu.: 558.0   3rd Qu.:221.0
              Max.   :353    Max.   :1568.0   Max.   :748.0
```

To apply the EM algorithm, we will use the same "mclust" package. The summary command with mclust object generates:

- log.likelihood: This is the log likelihood of the Bayesian information criterion (BIC) value – indicating the *goodness* of the model
- n: This is the number of X points
- df: This is the degrees of freedom
- BIC: This is the Bayesian information criterion; low is good
- ICL: Integrated complete X likelihood – a classification version of the BIC.

First, we need to extract the appropriate data before we can use the EM algorithm on it.

```
> data("diabetes")
> head(diabetes)
  class glucose insulin  sspg
1 Normal     80     356   124
2 Normal     97     289   117
3 Normal    105     319   143
4 Normal     90     356   199
5 Normal     90     323   240
6 Normal     86     381   157

> class.dia = diabetes$class
> table(class.dia)
class.dia
Chemical  Normal  Overt
      36      76     33

> X = diabetes[,-1]
> head(X)
```

```
  glucose insulin sspg
1      80     356  124
2      97     289  117
3     105     319  143
4      90     356  199
5      90     323  240
6      86     381  157

> clPairs(X, class.dia)
```

The above steps generate the output shown in Figure 10.7. Here, "clPairs" is a function for generating pairwise scatterplots showing classification. It is a pictorial representation of how two forms of data categories (in this case, diabetes class and glucose, insulin, sspg) are related.

Now we will use the Mclust function to fit a (density estimation) model.

```
> fit <- Mclust(X)
fitting ...
 |==========================================================| 100%
```

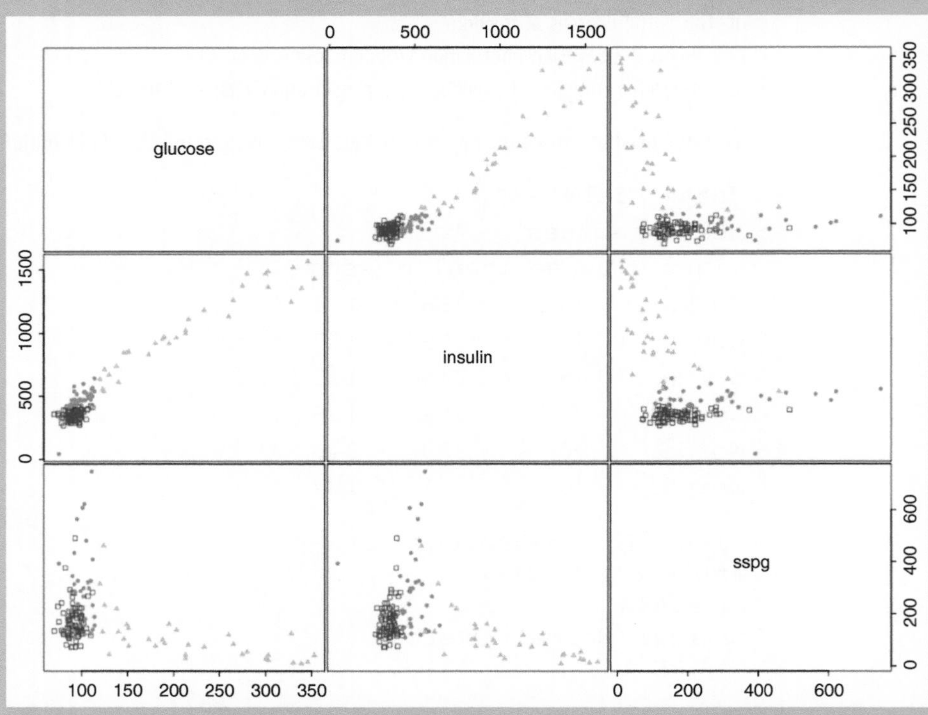

Figure 10.7 Pairwise scatterplots showing classification.

```
> fit
'Mclust' model object:
best model: ellipsoidal, varying volume, shape, and orien-
tation (VVV) with 3 components

> summary(fit)
----------------------------------------------
Gaussian finite mixture model fitted by EM algorithm
----------------------------------------------
Mclust VVV (ellipsoidal, varying volume, shape, and orienta-
tion) model with 3 components:
log.likelihood    n   df        BIC        ICL
     -2307.883  145   29  -4760.091  -4776.086

Clustering table:
1   2   3
82  33  30
```

What just happened? We created a model that tried to fit the data using the EM algorithm. Now that we have created a model for our dataset, we need to evaluate the goodness of the model. There are several criteria for evaluating this, such as the **Akaike information criterion** (AIC), the **Bayesian information criterion** (BIC), and **log likelihood**, etc. AIC provides an estimate of the relative information loss by a given model when representing the process that generated the data. Let us say, given some data, a model has been generated, where k is the number of estimated parameters. If $\hat{L}$ is the maximum value of the likelihood function for the model, then the AIC value is calculated as

$$\text{AIC} = 2k - 2\ln(\hat{L}). \tag{10.5}$$

BIC, on the other hand, estimates the posterior probability of a model being true from a certain Bayesian setup. A lower BIC means that a model is considered more likely to be a better model. The formula for BIC is

$$\text{BIC} = (\ln n)k - 2\ln(\hat{L}). \tag{10.6}$$

Both AIC and BIC are penalized-likelihood criteria. What this means is that the higher the number, the worse the model. The only significant difference between AIC and BIC is the choice of log n versus 2.

So, let us visualize this model with the following components:

- The BIC values used for choosing the number of clusters/components (Figure 10.8)
- A plot of the clustering
- A plot of the classification uncertainty (Figure 10.9)
- The orbital plot of clusters (Figure 10.10)

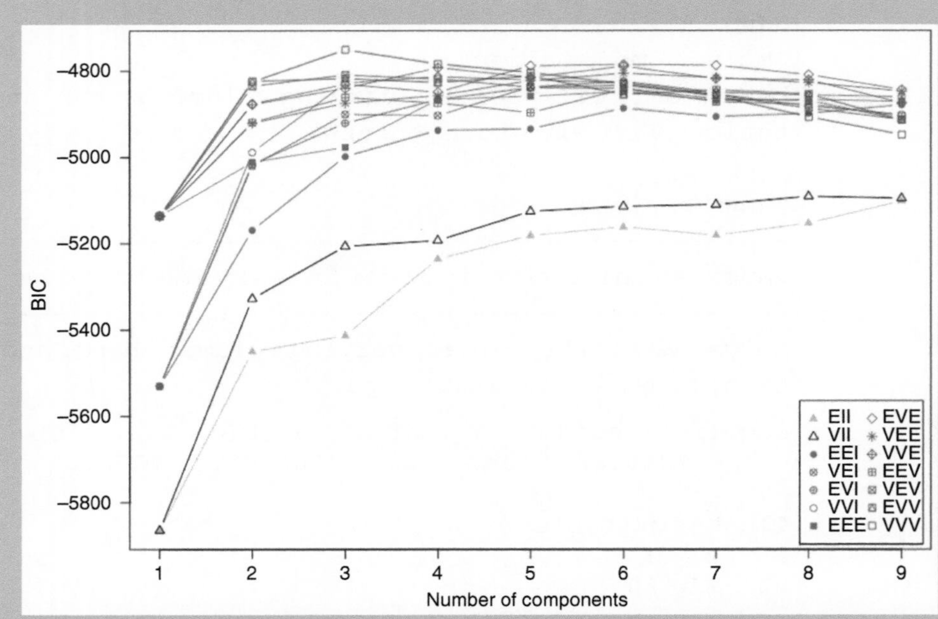

Figure 10.8 Plot showing number of components and corresponding BIC.

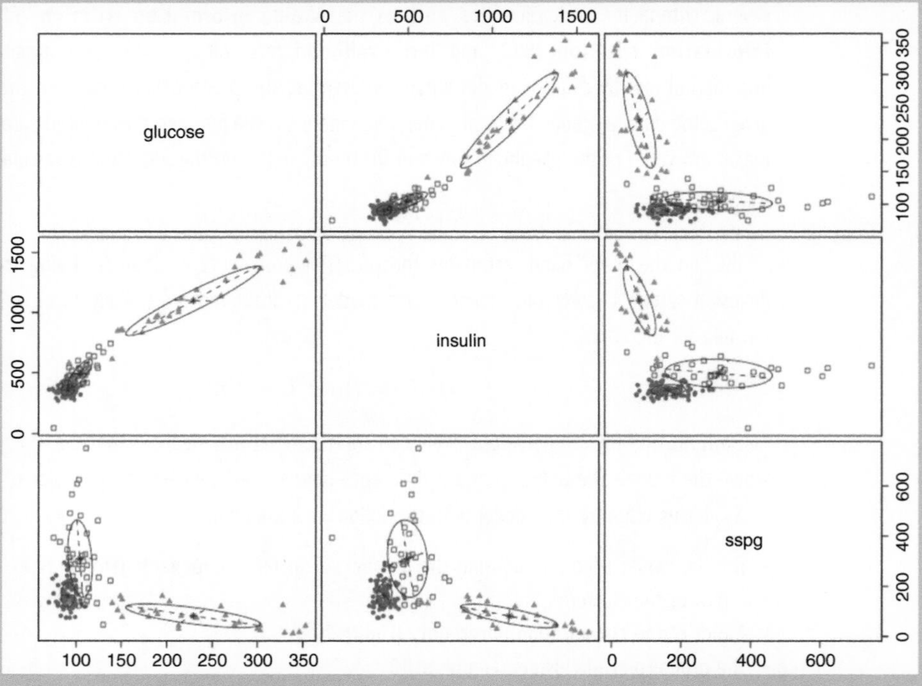

Figure 10.9 Classification plot.

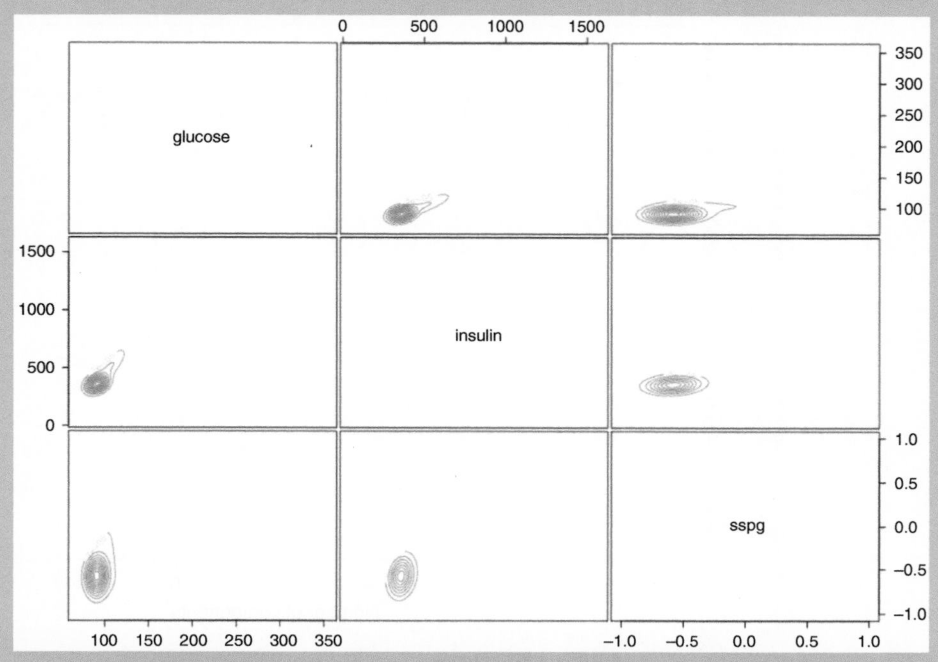

Figure 10.10 Density plot.

```
> plot(fit, what = "BIC")
> #table(class, fit$BIC)
> #2: classification
> plot(fit, what = "classification")
> plot(fit, what = "density")
```

You can try and plot the classification uncertainty in the same way. The mclustBIC function from the mclust package uses BIC for EM initialized by model-based hierarchical clustering for parameterized Gaussian mixture models (Figure 10.11).

```
> BIC = mclustBIC(X)
fitting ...
 |=================================================| 100%

> summary(BIC)
Best BIC values:
           VVV,3          VVE,3           EVE,4
BIC     -4760.091  -4775.53693   -4793.26143
BIC diff    0.000    -15.44628     -33.17079

> plot(BIC)
```

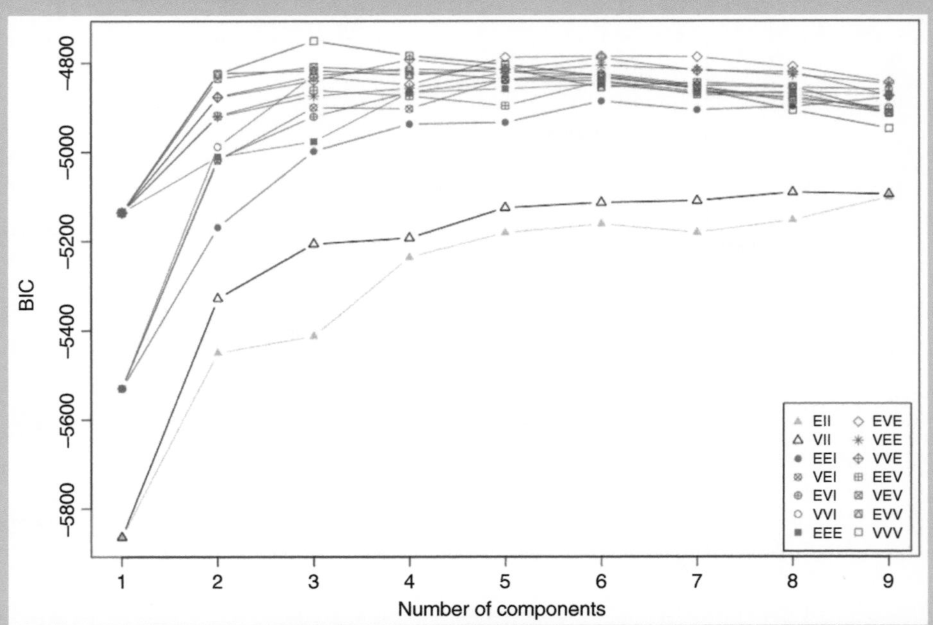

Figure 10.11 Visualizing BIC criterion.

The mclustICL from mclust uses ICL (integrated complete-data likelihood) for parameterized Gaussian mixture models fitted by the EM algorithm initialized by model-based hierarchical clustering (Figure 10.12).

```
> ICL = mclustICL(X)
fitting ...
|==========================================================|
100%

> summary(ICL)
Best ICL values:
              VVV,3         VVE,3          EVE,4
ICL      -4776.086  -4793.27143   -4809.16868
ICL diff     0.000    -17.18553     -33.08278

> plot(ICL) # Only ICL plot
```

Many of these constructs (e.g., density plot, ICL) are out of scope for this book, but I still wanted to draw your attention to these as a way to demonstrate that, since EM does not have a clear way to assess how well the model is built, like we are able to do for our classification models, we need several ways to look into the *goodness* of the model. Keeping aside some of the metrics and plots in the above explanation

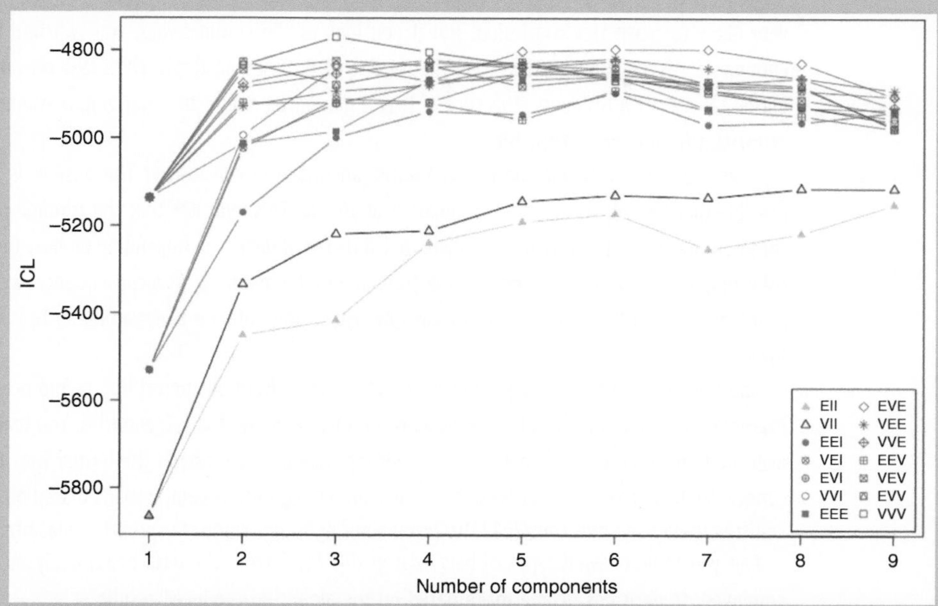

Figure 10.12 Visualizing integrated completed likelihood criterion.

that are out of scope for us, I hope at least log likelihood, AIC, and BIC are clear to you and that you could compute those for a model in order to say how well that model captures underlying data.

Try It Yourself 10.3: EM

Use the User knowledge modeling dataset from OA 10.2. Use the EM algorithm to find the MLE parameters of the model. Report the AIC and BIC values.

FYI: Bias and Fairness

At several places in this book we have discussed the issues of bias and fairness in different contexts. We will continue that topic here as we wrap up our coverage of machine learning.

Where Does Bias Come From?

Bias in data science may come from the source data, algorithmic or system bias, and cognitive bias. Imagine that you are analyzing criminal records for two districts. The records include 10,000 residents from district A and 1000 residents from district B. Of these, 100 district A residents and 50 district B residents have committed crimes in the past year. Will you conclude that people from district A are more likely to be criminals than people from district B? If simply comparing the number of criminals in the past year, you are very likely to reach this conclusion. But if you look at the criminal rate, you will find that district A's criminal rate is 1%, which is less than that of district B. Based on this analysis, the previous conclusion is biased for district A residents. This type of bias is generated due to the analyzing method; thus, we call it **algorithmic bias** or **system bias**.

Does the criminal-based analysis guarantee an unbiased conclusion? The answer is no. It could be possible that both districts have a population of 10,000. This indicates that the criminal records have the complete statistics of district A, yet only partial statistics of district B. Depending on how the reports data is collected, 5% may or may not be the true criminal rate for district B. As a consequence, we may still arrive at a biased conclusion. This type of bias is inherent in the data we are examining; thus, we call it **data bias**.

The third type of bias is **cognitive bias**, which arises from our perception of the presented data. An example is that you are given the conclusions from two criminal analysis agencies. You tend to believe one over another because the former has a higher reputation, even though the former may have the biased conclusion. Read a real-world case of machine learning algorithms being racially biased on recidivism here:

https://www.nytimes.com/2017/10/26/opinion/algorithm-compas-sentencing-bias.html

Can you think of what types of bias exist in this case? From the data being analyzed, the algorithms employed, to decisions people make based on the algorithm-produced results.

In reality, due to multiple factors such as data distribution, collection process, different analyzing methods, and measurement standards, it is easy to end up with a biased dataset and biased conclusions about the data. We need to be careful when dealing with data and the techniques we employ for data analysis.

Bias Is Everywhere

With the explosion of data and technologies, we are immersed in all kinds of data applications. Think of the news you read every day on the Internet, the music you listen to through service providers, the ads displayed while you are browsing webpages, the products recommended to you when shopping online, the information you found through search engines, etc. Bias can be present everywhere without people's awareness. Like "you are what you eat," the data you consume is so powerful that it can in fact shape your views, preferences, judgements, and even decisions in many aspects of your life.

Say you want to know whether some food is good or bad for health. A search engine returns 10 pages of results. The first result and most of the results on the first page are stating that the food is healthy. To what extent do you believe the search results? After glancing at the results on the first page, will you conclude that the food is beneficial or at least the benefits outweigh the harm? How likely is it that you will continue to check results on the second page? Are you aware that the second page may contain results of the harm of the food, so that results on the first page of results are biased? As a data scientist, it is important to be careful to avoid biased outcomes. But as a human being who lives in the world of data, it is more important to be aware of the bias that may exist in your daily data consumption.

Bias vs. Fairness

It is possible that bias leads to unfairness, but can it be biased but also fair? The answer is yes. Consider bias as the skewed view of the protected groups: fairness is the subjective measurement of the data or the way data is handled. In other words, bias and fairness are not necessarily contradictory to each other. Consider the employee diversity in a US company. All but one employee are US citizens. Is the employment structure biased toward US citizens? Yes, if this is a result of the US citizens being favored during the hiring process. Is it a fair structure? Yes and no. According to the Rooney rule, this is fair since the company hired at least one minority. While according to statistical parity, this is unfair since the number of US citizens and non-citizens are not equal. In general, bias is easy and direct to measure, yet fairness is subtler due to the various subjective concerns. There are just so many different fairness definitions to choose from, let alone some of which are contradictory to each other.

Check out the tutorial at https://www.youtube.com/watch?v=jIXluYdnyyk for some examples and helpful insights of fairness definitions from the perspective of a computer scientist.

10.5 Introduction to Reinforcement Learning

Born out of behaviorist psychology experiments performed almost a century ago, **reinforcement learning** (RL) attempts to model how software agents should take actions in an environment that will maximize some form of cumulative reward.[1]

Let us take an example. Imagine you want to train a computer to play chess against a human. In such a case, determining the best move to make depends on a number of factors. The number of possible states that can exist in a game is usually very large. To cover these many states using a standard rules-based approach would mean specifying a lot of hard-coded rules. RL cuts out the need to manually specify rules, and RL agents learn simply by playing the game. For two-player games, such as backgammon, agents can be trained by playing against other human players or even other RL agents.

In RL, the algorithm decides to choose the next course of action once it sees a new data point. Based on how suitable the action is, the learning algorithm also gets some incentive a short time later. The algorithm always modifies its course of action toward the highest reward. Reinforcement learning is common in robotics, where the set of sensor readings at one point in time is a data point, and the algorithm must choose the robot's next action. It is also a natural fit for Internet-of-Things (IoT) applications.

The basic reinforcement learning (RL) model consists of the following (and see Figure 10.13):

1. a set of environment and agent states S
2. a set of actions A of the agent
3. policies of transitioning from states to actions

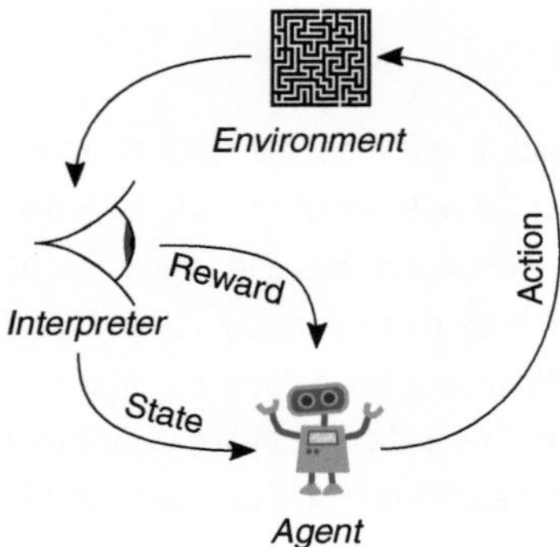

Figure 10.13 The typical framing of a reinforcement learning (RL) scenario (an agent takes actions in an environment that is interpreted into a reward and a representation of the state which is fed back into the agent.) (Source: Wikipedia.[2])

4. rules that determine the *scalar immediate reward* of a transition and
5. rules that describe what the agent observes.

An RL agent interacts with its environment in discrete time steps and in a particular order.

1. At each time t, the agent receives an observation o_t, which typically includes the reward r_t.
2. It then chooses an action a_t from the set of actions available, which is subsequently sent to the environment.
3. The environment moves to a new state s_{t+1} from s_t and the reward r_{t+1} associated with the *transition* s_t, a_t, s_{t+1} is determined.
4. The goal of a reinforcement-learning agent is to collect as much reward as possible. The agent can choose any action as a function of the history and it can even randomize its action selection.

Let us take a real-life example and see how reinforcement learning (RL) works. We will follow it up with a simple process to create a model using reinforcement learning in R.

First, take a step back and think about how we learn, specifically in a traditional classroom or educational environment. If you are using this book for such an educational purpose, you could consider me as a teacher and yourself as a student. I have followed the practice of explaining a given concept first and reinforcing the ideas with some follow-up examples. The students, once they go through the topic and follow the examples, are expected to solve similar questions from the end-of-chapter exercise section themselves. The RL algorithm tries to mimic this exact process.

So, how do you teach a machine to learn a new concept? To understand this, you need to break down the process of learning into smaller tasks and go through them step-by-step. For each step, you should have a set of "policies" for the machine to follow. A set of reward and penalty rules are defined which the machine uses to assess its performance. The training limit specifies the trial-and-error experiences which are used by the machine to train itself. Within this limit, the machine learns by continuously taking each of the possible actions and computing the change in reward after each action. This computation follows the "Markov process," which implies that the decision the machine makes at any given state is independent of the decision the machine made at any previous state. Over time, it starts seeking the most reward and avoiding the penalties.

Hands-On Example 10.5: Reinforcement Learning

Now that you are aware of how RL works, it is time to do a hands-on example in R to reinforce the concept. First, you have to download the required packages. The RL package in R is experimental at this stage, and therefore part of developmental tools, which you need to install first. Here is how to get hold of the RL package:

```
install.packages("devtools")
library(devtools)
install_github("nproellochs/ReinforcementLearning")
library(ReinforcementLearning)
```

Fortunately, the package also comes with a toy game, called tic-tac-toe, with data generated in its pre-built library. The dataset contains more than 400,000 rows of steps for tic-tac-toe. We are going to use the same dataset for this demonstration. You can build the reinforced model by executing the following steps. Let us start by loading the dataset:

```
# Load the dataset
data("tictactoe")
# View the dataset
View(tictactoe)
```

As you can see, the dataset has information about various states in a game, actions to be taken, and their corresponding reward. It is like you are teaching a child what to do and what not to do in a given situation in a tic-tac-toe game. Using this information, we can train a model:

```
# Perform reinforcement learning on tictactoe data
tic_tac_toe_model <- ReinforcementLearning(tictactoe,
s = "State", a = "Action", r = "Reward", s_new = "NextState",
iter = 1)
```

This line uses the supplied dataset for training a model based on the reinforcement learning approach. Since the dataset is really large, it will take a few minutes to complete the training. When the training is complete, you can inquire about the policy and the associated rewards the model has learnt. To inquire about the optimal policy, enter:

```
tic_tac_toe_model$Policy
```

What you see in this output is a long set of rules/policies that the model has learned; it has figured out the optimal actions to take (represented with c1, c2, etc.) given a state in the game. Note that this may be different for each run and each time it will print a large matrix of all the possible steps in that state. To find the reward for this run, execute the following line:

```
tic_tac_toe_model$Reward
[1] 5449
```

In this case, the reward is computed as 5449, but this may vary for each run.

You have to admit that this was easy to run! But what do we really take away from this example? Well, in the future, if you find yourself needing to use some form of reinforcement learning, you could construct a dataset such as the one used here, containing states, actions, where those actions lead to (next states), and corresponding rewards, which can then be used with a process similar to the one shown above for building a model.

Summary

If it has not been obvious to you so far, let me state it – data science often is just as much about art as it is about science. That means, at times, we do not have a clear and systematic way to address a problem and we have to get creative. Several techniques we saw in unsupervised learning in this chapter fall under that category. Essentially, you are given some data or observations without clear labels or true values, and you are asked to understand, organize, or explain that data. Such scenarios leave you in a position where you have to make design choices.

For instance, when working with the StoneFlakes data, we had to make choices about where to draw different thresholds for clustering. And that is not all. Often, we do not even know that clustering is the right technique to use for a given problem. Using machine learning for solving data problems is much more than simply running a classifier or a clustering algorithm on a dataset; it requires first developing an understanding of the problem at hand and using our intuition and knowledge about various machine learning techniques to decide which of them to apply. This takes practice, but I hope the chapters in this part of the book, along with dozens of hands-on examples and practice problems, have given you a head start.

FYI: Deep Learning

Now that we have massive amounts of storage, computational power at our disposal, along with the architecture to store, access, and analyze the big data in a distributed system, we need a new generation of algorithms to mine the insights from the data by leveraging these tremendous amounts of resources fully. Fortunately, there is a recent spinoff of traditional neural networks which does that. These new types of neural networks are called deep neural networks or deep learning models.

Simply put, deep learning is a new branch of the machine learning technique that enables computers to follow the human learning process, that is, to learn by example. In the deep learning technique, the model is trained by a large set of labeled data and neural network architectures that contain many hidden layers. The model learns to perform classification tasks directly from images, text, or sound. Deep learning models can achieve state-of-the-art accuracy, sometimes exceeding human-level performance. Deep learning is a key technology behind the current research in driverless cars, enabling them to distinguish a pedestrian from a lamppost, or to recognize the traffic symbols, etc. Deep learning has received lots of attention lately and for good reason. So far, it has achieved results that were not possible before, especially image classification or related tasks.

So, the question is, how does deep learning attain such impressive results? While deep learning was first proposed in the 1980s, it has only recently become a success, for two reasons:

- Deep learning requires large amounts of labeled data, which nowadays has become available due to the large number of sensors and electronics that we use in our daily lives, and the huge amount of data those sensors routinely generate. For example, driverless car development requires millions of images and thousands of hours of video.
- Deep learning requires substantial computing power, including high-performance GPUs that have a parallel architecture, efficient for deep learning. When combined with cloud computing or distributed computing, this enables the training time for a deep learning network to be reduced from the usual weeks to hours or even less.

How does deep learning work? The term "deep" in deep learning usually refers to the number of hidden layers in the neural network, which defines the underlying architecture of any deep learning framework. Traditional neural networks that we have seen in the previous chapter contained only two or three hidden layers, while deep networks can have as many as 150.

One of the most popular types of deep neural networks is known as convolutional neural networks (CNN or ConvNet). A CNN convolves learned features with input data, and uses 2D convolutional layers, making this architecture well suited to processing 2D data, such as images.

For further introduction and exploration of deep learning, you could check out this "weird" (more accessible) explanation on a Towards Data Science blog:
https://towardsdatascience.com/a-weird-introduction-to-deep-learning-7828803693b0

Key Terms

- **Unsupervised learning:** Unsupervised learning is where the outcomes of test cases are based on the analysis of training samples for which explicit class labels are absent.

- **Clustering:** Clustering is the assignment of a set of observations into subsets (called clusters) so that observations in the same cluster are similar in some sense.
- **Dendrogram:** A dendrogram is a representation of a tree structure.
- **Maximum likelihood estimator (MLE):** This is a way to assess the quality of a statistical model based on the probability that model assigns to the observed data. The model that has the highest probability of generating the data is the best one.
- **Log likelihood:** This is a measure of estimating how likely (or with what probability) a given model generated the data we observed. In other words, it is a measure for the *goodness* of a model.
- **Akaike information criterion (AIC):** Similar to log likelihood, except it penalizes a model for having a higher number of parameters.
- **Bayesian information criterion (BIC):** Similar to AIC, except it also includes a penalty related to the sample size used for the model.
- **Reinforcement learning:** This is a branch of machine learning that attempts to model how agents should take actions in an environment that will maximize some form of cumulative reward.

Conceptual Questions

1. What is unsupervised learning? Give two examples of data problems where you would use supervised learning.
2. How is divisive clustering different from agglomerative clustering?
3. EM seems like a typical clustering approach, but it is not. What is so special about unsupervised learning with EM? [Hint: Think about the nature of the data and the problem.]

Hands-On Problems

Problem 10.1 (Clustering)

Under the life-cycle savings hypothesis as developed by Franco Modigliani, the savings ratio (aggregate personal savings divided by disposable income) is explained by per-capita disposable income, the percentage rate of change in per-capita disposable income, and two demographic variables: the percentage of the population less than 15 years old, and the percentage of the population over 75 years old. The data are averaged over the decade 1960–1970 to remove the business cycle or other short-term fluctuations.

The following data were obtained from Belsley, D. A., Kuh, E., & Welsch, R. E. (1980). *Regression Diagnostics*. John Wiley & Sons, New York. They in turn obtained the data from Sterling, A. (1977) Unpublished BS Thesis. Massachusetts Institute of Technology. You can download it from OA 10.3.

The dataset contains 50 observations with five variables.

I. Sr: numeric, aggregate personal savings
II. pop15: numeric, percent of population under 15
III. pop75: numeric, percent of population over 75
IV. dpi: numeric, real per-capita disposable income
V. ddpi: numeric, percent growth rate of dpi

Use a clustering algorithm (agglomerative and/or divisive) to identify the similar countries.

Problem 10.2 (Clustering)

For this clustering exercise, you are going to use the data on women professional golfers' performance on the LPGA, 2008 tour. The dataset can be obtained from OA 10.4 and has the following attributes:

i. Golfer: name of the player
ii. Average Drive distance
iii. Fairway Percentage
iv. Greens in regulation: in percentage
v. Average putts per round
vi. Sand attempts per round
vii. Sand saves: in percentage
viii. Total Winnings per round
ix. Log: Calculated as (Total Win/Round)
x. Total Rounds
xi. Id: Unique ID representing each player

Use clustering (agglomerative and/or divisive) on this dataset to find out which players have similar performance in the same season.

Problem 10.3 (EM)

Obtain the slump dataset available from OA 10.5. The original owner of the dataset is I-Cheng Yeh (icyeh@chu.edu.tw; Yeh, I-C. (2007). Modeling slump flow of concrete using second-order regressions and artificial neural networks. *Cement and Concrete Composites*, 29(6), 474–480).

This dataset is about a concrete slump test. Concrete is a highly complex material. The slump flow of concrete is not only determined by the water content but is also influenced by other ingredients.

There are seven attributes and three outcome measures in the dataset (component kg in one cubic meter [1 m^3] concrete):

Cement
Slag
Fly ash
Water
SP
Coarse Aggr.
Fine Aggr.
Slump (cm)
Flow (cm)
28-day Compressive Strength (MPa)

The task is to predict maximum slump, flow, and compressive strength (each separately) from the amount of ingredients. Use the Mclust algorithm to run EM on this data and comment on how well you are able to explain those three outcome variables using the seven ingredients.

Problem 10.4 (EM)

For this problem, the dataset to be used is on SGEMM GPU kernel performance (download it from OA 10.6), which was measured in terms of the running time of a matrix–matrix product $A * B = C$, where all matrices have dimension of 2048×2048, in a parameterizable SGEMM GPU kernel with 241,600 possible parameter combinations. The experiment was run on a desktop workstation running Ubuntu 16.04 Linux with an Intel Core i5 (3.5 GHz), 16 GB RAM, and an NVidia Geforce GTX 680 4 GB GF580 GTX-1.5 GB GPU. For each tested combination, four runs were performed, and the results of each run were reported. All four runtimes were measured in milliseconds. Apart from these four output performance measurements, the dataset also contains the following 14 features that describe the parameter combination:

i. Input features 1 and 2, MWG, NWG: Per-matrix 2D tiling at workgroup level
ii. Input feature 3, KWG: Inner dimension of 2D tiling at workgroup level
iii. Input features 4 and 5, MDIMC, NDIMC: Local workgroup size
iv. Input features 6 and 7, MDIMA, NDIMB: Local memory shape
v. Input feature 8, KWI: Kernel loop unrolling factor
vi. Input features 9 and 10, VWM, VWN: Per-matrix vector widths for loading and storing
vii. Input features 11 and 12, STRM, STRN: Enable stride for accessing off-chip memory within a single thread: $\{0, 1\}$ (categorical)
viii. Input features 13 and 14, SA, SB: Per-matrix manual caching of the 2D workgroup tile: $\{0, 1\}$ (categorical)

First, from the four runtimes, which ones seem more accurate than others on measuring the GPU kernel performance in this experiment? Next, use EM on this dataset to predict the runtimes from the input parameter combinations.

Further Reading and Resources

If you are interested in learning more about unsupervised learning methods, following are a few links that might be useful:

1. Data mining cluster analysis: advanced concepts and algorithms: https://www-users.cs.umn.edu/~kumar001/dmbook/dmslides/chap9_advanced_cluster_analysis.pdf
2. Advanced clustering methods: http://www.cse.psu.edu/~rtc12/CSE586/lectures/meanshiftclustering.pdf
3. An advanced clustering algorithm (ACA) for clustering large data set to achieve high dimensionality: https://www.omicsonline.org/open-access/an-advanced-clustering-algorithm-aca-for-clustering-large-data-jcsb.1000115.pdf
4. Expectation-maximization algorithm for clustering multidimensional numerical data: https://engineering.purdue.edu/kak/Tutorials/ExpectationMaximization.pdf

Notes

1. Wikipedia on reinforcement learning: https://en.wikipedia.org/wiki/Reinforcement_learning
2. Wikipedia reinforcement learning diagram: https://en.wikipedia.org/wiki/File:Reinforcement_learning_diagram.svg

PART IV

APPLICATIONS, EVALUATIONS, AND METHODS

We finally come to the last part of this book, which is designed with two purposes in mind: to consolidate and apply the tools and techniques that we already know, and to extend our conceptual and practical understanding of data science by providing more nuanced descriptions of methods for data collection and evaluation of models. This part takes the techniques from Part I, as well as the tools from the Parts II and III to start applying them to problems of real-life significance.

In Chapter 11, we take this opportunity by applying various data science techniques to several real-life problems, including those involving social media, finance, and social good. In addition to practicing various statistics and the machine learning techniques that we learned in earlier chapters, this chapter also introduces ways to extract data using the Application Programming Interface (API).

Chapter 12 provides additional coverage into data collection, experimentation, and evaluation. There are two major sections in this chapter. One section is an overview of some of the most common methods for collecting/soliciting data, and the other provides information and ideas about how to approach a data analysis problem with broad methods. The latter section also provides a commentary on evaluation and experimentation.

11 Hands-On with Solving Data Problems

"In God we trust. All others must bring data."

— W. Edwards Deming

What do you need?

- Intermediate-level understanding of and practice with Python (see Chapter 5).
- Intermediate-level understanding of and practice with R (see Chapter 6).
- Practice with machine learning in R (see Chapters 8–10).

What will you learn?

- Applying skills in data science and machine learning to real-life problems.
- Accessing data from social media services using APIs.

11.1 Introduction

So far in this book we have taken one topic or tool at a time and looked at how we could tackle a given data problem. Now, it is time to start bringing them together to develop a deeper understanding of the nature of data problems and methods, as well as extend our reach and skillset to address new problems that may emerge. There is, of course, no way we could cover all that you would encounter in real life, but we can certainly try to go through a few examples to see where you could take your data science skills.

This chapter will provide a few applications based on the preceding parts of the book. Specifically, we are going to look at four different problems: one about exploring some clinical data; two related to popular social media services, Twitter and YouTube; and the fourth related to the online rating and reviewing service, Yelp. My hope is that, in addition to applying our problem-solving skills, we will also pick up a few new things, including social media data collection (Twitter, YouTube) and large data analytics (Yelp).

An important thing to note here is that at this point we are almost tool-agnostic. What this means is that we are not going to worry about what is the best tool or programming language to use for any of these problems. And while almost everything here could be done using Python or R (or possibly another language), I have made some design choices to go with one or the other for a given problem. This means that at this point, if you have only been exposed to one of Python or R and not the other, you may not be able to follow half the material in this chapter. In that case, to get the most out of this chapter, I would suggest taking the data and the problem for the example where your favorite programming language is not used and try solving that problem using what you are familiar with. Consider that as your try-it-yourself assignment! Besides, at this point in the book, we are all about exploring and experimenting.

Let us begin.

Hands-On Example 11.1: Exploring Clinical Data

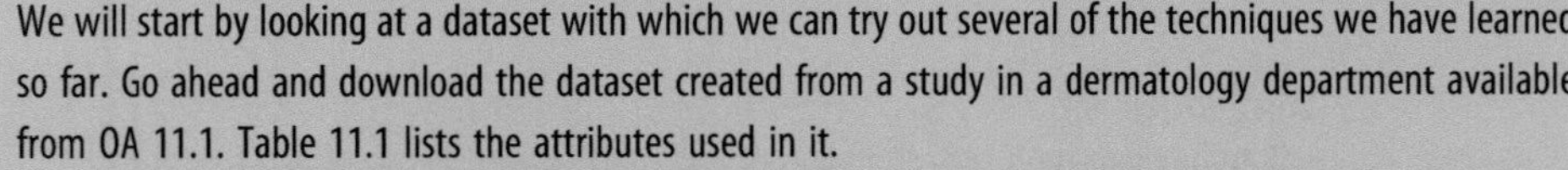

We will start by looking at a dataset with which we can try out several of the techniques we have learned so far. Go ahead and download the dataset created from a study in a dermatology department available from OA 11.1. Table 11.1 lists the attributes used in it.

This database contains 34 attributes, 33 of which are linear-valued and one of which (Age) is nominal. The 35th attribute is the class label, i.e., the disease name. The names and ID numbers of the patients were removed from the database.

Table 11.1 Explanation of various attributes of the dataset with clinical data.

Clinical attributes (take values 0, 1, 2, 3, unless otherwise indicated)	
1	erythema
2	scaling
3	definite borders
4	itching
5	Koebner phenomenon
6	polygonal papules
7	follicular papules
8	oral mucosal involvement
9	knee and elbow involvement
10	scalp involvement
11	family history (0 or 1)
34	age (linear)
Histopathological attributes (take values 0, 1, 2, 3)	
12	melanin incontinence
13	eosinophils in the infiltrate
14	PNL infiltrate
15	fibrosis of the papillary dermis
16	exocytosis
17	acanthosis
18	hyperkeratosis
19	parakeratosis
20	clubbing of the rete ridges
21	elongation of the rete ridges
22	thinning of the suprapapillary epidermis

Table 11.1 (cont.)

23	spongiform pustule
24	Munro microabcess
25	focal hypergranulosis
26	disappearance of the granular layer
27	vacuolization and damage of basal layer
28	spongiosis
29	sawtooth appearance of retes
30	follicular horn plug
31	perifollicular parakeratosis
32	inflammatory mononuclear infiltrate
33	band-like infiltrate

The differential diagnosis of erythemato-squamous diseases is a real problem in dermatology. They all share the clinical features of erythema and scaling, with very little differences. The diseases in this group are psoriasis, seborrheic dermatitis, lichen planus, pityriasis rosea, chronic dermatitis, and pityriasis rubra pilaris. Usually a biopsy is necessary for the diagnosis, but unfortunately these diseases share many histopathological features as well. Another difficulty for the differential diagnosis is that a disease may show the features of another disease at the beginning stage and may have the characteristic features at the following stages.

Patients were first evaluated clinically with 12 features. Afterwards, skin samples were taken for the evaluation of 22 histopathological features. The values of the histopathological features are determined by an analysis of the samples under a microscope.

In the dataset constructed for this domain, the family history feature has the value 1 if any of these diseases has been observed in the family, and 0 otherwise. The age feature simply represents the age of the patient. Every other feature (clinical and histopathological) was given a degree in the range of 0 to 3. Here, 0 indicates that the feature was not present, 3 indicates the largest amount possible, and 1, 2 indicate the relative intermediate values.

Assuming that the list of diseases in this group is complete (total 6 types), let us explore this dataset for a variety of analyses leading to different insights.

Step 1: Load the Data

We will use R for our analyses. At this point, it is important that you know enough about R to comfortably try the commands below without needing any explanation. (Refer to Chapter 6 if necessary.) Let us start by loading the data.

```
derm <- read.csv(file.choose(), header=T, sep='\t')
```

Variables "Age" and "Disease" should be numerical and categorical respectively, and it would make things easier if we turn those into their expected types. The following lines should do it.

```
derm$Age <- as.integer(derm$Age)
derm$Disease <- as.factor(derm$Disease)
```

Essentially, we have overridden the “Age” and “Disease” variables with these lines, turning their category labels to numbers.

Step 2: Visual Exploration of the Data

Let us now do some visual exploration. For simplifying our code further, we will first attach the dataset to our current environment and then ask for a plot.

```
attach(derm)
plot(derm$Disease, derm$Age, col = rgb(0.2,0.4,0.6,0.4),
xlab="Disease", ylab="Age", main = "Disease and Age")
```

The result is shown in Figure 11.1. The plot indicates that age is not a very good indicator when it comes to disease. Type 6 only appears at the low and high ends of the range of age; types 1 and 5 occur along the entire age range; and types 2, 3, and 4 occur less often at the higher end of the age range but still span a wide range of ages. As such, we can expect there to be some relationship with age, even if it is not very strong.

Step 3: Regression with Gradient Descent

We will now attempt to learn the relationship between age and disease. Remember, there are six different diseases here. To simplify things, we will look at only one of these diseases. Let us extract the data pertaining only to disease 1.

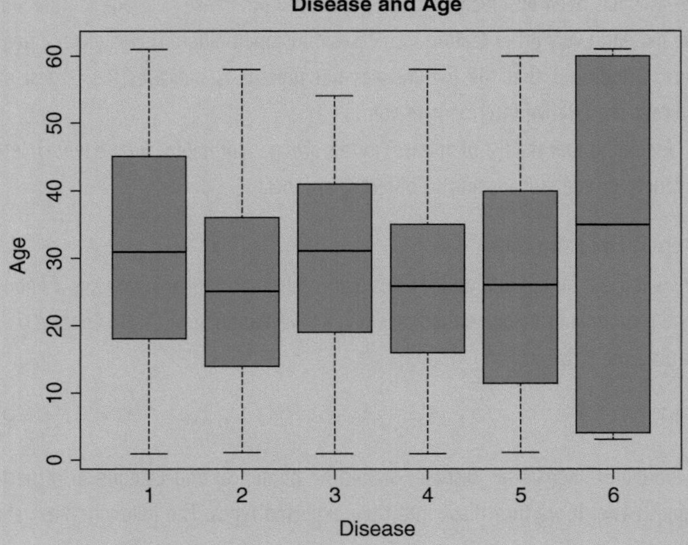

Figure 11.1 Distribution of age per disease.

```
derm$Disease1 <- ifelse(Disease==1,1,0)
```

This one line looks through the dataset and extracts only those records where the Disease=1, assigning "1" for those rows in the newly created "Disease1" column, and marking "0" for the rest. To use this slightly modified dataset, let us detach the old one and reattach the new one, which is still called "derm."

```
detach(derm)
attach(derm)
```

We could use a simple linear regression with the "lm" (linear model) function, but let us do something more complicated. Let us use the gradient descent approach to solving regression. For this, first we need our cost function.

```
cost1 <- function(X, Disease1, theta) {
       sum(X%*%theta - Disease1)^2/(2*length(Age))
}
```

Next, we need to initialize our model parameters (theta), number of iterations (let us keep them under 200), and learning rate (0.01 is a good choice). We will also store values of cost and theta values as we iterate through the gradient descent process.

```
theta <- matrix(as.double((c(0,0)), nrow=2))
num_iterations <- 200
alpha <- .01
cost_history <- double(num_iterations) # number with total
error at each iteration [will want to find minimum]
theta_history <- list(num_iterations) # matrix with values
per above at each iteration
X <- cbind(1,matrix(Age))
```

You can refer to Chapter 8 if you need to refresh your memory about all of these elements. Now we are ready to start the process. Here is the code for running through gradient and trying to find a minimal value of cost:

```
for (i in 1:num_iterations) {
    error <- (X %*% theta - Disease1)
    delta <- t(X) %*% error/length(Disease1)
    theta <- theta - alpha*delta # delta essentially is slope
    cost_history[i] <- cost1(X, Disease1, theta)
    theta_history[[i]] <- theta
}
```

The learned model is stored in "theta." Let us print it out.

```
print(theta)
```

```
                 [,1]
[1,] -3.519192e+290
[2,] -1.294364e+292
```

This gives us our regression equation as:

```
Disease1 = -3.519192e+290 - 1.294364e+292*Age
```

We should note that what we have done here (linear regression) is not the most ideal processing we should do, as "Disease1" is a categorical variable, even with numerical values to represent those categories. Think back – when you have a categorical or discrete variable for your outcome, what kind of analysis makes more sense? If you came up with "classification," you are well-trained! Let us go ahead and do that next.

Step 4: Classification with Random Forest

There are several ways we could do classification – in this case, using various features to predict which disease a person is diagnosed with. But we will try one of those ways – random forest. Make sure you have the "randomForest" package installed before starting the following block of code.

First, we will split the data into training (70%) and testing (30%) randomly.

```
set.seed(123)
dermsample <- sample(2, nrow(derm), prob = c(0.7,0.3),
replace = T)
dermTrain <- derm [dermsample == 1,]
dermTest <- derm [dermsample == 2,]
```

Now, we can go ahead and run the random forest algorithm and print the resulting forest.

```
dermForest <- randomForest(Disease ~ ., data = dermTrain)
print(dermForest)

Call:
randomForest(formula = Disease ~ ., data = dermTrain)
                  Type of random forest: classification
                        Number of trees : 500
No. of variables tried at each split : 6

     OOB estimate of error rate       : 0%
Confusion matrix:

   1  2  3  4  5  6 class.error
1 71  0  0  0  0  0           0
2  0 40  0  0  0  0           0
3  0  0 51  0  0  0           0
4  0  0  0 37  0  0           0
5  0  0  0  0 38  0           0
6  0  0  0  0  0 13           0
```

And the results are pretty astounding. We have a perfect score (error 0%) for this classification. Your scores may be slightly different, as there is randomization involved here. But still, chances are you got quite a high classification accuracy. This is not always a good thing. While random forest is meant to address overfitting the data, there may be other factors (including the nature of our data) that could make it do overfitting and overlearning. This could result in high classification accuracy on the given data, but may not work so well for unseen data in the future.

Step 5: Clustering with *k*-Means

Finally, let us pretend that we do not know the labels of the diseases and try to organize or explain the data. Such an objective fits squarely in clustering. As we know from Chapter 10, we have several options for clustering. Here, we will use one of the most popular options – *k*-means.

We have 34 features to work with here. How is that? In the original data we have 35 columns, with the last one being the true label of a disease. For the purpose of clustering, which is an unsupervised learning technique, we will ignore that 35th column.

It is very easy to use *k*-means with R. We just call the "kmeans" function, show it the data, and tell it how many clusters we would like to see. Now, normally, we may have to determine the number of clusters in some iterative way, or we may have some ideas or intuition behind what would make a good number. But here, we already know there are six different diseases, so while it is *cheating*, we will go ahead and ask for six clusters.

```
clusters <- kmeans(derm[,1:34], 6)
```

You can print out these clusters (simply enter "clusters" at the R console) to see how different data points are assigned to one of the six clusters. One of the lines from that output would look something like this:

```
Within cluster sum of squares by cluster:
[1] 1224.242 2962.476 1061.943 2390.171 2878.805 2098.899
 (between_SS / total_SS = 86.6%)
```

What this indicates is one way to say something about the "goodness" of our clustering. On its own, this information (86.6%) is not comprehensive enough to draw any conclusions, but you can try different techniques or even the same technique of clustering with different parameters (e.g., setting a different value for number of clusters in *k*-means) and compare this value. A good clustering has low within-cluster sum of squares (SS), so the lower the better.

What we saw was just the tip of the iceberg. There are plenty more analyses that can be done and many more insights that could be developed. But we will leave this here. If you are curious or want more practice, I encourage you to continue working with this dataset and try the following:

- Generate more descriptive statistics for various variables or factors.
- Use kNN and decision trees on the clinical attributes and histopathological attributes to classify the disease type and report your accuracy.
- Try other clustering approaches to see how well different attributes can help determine the disease type.

Try It Yourself 11.1: Clinical Data

In the Hands-On Example 11.1, we did linear regression using the gradient descent approach. Re-do this regression using a different technique (e.g., linear model).

Similarly, re-do classification using something other than random forest (e.g., kNN, decision tree), and clustering using something other than *k*-means (e.g., agglomerative approach, EM).

Compare your regression and classification results with those in the Hands-On Example 11.1.

11.2 Collecting and Analyzing Twitter Data

We will now look at a couple of applications involving social media services. As we go through them, we will not only be practicing what we already know, but also be picking up a few new concepts of data collection and analysis.

I am assuming that you know enough Python by now (having gone through Chapter 6) and are familiar with Twitter. To collect data from Twitter, we will need to ask it nicely! Specifically, we will have to register ourselves with Twitter and use their language. This language is called the Application Programming Interface (API).

Step 1: Signing Up for Using Twitter APIs

Using APIs is a common way to access data from various Web services. Most services, including of course social media, provide their own APIs, so developers could call for its services and data. To do so, first you need to sign up for an account. Let us go ahead and do that.

First, to learn about Twitter APIs, you can go to Twitter Docs.[1] Here, you will see different categories of APIs for different kinds of applications that one could develop. We are going to use the Search APIs, but right now, that does not matter.

Make sure you have a Twitter developer account. If you do not have one, you can sign up from the developer platform.[2] You can associate your developer account with your regular, free Twitter account. Once you apply for the developer account, Twitter typically takes a few days to approve. You can see the options I have chosen while applying for the account in Figures 11.2 and 11.3.

In the "use case details" section, you also need to provide detailed description of in what capacity and which purpose you are planning to use the API.

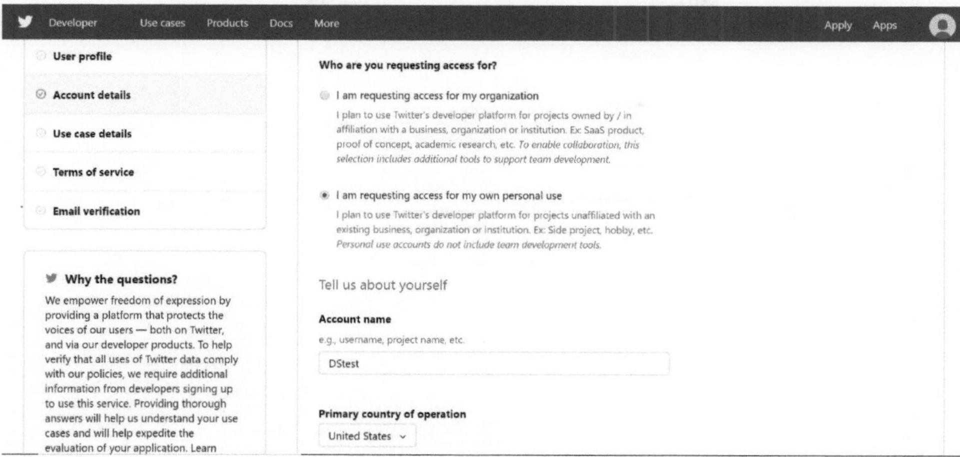

Figure 11.2 Applying for Twitter developer account – part 1.

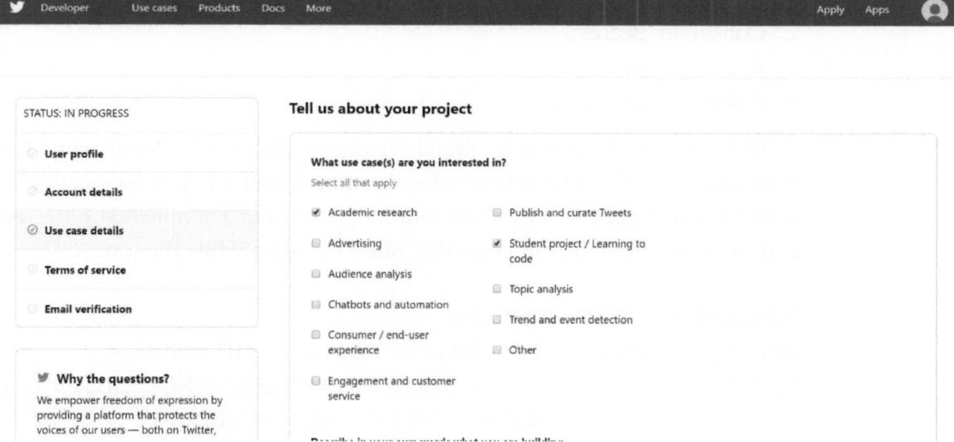

Figure 11.3 Applying for Twitter developer account – part 2.

Once you get approval for the developer account, go to Twitter Apps.[3] This is where you can see your existing apps that use Twitter APIs. If this is your first time here, then chances are you see nothing! But let us create something. Go ahead and click "Create an app." It should bring up a form, where you can pretty much enter anything. So, without worrying too much about what name and website your app should have, just go with some reasonable entries in that form (see Figure 11.4).

Step 2: Get Your Keys and Tokens

Once you get through the form in Figure 11.4, Twitter would have generated four important pieces of information for you. They are:

Figure 11.4 Signing up to use Twitter APIs.

1. Consumer_key
2. Consumer_secret
3. Access_token
4. Access_token_secret

The consumer keys can be found on your application's Details page located at Twitter "OAuth Settings".[4] The access tokens can be found on your application's Details ("Your access token") page.[5] Copy these four long strings in a simple text file – one line at a time, and call it auth.k. For reference, the following is how this file looks.

```
A2hLb3UTk6OZ1TwGCNOmgw
NCo8TyH13GQ0BCYt2revG3y8v8IHG3Ki3UrHTe1KJ8
51000978-si9zmRyZ4a9scK91nAuMUOZhUdYewMpepmLbPv02g
Dl6v15svy2uUI55idMAkU9GRwABoQ9ZQCv7cNhq5Fs
```

That's right – four lines of some garbled-up strings! Make sure you do not simply copy these specific strings (they will not work). Instead, retrieve your own unique strings and store them in that file (auth.k).

Step 3: Get the Twitter Search Python Script

Now, we can write a script in Python to use these authentication codes or keys to call Twitter and get some data, but that would involve a number of things we have not studied in this book. Fear not, someone has already developed such a script. Is this cheating?! Well, yes and no. Mostly no, for us, because reusing someone's code for our purposes (academic) is fine, as long as you are not taking credit for that code! In fact, in real-life projects, you will, most times, find yourself taking some existing code, stitching together or changing just enough of it to get your tasks done. This itself is a very important skill. So, while we are not writing this script from scratch (something we have done thus far in this book), it is important for us to understand how we could take existing modules and plug them into our application to create something more, different, or better.

Hands-On Example 11.2: Twitter

Go ahead and grab the script twitter_search.py from OA 11.2. You can open it up if you like. Chances are you will recognize at least some of the code. See if you can find a mention of the auth.k file. This Python script is expecting auth.k as an input. You will also find that the script is storing the output in a file called results.csv. Of course, you can change these settings. But beware – if you change the "auth.k" string to something else, you need to give that name to your file with those four strings.

Now we are ready to run the script. There are two ways to do that – using the console or terminal, and through Spyder. First, let us make sure our auth.k and twitter_search.py are at the same location. Open your terminal window and navigate to that location. If you are on a UNIX, Linux, or Mac system, this can be accomplished using appropriate "cd" commands on your terminal. On a Windows machine, you will need to do something different. See Chapter 4 for more details.

Once you are at the right location, you can issue the following command:

```
python ./twitter_search.py brexit -c 100
```

Here, the first term is "python," which evokes the Python interpreter. Of course, we are assuming that you already have Python installed. The second term is a reference to the Python script in the current directory ("./" makes sure it is the current directory). The third term is the search word/phrase we want to run on Twitter. And finally, "-c 100" says that we want to retrieve 100 tweets.

When running the command above, the script collects 100 tweets that include "brexit" in their text and writes the tweets in a file named "result.csv," with six columns – created time, text, retweet count, hashtag, followers count, and friends count. Where is all that? It is in a file named result.csv. It should be in the current directory. Go ahead, open it up to make sure you got some data. Now, try running the above command with different search parameters (keywords, number of results). Note that we can only get up to 180 results at a time from Twitter. So, asking for anything more than 180 will result in getting only 180 tweets. There are ways to overcome this, but we will not go there.

There is another way to run this script, and that's through Spyder. First, open the Python script twitter_search.py in your Spyder. Then go to Run > Configuration per file . . . in your menu. Note that this option may appear slightly differently depending on the version and the system on which you are using Spyder, but it will look something like Figure 11.5. Here, make sure your script (twitter_search.py) is selected, then check "Command line options": and provide that string after the name of the script (brexit -c 180). Go ahead and hit "Run." This should result in the same thing (result.csv in the current working directory).

Now that we know how to extract data from Twitter, let us integrate it into a larger project that collects as well as analyzes such data. Essentially, we can have two separate parts here: one that collects the data and another that analyzes it. We already saw the first part. Now, let us add the second part to it. Before we

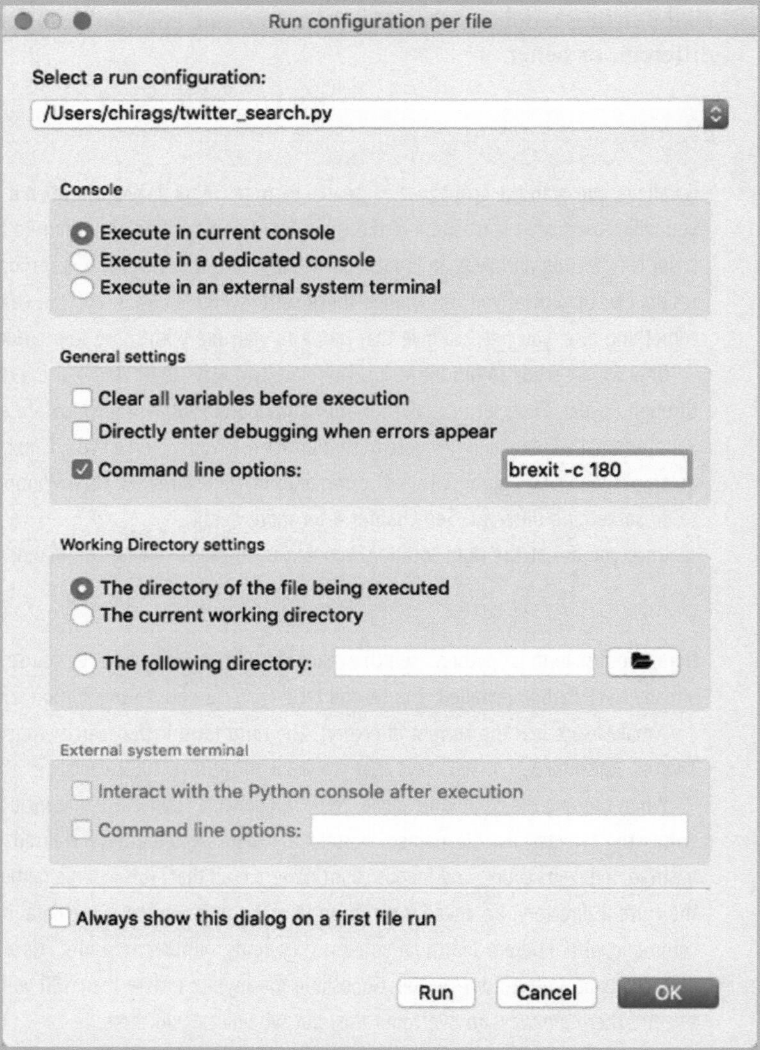

Figure 11.5 Running a Python script with run parameters.

begin, it is important to consider if we really want these two parts to be in one script or should we just keep them separate. Let us look at the latter option first.

Given that we were already able to download data from Twitter, now let us explore it. Remember – the data is stored in the result.csv file. We will open this up in a Python script and then perform various explorations. For instance, we may want to see if there are any relationships among number of followers, number of friends, and number of retweets.

At the time when I ran such correlations with the data that I gathered (180 tweets related to "brexit"), I got correlation of 0.55 between number of friends and number of followers. This indicates a medium-level positive correlation. On the other hand, my correlation between number of followers and number of retweets was −0.08. That's very close to zero and indicates almost no relation between these two variables. So, let us go ahead with exploring the connections between number of followers and number of friends. This includes creating a regression model. Since this is something we have done quite a bit before, I will not go into the details. But the following is the full code for performing this analysis. There are in-line comments that should help you understand the code.

```
# Load numpy and pandas for data manipulation
import numpy as np
import pandas as pd
import matplotlib.pyplot as plt

# Load statsmodels as alias "sm"
import statsmodels.api as sm

# Load the data downloaded from Twitter
df = pd.read_csv('result.csv', index_col=0)

# Let us look at some correlations
print("Correlation coefficient =",
np.corrcoef(df.followers,df.friends)[0,1])
print("Correlation coefficient =",
np.corrcoef(df.followers,df.retwc)[0,1])

# Create a scatterplot of followers vs. friends
plt.scatter(df.followers, df.friends)

# Use regression analysis for predicting number of fol-
lowers (y)
# using number of friends (X)
y = df.followers # response
X = df.friends # predictor
X = sm.add_constant(X) # Adds a constant term to the pre-
dictor

lr_model = sm.OLS(y, X).fit()

print(lr_model.summary())

# We pick 100 hundred points equally spaced from the min to
the max
X_prime = np.linspace(X.friends.min(), X.friends.max(),
100)
X_prime = sm.add_constant(X_prime) # add constant as we did
before
```

```
  # Now we calculate the predicted values
  y_hat = lr_model.predict(X_prime)
  plt.figure(1)
  plt.subplot(211)
  plt.scatter(df.followers, df.friends)
  plt.subplot(212)
  plt.scatter(X.friends, y) # Plot the raw data
  plt.xlabel("Friends")
  plt.ylabel("Followers")
  plt.plot(X_prime[:, 1], y_hat, 'red') # Add the regression
line, colored in red
```

Figure 11.6 also shows the outcome for scatterplot and the regression line. Of course, yours may look quite different from this, as you will be doing the data collection at a different time than I have done.

Now, what if we wanted to combine both of these parts – collecting the data and analyzing it? Sure, we could just copy both the scripts in one file. But there is an easier way to do it. We can evoke the first script in the second file before running the code for the second part. In fact, it is possible to evoke any external commands in Python using the "os" package. Here is how:

```
import os
os.system("python twitter_search.py brexit -c 180")
```

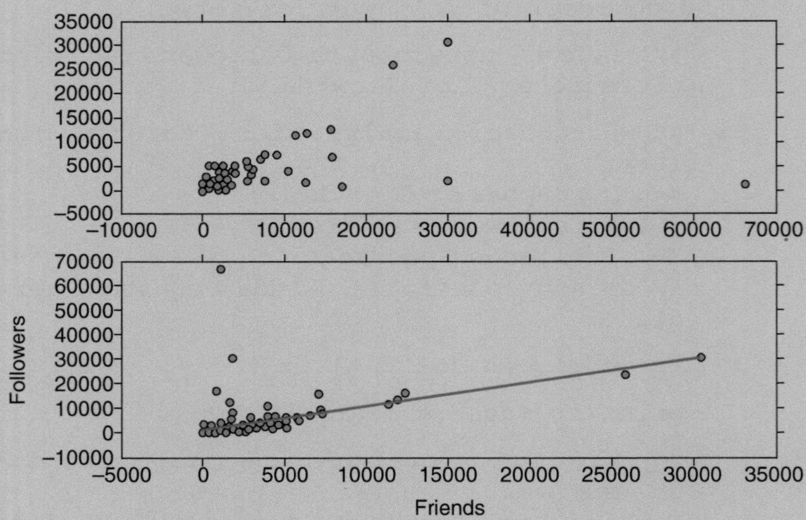

Figure 11.6 Scatterplot and regression plot for friends vs. followers.

You see what we did (and how easy it was)? The first line imports the package "os" (Operating System). The second line uses its function "system" to run a command that we would normally run on a console. Of course, you have to make sure that the path to the script (twitter_search.py) is correct. Here, we are assuming that this script is in the current directory. So, adding these two lines at the top of the previous script will ensure that, when you run that analysis script, you also get a fresh batch of data. The downside is now you have these two processes combined, and so even if you want to use the same data to run a different analysis, you end up getting new data every time you run the analysis script. The lesson? Choose wisely!

Let us now see a different kind of analysis we could do on tweets. If you have been a Twitter user, or simply following the news, you know that people express all kinds of opinions and sentiments on Twitter. So how about analyzing those sentiments? For this, we will use a package called TexBlob, which has a number of very useful functions for processing textual data. To use those functions, we need to convert a string (text) to an object of TextBlob type. And then it is really easy from there.

First, start by collecting some data as we did before:

```
import os
os.system("python twitter_search.py brexit -c 180")
```

Now, we are going to open up that data in a dataframe:

```
import pandas as pd

# Load the data downloaded from Twitter
df = pd.read_csv('result.csv', index_col=0)
```

Next, we use the TextBlob package to go through the dataframe one row at a time and find the text – in this case a tweet stored in a variable or column named "text". Once we have that tweet, convert it into a TextBlob object, and then we can ask it to analyze that string for subjectivity and polarity.

```
from textblob import TextBlob

for index, row in df.iterrows():
    tweet = row["text"]
    text = TextBlob(tweet)

    # Sentiment analysis
    subjectivity = text.sentiment.subjectivity # Runs
    from 0 to 1
    polarity = text.sentiment.polarity # Runs from -1 to 1
    print (tweet,subjectivity,polarity)
```

Here, the subjectivity score runs from 0 to 1; if it is "0," the text is completely objective. The polarity score runs from −1 to +1, just like the correlation scores. Any value close to "0" means there is a lack of positive or negative opinion or sentiment in that tweet.

Try It Yourself 11.2: Twitter

In the Hands-On Example 11.2, we explored the relationship between number of friends and number of followers for a Twitter user. But there may be other important or interesting relationships. Form a new hypothesis that involves numerical quantities (e.g., "The more posts one makes, the more followers one has"). Extract appropriate data by querying Twitter using the API. Then create an appropriate visualization (e.g., scatterplot), and perform an appropriate statistical test (e.g., correlation) to test your hypothesis. Present your thoughts on the findings in a few sentences, supported with various outcomes of your code.

11.3 Collecting and Analyzing YouTube Data

Now let us look at another popular social media service – YouTube. Once again, we need to sign up with this service to use their APIs for accessing the data.

Step 1: Signing Up for Using YouTube APIs
As before, let us begin by signing up for a YouTube developer account. Since YouTube is a Google service, you would be essentially signing up for using Google APIs.

Go to the Google API client library[6] to get started. Here, you will see three main steps to follow: (1) sign up for a Google account if you do not have one; (2) create a project in the Google API Console (Figure 11.7); and (3) install a Python package.

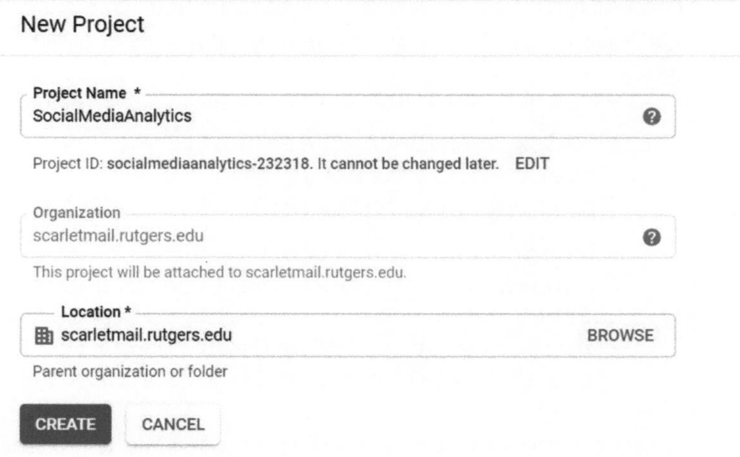

Figure 11.7 Creating a project in the Google API Console.

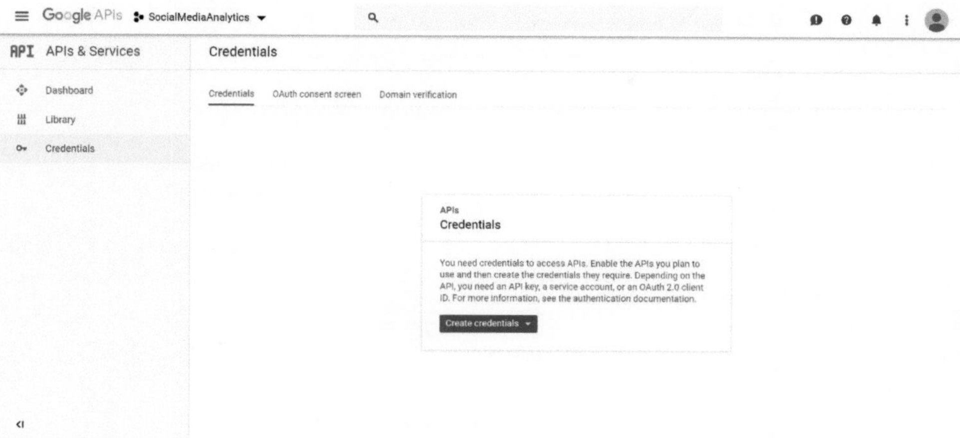

Figure 11.8 Library of APIs available for a Google project.

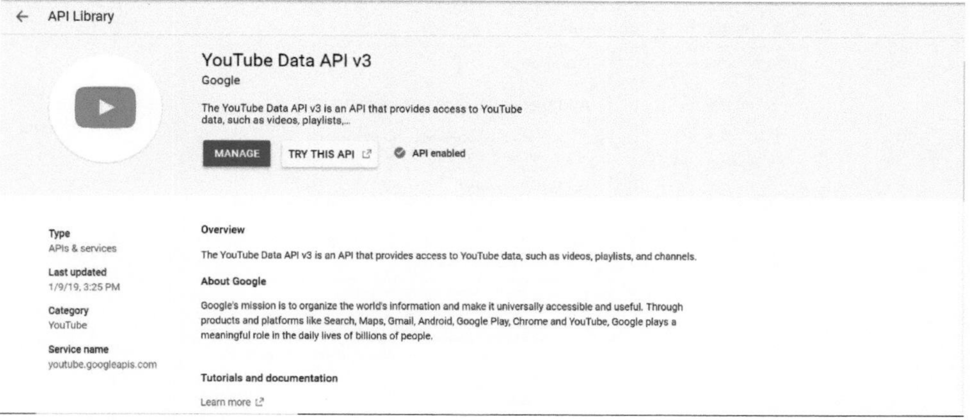

Figure 11.9 Enabling YouTube Data APIs.

Step 2: Select the Correct API and Get Your API Key

Once you create your project, you will see something like Figure 11.8. Here, you can see all kinds of Google APIs that are available to you from the Library option under APIs & Services. Select the "YouTube Data API v3." Go ahead and click "Enable" to have these specific APIs available to your project. This will bring up a screen much like what you see in Figure 11.9. Click on "Manage" and you will see a screen like what is shown in Figure 11.10.

At this step, you need to create credentials before you can use the API. Go ahead and click the "CREATE CREDENTIALS" button, and select the YouTube DATA API v3 from the list of options. Here, you can configure the credentials depending on your project or purpose. You can see in Figures 11.11 and 11.12 what options I have chosen.

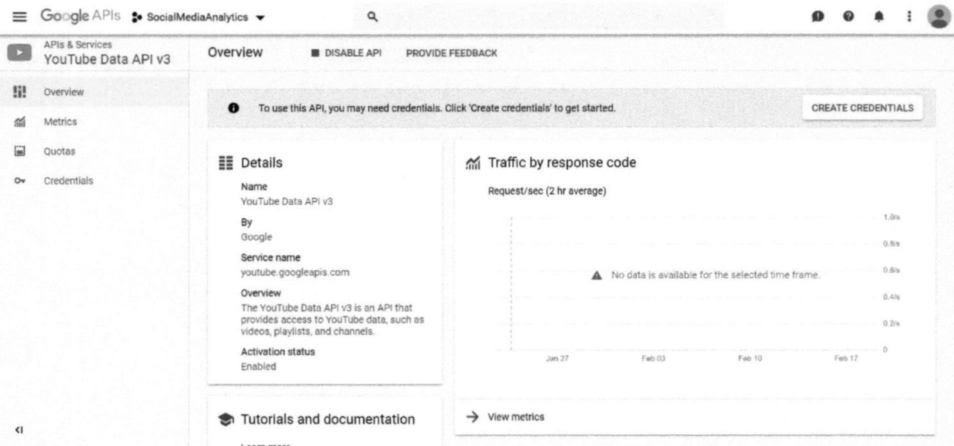

Figure 11.10 YouTube Data APIs enabled, but not yet available for the project.

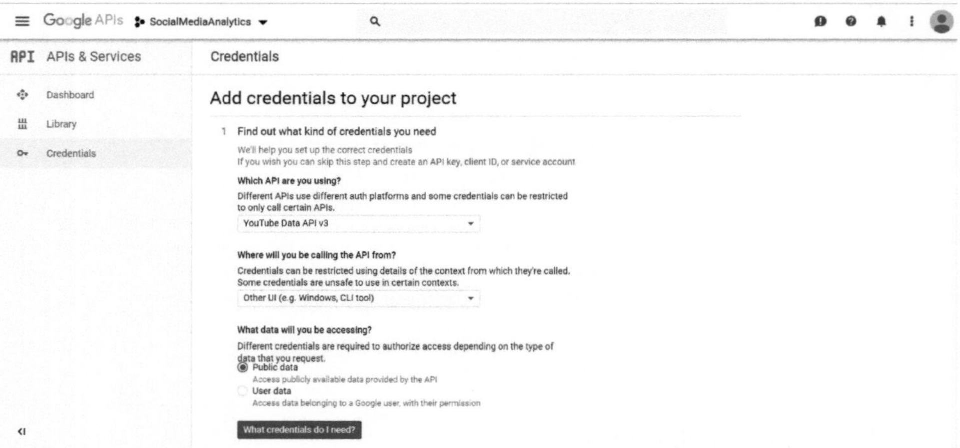

Figure 11.11 Creating credentials for using the YouTube Data APIs – part 1.

Once you go through these steps, you should now have the API key for your application (Figure 11.13). It looks like this:

```
PIzaQyCsNBE34ffoYhN9WTk9mqMqexhYmO0LuRz
```

Save this information somewhere.

Step 3: Install the Packages

In addition to our usual needs, we will need two packages here: google-api-python-client[7] and unidecode.[8] You can install them using Anaconda, as you have done before. Or, you can use "pip" on your terminal or command line (on a Mac or a UNIX system):

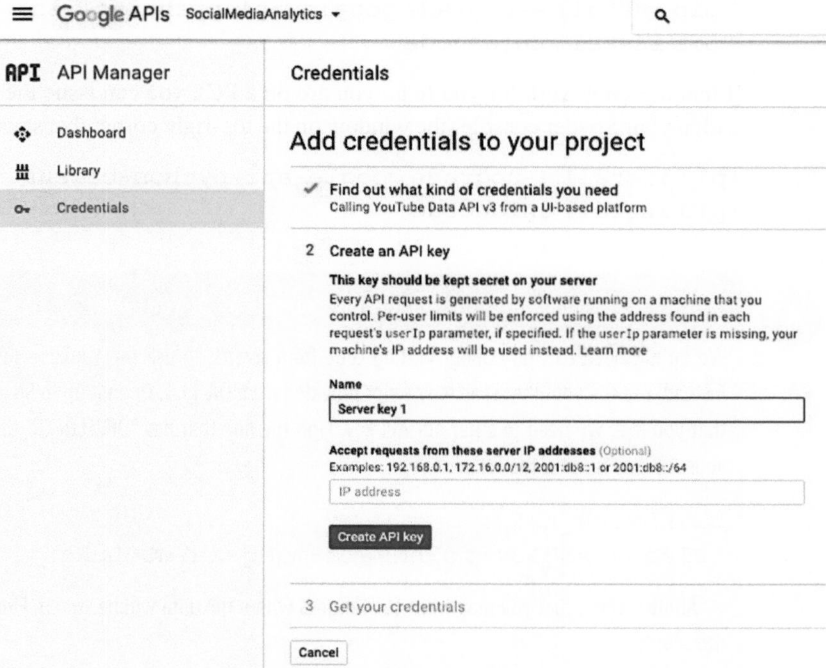

Figure 11.12 Creating credentials for using the YouTube Data APIs – part 2.

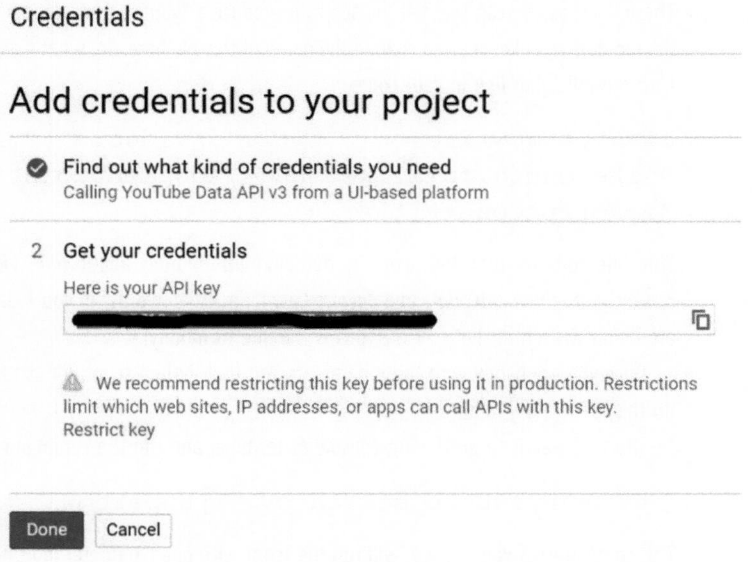

Figure 11.13 Getting the credentials (API key).

```
$ pip install --upgrade google-api-python-client
$ pip install unidecode
```

If that does not work for you (e.g., you are on a PC), you can issue the following command within your Spyder console (the window on the top-right corner that says "IPython console"):

```
!pip install --upgrade google-api-python-client
!pip install unidecode
```

Hands-On Example 11.3: YouTube

We do not need to worry about writing code from scratch to use the YouTube APIs and get some data. Instead, use the youtube_search.py script provided from OA 11.3. Open it up in Spyder or any editor or IDE that you like. We need to enter our API key. Find the line that has "DEVELOPER_KEY" variable and assign your API key to it as the following:

```
DEVELOPER_KEY =
"PIzaQyCsNBE34ffoYhN9WTk9mqMqexhYmO0LuRz"
```

Another thing that you may want to change is where the data will be stored. Find the following lines in the script:

```
csvFile = open('youtube_results.csv','w')
csvWriter = csv.writer(csvFile)
```

These lines, as you can see, tell the script to produce a "youtube_results.csv" file and dump the obtained data in it. If you like, you can change the name of this file here. So, what's really being written to the file? Find the following line in your code:

```
csvWriter.writerow(["title","videoId","viewCount",
"likeCount","dislikeCount","commentCount",
"favoriteCount"])
```

This line tells us that the script is dumping information about *title*, *videoId*, *viewCount*, *likeCount*, *dislikeCount*, *commentCount*, and *favoriteCount*. In other words, if you want to change what columns are being written in that CSV file, this is the line to modify.

Once you are happy with these parameters in that Python script, let us run it. There are three ways to do this, as we saw before.

The first way is to go to your console or terminal and run the command:

```
$ python youtube_search.py --q superbowl
```

This command, as you can see, will run the script with one parameter indicated using "-q", and that's the query (here, "superbowl").

Alternatively, you can go to the Spyder Run Configuration option and enter your command-line options (see Figure 11.14).

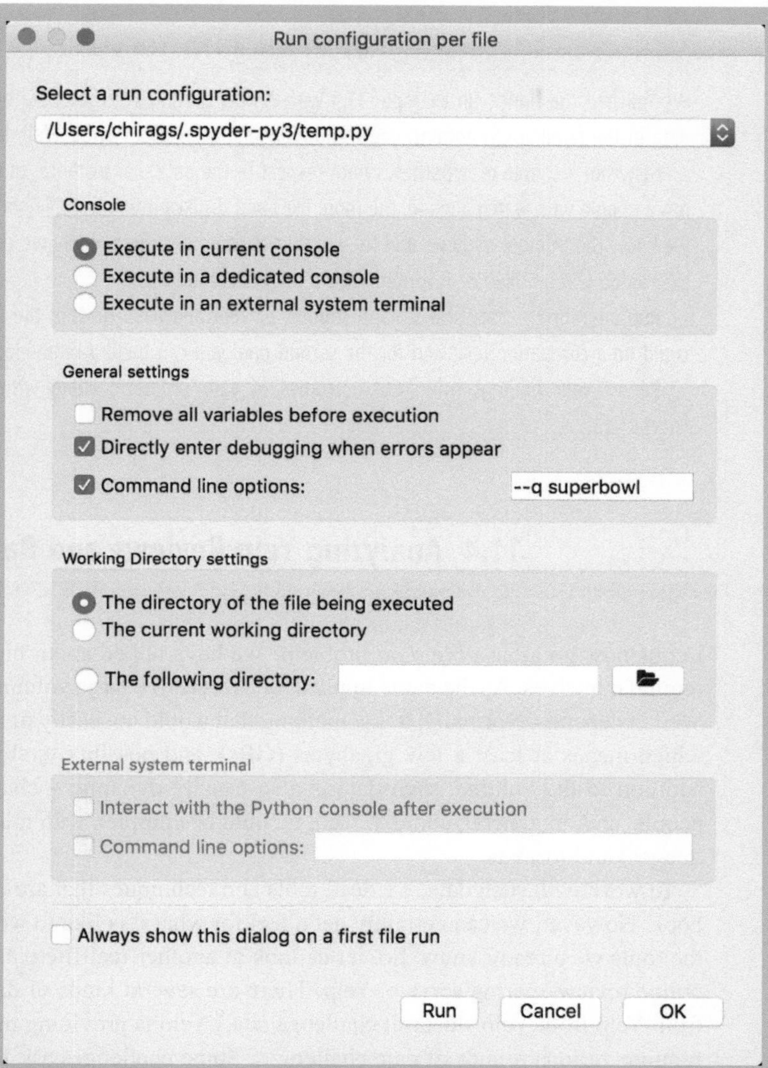

Figure 11.14 Run configuration window in Spyder. This is where you can enter your command-line options/arguments/parameters.

Finally, if you are using this data to do further analysis and want to integrate the data collection in that analysis script, you can use the following code at the top of the script:

```
import os
os.system("python youtube_search.py --q superbowl")
```

This will get you the data and store it in a CSV file in the current directory. Make sure to open that same file in the code that follows for further processing, just as we did with Twitter data analysis before.

Try It Yourself 11.3: YouTube

We finished the Hands-On Example 11.3 with simply getting YouTube data because, once you have the data in the familiar CSV format, you can do all sorts of analyses on it. Well, let us do that then.

Generate a couple of hypotheses with respect to the data. For instance, one hypothesis could be "The more people who watch a video, the more likes and dislikes it will have." Another hypothesis could be "If we know the number of views and the number of comments on a video, we can predict how many times that video will be liked or favorited with a reasonable accuracy."

Run appropriate statistical tests in support of your analysis. [Hint: In the first hypothesis above, you could do a correlation test; and for the second one, you can build a regression model.]

Report your findings using the outcomes of your program, along with your interpretations and conclusions.

11.4 Analyzing Yelp Reviews and Ratings

Let us now go after a *big data* problem. We have talked about big data before, but let us remind ourselves. As the name implies, this refers to a large volume of data. What is large? Well, it depends. Normally, it is something that would not easily fit in your memory (RAM), which means at least a few gigabytes (GBs), and possibly terabytes (TBs), or more. In addition to the volume, such data is also usually dynamic – changing with time, place, people, and, in general, context. And, it could be complex with multiple types (text, audio, images) and formats.

To work with such data, we need tools and techniques that are beyond the scope of this book. However, we can certainly get a feel for what it is like to work with such data using the tools we already know. So, let us look at another real-life dataset – this time from an online review-sharing service, Yelp. There are several kinds of datasets one could obtain from Yelp from Yelp's dataset challenge site.[9] Yelp is providing these datasets as a part of running various rounds of data challenges. Some challenges ask for creating a new/better recommendation technique, whereas some ask for image classification. If you tackle one of these challenges and your submission makes it in the top 10, you could win thousands of dollars!

For our purposes, we will limit to something less attractive – processing a dataset to derive interesting insights from it. I encourage you to download a dataset directly from Yelp. More than likely, it will come in JSON (JavaScript Object Notation) format. To make things easier, we will want to convert it to CSV. I am providing you two Python scripts that you could use to convert user-related and business-related JSON datasets to CSV (get them from OA 11.4 and 11.5). Keep in mind that, since the datasets are going to be large, your Python script may take a long time, and, in some cases, may fail to finish processing. This happens because of the limited power and memory that your computer will have. Unless you are a savvy programmer who knows how to work on a high-performance cluster, you may have to stop right here. Well, that is not good! So, I encourage you to use two datasets that I have already converted into CSV format (available from OA 11.6 and 11.7). Sure, they are not as large, but they are still the largest datasets we have worked with so far – in tens of megabytes (MBs).

Hands-On Example 11.4: Yelp

Let us use R (RStudio) for this project. First, we are going to load up Yelp's business dataset as follows:

```
library(ggplot2)
business_data <- read.csv(file='yelp_academic_dataset_
  business.json.csv')
ggplot(business_data) + geom_bar(aes(x=state),
fill="gray")
```

This should generate a bar chart as shown in Figure 11.15. Note that running the above processes could take a few seconds – something that perhaps has not happened before. Be patient.

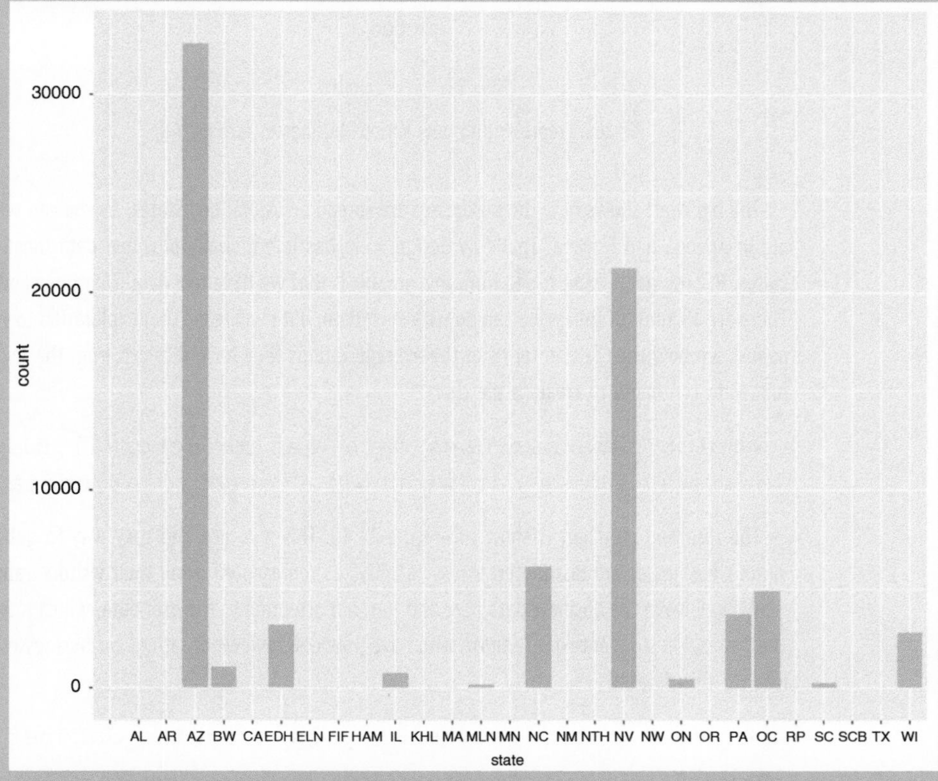

Figure 11.15 Yelp business data spread across different States.

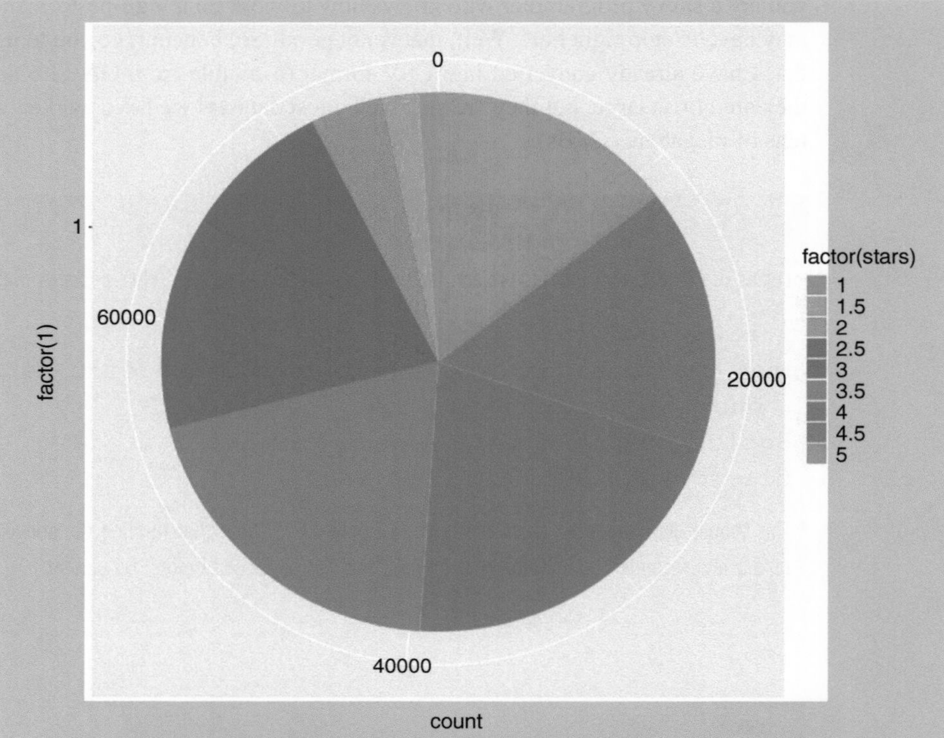

Figure 11.16 Pie chart representing how various businesses fare on Yelp.

The bar chart shows how the businesses are spread across various States. As you can see, most of them are in Arizona and Nevada. That's by design. Yelp has intentionally provided data mostly for these two states. But the good thing to see from this graphic is that we have *real* data from thousands of businesses. There are all kinds of things we can do with such data, but I will leave that exploration to you. For now, let us just see how they fare in terms of the average ratings they have received from the reviewers. Run the following command to create a pie chart:

```
ggplot(data=business_data, aes(x=factor(1),fill = factor
(stars))) + geom_bar(width=1) + coord_polar(theta="y")
```

The resulting pie chart is shown in Figure 11.16. This is a nice and easy way to get a sense of how various businesses are distributed across "quality" as represented using their visitors' ratings.

We will leave the business data here and turn our attention to the user data, which is more interesting. The "users," in this context, are those who have provided reviews or ratings for businesses on Yelp. Let us load up this dataset:

```
user_data <- read.csv(file='yelp_academic_dataset_user.
json.csv')
```

You will notice that the "user_data" dataframe has more than half-a-million records and 11 columns (variables or attributes). This is certainly a good amount of data to work with. If you are curious, you can open up this dataframe in RStudio (click on "user_data" in the "Environments" panel on top-right). There are several numerical variables here for us to work with. Let us look at the votes. Specifically, there are three columns or variables named "cool_votes," "funny_votes," and "useful_votes." We can extract those columns using the following command:

```
user_votes
<-user_data[,c("cool_votes","funny_votes",
"useful_votes")]
```

Let us see if there is any relationship among these three variables by running a correlation analysis:

```
cor(user_votes)
```

This generates the following outcome:

```
               cool_votes  funny_votes useful_votes
cool_votes      1.0000000    0.9764113    0.9832708
funny_votes     0.9764113    1.0000000    0.9546541
useful_votes    0.9832708    0.9546541    1.0000000
```

We can ignore the diagonal, as it indicates self-relation, which is always going to be a perfect 1.0. But if we look at the other numbers, we see that there are strong positive correlations among these three variables. In other words, the more someone's reviews receive votes for being "funny," the more "cool" and more "useful" votes they receive. If you've ever wondered if it is cool or useful to be funny, here's your proof that it is!

Since we have such a high correlation here, it should be easy to build a good regression model in which you can use one or two of these variables and predict the third one. I will leave this to you to explore.

Let us move on to some other forms of exploration. Does writing more reviews bring me more fans? Let us do a correlation:

```
cor(user_data$review_count, user_data$fans)
```

That gives a value of 0.58. That's about medium-strong correlation. Not so good as the correlations among the kinds of votes, but not too bad either. Let us visualize these two variables by creating a scatterplot:

```
ggplot(user_data, aes(x=review_count,y=fans)) + geom_
  point()
```

The result is shown in Figure 11.17. Once again, it may take a little while to get this plot, as your machine is trying to render more than half-a-million points on that graph plane.

Similarly, if we look at correlations between "useful_votes" and "review_count," we get 0.66, whereas the correlation between "useful_votes" and "fans" comes out to be 0.79. These are high numbers, giving

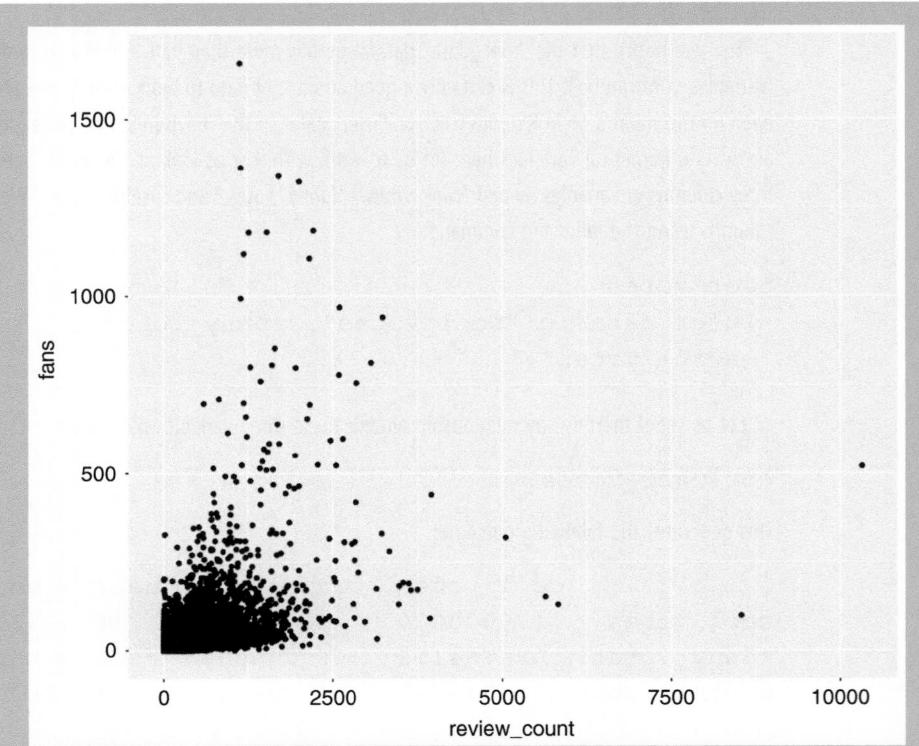

Figure 11.17 Scatterplot showing number of reviews and fans for reviewers.

us some confidence that we could make a good prediction of "useful_votes" using variables "review_-count" and "fans." So, let us go ahead and do regression.

```
my.lm = lm(useful_votes ~ review_count + fans, data =
  user_data)
```

Where is the regression model? Let us extract the coefficients and print them out:

```
coeffs = coefficients (my.lm)
coeffs
 (Intercept)  review_count       fans
 -18.259629      1.419287  22.686274
```

This gives us the following regression equation:

```
useful_votes = -18.26 + 1.42*review_count + 22.69*fans
```

If you like, you can go ahead and plug in some values of "review_count" and "fans" to see what your prediction for "useful_votes" is, and how far you are from the actual value in the dataset. It is not too bad for most values. In other words, based on how many reviews one writes and how many fans they have, we could predict how many "useful" review votes they would get. But, as we saw before, "review_count" and "fans" also have a decent correlation, which means they are not completely independent of each other and there may be some interaction effect going on. Thankfully, R allows us to easily capture this. We just change our linear regression equation and add this interaction effect – represented as `review_count*fans`:

```
  my.lm = lm(useful_votes ~ review_count + fans + review_-
count*fans, data = user_data)
  coeffs = coefficients (my.lm)
  coeffs
  (Intercept)     review_count fans      review_count:fans
  -13.377752509  1.387775538  18.060456934    0.003634949
```

Now, we have a coefficient for that interaction effect for a new regression model. Fortunately, that coefficient is quite small, indicating that while "review_count" and "fans" have some dependence, it is not going to hurt us much if we ignore that factor.

Finally, let us see if we could organize this large set of users into some meaningful clusters. We have several things to look at, but we will limit ourselves to how many reviews they have written and how many fans they have. Essentially, we could see how some people are more active or popular on Yelp. We will use the "kmeans" clustering algorithm, which we have used before:

```
userCluster <- kmeans(user_data[, c(3,11)], 3, nstart = 20)
```

Here, we are using "review_count" (feature or column #3) and "fans" (feature or column #11) as features to represent a data point and perform clustering.

After the clustering process is finished, we can print out the cluster centers/centroids and their sizes using the following commands:

```
userCluster["centers"]
$centers
 review_count        fans
1     14.35739   0.5011401
2    998.91922  84.9894403
3    268.16072  14.3641892

userCluster["size"]
$size
[1] 528904 1894 21541
```

Finally, let us replot that scatterplot from Figure 11.17 with this clustering information:

```
  ggplot(user_data, aes(review_count,fans,color =
userCluster$cluster)) + geom_point()
```

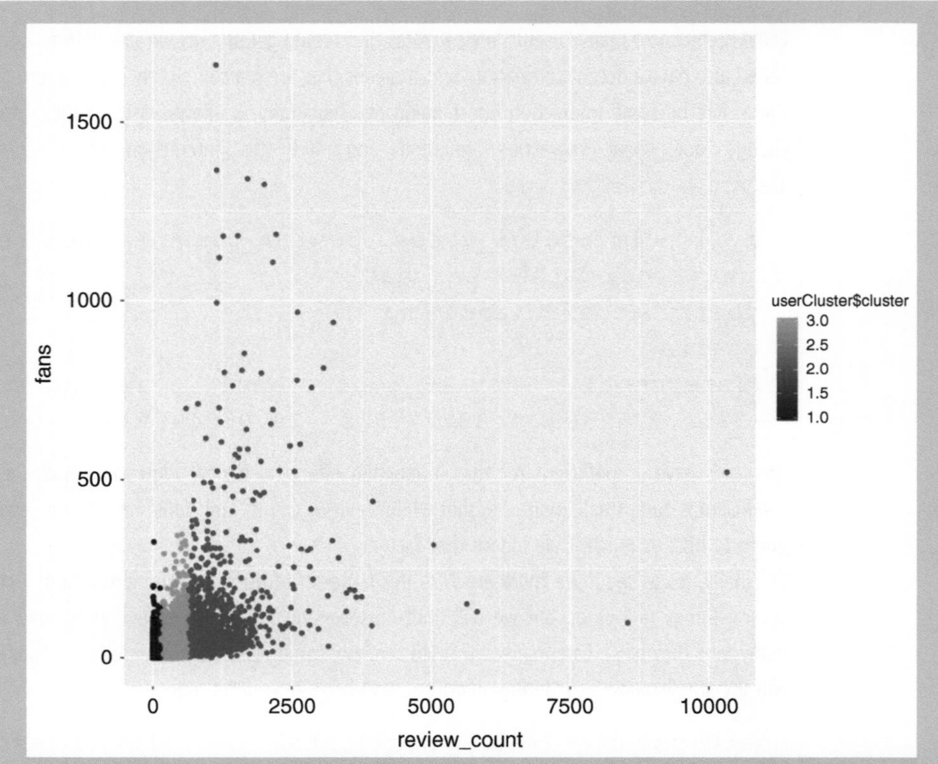

Figure 11.18 Clustering result for individuals on Yelp according to reviews and fans counts.

The result can be seen in Figure 11.18. Do you see three distinct classes here? Perhaps around low, medium, and high levels of activities and popularity? Perhaps there are five clusters instead of three. Go ahead and try rerunning your clustering analysis and see if that gives you more *meaningful* organization. After all, we are here to explore and provide our interpretations!

Try It Yourself 11.4: Yelp

In the Hands-On Example 11.4, we explored the data using review count and number of fans for a given user. Identify a different pair of relationships to explore. For instance, you could look at review count and number of useful votes.

Start by finding correlation between these two numerical variables. Next, plot the users along these two variables using a scatterplot.

Finally, perform clustering (you decide how many clusters) and report if there are any meaningful patterns you see. Is this a better way to organize and represent the user groups than what we did above?

FYI: Ethics and Privacy in Data

You may have heard about Bernie Madoff, who ran a "Ponzi" scheme in New York City in which many people invested their life savings and then lost it all in the 2008 economic crisis. Perhaps you have heard of Elizabeth Holmes, who in 2003 founded a company called Theranos in Palo Alto, California. She was a wunderkind who dropped out of Stanford University on the strength of what she thought was the certain future for a blood-test technology she was developing. Hundreds of millions of dollars were invested by "believers" and a lot of media attention was given to the device, which turned out to be a fraud. Bernie Madoff and Elizabeth Holmes are infamous for operating above the law and hurting many people. Not everybody is operating out of the same moral playbook, but our society eventually outs "scofflaws" such as these.

Where do our values, ethics, and morals come from? Many will say they are built into our consciences, and others will say they are from religion. Society cannot operate without agreeing on a set of laws that govern our behavior and consequences for misbehaving. But we have learned that greed is alive and well.

Since the 2016 presidential election, we are more aware of the abuse of personal data. George Orwell's prophesy "Big Brother is watching," in his novel, *Nineteen Eighty-Four* (published in 1949), seems to have come true. When we signed up to use social media platforms, some of us did not realize we were signing away our rights to how our information is used. Some people are outraged and some are resigned to this reality. But, big businesses like Facebook and Google are working on ways to protect people's privacy and information from identity theft and other abuses. These efforts are almost controversial. Who determines what is right or ethical? This issue has been debated from the days of Socrates and is likely to continue being contentious for some time to come. A fuller discussion of this topic is beyond the scope for us, but I hope that as you pursue your studies or career in data science, you keep the importance of ethical challenges in mind.

Here is some reading to check out if you are interested in such issues.

Olteanu, A., Castillo, C., Diaz, F., Kiciman, E. (2018). Social data: biases, methodological pitfalls, and ethical boundaries. *Frontiers in Big Data*, 11 July. https://doi.org/10.3389/fdata.2019.00013

Spielkamp, M. (2017). Inspecting algorithms for bias. *MIT Technology Review*. 12 June.

Summary

Remember, in Chapter 1 we discussed the *3V model*? As a reminder, the three Vs were velocity, volume, and variety. It is due to these characteristics of today's data that we have to be innovative in how we access, store, and process data. In addition, there are often concerns (as there should be) about ethics and privacy (see the FYI box above). All of these make it crucial for us to find effective ways to access and share data. In this chapter, we saw a primary way this happens today with a variety of services – using the Application Programming Interface (API). This method allows data providers to control who accesses the data, what kind of data they could access, and how much data they are provided. Of course, it also allows them to put a price on that data access process, creating a lucrative business of monetizing the massive amounts of data they have gathered from their users. Mitch Lowe, the CEO of MoviePass service, infamously blurted out about how the data collected from their users could be linked to create a much more profound profile of them to potentially recommend (or sell) services.[10] Such traits by companies that collect a lot of data are not uncommon.

But, of course, there are advantages of API-based services. It allows developers and data scientists to create apps and data analysis pipelines effectively and efficiently. Since different interfaces, platforms, and data pipelines could all use the same APIs, but for different purposes, the developers and data scientists get a robust way to access and use data. This ability also allows them to link various services in a cost-effective manner.

Due to changing uses of APIs and the ever-increasing demand for obtaining data from various services, each service has seen an evolution of their APIs. This often means the newer versions of a service's APIs provide more efficient ways of data access, better protection for privacy concerns, and more variety of data to meet the needs for new apps and analyses. At the same time, we have seen many services restricting their use of APIs, at least for free access, and starting to charge if one wants more data or greater access. So, while what we covered in this chapter should work for the time being, do not be surprised if some things start breaking for you; chances are – the service that you are using has changed its API structure or access limits. I can tell you from my personal experience with using APIs over many years – this happens more often than we would like to see. So, be prepared to adapt to this ever-changing landscape of data APIs. My hope is that this chapter has at least given you enough to get started and to know where to go to look for help if things do not work as you intended.

Key Terms

- **Application Programming Interface (API):** The API defines a set of functions or procedures for a developer to write programs that request services from an operating system (OS) or another application.
- **High-performance cluster (HPC):** A collection of tightly integrated computer processors that allow one to solve a complex problem, often involving a large amount of data, by distributing the workload onto those processors and combining the outcomes to create one solution.

Conceptual Questions

1. How will you convert a variable with category labels to one with numerical labels in R?
2. Clustering technique A gives within-clusters sum of squares (as a portion of the total sum of squares) as 78.4%, whereas the same quantity for technique B is 67.3%. Which one is a better clustering technique? Why?

3. What is API? Find at least two examples of APIs available from sites/sources not mentioned in this chapter.

4. How will you run a Python script that requires command-line arguments? Describe two different ways.

Practice Questions

Problem 11.1

Since we live in a politically charged environment, let us explore some of the political views and politicians as seen through the lens of Twitter.

Pick three topics or politicians (possibly controversial!) and collect 180 tweets for each of them. Give a summary (what you collected, how you did it). Do not put actual data.

Do exploratory analyses using Python to detect any trends and form hypotheses. Present (1) visual relationships among the variables explored, and (2) your hypotheses based on these relationships.

A good hypothesis is one that can be tested using the method(s) and other parameters we have here. An example: "The more followers one has, the more positive sentiment expressed in their tweets." You can visualize this using a scatterplot, find correlations, and even do regression (using "followers" as an independent variable to predict "sentiments").

Problem 11.2

For this exercise, we will focus even more on the problem and less on the amount and nature of data. On top of that, we will do cross-data and cross-platform analysis.

Imagine you are working as an aide or advisor for a candidate for an upcoming election. You are preparing the candidate for an open debate or a town-hall meeting and want to make sure he/she is aware of public opinions on some of the current issues. Pick two issues out of the following list to investigate: gun control; abortion; war; immigration; inequality.

For each of these topics, gather data from Twitter and YouTube using Python. How much data? Well, you decide! Perhaps 100 comments, perhaps 500 tweets, or a combination of these. What you are aiming to do is to provide a summary of what people are talking about, how much they are talking about it, and, if possible, who these people are. For instance, you could find that people with the most subjective things to say are talking a lot or they have many friends or followers. This could be interesting or important, since these people are likely spreading their understanding and opinions of the topic much more widely than regular users. So, it would serve your campaign well to know if these potentially influential people are for or against that issue.

Create a report with the description of (1) your data collection method, (2) your data analysis method, and (3) your findings.

Problem 11.3

Using R, create visualizations with different perspectives of the data we covered in this chapter, using Yelp dataset of "business" and "users." In other words, you are to try different variables for the visualization other than those used in the example.

Through this practice of data visualization with the Yelp dataset, did you find anything interesting that we did not cover in this chapter? For instance, you may have created a plot that shows some interesting patterns about one variable or interesting relationships between different variables. These are the kinds of observations that generate new ideas and innovations. Report this using appropriate graphs (unless you had them for the previous question) and a brief description.

Problem 11.4

Obtain the dataset containing statistics of hate crimes that happened within 10 days of the 2016 US election from OA 11.8. In that period, nearly 900 hate incidents were reported to the Southern Poverty Law Center, averaging out to 90 per day. By comparison, about 36,000 hate crimes were reported to the FBI from 2010 through 2015 – an average of 16 per day.

The numbers we have here are tricky; the data is limited by how it is collected and cannot definitively tell us whether there were more hate incidents in the days after the election than is typical. What we can do, however, is to look for trends within the numbers, such as how hate crimes vary by State, as well as what factors within those States might be tied to hate crime rates.

Following is the description of variables that are part of the dataset:

Header	Definition
State	State name
median_household_income	Median household income, 2016
share_unemployed_seasonal	Share of the population that is unemployed (seasonally adjusted), Sept. 2016
share_population_in_metro_areas	Share of the population that lives in metropolitan areas, 2015
share_population_with_high_school_degree	Share of adults 25 and older with a high-school degree, 2009
share_non_citizen	Share of the population that are not US citizens, 2015
share_white_poverty	Share of white residents who are living in poverty, 2015
gini_index	Gini Index, 2015
share_non_white	Share of the population that is not white, 2015
share_voters_voted_trump	Share of 2016 US presidential voters who voted for Donald Trump
hate_crimes_per_100k_splc	Hate crimes per 100,000 population, Southern Poverty Law Center, Nov. 9–18, 2016
avg_hatecrimes_per_100k_fbi	Average annual hate crimes per 100,000 population, FBI, 2010–2015

Use this data to answer the following questions. Use appropriate machine learning techniques or algorithms.

a. How does income inequality relate to the number of hate crimes and hate incidents?
b. How can we predict the number of hate crimes and hate incidents from race or nature of the population?
c. How does the number of hate crimes vary across States? Is there any similarity in number of hate incidents (per 100,000 people) between some States than in others – both according to the SPLC after the election and the FBI before it?

Note, for the first two questions:

- Choose the variables which you think are related to the predictors (income inequality, race, and nature of the population) to build your model. Justify your selection.
- Refine your model iteratively.

[Hint: You can use gradient descent, and/or add or remove variables in an incremental fashion.]

Notes

1. Twitter Docs: https://developer.twitter.com/en/docs
2. Twitter developer account access: https://developer.twitter.com/en/apply-for-access
3. Twitter Apps: https://developer.twitter.com/en/apps
4. Twitter Apps (OAuth settings): https://apps.twitter.com/
5. Twitter Details ("Your access token"): https://apps.twitter.com/
6. Google API client libraries: https://developers.google.com/api-client-library/python/start/get_started#setup
7. Google API Python client: https://developers.google.com/api-client-library/python/
8. Unidecode: https://pypi.python.org/pypi/Unidecode
9. Yelp's dataset challenge: https://www.yelp.com/dataset/challenge
10. CEO Mitch Lowe says MoviePass will reach 5 million subs by end of year: https://www.mediaplaynews.com/ceo-mitch-lowe-says-moviepass-will-reach-5-million-subs-by-end-of-year/

12 Data Collection, Experimentation, and Evaluation

"If your experiment needs statistics, you ought to have done a better experiment."
— Ernest Rutherford

What do you need?

- A general understanding of data collection and storage.
- Basic knowledge of statistical analysis methods.
- Concepts of building models and testing them in the context of machine learning.

What will you learn?

- Different methods for collecting human-focused data.
- Quantitative and qualitative approaches for analyzing data.
- Introduction to various common methods for evaluating data systems and models.

12.1 Introduction

We started this book with a glimpse into data and data science. Then we spent the rest of the book, especially Parts II and III, learning various tools and techniques to solve data problems of different kinds. Our approach to all of this has been hands-on. And now we have come full circle. As we wrap up, it is important to take a look at where that data comes from, and how we should broadly think about analyzing it. This final chapter, therefore, is dedicated to those two goals, as you will see in the next two sections. One section is an overview of some of the most common methods for collecting/soliciting data, and the other provides information and ideas about how to approach a data analysis problem with broad methods. Then the final section provides a commentary on evaluation and experimentation.

Note that, due to the limits of our scope, the descriptions of the methods for data collection, evaluation, or experimentation are not meant to be comprehensive. In other words, if you find yourself needing to design and execute a survey, perhaps what is presented here is not sufficient for you, especially if you have never done one before. But this should serve as a starting point. Sometimes knowing what to ask and where to look is half the battle!

12.2 Data Collection Methods

For the most part in this book we have assumed that the *right* kind of data is given to us, and we can go ahead with tackling a data problem. However, we may not always be so lucky. More realistically, we may be working in a field or a problem domain where prior data is not available, or what is available is not as useful for a given application. In this section, we will see how to go about designing new experiments and doing various quantitative and qualitative analyses to address emerging problems.

12.2.1 Surveys

Let us say you want to collect data that is specific to a problem or a question you are asking about how people think about something, for which data does not exist. A good method for collecting such data is conducting a survey. I am sure you have come across this method before, even if you have never practiced it yourself. When you hear the terms census, Nielsen ratings, or exit polls on an election night, these are all variations of surveys. A survey can be conducted in person, on paper, or online.

Snap Surveys Ltd.[1] says there are four reasons to conduct a survey:

1. Uncover answers
2. Evoke discussion
3. Base decisions on objective information
4. Compare results

A survey will give you targeted results – a potential gold mine of information. To get started, it is essential that first you know what question or problem you are tackling to strategize the questions. And what do you want to do with the results? If you need numbers (how many people think "ABC" or "XYZ"), creating multiple-choice closed-ended, or forced questions may be efficient. On the other hand, if you want public opinion about an issue, having respondents provide open-ended free text could be the better option.

12.2.2 Survey Question Types

Let us look at the kinds of survey questions you could ask.

Multiple-choice-type questions are going to be easiest for respondents to zip through, but what if your answer selections do not define how they would really answer? You might want to preface your questions by asking respondents to choose the answer that comes closest to how they would answer. On the one hand, you may think the more choices you offer (more is more) will be better, but on the other hand that may prove tiresome for the respondent to read through and they may lose patience.

Some of the basic demographic questions are often multiple-choice questions. Think about questions related to gender (Male/Female), age groups (e.g., 18–25, 26–30,

31–40, 41–50, >51), and employment (Employed, Not employed, Self-employed). Note that it is often a good idea to offer a *"Prefer not to answer"* option with each of these questions.

But multiple-choice questions are also used to get responses for other kinds of inquiries that are more complex. It is common to have such questions while eliciting information about various usability measures, including effectiveness, satisfaction, ease of learning, and engagement. For instance, one could ask customers/users about what was the most dissatisfying thing about a new service/interface using a multiple-choice question that has five possible answers: (1) input dialogue; (2) transaction confirmation screen; (3) speed of the interaction; (4) audible and visual feedbacks with each interaction; and (5) readability of the messages. One could design a survey such that, when a responder picks a choice, he/she gets a follow-up question based on that option to elicit more information.

Rank-order-type questions ask respondents to choose one thing over another in preference. These are usually things that come in paired comparisons, like price versus quality. These are fairly easy to answer but may not be very useful unless you are testing a hypothesis. For instance, if you think people may prefer one thing over another, you could float the idea in a rank-order question and your hypothesis may be affirmed. You probably want to include only one rank-order-type question in your survey, as people may not have the patience to answer carefully on more than one.

Here is an example of a rank-order question that may reveal more in the way of perception than truth.

> *Please rank the following five items in order, from most to least, using 1 for most and 5 for least. Please rank all five items.*
>
> *Off the top of your head, what would you think is the most ecologically mindful way for two people to travel from Miami to New York City, ranking from most ecologically mindful (1) to least ecologically mindful (5):*
>
> *Drive a Toyota Prius car; ride Amtrak at full passenger capacity; fly in a jumbo jet at full passenger capacity; ride a Greyhound bus at full passenger capacity; or ride a motorcycle for two. (Fill in the blanks with a shortened answer, as in "Prius," "Amtrak," Jet," "Bus," and "Motorcycle.")*
>
> *1.*
> *2.*
> *3.*
> *4.*
> *5.*

Rating or open-ended questions may work for your survey purpose. A **Likert** (pronounced *Ly*kert) **scale** (of 1 to 5) – widely used in scaling responses in surveys – gives respondents five statements and asks them to choose one that comes closest to how they feel, ranging from (1) strongly agree to (5) strongly disagree. Respondents are typically asked to pick one statement. This is more precise than a yes/no question but doesn't give you the reason behind the choice.

Here is an example of a Likert-scale question:

Please check the box that most closely expresses your opinion or feeling on the following question.

1. *The organization of the website make sense from the user's perspective.*

[]	[]	[]	[]	[]
strongly agree	*agree*	*neutral*	*disagree*	*strongly disagree*

An **open-ended question** is constructed so the respondent cannot answer "yes" or "no" but must give more information. Open-ended questioning is useful to master if you are interviewing people on camera and you need a good "sound bite." On a survey, you will need to create some space for the person to write a sentence or two. This might give you a response you could quote in your paper. Examples of open-ended questions are:

"What did you guys do last night?"

or

"What do you think would make this website more user friendly?"

On the other hand, an open-ended question will be more difficult to quantify as it will have more nuance, but it may be the most fruitful in giving you the reason behind the answer. Let us say you need to know how someone's vacation experience was in the Dominican Republic. If you ask, *"How was your experience?"* they could say, "Good!" But what would that tell you? Not much. Instead if you ask, *"Tell me your favorite thing about the Dominican Republic,"* you might get some interesting answers. You could follow up with *"What would have made your vacation experience even better?"* for some valuable insights.

Dichotomous (closed-ended) questions ask for "yes" or "no," or "true" or "false" answers. For instance,

"In the last 30 days, have you seen any ads on Facebook for shoes?" ______ yes ______ no

or

"Five plus three equals eight." ______ true ______ false

You could program your survey, depending on the answer, to jump to another question. If a person answered "yes" to seeing ads for shoes, then you could ask if they remembered the brand. If they say "no," then you could put some brand names in front of them and see if one might be the answer. This may not prove accurate, though, as familiarity with a brand name may influence the response.

12.2.3 Survey Audience

Just as it is important to figure out what kinds of questions to ask, it is imperative that you think about the people who will be taking your survey. If you are using an online survey service (see the next subsection) and broadcasting the survey, you may not be able to control who sees and responds to your survey. And since you do not see these people in person, it may be hard to assess if the responses you received were from the right kind of audience. In fact, it may not be easy to figure out if even a human took your survey, as there are many online bots these days spamming surveys. Will you also be able to track if the same individual responds to your survey more than once? Or, are they just randomly clicking around your multiple-choice questions? These are not easy questions to answer, but something that you should think about and plan for. For instance, you could use a service such as CAPTCHA[2] to verify that indeed a human is taking your survey. You could also insert a question or two somewhere in between real questions that tests if the respondent is paying attention. An example is "What is 1 + 1?"

You should also remember that you are asking *people* questions, and people usually like to talk about themselves or give their opinion. Who do you want to ask? How are you going to ask them to participate? Do you have a community on Facebook or Twitter? Are you connected to a community through school on Google Docs? Might a targeted email be more likely to get the people you want? Or, do you want to cast a wider net for responses from total strangers?

12.2.4 Survey Services

You could do your survey using mobile social media or old-fashioned email, or, even more old-fashioned, by handing out a piece of paper at the exit of an event and asking people to answer on the spot. (*"What did you think of the ending of the movie?"*) Some companies still use the US Postal Service to send hard-copy surveys in the mail. It depends on whom you are trying to reach.

As of this writing, there are probably more free survey services online you could try, but here are a few tried-and-true options. Of course, there are very expensive ones, too, in case you have the backing from a grant or a corporation to conduct a multiple-platform survey in various languages.

Microsoft's Office 365 offers a mobile-only option to conduct a survey using Excel.[3] If you are a subscriber, you can download the app and check it out.

SmartSurvey[4] is out of the UK and offers free plans but also student discounts if you want more bells and whistles. For free, you have options to create your own new survey or use a survey template, for which they have more than 50 varieties for questions related to realms as broad as client services, educational experiences, hospitality, and marketing. And there is a section of Web-ready surveys that you could tailor and shoot out via your social network or post to a website to gather information from visitors.

If you are devoted to Google, you probably know you can conduct a survey through Google Forms.[5] Just Google "Google Forms" and you will see the template gallery that can be tailored for personal, work-, or education-related surveys and assessments. They are free, easy, and fun, and look pretty, too. Try out a short one on your friends. And if you create one and use it, the survey and results will stay in your Google Docs for as long as you like, so you can conveniently revisit it or use it again. Another advantage of using Google for conducting surveys is Google also provides a decent set of data analytics and visualization tools.

If you are able to afford to pay for services or if your school or company already has a subscription, you could look into more refined and sophisticated tools available from SurveyMonkey[6] and Qualtrics.[7]

These days, many social media services also allow one to create an instant poll. For example, if you are a Twitter user and/or want some simple responses from your Twitter community, you can create a simple poll.[8] Of course, this will not suffice if you are looking for advanced options, more types of question types than multiple choice, or want to use pictures in your poll.

12.2.5 Analyzing Survey Data

Chances are you already know and have a favorite spreadsheet program such as Excel or Google Sheets. You can easily import your survey data (most tools allow this) into one of such programs. If you have used Google Forms to conduct your survey, the data is already in Google Sheets. See Table 12.1 for an example of such data. Or, you could write a report that summarizes your results. Perhaps include a chart that visualizes the range of responses; see Figure 12.1. There are lots of ways to do this, and a Google search will give you an array of options to consider for your results.

Table 12.1 An example of how survey results can be organized in Excel.

Row labels		Count for "I think this website is user friendly."
Neither Agree or Disagree	4	
Somewhat Agree	2	*Note the values*
Somewhat Disagree	2	*are the same for*
Strongly Agree	1	*"somewhat" and*
Strongly Disagree	1	*"strongly"*
Total	10	

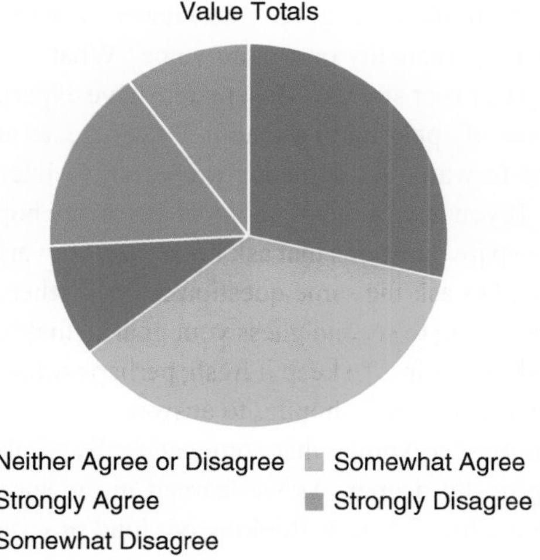

Figure 12.1 A simple visual of results from a Likert-type question.

12.2.6 Pros and Cons of Surveys

A survey offers another angle on your research. You may not want to base your entire thesis on the results, as they may be skewed due to the mood the respondents were in, but the results could indicate a direction for you to pursue.

What if you get results you did not expect? You may want to do another survey to see if the results were indicative. People may not answer the questions honestly. You can ask them to be honest, but you can't ask them to swear to be honest. You can boost the probability of honesty by telling them no one will know who answered what – that it is a blind survey and the responses will be pooled. Some of the questions may not get to the "why" behind the answer.

It probably makes sense to mix it up. Give respondents a variety of ways to answer. Try to ask more or less the same question or a couple of questions in different ways, from different angles, if you really need to know something specific. You may want to do a test run of a sample of questions before running the "official" survey to see if the results look promising.

12.2.7 Interviews and Focus Groups

Interviews and focus groups can deliver rich, targeted information with the benefit of the exact words of the interviewee. In person and in their own words, respondents may offer nuggets you will not get from a survey. And a direct quotation can be a compelling way to conclude a paper if it supports your findings. Interviews are generally done one on one and focus groups are just what they sound like – a group of people responding to focused questions or stimuli. Interviews may be better suited to more intimate-type questions, and focus groups may be ideal for testing something that is easy to talk about in public. There are reasons, as well as pros and cons, for using each.

12.2.8 Why Do an Interview?

When you think of a great interviewer, whom do you think of? Are you picturing a television personality or a radio voice? What is it that makes them good at bringing out revealing truths or stories? Most people have experience of being interviewed for a job or in the process of applying to a school. Of course, as an interviewee you prepare and put your best foot forward. As someone preparing to interview someone else, you also need to prepare. If you have a thesis about what you are hoping to answer, confirm, or explore, you should prepare questions that ask for answers in various ways. Not only a variety of types of questions, but ask the same question from another angle. You do not want the person you are interviewing to second guess your goal so that they give you predictable answers – what they think you want. To keep it fresh, perhaps some of your questions are "fillers" and some are what you are really hoping to answer.

If you want to know what someone really thinks, you may need to go for shadings of meaning or dig deeper. As we learned in the surveys section, some questions are open-ended and allow for some thinking out loud or writing a couple of sentences, and for other questions you are looking for yes/no or one answer.

12.2.9 Why Focus Groups?

Let us say you are a brand manager and you need to test a new cereal that is still in development with an established brand behind it. There is pressure to get the taste and texture just right. Research and Development has delivered what they think is a winning recipe, and the test kitchen has created it. You have different kinds of milk and milk substitutes for every possible preference. Now it is your job to try it out on a group of willing people in a focus group. You want to get at exactly what it is that would make the cereal great, not just good. You want to ask if it reminds them of any other cereal. You want to know if they like it and if they would buy it or what they think might make it better.

Focus groups can also be useful for brainstorming. If you need feedback on a developing logo for a new brand or a brand update, you could show variations and get reactions. You want a graphic that is memorable, not one that will be overlooked.

Just as in the interview, you will want people to sign an agreement that gives you permission to use their thoughts and words but protects their privacy. They would not be there if they did not agree to this in advance. You will also want to offer some form of remuneration.

You could invite 100 people and have the testing go all day, but the groups should probably be scheduled in increments of 8–10 so you can lessen the self-consciousness some people have about speaking in front of others. Tell them you are going to tape-record the session and how long it will last.

12.2.10 Interview or Focus Group Procedure

Let us say you want to know what it was like growing up in a single-parent household. Or, what are a person's feelings about high-school math. These questions might be well suited for an interview.

You will want to attract people to interview who fit the profile and are willing to talk about the subject.

Once you have crafted your questions, you might do a test-run on a friend or two to see if the questions generate answers you can work with.

Once you have gotten people to agree to be interviewed and they are in the room, you will want to start with an/a:

1. **Agreement.** Have them write out and sign their name and the date as well as their contact information under a statement that says they are competent and willing to divulge their thoughts/opinions today for the purpose of the interview. You should add that their identity and privacy will be protected. (You could get some formal legal language if it is a serious or very personal set of questions.) Also, this could be a step that is done outside of the interview room by another person if you have the personnel to help out.
2. **Ice breaker.** Help your interviewee relax by offering them water and asking how was their trip getting there. Share something of equal weight about yourself. Offer them a chair at a table where the power dynamic is equal (as opposed to setting up the

interview from behind a desk where they might feel like you are the boss.) Make sure the sun is not in their eyes, etc. You want them to feel safe and relaxed.

3. **Honest opinion.** Tell them upfront that you hope they are willing to tell the truth. Ask if it is alright if you tape-record the interview. Remind them that their identity will be protected and that you will ask them for permission to quote them anonymously after the process of interviewing others is complete if they have made a useful statement.
4. **Plan.** Tell them that you will be asking different kinds of questions from a prepared list and they can take their time answering, but that the entire interview will last no more than (whatever you initially told them when you asked for the interview), say, half an hour. If you go over time because a worthwhile conversation happened, ask for permission to continue. (They may need to leave.)

After it is finished, thank them and give them some form of remuneration. Perhaps cash – everyone gets the same – or a gift card for Starbucks.

12.2.11 Analyzing Interview Data

Once you have conducted your interviews or focus groups, hopefully you now have a rich resource in a recorded format. By way of illustrating the next step, let us consider the job of the court reporter. If you are a court reporter, your job is to sit through courtroom proceedings and capture the exact verbiage that transpires – from attorneys, witnesses, defendant, judge – on a stenotype machine. Then you go home and transcribe the paper from shorthand symbols back into words. You literally sit down at a computer and type, so a document with words can be emailed or printed out. Essentially, this process needs to happen with your interview recordings. Your interviews will not be on stenotype paper, but you can methodically listen to the recordings and type what you hear yourself, though it is time-consuming. (By the way, court reporters make a good living.) You could ask a student or a friend (and pay them) to listen to the recording and type it up. Or, you could use a professional transcription service that can turn your job into the written word in hours. They will charge you by the minute, but it will be worth it in time saved and attention to detail. Once you have your transcription (your content), then you can analyze it. You can excerpt the exact words, sentences, or interactions that get at what you are investigating or trying to define. Do you need to go in another direction with a different set of questions, or did you nail it? There are loads of transcription services out there, and they are very competitive (they want your business), so shop around to get the best deal.

12.2.12 Pros and Cons of Interviews and Focus Groups

Is the interview the most honest of conversations? Perhaps not. As we might do on a first date, we are usually putting forward our best selves. Most people want others to like them. So how would you get an honest answer from someone you are interviewing for a research project? You can set the scene for your best shot with preparation. You are not looking for a relationship with the person, but you want to project warmth and that you are genuinely interested in their answers. Prepare and then practice on your classmates or a friend before the real thing. The first couple of times you interview you will learn as you go what works and what does not seem to elicit what you need.

In focus groups, you are going to have the natural dynamic of some people dominating and some being more passive. Some will be tempted to piggyback on what someone else said. But, there will be interesting things that develop as a conversation ensues, and sometimes the stimulation of people thinking together, out loud (sometimes called brainstorming), can bring rich fodder for your project.

You may find using a set of interviews or focus groups a great way to help get a clearer working thesis or data for your research.

12.2.13 Log and Diary Data

The experience of your study participants might best be captured in a log or a diary for the flexibility it gives the user-participant. Perhaps your user-participants are students or workers with full-time jobs and they need to be able to give you time at their convenience. They could do the log on an app on their smartphone or the diary from their laptop at home. And, perhaps a structure with regular intervals works best for the kind of data you want to collect.

What is the functional difference between a log and a diary? Really, they have the same purpose, which is to capture data at regular intervals. One traditional use of a log is by a ship's captain to note things like weather, geospatial coordinates, and anything unusual at predictable times of day so that he or someone else can look back at the record for why they hit an iceberg! Or an athlete might use a log to note his/her progress while training for the Olympics. For a research study, you might use an activity log to capture specific data at regular check-ins to assess a quality over time.

Alternatively, you might use a diary if you want someone's experience or perceptions daily over a set time period. You might ask that a diary entry be made once a day, at the end of each day, over the course of your study or experiment. You might suggest a couple of sentences or a paragraph of text in the person's own words. See Table 12.2 for an example template for a log data collection, and Table 12.3 for a generic diary template.

Diary data can be captured in a structured manner as well. You can create a log or diary template that includes whatever buckets you want to track.

Table 12.2 A generic activity log template.

Name:
Date:

Time	Activity/ Task	Feeling/ Observation	Duration/ Measurement
10:00 am			
1:00 pm			
4:00 pm			
8:00 pm			

Table 12.3 A generic diary template.

Daily reflection for (Name): (Date): / /
What was your experience of doing "XYZ" today? If you had to summarize it in one word, what would it be? How might this work more efficiently/effectively if you did something differently? Share any other thoughts. Thank you!

Now, let us see how you could analyze such data. As you might do for interviews or focus groups, you could recruit participants through an announcement in class, a student newspaper notice, using social media, or email, passing out flyers, posting a notice on a bulletin board, or making phone calls. You need people who are willing to participate, and you should pay them something. You will need to prepare carefully considered questions or activities (or find/create an app) for your log or diary capture.

How will you quantify and analyze the results? You could assign numerical values to the range of responses (or words) you expect to collect. The numbers become your data points.

12.2.14 User Studies in Lab and Field

Who is a user? The user is you and me! Real people who will be using a product, such as a cellphone, a refrigerator, a car. What is a user interface (UI)? It is the designed relationship between the user and the product – essentially, a mechanism through which a user could interact with a system. When a product or an experiment involves testing the *goodness* of a UI, we ask questions such as: Is it intuitive? Is it awkward or inefficient? Is it aesthetically pleasing? The UI is a physical design as well as an interactive one. You want users of what you are designing to enjoy your product and to recommend it to others. How do you get there?

Test, test, test! If you want to test the performance of a new car or a website, you need some willing participants, or users. User studies can be done in a lab setting, where you have the most control and opportunity to observe, or "out in the field," where less control may be a more realistic gauge of the product.

You might want a lab-based setting for something that needs supervision or requires confidentiality. How a user interacts with a new product still in beta that may have bugs to be discovered might be moderated in a controlled situation, so you can witness the experience. Of course, there are also computer programs that track a user's experience, so you do not necessarily need to be present, unless witnessing the interaction firsthand is part of your information gathering. Is the artificiality of the lab setting a hindrance to yielding a natural interaction? Possibly, but this may not be important if you are after exacting specifications.

It is common in such studies to use hardware equipment such as an eye-tracker[9] for collecting data about where a user is looking on the screen, heart-rate monitors, electro-conductance monitors to measure emotional responses, and EEG monitors to collect data about brain activity. All of these have gotten quite sophisticated, becoming more powerful, more compact, and able to collect higher-resolution data than in the past.

Often, these things come with their own software that you can use for analysis. Or, they let you export the data in a format (such as XML and CSV) that can be understood by other analysis software. Figure 12.2 shows an example of a heat map that was generated by processing the raw data from an eye-tracker.

In addition to such hardware, you may also need software tools for logging various activities on a system (computer, mobile, etc.). There are several loggers available and some are free. One such example that my lab uses is Coagmento.[11] (Full disclosure: The author of this book is also the creator of Coagmento.) Coagmento can collect log data (websites visited, queries run, etc.) from within a Web browser.

A field-based study, where the user is out and about in their daily life – their normal context – interacting with the product, such as an app, and giving self-reported feedback, is a more "natural" situation that might be useful when you are looking for a big-picture experience. (Of course, if you are testing the results of crashing a sports car, you will want to use dummies!)

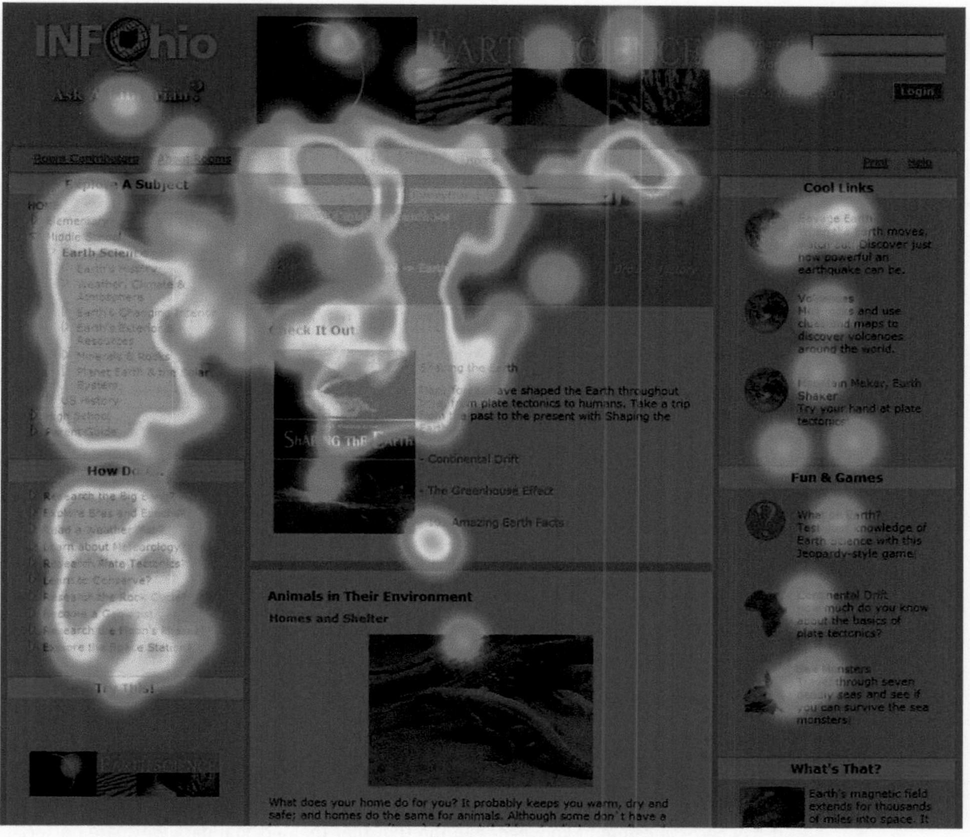

Figure 12.2 An example of a heat map generated from using eye-tracking data.[10] [Source: Johnny Holland "UX: An art in search of a methodology."]

User studies in both the lab setting or out in the field are likely to yield feedback on the quality of the user experience and not numerical data. Are you looking for attitudes about your product or behaviors around it? Try your test on a friend or colleague before getting your participants engaged.

12.3 Picking Data Collection and Analysis Methods

We will now turn our attention to analyzing the data. But wait, is that not what we have done throughout this book? Yes, we have. But we have often boxed ourselves in a specific kind of problem, eliminating the need to really think about what kinds of methods are needed for that analysis.

Here, we are going to take a step back and think more generally about data analysis methods. They can be broadly divided into quantitative methods and qualitative methods. What we have mostly encountered in this book are quantitative methods (except in some of the interviewing, focus groups, and diary data collection settings), but if you are serious about being able to address all kinds of data problems, it is important to know at least something about qualitative methods.

Both of these categories warrant their own books, but we are going to introduce them in just a couple of pages! So, I hope you understand that there is no way we are being comprehensive here. But let us have a bit of an introduction.

12.3.1 Introduction to Quantitative Methods

There are two broad categories of methods for data analysis we will now discuss. Quantitative methods use measuring techniques that result in numbers, or data. Qualitative methods, on the other hand, involve observations of behavior, attitudes, or opinions, resulting in an assessment of qualities (hence the qualification in parenthesis a couple of paragraphs earlier).

The formation of a theory usually begins with an observation that leads to a hypothesis. This is the inductive process in qualitative research, covered in the next subsection. Alternatively, in quantitative analysis, you test the hypothesis and collect numbers, information, or data, which you analyze to deduce another, perhaps closer-to-accurate hypothesis, and continue to evolve your working theory into a model. This is the deductive process. You need both quantitative and qualitative methods to get closest to a working theory. How do you think Albert Einstein arrived at his early-twentieth-century theory of relativity? Through observation, calculation, and deduction, and over many years, he refined his theory.

FYI: General Data Protection Regulation (GDPR)

It has become common knowledge in the USA that the personal data we share on social media has been collected and used for marketing purposes. The data is used to market to us directly and to add to the aggregate of marketing trends. It could be used in targeting goods and services back to us or in support of political agendas. While this may be a brilliant move on the part of these marketers to maximize the data that is right in front of them, it is offensive to consumers who did or did not read the fine print when they signed up for a service on X, Y, or Z social media platform. To the individual user, it may feel like an invasion of privacy and that there isn't a choice. While we may have gotten used to the notion that "Big Brother is watching"[12] in the USA, in the European Union (EU) this sense of a breach in trust has not been the norm or acceptable. In the EU, the culture has offered more protections for the individual. This level of protection is fast becoming what the rest of the world wants now that we know.

"Stronger rules on data protection mean people have more control over their personal data and businesses benefit from a level playing field."[13] The new rules (General Data Protection Regulation, or GDPR)[14] give consumers protection and control of their personal information; they were approved and adopted in 2016, but a two-year transition period elapsed and the rules were formally launched on May 25, 2018.

If you do business with the EU, then you must comply. "The GDPR not only applies to organisations located within the EU but it will also apply to organisations located outside of the EU if they offer goods or services to, or monitor the behaviour of, EU data subjects. It applies to all companies processing and holding the personal data of data subjects residing in the European Union, regardless of the company's location."[15]

The rules are designed to harmonize privacy laws across Europe, and empower all EU citizens to have data privacy. Organizations may face heavy fines for non-compliance; penalties include a fee of 4% or a maximum fine of €20 million.

Some organizations (public authorities; those that engage in large-scale monitoring; and those that deal in personal data) will need to appoint a staff Data Protection Officer (DPO) to keep on top of how their company processes data in keeping within the regulations. Take a look at what IBM is doing[16] to be responsible for their part.

Let us look into quantitative methods a little more. You may have already employed quantitative methods. For instance, if you used math to determine the volume of an object (assuming you took geometry in high school), that was an example of applying a quantitative method. In that case, you need to know an object's dimensions in order to perform that calculation. In a lab setting, you could use quantitative methods for counting the number of times something happens, or even quantifying – assigning numerical value to – attitudes or behavior. In a lab, as we discussed in the section about user studies, theoretically you have more control, and accuracy, in getting the measurements or data you need. These measurements can be done indirectly, that is, through a programmed or structured questionnaire or survey on a computer or on paper. Potentially you can get a larger pool of data this way and your analysis of it (your statistical inference) can yield results that support, or challenge you to refine, your theory.

A lot of quantitative analysis starts by first just describing the data – reporting what *is* rather than *why* or *how* it is. This is done using descriptive statistics. This includes things like the measures of central tendency (mean, median, mode) and the nature of the distribution of the data (range, variance, standard deviation). Often, this in itself could be very revealing. Seeing these descriptive statistics, one could form hypotheses or think about what further explorations to do (or not to do). What happens next depends greatly on the problem, the dataset, and the revelations obtained from the descriptive statistics. We will not go into the details because that's what we have done throughout this book – correlations, regression, classification, etc.

12.3.2 Introduction to Qualitative Methods

The word "**qualitative**" implies emphasis on the qualities of entities and on processes and meanings that cannot be experimentally examined or measured (if measured at all) for quantity, amount, intensity, or frequency. If you do cutting-edge research, every now and then you will come across scenarios where you will not have any definite idea about which variables are important to answer your research questions and how you can measure them. Sometimes, if you are lucky, you may have a hunch or there can be some clues in the existing literature. But what if you do not?

A good place to start would be observing the phenomenon and recording as much detail as you can without interfering. (This could take many hours, or years, as some scientists in the field of animal behavior have experienced.) In any case, it is going to take a long time. An alternative and probably less time-consuming way would be to ask other people to see what they think of the phenomenon. Ethnography, survey, and interview are types of *qualitative* inquiry.

Now that we have some data collected qualitatively, the next question is how to analyze them. A simple, straightforward answer is to quantify them – for example, converting the survey participants' responses into categories or numbers (as in the five possible responses on the Likert scale). But obviously, you can imagine that quantifying the field notes and ethnographic recordings is easier said than done. And oftentimes, when you quantify them, you lose some detail and the richness of the data.

Fortunately, there are qualitative methods to analyze such data as well. You can use something called *constant comparison* among your field notes to see what patterns are emerging from the data. Here, the idea is to develop a set of labels (what is often called "codes" in qualitative analysis) as you compare and contrast different data points.

As you begin to collect qualitative feedback about behaviors, attitudes, and opinions, another method you can apply is called *grounded theory*, a concept that came out of the social sciences in the 1960s. It is grounded because it is systematically tested and emerges slowly through constant comparison of the reality (data) of what you are collecting against the initial theory.

As we can see, qualitative research is important as you are beginning to explore your notions of what may become a model for your theory. Initially you might ask people (experts) for their thoughts and ideas, and uncover some problems you need to consider. What is the question you want to answer? You can organize a small field experiment to observe reactions directly about your initial theory. Next, you analyze your data either qualitatively or quantitatively. You are laying the ground for a working theory by thoughtful analysis. This careful process helps close the gap between your quantitative data and your initial hypothesis. Essentially, this is what Albert Einstein did.

Note that from the above narrative it may seem that the role of qualitative methods is somewhat limited and more of a backup option for a data science professional; for a researcher who cares more about explaining the models toward building new theories, qualitative methods can be a potent weapon.

12.3.3 Mixed Method Studies

In the previous subsections, both quantitative and qualitative research methods were discussed. However, it is important to note that both qualitative and quantitative methods have their own sets of weaknesses.

- Quantitative methods are often weak in understanding the context or setting in which data is collected and the results are less interpretable.
- Qualitative research, however, is time-consuming, and it may include biases from the data due to small sample sizes which may not lend itself to statistical analysis and generalization to a larger population.

Mixed method strategies can offset these weaknesses by allowing for both exploration and analysis in the same study, combining quantitative *and* qualitative methods into one research design in order to provide a broader perspective. Instead of preferring one method over the other, mixed methods emphasize the research problem and use all approaches available to generate a fuller understanding. In mixed method research designs, the quantitative data collected usually includes closed-ended information that undergoes statistical analysis and comparisons resulting in numerical representation. Qualitative data, on the other hand, is usually more subjective and open-ended. Such data allows the "voice" of the participants to be heard and the observations become more interpretable. Following is an example of how the methodologies can be mixed to provide a more thorough understanding of a research problem.

Imagine yourself as a budding information retrieval (IR) researcher, and you want to find the relationship between peoples' intentions of engaging in longer search episodes and their Web search behaviors. You may design a user study to collect data using a quantitative data instrument, such as query logs, the amount of time spent in each query segment, query reformulation strategies, etc. Based on the data you have collected, you may cluster similar search behaviors of participants presuming that each cluster will represent a unique intention of information seeking and different search intentions result in different search behavior. However, you still will not have any clue about which cluster represents what intention type. If you are lucky, you may find some hints from previous literature, but often with state-of-the-art research that is not the case. What you as a researcher can do in such situations is to follow up the study by interviewing a subset of the participants to learn more about their strategies and intentions while performing the search tasks. Thus, combining quantitative results with that from qualitative data may result in a more comprehensive answer to your research problem.

12.4 Evaluation

In this section, we will revisit some of the concepts that we have covered before when we analyzed data. The primary purpose of data analysis is often to make a decision or develop an insight. And in service of these goals, it is important to know how much we can really *trust* that data. More specifically, how much do we believe that the analysis we have performed or the model we have built is solid enough to accept the conclusions or recommendations from it? For instance, if we are building a classifier, we should know its accuracy. We have looked at this before when we discussed the problem of classification. But is the measure of accuracy enough? What if a given classifier model *overlearned* the data? In that case, it could give us a good accuracy value for the training data but may do poorly on new (test) data. Similarly, we could create a model so complex that it could become hard to generalize or explain even though it performs well.

When we are evaluating the *goodness* of our technique or model, we need to look at multiple measures of success and effectiveness. The same goes when we are trying to compare various models. Here, we will see some of the ways to accomplish these objectives.

12.4.1 Comparing Models

You have seen that the same weather dataset was used to explain multiple machine learning algorithms in previous chapters. And you have probably realized by now that the same dataset can be used by different algorithms to answer the same set of questions in very different ways. So, you might be imagining that when you have a real-world problem with many hundreds of variables and millions of instances, you would want to try multiple models before choosing the most appropriate one. Then, the question becomes how would you compare different models to pick the right one for the problem at hand? (Not that you can directly compare the weights of a neural network to the decision rules of a tree and come up with a right answer, and especially not with a big dataset.) Obviously, there has to be some mechanism to test the goodness of your model to say how well it can explain the data. Fortunately, there are plenty of metrics to evaluate the goodness of a model. Following are a few.

Precision: In any classification problem, precision (also called positive predictive value) is the fraction of correctly classified instances among all the classified instances. Suppose you have designed a fact checker that can read any statement and decide whether the statement is true or false. In this case, four kinds of classification situations can happen. The statements which are really true can be classified as true (also known as true positive, TP); the correct statements can be misclassified as false (false negative, FN); the incorrect statements can be misclassified as true (false positive, FP); and incorrect statements can get classified as false (true negative, TN). In this case, precision is defined as

$$\text{Precision} = \frac{\text{TP}}{\text{TP} + \text{FP}}. \tag{12.1}$$

Precision can be used as a measure of exactness or *quality* of the model.

Recall: Now, what if you have a model that is 100% precise; then there is no FP. However, there is no guarantee that minimizing FP results in low FN. Typically, if you decide to create a strict fact checker, it may be biased toward predicting most of the instances as negative (given that a majority of statements are actually true), therefore having a low FP, but at the cost of high FN. To help in those scenarios, you can use another evaluation scheme to test the completeness of your model, known as recall. For any classification scheme, recall can be calculated as

$$\text{Recall} = \frac{\text{TP}}{\text{TP} + \text{FN}}. \tag{12.2}$$

Ideally, one would like a model that has high precision and high recall. However, it often happens that precision and recall values are complementary. When the model is designed to have high precision, it typically has low recall; and models with low precision have high recalls. So how do you strike a balance? You take a harmonic mean of them, which is also known as the F-measure, which is calculated as

$$F\text{-measure} = 2 \times \frac{\text{precision} \times \text{recall}}{\text{precision} + \text{recall}}. \tag{12.3}$$

It is important to note here that not all problems require a high-accuracy solution. In some cases, you may want really high precision even at the cost of low recall. For example, a bank wants to use their data to design an algorithm to predict loan applicants who may become willful defaulters. In that case, it might be more important that your algorithm has high precision, even at the cost of denying loans to some customers who may not be willful defaulters. Considering this, it might be helpful if some metric informs us how the rates of true positive and false positive change over various settings of the model.

Fortunately, you can use the receiver operating characteristic (ROC) curve for that. In the ROC curve the true positive rate (TPR) is plotted against the false positive rate (FPR) at various thresholds. The area under the curve represents the goodness of the model. To visualize this, consider Figure 12.3.

The graph in Figure 12.3 shows three ROC curves representing excellent, good, and worthless models plotted on the same graph. The accuracy of the test depends on how well the test separates the group being tested. The yellow line (excellent) has the largest amount of area under the curve, and therefore is the most desired one for the problem.

AIC (Akaike Information Criterion): There are other criteria to compare the accuracy of different models. For example, simple models are less expensive, easier to explain and less computationally intensive, whereas complex models are more resource-hungry to build, less explanatory but often provide better performance. So, depending on the problem, you may want to balance the simplicity and the goodness of fit. AIC, borrowed from information theory, is a measurement of the relative information lost for a model explaining the process that generated the data. While doing so, it deals with the trade-off between the goodness of fit of the model and the simplicity of the model. Unlike precision and recall, AIC cannot be used to judge the absolute quality of a model; it can be used only to

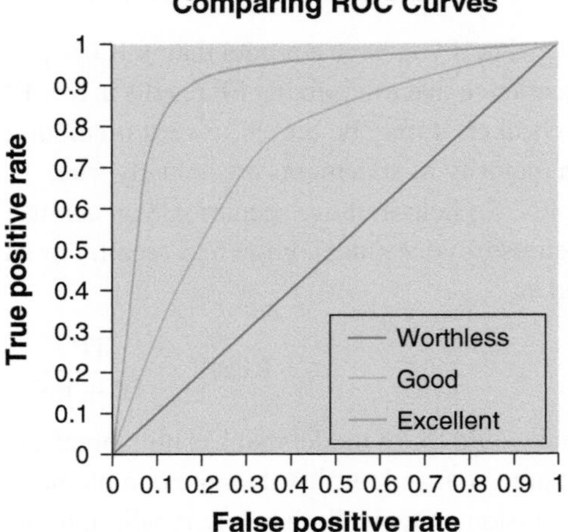

Figure 12.3 ROC curve. (Source: University of Nebraska Medical Center.[17])

understand the relative quality of a model compared to other models. Thus, there may not be any difference in results between the case where all candidate models perform poorly, and where candidate models perform superbly.

BIC (Bayesian Information Criterion): While fitting models, it is possible to increase the likelihood criteria by adding more parameters, but doing so may result in overfitting. Both AIC and BIC attempt to solve this problem by introducing a penalty for the number of parameters in the model. Therefore, the more complex the model is, the higher the penalty, and the lower the BIC, the better the model. However, the way the penalty is introduced is a little different in BIC from AIC. BIC penalizes more severely than AIC when introducing a new parameter to the model. AIC approximates a constant plus the relative distance between the actual likelihood function of the data and the likelihood function of the fitted model. So, the lower the AIC, the closer is the model representing the true nature of the data. Compared to that, a lower BIC also means the model is more likely to be the true model. However, BIC is calculated as a function of the posterior probability of a model being true, under a certain Bayesian setup.

So, what's the bottom line? In general, it might be best to use AIC and BIC together to select the most appropriate model. For example, in selecting the number of latent classes in a model, if BIC points to a four-class model and AIC points to a two-class model, it makes sense to select from models with two, three, and four latent classes.

12.4.2 Training–Testing and A/B Testing

You have seen in various instances in the preceding chapters that, once a model is built on training data, it was tested on a test sample. This test sample is usually a smaller dataset compared to the training set, which the model did not see before. The reason behind such a strategy is to test the model's generalizability. In its purest form, generalizability is for making predictions based on known observations. Generalizability can happen in two ways.

Sometimes when researchers talk about generalizability, they are predicting for a larger population from the result of a study sample given the population represented by the sample. For instance, consider the question, "What percentage of the American population supports the Democratic party?" It would be impossible for the researcher to put this question to every single person who has a voting right and come to a definite number. Rather, the researcher can survey some people and extend their result to the population. In this case, it would be important for researchers to survey people who represent the population at large. Therefore, it must be ensured that survey respondents include relevant groups from the larger population in correct proportions.

Second, the concept of generalizability can help the move from scientific observations to theories or hypotheses. For instance, in the 1940s and 1950s, British researchers Richard Doll and Bradford Hill found that 647 out of 649 lung cancer patients in London hospitals were smokers. This observation prompted many later research studies to use larger sample sizes, with different groups of people and different amount of smoking, and so on. When the results from these studies found similarity across persons, groups, time, and place, the observation was generalized into a theory: cigarette smoking causes lung cancer.

In this case, the first kind of generalizability is being applied. To test the generalizability, an important step is to separate data into training and testing sets. Typically, when dividing a dataset into a training set and test set, there are a couple of important factors that need to be handled. First, as demonstrated in various examples in previous chapters, a bigger chunk of the data goes for training, and a smaller portion is set aside for testing. Moreover, the separation has to be unbiased. Specifically, the data should be randomly sampled to help ensure that the testing and training sets are similar in terms of variation and representing the population.

Sometimes you may come across other variations of this separation, such as training–testing–validation sets. In this case, the training is done a little bit more rigorously. As you have seen before, some of the data mining models may introduce some form of bias such as overfitting while creating the data. To reduce the effect of bias, a validation set is used. Take the example of the decision tree algorithm. During the training phase, the training dataset is used to adjust the decision boundaries. However, such adjustment may introduce overfitting into the model, especially on the occasion when the model would try to reduce the error in each iteration and would not stop until the point it becomes lowest. And while doing so, it may lose generalizability. This occurs when the decision boundaries are adjusted so well that the model can explain the current dataset, but cannot do so for other samples of the same population.

In those cases, a separate validation set is used to reduce the overfitting. As the name suggests, it is for validating the accuracy of the model before you test it on a larger population. In the previous example of the decision tree model, you will not adjust the decision boundaries any more with a validation set. Rather, you will verify that any increase in accuracy over the training dataset actually yields an increase in accuracy over a dataset that has not been shown to the model before, or at least the model has not been trained on it.

The above discussion on training and testing is all about knowing which variables are important for your model and figuring out to what extent. However, often you may come across scenarios where you will not be able to decide or even guess which variable to choose among many, or which version of the same variable is more effective in explaining the response. What then? Fortunately, there is a way to test the importance of competing alternative variables and decide which one is best. This is known as A/B testing, typically used with Web analytics for figuring out the best online or direct mail promotional and marketing strategies for a business. A/B testing is a controlled experiment with two variants, A and B, where the subject's response is tested by comparing the response of variable A against variable B, to determine which of the two variables is more effective. Let us take an example and see how it works.

A food delivery startup wants to generate sales through its website by running an advertising campaign with discount codes. The company is not sure which is the best channel for its customer acquisition, personal email or social media. So, it creates two versions of the same advertisement, one meant for its social media channel, "Use this promotional offer code AX! Hurry," and the other meant for personal email campaign, "Use this promotional offer code AY! Hurry," and everything else about the advertisements remains the same. The company now can monitor the success rate of each channel by analyzing the use of the promotional code and come up with better strategies for new client acquisition.

Note that A/B testing does not mean you get to experiment with only two (A and B) conditions. You can have several conditions/treatments. Of course, having many conditions will increase the complexity of your study design and analysis, and create a larger demand for samples/recruitments. This may become prohibitively expensive for academic research, but for a professional website or a service that has a large number of users (tens or hundreds of millions), this may not be a big issue. Not surprisingly, A/B testing today is a popular method for evaluation in various commercial organizations.

12.4.3 Cross-Validation

An alternative to such predefined separate training and testing data to validate generalizability is the cross-validation technique, sometimes called rotation estimation. In this technique, the original sample is partitioned into a training set to train the model, and a test set to evaluate it, often due to lack of a pre-existing test set. There are different variations of cross-validation used in practice.

The simplest kind of cross-validation is the holdout method. In this case, the sample is separated into two disjoint sets, called the training set and the testing set. A model is built using the training set only. Then this model is asked to predict the output values for the test set, which it has never seen before. The errors it makes in predictions are accumulated. This gives what is often called *mean absolute test set error*. Obviously, we want as little error as possible, and thus this error serves as an evaluation measure of the model.

An improvement over the base holdout method is k-fold cross-validation. In this case, the dataset is divided into k subsets. The evaluation is done k number of times. Each time, one of the k slices is kept aside for testing and the other $k-1$ subsets put together to be used as the training set. Thus, it can be seen as the holdout method being repeated k times here. The average error across all k trials is computed, which is the overall accuracy of the model. The advantage of k-fold cross-validation is that the model is less biased from how the data gets divided between training and test sets. Every data point gets a chance to be in a test set exactly once and in the training set $k - 1$ times. Therefore, the variance of the resulting estimate is reduced as k is increased. The disadvantage of this over the holdout method is that for k-fold cross-validation the training algorithm has to be run k times compared to just once in the holdout method, and it takes k times as much computation to make an evaluation.

Leave-one-out cross-validation is another logical extreme variation of k-fold cross-validation, where k is equal to the number of data points (N) in the set. As a result, the function approximator is used to train on all the data except for one point, which is kept aside for testing, and this process is repeated for each data point used exactly once as test case, in total N number of times. As before, the average error in N evaluations is computed and used as the overall error of the model. The evaluation provided by leave-one-out cross-validation method (LOO-XVE) is good, but it seems very expensive to compute, especially when the number of data points is large, which is often the case. Fortunately, learners that are locally weighted can make LOO predictions at the same cost as they take for regular predictions. That means computing the residual error takes as much time as the LOO-XVE, and the latter is a much better way to evaluate models.

FYI: Misinformation and Fake News

How many times have you heard the term "fake news" being discussed in the living room, at school, or in the news? The news media in the current world is not just limited to newspapers and news channels but also includes social media platforms like Facebook, Twitter, and many others like them.

Have you heard of the terms *misinformation* and *disinformation*? While both involve the spread of false information, the former is not meant to mislead you intentionally. So, when a person wants to manipulate others and spreads some false information for that purpose (maybe by tweeting), that is disinformation. If you read the tweet and decide to like or retweet it, you are unknowingly helping the spread of that false news, which is called misinformation.

The spread of such misinformation can be used to influence public opinion around important social, political, and environmental issues like vaccinations, elections, global warming, and green energy. To tackle the spread of false information, we will need to combine public awareness with technology. Educating people on how to check the authenticity of any information before sharing it is one such step. As the massive amounts of social media data make it impossible to manually curate such information, we could also build simple systems which can identify fake news content automatically and stop such news from propagating.

It might also be useful to know that fake news may involve political satires, parodies, propaganda, and biased reporting. More importantly, it may not be limited to text but may include doctored videos and photoshopped images.

Do you want to test your skills in identifying fake news? Try to identify the authenticity of the following news items (used from http://factitious.augamestudio.com/#/):

1. Can't stop gaming? The WHO may soon consider video game addiction a mental disorder.
2. India has the highest number of selfie deaths in the world.
3. Trump suggests immigrants wear identifying badges.
4. China assigns every citizen a "Social Credit Score" to identify who is and isn't trustworthy.

The answers are True, True, Fake, and True.

You may also like the online game on fake news on the same site: http://factitious.augamestudio.com/#/.

Misleading information can cause tremendous damage to personal and social lives. So, the next time you see a news headline that is suspicious, check the entire news before sharing it. Spelling and grammatical errors, strong and abusive language, and informal writing style – these are all telltale signs of "fake news."

Remember: Do not trust news by its headline!

Summary

Data science is just as much about what happens before data and what happens after data as it is about what you do with the data. Let me clarify. For most of this book we have focused on the phase that starts with having the *right* kind of data and applying various analyses. However, in reality there is a lot that needs to happen before one stumbles upon that *right* kind of data for a given problem. And a lot has to happen after the data is processed/analyzed in some way. In this chapter, we talked about those pre-data and post-analyses phases. We saw that there are many ways to collect data, each with its own advantages and disadvantages, costs and benefits. In the end, which method to use depends on the need, budget (time and money), and other practical considerations. It is also common to use multiple methods for data collection, resulting in datasets that are in different formats and could tell different stories, when analyzed.

Similarly, there are different ways to analyze the data. Broadly speaking, there are quantitative and qualitative approaches. In this book, we focused primarily on quantitative methods, and when you look around in the broad field of data science, those are what you would find most times. Remember, data science stemmed from statistics! That being said, it is also important to know at least some basics of qualitative methods, as we may end up with data (e.g., collected from interviews) that may need to be analyzed qualitatively.

Finally, we saw that sometimes we have to do meta-analysis after processing or analyzing the data. This involves rethinking our evaluation strategy and comparing various techniques or models used in the data analysis. It is very common to find that there are no exact answers or perfect models. Instead, we are left with a decision to make – should we go with a better fitting model that has more complexity or a simpler model with less accuracy? Do three classes make more sense than five classes, even though five classes categorize the data better? How do we ensure that the models we have built are general enough to be used for new data that will come? There are no standard answers to these questions. But hopefully, this chapter has given you a start toward asking the right questions and making some informed decisions.

Key Terms

- **Likert:** A Likert scale is a type of psychometric rating scale commonly involved in research that employs questionnaires. With the scale, respondents are asked typically to rate items on a level of agreement.
- **Grounded theory:** Grounded theory is a systematic methodology mostly used in the social sciences which is used to construct theories through methodical gathering and analysis of data.
- **Quantitative method:** The quantitative method focuses on collecting numerical data and analyzing it objectively. It typically involves objective measurement and analysis of data collected through questionnaires, surveys, or by manipulating pre-existing statistical data employing computational techniques.
- **Qualitative method:** The word qualitative implies emphasis on the qualities of entities and on processes and meanings that cannot be experimentally examined or measured (if measured at all) for quantity, amount, intensity, or frequency. Most qualitative methods (e.g., ethnography) involves observing the phenomenon of interest and recording as much detail as possible without any interference.
- **Constant comparison:** The constant comparison is an inductive method of data coding, used for categorizing and comparing qualitative data for analysis purposes.
- **Precision:** In any classification problem, precision is the fraction of correctly classified instances among all the classified instances.
- **Cross-validation:** In the cross-validation technique, the original sample is partitioned into a training set to train the model, and a test set to evaluate it, often due to lack of a pre-existing test set.

Conceptual Questions

1. Compare surveys and interviews methods, citing their pros and cons.
2. What is quantitative method of data collection and analysis? Give two examples.
3. What is qualitative method of data collection and analysis? Give two examples.
4. What is an advantage of focus group method over interviews?
5. How do AIC and BIC differ?

6. What does a receiver operating characteristic (ROC) curve represent? Describe how you could use it in deciding which system/classifier to use for a given situation.

Further Reading and Resources

1. Patton, M. Q. (2014). *Qualitative Research & Evaluation Methods*, 4th ed. Sage: https://us.sagepub.com/en-us/nam/qualitative-research-evaluation-methods/book232962
2. Kalof, L., Dan, A., & Dietz, T. (2008). *Essentials of Social Research*. McGraw-Hill Education: https://books.google.com/books/about/Essentials_Of_Social_Research.html?id=6GsLKDQHIncC
3. SAGE. (2018). SAGE Research Methods: http://sagepub.libguides.com/research-methods/researchmethods
4. Labaree, R. (2013). Organizing Your Social Sciences Research. Paper 1. Choosing a Research Problem: http://libguides.usc.edu/writingguide/researchproblem
5. Labaree, R. (2013). Organizing Your Social Sciences Research. Paper 6. The Methodology: http://libguides.usc.edu/writingguide/methodology

Notes

1. Snap Surveys: The 4 Main Reasons to Conduct Surveys: https://www.snapsurveys.com/blog/4-main-reasons-conduct-surveys/
2. Captcha Bot Detector: https://captcha.com
3. Microsoft 365 Surveys: https://support.office.com/en-us/article/Surveys-in-Excel-hosted-online-5FAFD054-19F8-474C-97EC-B606FCDA0FF9
4. Smart Survey: https://www.smartsurvey.co.uk/signup
5. Google Forms surveys: https://www.google.com/forms/about/
6. SurveyMonkey: https://www.surveymonkey.com/
7. Qualtrics: https://www.qualtrics.com/
8. Twitter polls: https://help.twitter.com/en/using-twitter/twitter-polls?lang=en
9. Wikipedia entry on eye tracking: https://en.wikipedia.org/wiki/Eye_tracking
10. Source of heat map: "UX: An art in search of a methodology": http://johnnyholland.org/2009/10/ux-an-art-in-search-of-a-methodology/
11. Coagmento: http://coagmento.org
12. "Big Brother is watching" is a concept English author George Orwell introduced in his novel *Nineteen Eighty-Four* (published in 1949).
13. European Commission: 2018 reform of EU data protection rules (official): https://ec.europa.eu/commission/priorities/justice-and-fundamental-rights/data-protection/2018-reform-eu-data-protection-rules_en
14. EU General Data Protection Regulation portal: https://www.eugdpr.org
15. GDPR FAQs: https://www.eugdpr.org/gdpr-faqs.html
16. IBM Corporation: IBM Data Privacy: Consulting Services GDPR Readiness Assessment: https://www-01.ibm.com/common/ssi/cgi-bin/ssialias?htmlfid=WGD03104USEN&
17. The area under an ROC curve (courtesy of University of Nebraska Medical Center): http://gim.unmc.edu/dxtests/roc3.htm

Appendix A: Useful Formulas from Differential Calculus

Generally speaking, for a function $y = x^n$:

$$\frac{d}{dx}x^n = nx^{n-1}.$$

Let us list a few more rules:

$$\frac{d}{dx}cy = c\frac{dy}{dx}, \text{ where } c \text{ is a constant,}$$

$$\frac{d(u+v)}{dx} = \frac{du}{dx} + \frac{dv}{dx},$$

$$\frac{d(uv)}{dx} = u\frac{dv}{dx} + v\frac{du}{dx},$$

$$\frac{d}{dx}\left(\frac{u}{v}\right) = \frac{u\frac{du}{dx} - u\frac{dv}{dx}}{v^2},$$

and

$$\frac{dy}{dx} = \frac{dy}{du}\frac{du}{dx}.$$

If $y = f(u) = u^n$ and $u = d(x)$, then:

$$\frac{dy}{dx} = \frac{d}{dx}u^n = nu^{n-1}\frac{du}{dx}.$$

Sometimes we have functions with multiple variables. At that time, we take a derivative with respect to one of the variables and treat the other variables as constants. This is called a partial derivative. A partial derivative with respect to x means we disregard all other letters as constants, and just differentiate the x parts. Here is an example:

$$f(x,y) = 3y^2 + 2x^3 + 5y$$
$$\frac{\partial f}{\partial x} = 6x^2.$$

And here is what happens if we take the partial derivative of f with respect to y:

$$f(x,y) = 3y^2 + 2x^3 + 5y$$
$$\frac{\partial f}{\partial x} = 6y + 5.$$

Further Reading and Resources

To know more about these formulas, proofs, or some more advanced formulas that are relevant to the chapters, you can read from the following pointers:

1. Adams, R. A. (2003). *Calculus: A Complete Course*, 5th ed. Pearson Education.
2. Math is Fun: Introduction to derivatives: https://www.mathsisfun.com/calculus/derivatives-introduction.html
3. University of Texas: Basic differentiation formulas: https://www.ma.utexas.edu/users/kit/Calculus/Section_2.3-Basic_Differentiation_Formulas/Basic_Differentiation_Formulas.html

Appendix B: Useful Formulas from Probability

The probability of an event is calculated as:

$$\text{Probability } P = \frac{\text{Number of ways the event can happen}}{\text{Total number of outcomes}}.$$

For mutually exclusive events A and B:

$$P(\text{A or B}) = P(\text{A} \cup \text{B}) = P(\text{A}) + P(\text{B}).$$

For independent events A and B:

$$P(\text{A and B}) = P(\text{A} \cap \text{B}) = P(\text{A})P(\text{B}).$$

The conditional probability of an event A is defined by the likelihood of occurrence of A, given the occurrence of some other event B. It is defined as:

$$P(\text{A}|\text{B}) = \frac{P(\text{A} \cap \text{B})}{P(\text{B})}.$$

Here $P(\text{A}|\text{B})$ represents the conditional probability of A given B; $P(\text{A} \cap \text{B})$ denotes the probability of occurrence of both A and B, and $P(\text{B})$ is the probability of the event B.

Bayes' theorem is a formula that describes how to calculate the probabilities of hypotheses when given evidence. It follows simply from the axioms of conditional probability. Given a hypothesis H and evidence E, Bayes' theorem states that the relationship between the probability of the hypothesis $P(\text{H})$ before getting the evidence and the probability $P(\text{H}|\text{E})$ of the hypothesis after getting the evidence is:

$$P(\text{H}|\text{E}) = \frac{P(\text{E}|\text{H})}{P(\text{E})} P(\text{H}).$$

Further Reading and Resources

To know more about these formulas, proofs, or some more advanced formulas that are relevant to the chapters on machine learning, you can read from the following pointers:

1. Jaynes, E. T. (2003). *Probability Theory: The Logic of Science.* Cambridge University Press.

2. Online Statistics Education: An Interactive Multimedia Course of Study: http://onlinestatbook.com/2/probability/basic.html
3. Introduction to Probability by Bill Jackson: http://www.maths.qmul.ac.uk/~bill/MTH4107/notesweek3_10.pdf
4. RapidTables: Basic probability formulas: https://www.rapidtables.com/math/probability/basic_probability.html

Appendix C: Useful Resources

C.1 Tutorials

- Unix Primer – Basic Commands in the Unix Shell: http://www.ks.uiuc.edu/Training/Tutorials/Reference/unixprimer.html
- The Python Tutorial: https://docs.python.org/2/tutorial/
- Getting Started with MySQL: https://dev.mysql.com/doc/mysql-getting-started/en/
- Introduction to PHP: http://www.w3schools.com/PHP/php_intro.asp
- An R Primer for Introductory Statistics: http://www.stat.wisc.edu/~larget/r.html
- Statistics – Statistical Primer for Psychology Students: http://www.mhhe.com/socscience/intro/cafe/common/stat/index.mhtml
- Primer in Statistics: http://www.micquality.com/downloads/ref-primer.pdf
- Daniel Miessler: The Difference Between Machine Learning and Statistics: https://danielmiessler.com/blog/differences-similarities-machine-learning-statistics/
- Primer for the Technically Challenged by Stephen DeAngelis:
- Part 1: https://www.enterrasolutions.com/blog/machine-learning-a-primer-for-the-technically-challenged-part-1/
- Part 2: https://www.enterrasolutions.com/blog/machine-learning-a-primer-for-the-technically-challenged-part-2/
- An Introduction to Machine Learning Theory and Its Applications: A Visual Tutorial with Examples: http://www.toptal.com/machine-learning/machine-learning-theory-an-introductory-primer

C.2 Tools

- Cygwin (http://www.cygwin.com/) (Windows) – for Linux-like environment on Windows
- WinSCP (http://winscp.net/eng/index.php) (Windows) – SSH and FTP client. Instructions: http://winscp.net/eng/docs/guides
- PuTTY (http://www.chiark.greenend.org.uk/~sgtatham/putty/download.html) (Windows) – SSH client. Instructions: https://mediatemple.net/community/products/dv/204404604/using-ssh-in-putty-

- Fugu (https://download.cnet.com/Fugu/3000-7240_4-26526.html) (Mac) – FTP client. Instructions: http://www.cs.cmu.edu/~help/macintosh/fuguhowto.html
- FileZilla (https://filezilla-project.org/download.php) (Mac) – FTP client. Instructions: https://wiki.filezilla-project.org/FileZilla_Client_Tutorial_(en)
- MySQL downloads (http://dev.mysql.com/downloads/mysql/) (All platforms)
- MySQL GUI tools (http://dev.mysql.com/downloads/gui-tools/5.0.html) (All platforms)
- MySQL Workbench (http://www.mysql.com/products/workbench/) (All platforms) – MySQL GUI client. Instructions for setting up SSH Tunnel: https://mikefrank.wordpress.com/2009/12/14/mysql-workbench-5-2-and-ssh-mini-faq/
- Sequel Pro (http://sequelpro.com) (Mac) – MySQL GUI client
- PHP (http://php-osx.liip.ch/) (Mac)
- MAMP (http://www.mamp.info/) (Mac, Apache, MySQL, PHP)
- PHP (http://www.php.net/downloads.php) (Windows)
- Eclipse (https://www.eclipse.org/downloads/packages/installer) (All platforms) – Integrated Development Environment (IDE) for all kinds of programming needs
- PHP Eclipse plugin (http://sourceforge.net/project/showfiles.php?group_id=57621) (All platforms)
- Python (https://www.python.org/downloads/) (All platforms)
- Spyder (https://github.com/spyder-ide/spyder) (All platforms) – Scientific PYthon Development EnviRonment
- PyDev (http://www.pydev.org) (All platforms) – Python IDE for Eclipse
- R (https://www.r-project.org/) (All platforms)
- RStudio (https://www.rstudio.com/products/rstudio/download/) (All platforms) – an IDE for R

Appendix D: Installing and Configuring Tools

D.1 Anaconda

There are plenty of ways to work with Python and Python-related tools. If you already have your favorite way or tool (e.g., Eclipse), feel free to continue with that. If, however, you are new to Python or want to try something different, I suggest the Anaconda framework.

It is available from https://www.anaconda.com/distribution/ and provides a host of tools, including Python itself. And then it has hundreds of the most popular Python packages, including a large set for doing data science.

Once you install Anaconda, start the "Navigator" utility. The Navigator will list all the Python-related tools you have on your machine, allowing you to launch and manage them from this one place.

See the screenshot in Figure D.1. A couple of utilities that are very useful for us are ipython-notebook and spyder. They are covered next.

D.2 IPython (Jupyter) Notebook

The IPython (stands for Interactive Python) Notebook is a nice little utility for trying Python. It allows you to interactively write, execute, and even visualize your Python code. In addition, it helps you document and present your work, so it is good for learning and teaching!

You can get it from http://ipython.org/notebook.html. Installation instructions can be found at http://jupyter.readthedocs.org/en/latest/install.html. Note that IPython now goes by the name Jupyter. So, if you ever worked in IPython before, do not let this confuse you.

One nice thing about the Notebook is that it runs in your Web browser, making it easy to access and have cross-platform compatibility.

See the screenshot in Figure D.2. As you can see, you can not only write and run your code, you can also edit and format it.

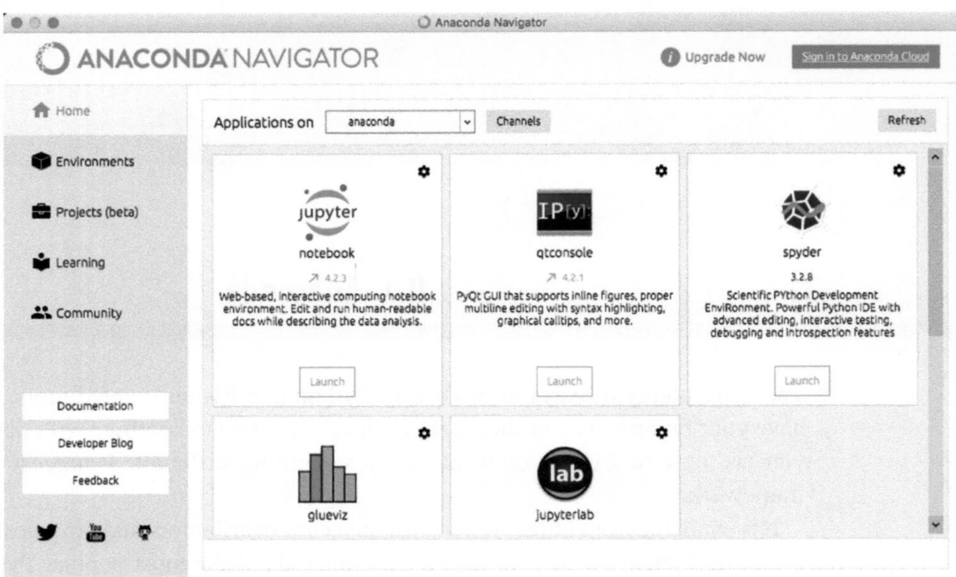

Figure D.1 A snapshot of Anaconda Navigator.

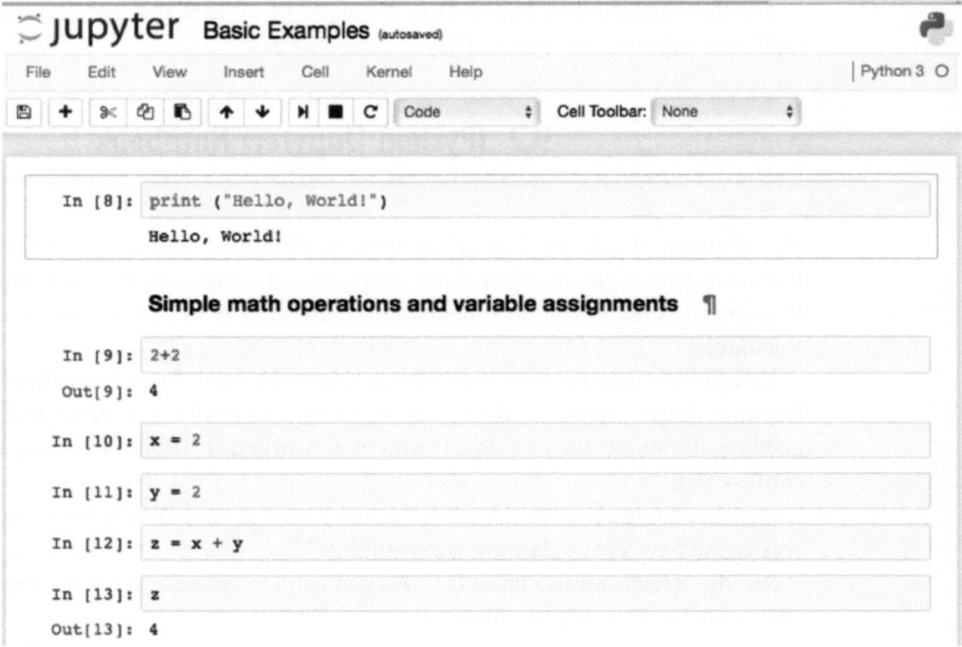

Figure D.2 A snapshot of IPython Notebook.

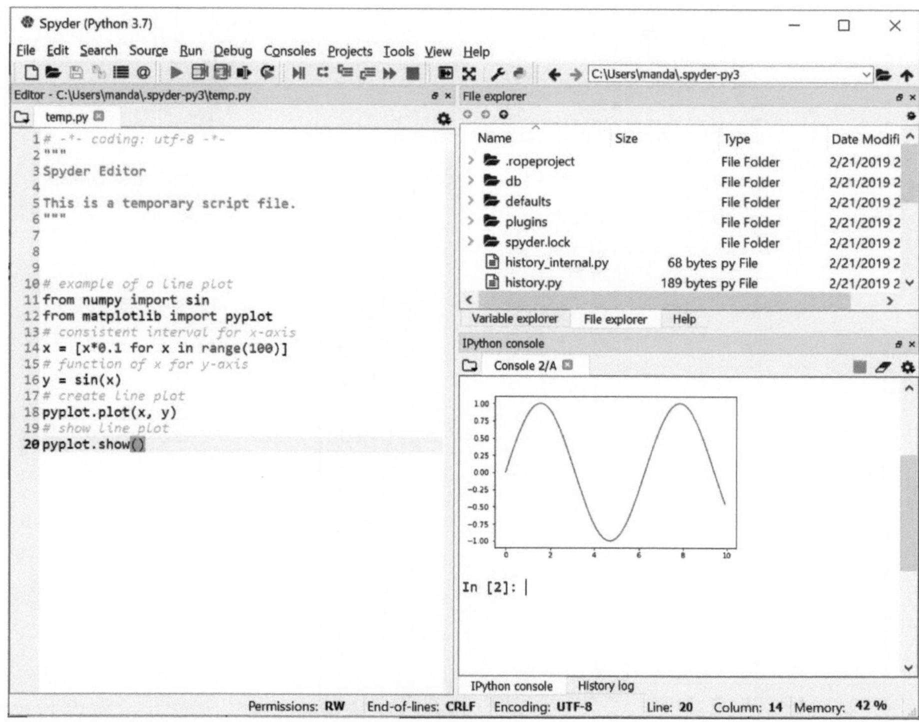

Figure D.3 A snapshot of Spyder.

D.3 Spyder

Continuing the tradition of switching an "i" with a "y," next we have "Spyder"! This is a full-fledged IDE (Integrated Development Environment) that allows you to write, run, debug, get help, and pretty much do everything you would ever want to do with Python programming.

If you have ever used any IDE like Eclipse, this should feel familiar. As you can see in the screenshot in Figure D.3 (taken from Spyder's project page), there are several windows, including one with an editor, one with online help, and another with results (console).

You can get Spyder from https://github.com/spyder-ide/spyder. Once installed, Spyder, like ipython-notebook, will also show up in Anaconda.

D.4 R

R is a free, open-source, and rigorously developed (and supported) programming environment (see Figure D.4). It is ideal for data science applications because it allows for a very

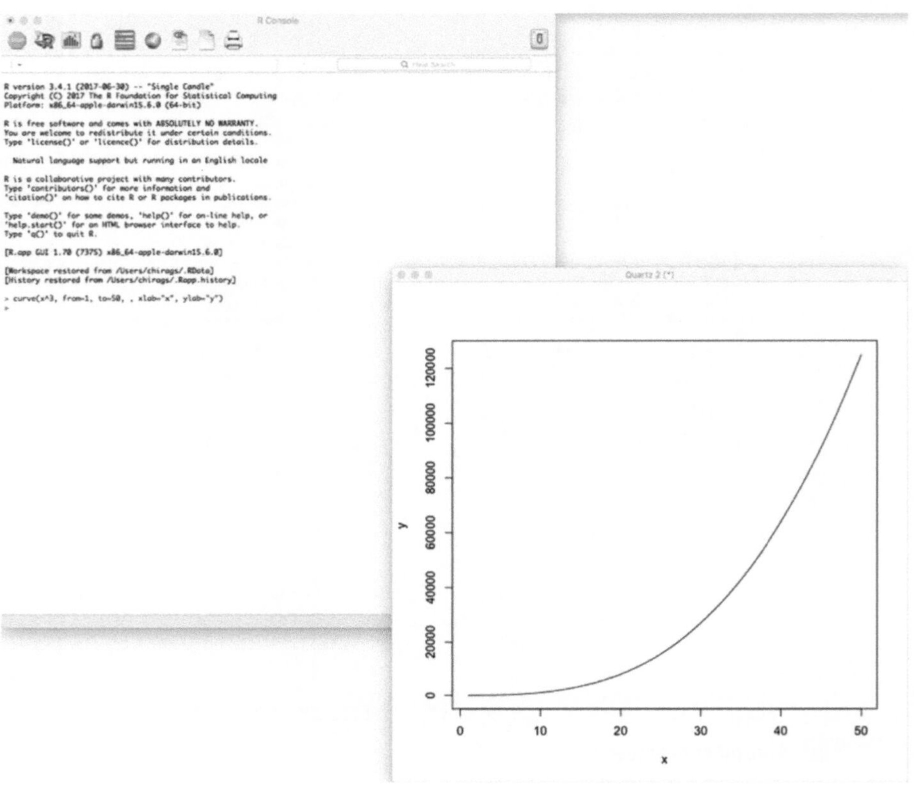

Figure D.4 A snapshot of R.

easy way to load up and process the data, yet is quite powerful for both analyses and visualization. Go to https://www.r-project.org/ to learn more and download.

D.5 RStudio

A great way to use R is through an R IDE called RStudio, which is available for free download from https://www.rstudio.com/products/rstudio/download/.

As the screenshot in Figure D.5 shows, RStudio has four main windows. Top-left is where you can see datasets or R script files. Bottom-left is where you can find the console. You can type R commands at the prompt here. In the top-right window, you can see either the variables and functions that are loaded in the environment, or the history of all the commands you have tried in the console. Finally, the bottom-right window displays several useful things, including plots, help, and a list of packages. There is also a file browser.

If or when needed, you can install a package or library for R using Tools > Install packages.

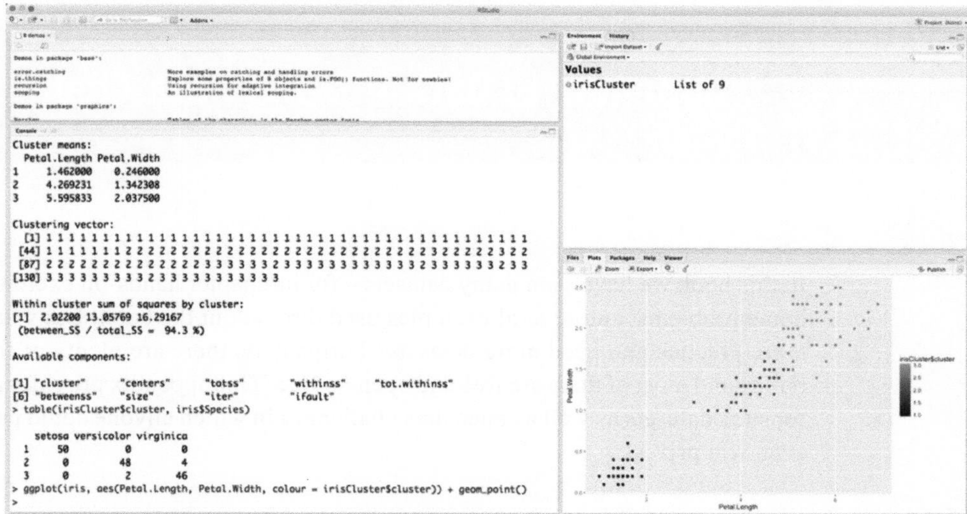

Figure D.5 A snapshot of RStudio.

Appendix E: Datasets and Data Challenges

In this book we have seen many datasets – for in-chapter hands-on exercises, for try-at-home problems, and several examples used throughout the book. But what if you want more practice and need more datasets? Fortunately, there are plenty of them available online and most of them are free and open-source. This appendix provides a few pointers for such datasets as well as open data challenges in which anyone could participate, and even win prizes!

E.1 Kaggle

Kaggle (https://www.kaggle.com/) is a great place to hone your data science skills. It is an online community of data scientists, machine learning, and AI researchers that was acquired by Google in 2017. Kaggle started its journey as a platform to share machine learning problems or challenges, which also morphed into a data sharing platform later. Users can find datasets, publish new ones, collaborate with other data scientists and machine learners from the community, enter competitions to solve data challenges, build new models, explore existing ones, share results with the community, and do many other things. Following are a few of the most popular services available from Kaggle.

Kaggle Kernels: Kernels are cloud-based workbenches to share code snippets with the community, which allow others to replicate the experiment, confirm the outcomes, and thus promote the reproducibility of the research. The code snippets shared in Kaggle are written in Python or R. Over 150,000 "kernels" have been shared on Kaggle so far.

Hosting Datasets: Kaggle is a great platform to share datasets with the community. Although not all datasets hosted in Kaggle are technically open datasets (without any copyrights), at the very least it enables fellow researchers to explore data collected by others, thus providing a way-point to improve education and building tools to solve other real-world problems.

Kaggle Learn: Kaggle also supports an online micro-course on AI education.

Jobs Board: This service allows potential recruiters to post job listings on data science, machine learning, and related areas. Of course, that means if you are looking for data science jobs, this could be one of the places you check. For more on data science jobs, refer to Appendix G.

E.2 RecSys

RecSys is an ACM (Association of Computing Machinery) conference on recommender systems that was organized for the first time in 2007. A recommender or recommendation system seeks to predict a user's "preference" for an item and filters information accordingly. For example, when you browse for a product in Amazon that you are interested in purchasing, it also shows you a list of additional products that you might be interested in based on your search log. The recommendation algorithm in the background, which in Amazon's case is known as collaborative filtering, is responsible for generating this list. Even though e-commerce websites are the most obvious and popular use of recommender systems, their application is by no means limited to e-commerce applications. A variety of popular services such as movie recommendation (Netflix), music recommendation (Spotify), search queries recommendation (e.g., Google search) run some form of recommendation system in the background.

RecSys 2019, the thirteenth and latest edition of the conference, challenges the research community to develop a session-based and context-aware recommender system on travel recommendations from various user inputs to provide a list of accommodation that will best match the user's preference. The dataset is collected from Trivago, a platform that compares accommodation and prices from various travel booking websites. Trivago provides aggregated information about the characteristics of each accommodation from different booking websites to help prospective travelers to make an informed decision and find their ideal place to stay. The dataset is available at https://recsys.trivago.cloud/ and can be downloaded upon registering for the challenge. The participants can develop their predictive model using the training data downloaded from the link, and submit their system, which will be reviewed by the organizers offline based on a private test set. Based on the result, the participants will also have the opportunity to submit a paper discussing their system. Thus, RecSys not only provides an important junction for promoting state-of-the-art industry research on recommender systems, but at the same time also provides academics with scope to advance their education on data science.

E.3 WSDM

Web Search and Data Mining (WSDM, pronounced as "wisdom") is another premier ACM conference on search and data mining. Like RecSys, WSDM also hosts several competitions or tasks on data mining every year. Each of these tasks is based on current real-world challenges. In its twelfth iteration, WSDM 2019 hosted challenges on fake news classification, intelligent flight schedules development, sequential skip prediction, and retention rate of Baidu Haokan app users. Participating in these competitions not only gives us a sneak-peak of cutting-edge problems currently being faced by the industry, but also provides an opportunity to collaborate with fellow researchers and work toward developing state-of-the-art solutions. Note: datasets for WSDM, 2019 challenges are hosted in Kaggle.

E.4 KDD Cup

ACM Special Interest Group on Knowledge Discovery and Data Mining (SIGKDD) is a leading professional organization of data miners. The annual Data Mining and Knowledge Discovery competition or KDD Cup is organized by ACM SIGKDD. KDD is widely considered the most influential community in data mining research. Every year KDD hosts competitions in multiple tracks, ranging from regular machine learning challenges to data mining problems for medical diagnosis. Usually the competitions last two to four months. In 2019 SIGKDD hosted the twenty-fifth edition of the KDD cup. You can learn more about the tracks from this link: https://www.kdd.org/kdd2019/kdd-cup.

Appendix F: Using Cloud Services

You may have noticed that some of the services and tools used in this book, especially in Chapter 4, require a UNIX environment and are not easily supported by other operating systems such as Windows, or Mac OS. The handy way out in such situations is either to make your system multi-boot (multiple operating system installed on the same machine) or to use a virtual environment. Unfortunately, both of these options also come with limitations, and they are not exactly equivalent of multiple systems with one environment installed in each system. Fortunately, there is an alternative, thanks to recent cloud service offerings by major technology companies such as Google, Microsoft, Amazon, etc.

Cloud computing is a paradigm that enables ubiquitous access to both lower-level shared pools of configurable system resources and higher-level services that can be rapidly provisioned with minimal management effort. Simply put, cloud computing is the delivery of computing services such as storage, databases, servers, networking, analytics, as well as a high-speed network, typically the Internet ("the cloud"). Providers offering such services are called cloud providers and typically charge the user for cloud services based on usage and the type of services being used, akin to being billed for utilities at home.

Outside the context of this book, you are probably using cloud computing right now even if you do not recognize it. If you are watching shows on Netflix, listening to music on Spotify, playing online games, or storing pictures in iCloud, you have been using cloud-based content, processing, and services. Even while using "simple" services such as email, it is likely that behind the scenes cloud computing is making it all work seamlessly. Even though the first commercial cloud computing services are just a little over a decade old at this point,[1] cloud computing is being embraced by astonishingly larger numbers of organizations – from small startups to global corporations, and from government agencies to non-profits. Here are a few barebones services for which cloud services are used:

- Store data with options for backup and recovery
- Analyze the data to identify patterns and make predictions
- Stream audio and video services
- Create new applications and services

Even though the above list is far from comprehensive, what you can imagine is that not all the services require the same type of support. Based on the type of support required by the cloud users, most of the cloud computing services can be broadly categorized into three types:

- **Infrastructure-as-a-Service (IaaS):** This is the most basic category of cloud computing services with bare minimum support required from the service provider. In this type of arrangement, you typically rent some IT infrastructure, ranging from servers and virtual machines (VMs) to storage and networks, from a cloud provider based on your requirement on a pay-as-you-use basis. One simple example of IaaS that we use almost daily is Google Drive or Dropbox to store files and data.
- **Platform-as-a-Service (PaaS):** Platform-as-a-service (PaaS) refers to the type of services that supply an on-demand environment to develop, test, and manage software applications as required by the cloud user. PaaS is designed for developers to simplify the process of developing applications without worrying about setting up or managing the underlying IT infrastructure of servers, storage, network, and databases needed for development. Unlike IaaS, PaaS not only includes the infrastructure but also provides middleware, development tools, business intelligence (BI) services, database management systems, and more, to support the complete application development lifecycle: building, testing, deploying, managing, and updating. Google Cloud Platform (GCP), Microsoft Azure, and Amazon Web Services (AWS) are popular examples of such platforms. We will discuss more on PaaS in the following sections.
- **Software-as-a-Service (SaaS):** Software-as-a-service (SaaS) is a new mode of delivering software applications over the Internet, on demand, and mostly by subscription. In SaaS, apart from maintaining the underlying infrastructure, cloud providers also host and manage the application and handle any maintenance, such as providing software upgrades and security patches. End-users of such applications typically connect to the application over the Internet, usually with a Web browser on their phone, tablet, or PC. Immunet™ antivirus originally developed by Cisco, and later acquired by Sourcefire, is an example of such an application built on SaaS.

F.1 Google Cloud Platform

Google Cloud Platform (GCP) is a host of cloud computing services that run on the same infrastructure that Google uses internally for its own end-user products, such as Google Search, Gmail, and YouTube. Alongside a set of management tools, GCP provides a series of modular services that includes computing, data storage, data analytics, and machine learning. Thus, you can use it for IaaS services as well as for PaaS services. However, in this section we will mostly cover how to use GCP as a virtual machine and use it as PaaS, which Google calls Compute Engine. To use the services, you need to visit https://cloud.google.com, where you can sign in using your Gmail account. If you do not have one, you need to sign up first to create a new account. If this is your first account in GCP, you will get $300 worth of credit for signing up, which should be just about enough to complete a small demo project. However, (full disclosure) you do need a credit card when you sign up in GCP for

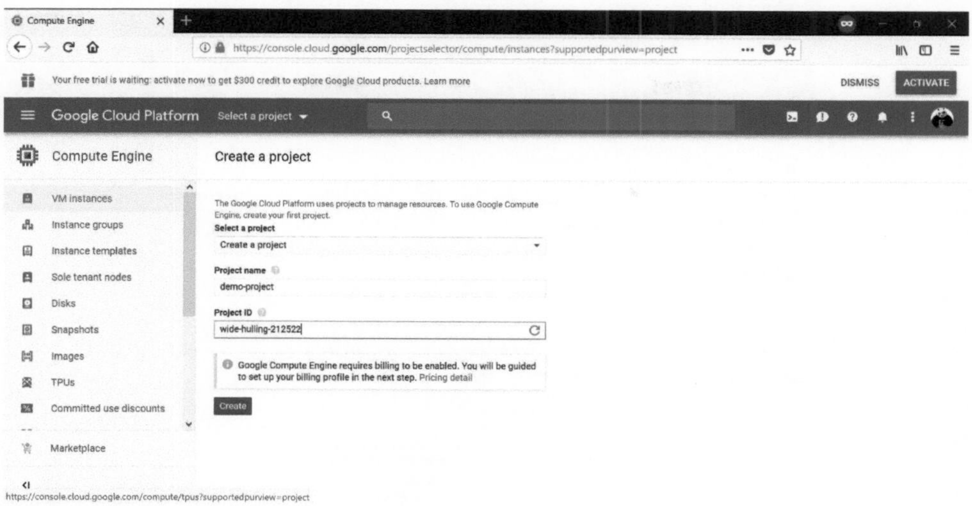

Figure F.1 Creating a new project in GCP.

the first time, but your card will be charged only after you exhaust your initial $300 sign-up bonus.

Once you log in, you need to head over to Console, where you will find the location of Compute Engine, Cloud Storage, App Engine, and links for many other cloud service functionalities. To create a virtual machine, you need to click on the Compute Engine link, which should redirect you to your list of projects running on GCP. Assuming this is your first project, you will need to create a project first, and assign it a name. For this demonstration, I have created one with the name "demo-project" as shown in Figure F.1. Note, apart from the project name, the project also needs to have some unique project ID, you can use the ID assigned by Google, or you can modify it to some other combination that might be more meaningful toward the goal of the project. Once you hit the "create" button, usually it takes a few minutes to complete this step.

Once you create the project it will be displayed under the list of current projects; if you select this, it will take you to your personal information page that you need to fill out, including your billing information. If it is set up correctly and your account is enabled, you are all set to create your virtual machine on Google's infrastructure.

To create the virtual instance, click on the VM instances > Create button. This will take you to the instance specification page. You can modify the Region of the instance as the one closest to your geographic location, machine type, and the Linux distribution of your choice in the specification, as shown in Figure F.2. You can further customize in advanced settings the machine type, which includes altering the number of CPUs, GPUs, and the amount of memory for your instance. Please note, the more customized and powerful configuration you have for your virtual machine, the higher is the cost. As shown in the figure, the configuration I have chosen for this demonstration will cost $99.09 per month to maintain.

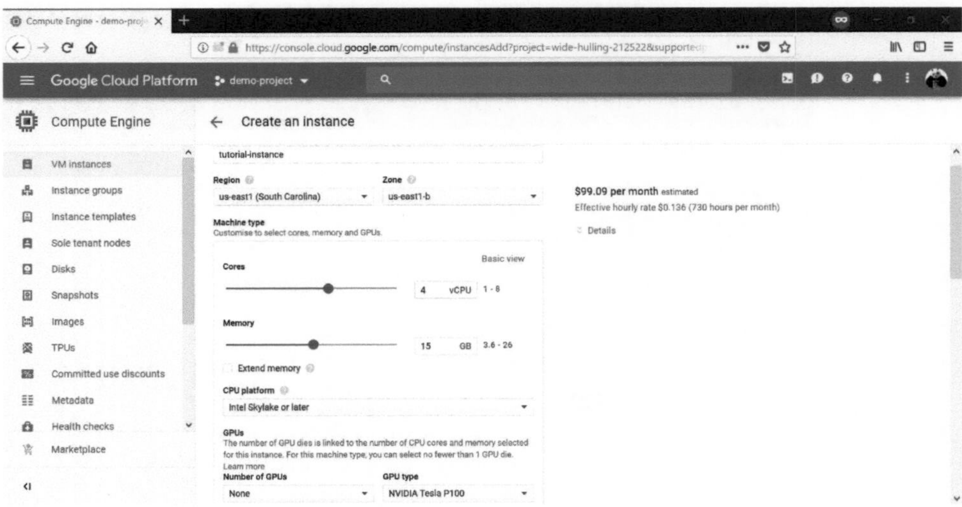

Figure F.2 Creating a virtual machine on GCP.

Now, before you hit the create button to complete creating the virtual instance, you need some arrangement to securely access this instance. Since the virtual instance is essentially going to be an equivalent of a UNIX platform, one possible arrangement can be using the secure shell. Recall from the SSH section in Chapter 4 that you need a tool to use an SSH client service if you are using a PC. There are plenty of such tools available for free on the Web. For this exercise I am going to use PuTTY. Once you have downloaded and installed PuTTY, search for PuTTYgen. Run PuTTYgen and move your mouse randomly to generate your unique SSH key. You can modify the key comment, as I did in Figure F.3, to further personalize your SSH key. Do not forget to save the private key in your local machine and use some passphrase to secure it.

Next, copy the public key from PuTTYgen and add it as the Security key to your virtual instance under the Management, Security, Disks, Networking, Sole Tenancy section in GCP and hit the Create button, as shown in Figure F.4. Once the setup of the instance is complete, it will be shown under the list of virtual instances that has been created under your GCP account, a green tick mark left to its name indicating its current running status along with its external IP address. You will need this address to connect the virtual instance from your local machine.

Since you have the virtual instance up and running, let us connect to it from your virtual machine. To do this open PuTTY from your system, go to SSH > Auth and browse for the private key that you have stored while generating the SSH private key, move back to the Session > Host Name (or IP address), paste the external IP address of your virtual instance here, as shown below in Figure F.5, to open the connection. This should pull up a terminal prompting you for the login name, which should be the same as the Key-comment in PuTTYgen, chirag-demo, in my case. Once you provide the login name, it should prompt

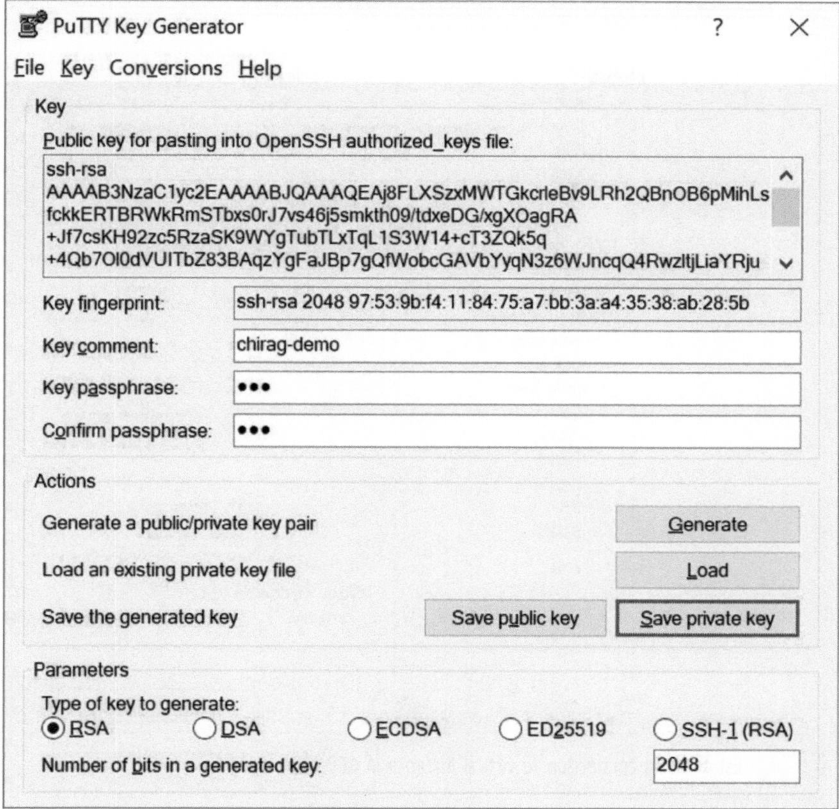

Figure F.3 Using the PuTTYgen to generate the ssh key.

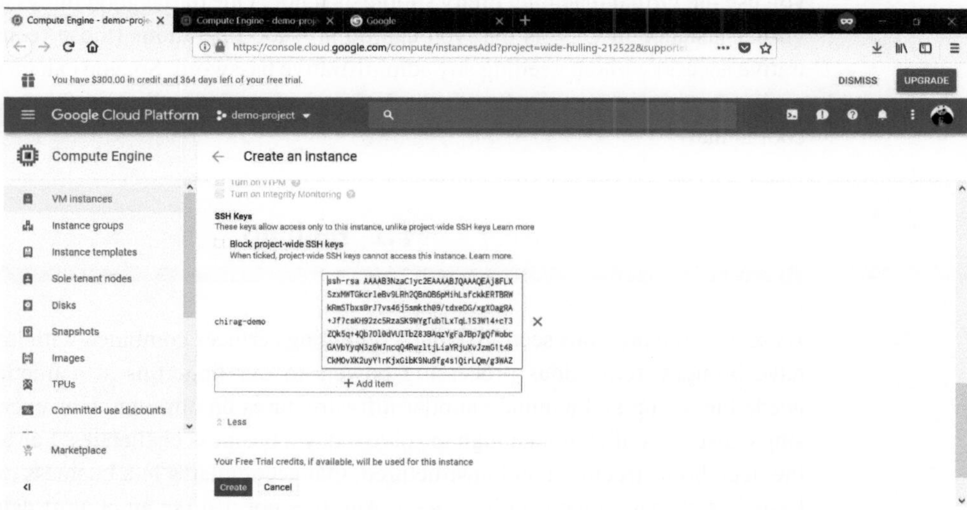

Figure F.4 Adding the SSH key to your virtual machine.

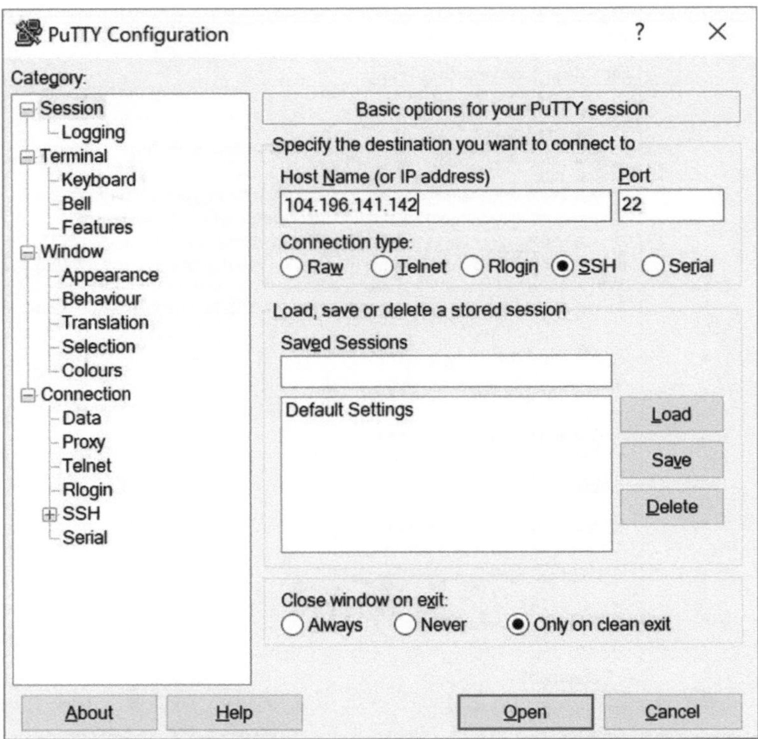

Figure F.5 Establishing connection to virtual instance in GCP using PuTTY.

for the passphrase, which is the same passphrase you used in PuTTYgen to store your private key. Once these two credentials are correctly provided, it should authenticate and let you use the virtual machine. Pretty simple, is it not? One of the good things about using the virtual instance in GCP is that you can do all sudo operations (those requiring administrative access) without needing any administrative password. So, you can install all types of packages you might need to handle the data analysis and visualization for your project. How cool is that?

F.2 Hadoop

As seen in the previous section, cloud computing services combined with low-cost storage have brought tremendous processing powers to our fingertips at a fraction of the cost needed to set up and maintain similar infrastructures on our own. However, large processing capacity is often not enough to solve today's business challenges. For better or worse, the data, both structured and unstructured, that accumulates in a business on a day-to-day basis has grown by many-fold as well. And it is not just the amount of data but what the organization does with that data that matters. Fortunately, there is a set of open-source programs and procedures, called Hadoop, which anyone can use as the "backbone" of their large-quantity data, called "big data" operations.

Simply put, Hadoop is a distributed processing framework that manages data processing and storage for big data applications, often running in high-performance clustered systems. The good thing about Hadoop and the principle reason why it is so popular is its modular nature. The whole system consists of four modules, described below, each of which carries out a specific task essential for the big data analytics at hand.

1. Distributed File System

A "file system" defines how the computer is going to store any data so it can be found and used later. Normally it is specified by the computer's operating system; however, Hadoop can use its own file system, which sits "above" the file system of the host computer – meaning the data can be accessed using any computer running any supported OS. Thus, Hadoop enables the data to be stored in an easily accessible format, across a large number of linked storage devices, supporting distributed computing.

2. MapReduce

As the data is distributed into multiple systems in Hadoop, it needs something to aggregate this data, reading it from the database and putting it into a format suitable for analysis (map). The MapReduce module does just that. In simple terms, MapReduce refers to two separate and distinct tasks that this Hadoop module performs. The first is the map job, which takes a set of data as input and converts it into another set where individual elements are broken into tuples (key-value pairs). The second is the reduce job, which combines the data tuples from the map output and combines them into a smaller set of tuples. As the name implies, the reduce job is always performed after the map job.

3. Hadoop Common

The Hadoop Common module provides the tools (in Java) required for the user's underneath computer systems (Windows, Unix, or whatever is installed) to read the data stored in the Hadoop file system.

4. YARN

The final module is YARN, which manages resources of the systems storing the data and running the analysis. It is the architectural center of Hadoop that allows multiple data processing engines, such as interactive SQL, real-time streaming, and batch processing, to handle data stored in a single platform.

Various other libraries or features have come out as part of the Hadoop "framework" over recent years, but Hadoop Distributed File System, Hadoop MapReduce, Hadoop Common, and Hadoop YARN remain the principal four.

F.3 Microsoft Azure

Now that I have explained the use of cloud services and the Hadoop framework for data storage and processing, it is only logical that I demonstrate the Hadoop in the cloud environment. However, for this exercise I am not going to use GCP, but I will take this opportunity to introduce you to another cloud platform, called Microsoft Azure, which offers similar functionalities and services as GCP. In the following example, I am going to demonstrate how to process a big dataset with Hadoop in Azure HDInsight cluster.

If you do not have a current Azure subscription or have never used Azure before, you can sign up for the Visual Studio Dev Essentials program at https://visualstudio.com/dev-essentials, which should give you $25 of Azure credit per month for a year. The HDInsight within Azure platform is a fully-managed cloud service that makes massive amounts of data processing easy, fast, cost-effective, and reliable. You can use many popular open-source frameworks including Hadoop, Spark, Hive, LLAP, Kafka, Storm, and R, etc., with HDInsight. Note that HDInsight clusters consume credit even when not in use, so make sure to complete the following exercise as soon as possible, if not in one sitting, and be careful to delete your clusters after each use if you do not intend to put them to immediate use, otherwise you may run out of credit before the month ends.

Alternatively, you can follow the steps below to create a free 30-day trial subscription that will give you enough free credit in your local currency to complete the exercise. Note, you will need to provide a valid credit card number for verification (and to sign up for Azure), but you will not be charged for Azure services.

1. You will need to have a Microsoft account that has not been previously used to sign up for Azure. If you do not have one, you can create one at https://signup.live.com by following the directions.
2. Once your Microsoft account is ready, visit the link http://aka.ms/edx-dat202.1x-az and follow the instructions to sign up for a free trial subscription to Microsoft Azure. To complete this step:
   a. First, you will need to sign in with your Microsoft account if you're not already signed in.
   b. Microsoft will verify your phone number and payment details. As said before, your credit card will not be charged for any services as long as you use the services during the trial period, and the account will be automatically deactivated at the end of the trial period, unless you explicitly change the settings to keep it active.

Once you are done setting up your Azure account, you should land at the centralized portal dashboard where you have links for accessing all the resources and services, as shown in Figure F.6.

Next, to use the HDInsight cluster, click on Create a resource > Analytics > HDInsight. Within HDInsight there are many custom settings available for tweaking the system according to the project requirements. However, for this tutorial, I will stick to the Basic setting, provide some cluster name, in this case cloud-hadoop-tutorial, as shown in Figure F.7, choose

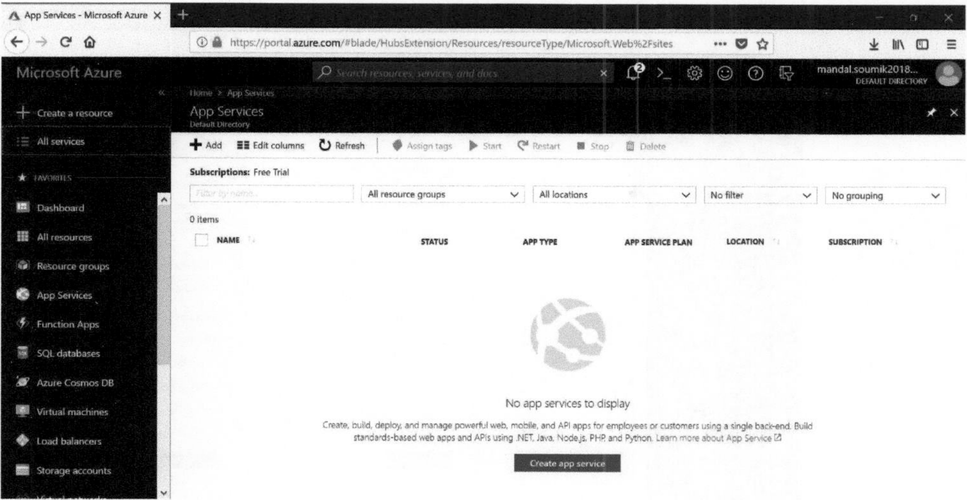

Figure F.6 Interface of the Azure portal.

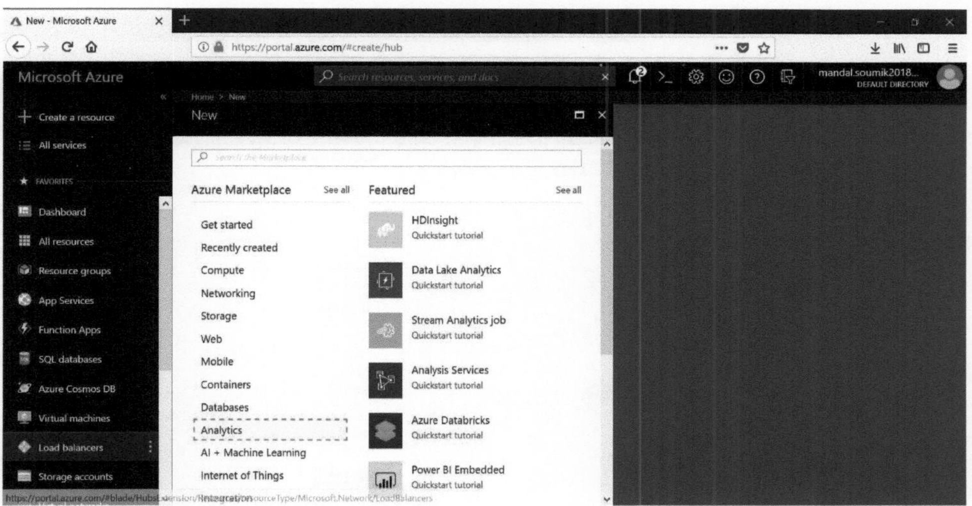

Figure F.7 Using HDInsight cluster in Azure.

the cluster type as Hadoop, go with the default operating system, and Hadoop version (2.7.3) as provided by the system. Do not forget to provide some resource group name while completing this step. You can use different resource groups for different projects. Alternatively, if two or more projects require the same kind of resource and services in Azure, you can use the same resource group.

In the Next step, you will configure the Storage setting in Azure. To do this, first select the Primary storage type as Azure Storage, Use the Create new link to create a new storage

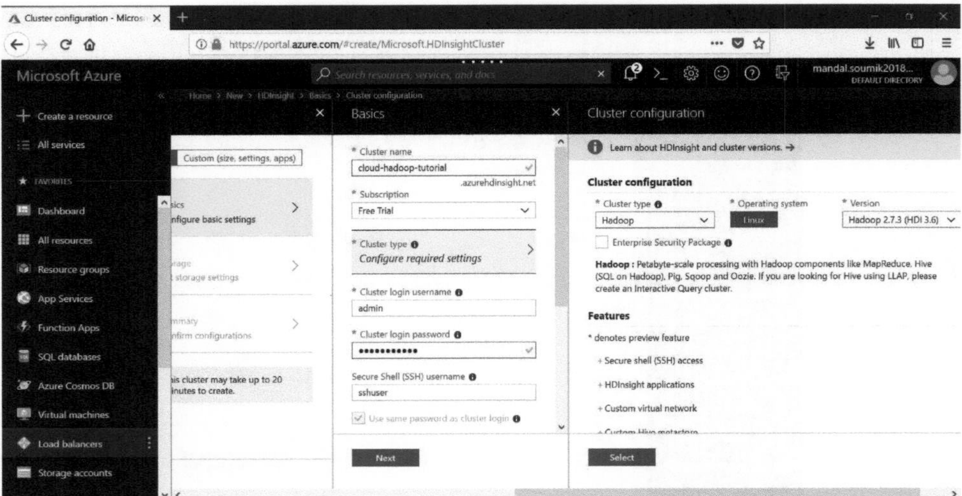

Figure F.8 Configuring the storage options in HDInsight.

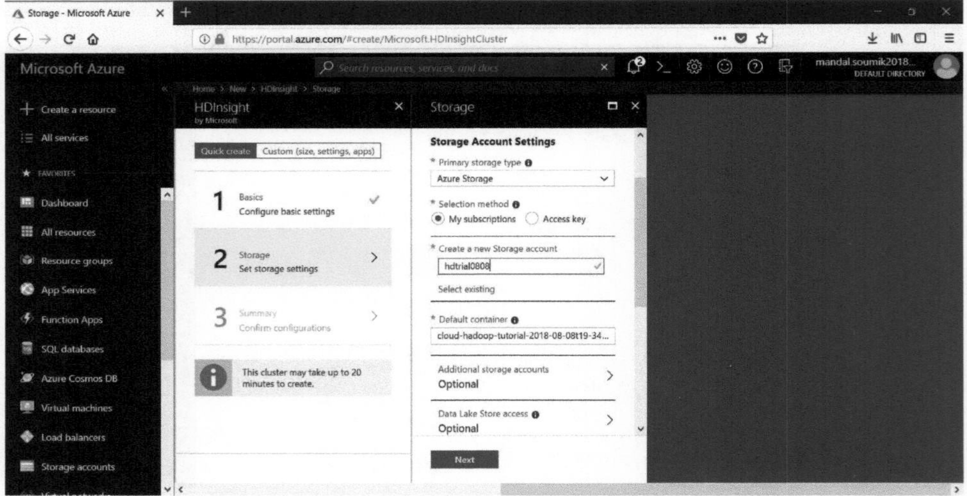

Figure F.9 Overview of the cluster details.

account, and provide some name, “hdtrial0808”, as shown in Figure F.8; and for the rest of the settings, stick to the default values. In the Next step, in the Summary page, you can verify all the major configuration settings that you have chosen, and after you hit the Create button at the bottom, it will take roughly 15–20 minutes to create the cluster instance.

Once the cluster creation is complete and successfully deployed, you should be able to see it in the Overview page, as shown in Figure F.9.

The HDInsight Hadoop cluster that you just created can be provisioned as Linux virtual machines running in Azure. When using a Linux-based HDInsight cluster, as we did in the last setup, you can connect to Hadoop services using a remote SSH session. And if you plan to use a PC to access the Linux HDInsight, you must install an SSH client such as PuTTY.

To connect to the HDInsight cluster, click on the SSH+ Cluster login option, select the hostname from the dropdown (should be *your_cluster_name-ssh.azurehdinsight.net*), and copy it. Next, open PuTTY, go to Session, paste the Host Name, and click the Open button. This will bring up a prompt that will ask for the SSH username and password you specified when provisioning the cluster (not the cluster login). Once it successfully authenticates your credentials, you should be able to access the cluster pretty much the same way as in GCP.

To use any functionalities from the Hadoop framework, you need to go to Cluster dashboards in the Overview page; from Cluster dashboards, click on the Ambari views. This will open a new tab which will prompt for your Hadoop username and password. The default username is admin, unless you have changed it while configuring the HDInsight cluster. Alternatively, you can also browse the link http://<your_cluster_name>.azurehdinsight.net to arrive at the same page. The Ambari views will have links to all the Hadoop functionalities, including YARN, MapReduce2, and Hive, that you may need to manage your big data. If you are curious about any of these specific functions or would like to know more about how to use these components, you can refer to the official Azure documentation.[2]

F.4 Amazon Web Services (AWS)

Amazon Web Services (AWS), a subsidiary of Amazon.com, also provides on-demand cloud computing platforms to individuals, and organizations, on a subscription basis. The cloud service, named Amazon Elastic Compute Cloud (Amazon EC2) provides similar functionalities as GCP and Microsoft Azure. There are several ways to connect to Amazon EC2, such as through AWS Management Console, the AWS Command Line Tools (CLI), or AWS SDKs. In this demonstration I will use the AWS Management Console.

1. First, you need to create an AWS account if you do not already have one. To connect to your existing account, or to create a new one, go to https://portal.aws.amazon.com and follow the steps as per directions. Note, the later steps will ask for your address, phone number, and credit card details for verification purposes. Like GCP and Microsoft Azure, Amazon will not charge you unless your usage exceeds the AWS free tier limits.[3]
2. Once you are done setting up your AWS account, navigate to the Amazon EC2 Dashboard and choose Launch Instance to create and configure your virtual machine (Figure F.10).

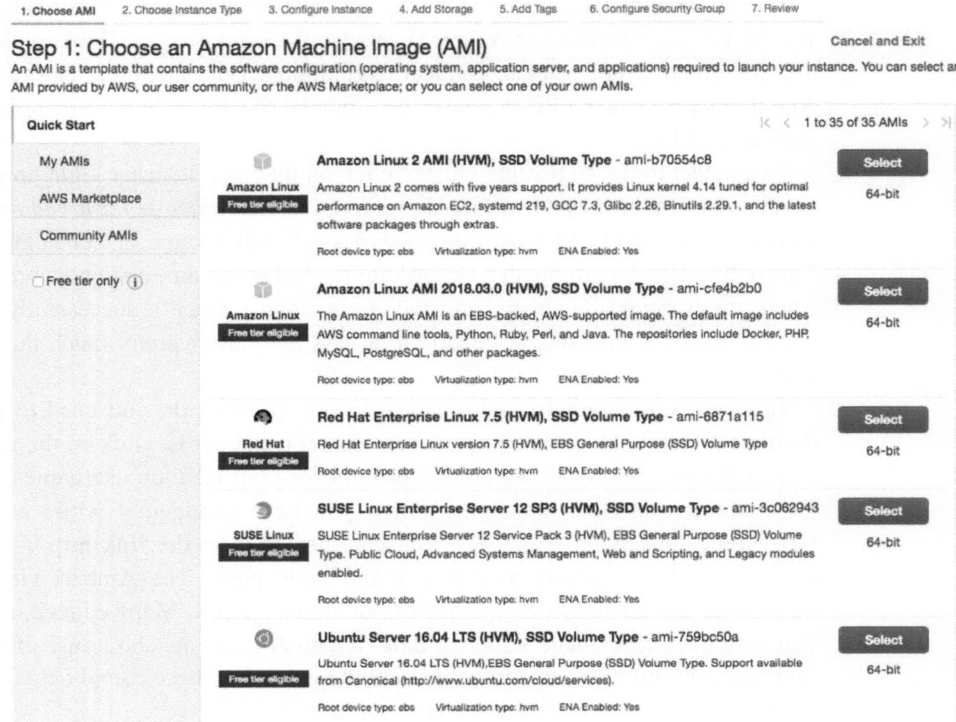

Figure F.10 Creating a virtual machine with AWS.

3. While configuring the virtual instance, you will have the following options:
   a. Choose an Amazon Machine Image (AMI): In step 1 of the wizard, you have to choose the preferred OS to be installed in your virtual machine. If you are not sure about which AMI to go for, the recommended free-tier eligible image is Amazon Linux AMI.
   b. Instance type: In step 2 of the wizard, you need to choose the instance type. The recommended instance for free-tier AWS accounts is t2.micro, which is a low-cost, general-purpose instance type that provides a baseline level of CPU performance.
   c. Security group: Use this option if you want to configure your virtual firewall.
   d. Launch instance: In the final step of configuring the instance, review all the modifications you have made before hitting the Launch button.
   e. Create a key pair: To securely connect to your virtual machine, select Create a new key pair option and assign a name. This will download the key pair file (.pem). Save this file in a safe directory, as you will need it later to log in to the instance.
   f. Finally, choose the Launch Instances option to complete the setup (Figure F.11).

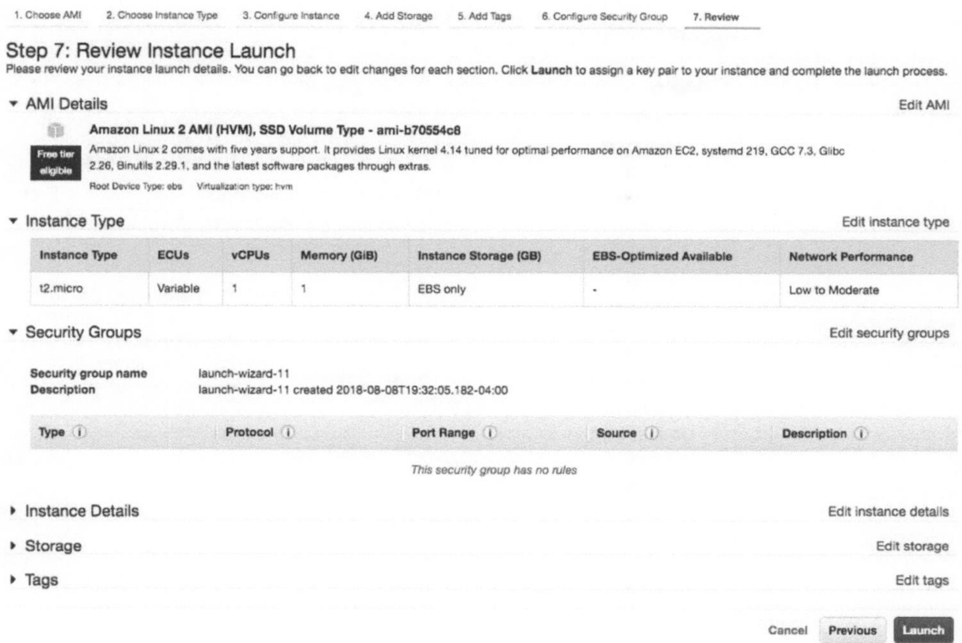

Figure F.11 Launching a virtual machine on AWS.

Accessing your virtual instance in EC2 from a PC is similar to what we have seen for GCP and Azure. You need to use an SSH client, PuTTY. However, there is an extra step involved while accessing instance in EC2. Since PuTTY natively does not support the .pem format, which AWS uses for authentication, you need to convert the .pem file to a PPK format (PPK = PuTTY Private Key), first. You can do this using the PuTTYgen utility. On the PuTTYgen dialog box, click on the Load button, then navigate to the .pem file that you downloaded while setting up your instance. Please note, while browsing for your .pem file in your local directory, be sure to select All Files in the dropdown list located on the right of the File name field. Once loaded, PuTTYgen will convert your file into .ppk format. To save this .ppk file, click on the Save private key option. The utility might yell at you if you try to save the key without a passphrase. Ignore that by selecting Yes, and be sure to provide a name and store it in a directory that you will remember.

Now that you have converted the .pem file from AWS to a .ppk file in PuTTY, you are ready to securely log in to your instance by using SSH from PuTTY. To do this, start PuTTY, and click on Session, to provide the Host Name. The Host Name should be in the format of user_name@public_dns_name, as shown in Figure F.12. The default username for Amazon Linux AMI is ec2-user.

Next, navigate to the Auth button under SSH, browse for the private key (.ppk file) that you saved earlier, and Open the connection. If you followed every step above correctly, you should see a new terminal appear displaying your command-line SSH session as shown in Figure F.13.

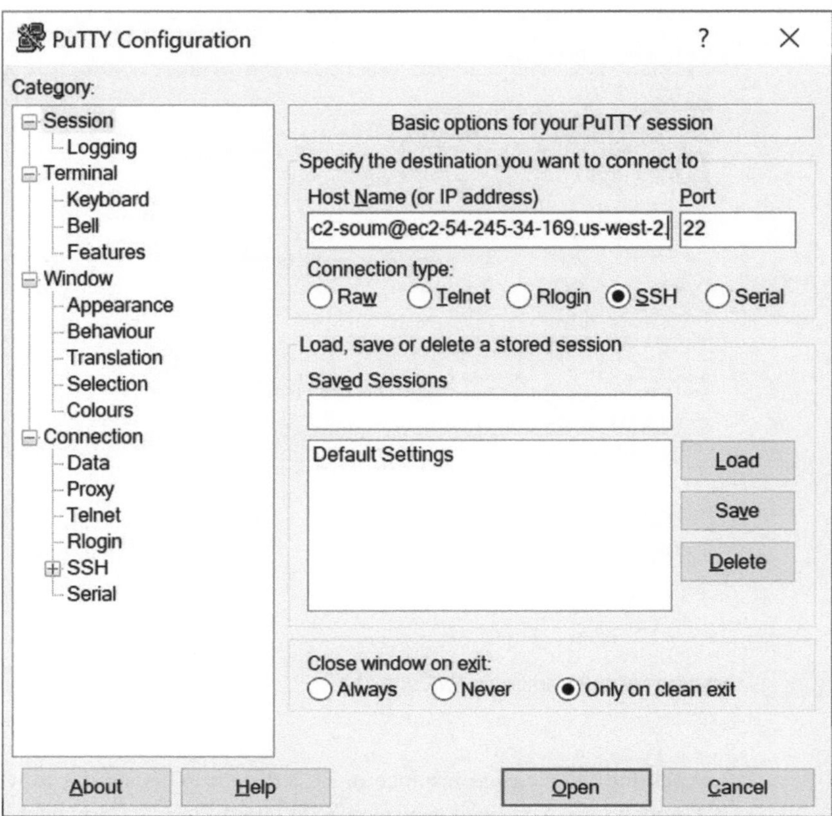

Figure F.12 Connecting AWS EC2 instance from PC using PuTTY.

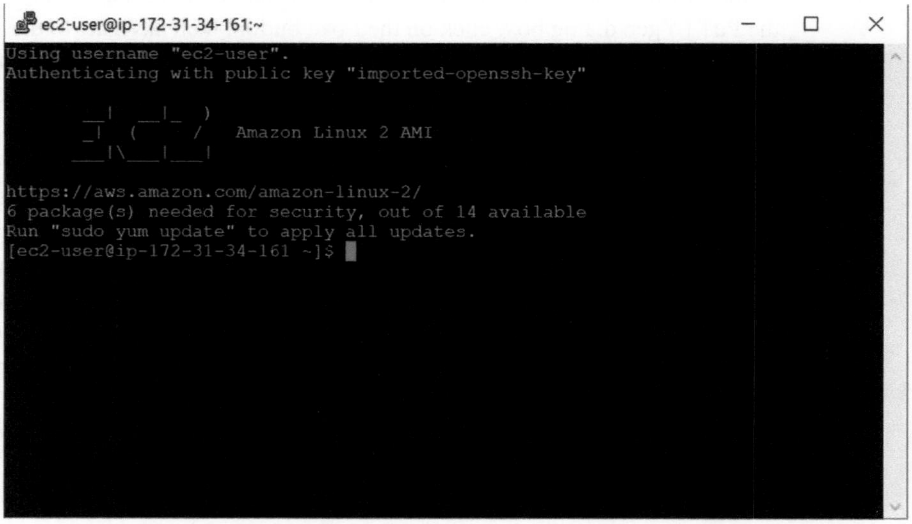

```
ec2-user@ip-172-31-34-161:~
Using username "ec2-user".
Authenticating with public key "imported-openssh-key"

       __|  __|_  )
       _|  (     /   Amazon Linux 2 AMI
      ___|\___|___|

https://aws.amazon.com/amazon-linux-2/
6 package(s) needed for security, out of 14 available
Run "sudo yum update" to apply all updates.
[ec2-user@ip-172-31-34-161 ~]$
```

Figure F.13 SSH session connected to AWS EC2 instance.

Appendix G: Data Science Jobs

We have presented a lot of information about what data science is and the essential skills to be a data scientist. But, what kinds of jobs are available to leverage your new data science skills? If you perform a job search within LinkedIn with the keyword "data scientist," you will retrieve over 24,000 job postings within the United States. If you begin to explore these data scientist positions, you will see many of the following keywords that are used to describe the job title or role: data scientist; chief data scientist; and data engineer. Additionally, if you begin to explore the details of these available positions and the desired skills, you may see the following: statistical analysis; predictive modeling; data-driven storytelling; manipulating large datasets using Python or R; working in Linux environments; SQL; and machine learning. You might be surprised to see that you have already interacted with many of these concepts because you encountered them in this book – Part I (Chapters 1–3) for conceptual introductions to data and data science, Part II (Chapters 4–7) for practical tools, and Part III (Chapters 8–10) for machine learning. But just to develop a more specific idea about what kind of jobs are available, what they expect, what you already have or can have from this book, and what you may want to pick up next, we will examine the data science job market a bit more closely.

Glassdoor identifies three categories of data science jobs: those for core data scientists, those for researchers, and those for big data specialists.[4] The core data scientist jobs, which are the most common (more than 70%), primarily require skills related to python, R, and SQL – all of which are covered in this book. This kind of job also often expects one to know a bit of data cleaning or pre-processing (Chapter 2), machine learning (Chapters 8–10), and using integrative services (Chapter 11). Glassdoor estimated that, in 2017, this category of jobs had an average salary of \$116,203. The researcher category made slightly less, and the big data specialist category made slightly more. Those two categories are less common and often require more specialized skills (e.g., Java, Hadoop) that are in line with the sector in which they are situated. In general, Glassdoor found that, across all the data science-related job postings, the three most common skills were Python (72%), R (64%), and SQL (51%). All of these have devoted chapters and tons of exercises throughout this book, but if you are interested in pushing your skills to the next level, you know which ones to focus on. Beyond that, I would recommend developing a better understanding of the sector or the industry where you want to find a data science job. Of course, doing such prodding could require quite a bit of work, so let me get you started with a few pointers in some of the domains.

You might be surprised to learn that your new data science skills can actually be utilized within many employment arenas. So, to demonstrate this, I have listed below four employment categories and the typical roles that require data science skills. Data science skills and positions can be found in marketing and public relations, corporate retail and other sales business models, legal, and the health and social services industries. In the sections below, I have outlined the general purpose of typical data science roles within each of these industries, the job title keywords you should search for, and the desired skills employers are seeking within a potential candidate.

G.1 Marketing

Data science jobs in marketing can assist in shaping customer profiles and designing strategies to target the core customer. The types of datasets that exist within marketing can range from profile information, such as age, education, and location of customers, to social media comments, to customer support logs. These datasets can be enormous and would require unrealistic amounts of time for any human to manually review and categorize each data point to derive meaning that will inform the development of marketing strategies and initiatives. This is where your skills as a data scientist will come in handy! You can use Python or R to wrangle the data associated with each customer to identify the key attributes of a company's core customer. Is the customer a particular age, gender, or race? Does this customer typically have children? Does the customer live in certain geographical areas such as urban, suburban, or rural? Your ability to handle large datasets will assist in painting the picture to reveal who that core customer is.

If you are interested in positions that are within the marketing industry, you should use the following keywords in your job search: marketing data scientist; marketing analytics; SEO; customer engagement; data wrangling; and predictive analytics. When you perform a job search with any combination of those keywords, you will find that employers are seeking applicants with the following skills: SQL; data visualization; Python; R; predictive modeling; statistical learning methods; machine learning methods; data-driven decision-making; storytelling; and excellent written and verbal communication.

For more details, you may start your exploration from the following links:

- https://www.martechadvisor.com/articles/marketing-analytics/5-musthave-skills-of-a-marketing-analytics-manager/
- http://www.data-mania.com/blog/data-science-in-marketing-what-it-is-how-you-can-get-started/
- https://www.business2community.com/marketing/3-great-examples-of-data-science-in-marketing-02052176
- https://www.ngdata.com/what-is-marketing-analytics/

G.2 Corporate Retail and Sales

Data science is also applicable to corporate retail and sales. All retailers have a core customer that they are marketing to. The job of a retailer is to cater their product assortments to meet the needs of its core customer in order to drive sales. Datasets within retail will include the purchase history of its customers: What did she purchase? When did she purchase it? Did the transaction occur after a major advertising campaign was launched? What items were purchased together? Were coupons or other promotions used? Retailers can also benefit from assessing pricing strategies from a structured, scientific approach, instead of the traditional process to determine margin based on production and operational costs. Are there certain types of customers who are willing to pay more on types of products based on the perceived value? Who is that customer, and what other information can you analyze to identify how to engage with her in the future to encourage loyalty? These are complex questions that can easily be analyzed and answered through the use of your knowledge of data science. You can also use data science to understand the purchasing habits of customers and how products relate to one another. Are there specific items that are commonly purchased together in transactions across all customer types? Where do these items reside on the store website or within the brick-and-mortar location? Do these items physically sit next to each other on a shelf or the website page? Or are they naturally purchased together by the customer? Data science can assist in analyzing the details of customer transactions and identify ways to drive sales just by physically relocating items in the store that customers tend to purchase together.

If you are interested in positions that are within the corporate retail and sales industry, you should use the following keywords in your job search: business intelligence; metrics; price indexing; planning analytics; analysis; retail business reporting; data mining; and product analytics. When you perform a job search with any combination of those keywords, you will find that employers are seeking applicants with the following skills: SQL; data visualization; data-driven decision-making; excellent written and verbal communication; XML; Oracle; and execute A/B multivariate tests.

For more details, you may start your exploration from the following links:

- https://www.cio.com/article/3055833/retail/why-data-scientist-is-the-hottest-tech-job-in-retail.html
- https://www.kdnuggets.com/2018/02/data-science-improve-retail.html
- https://www.retaildive.com/ex/mobilecommercedaily/5-businesses-that-benefit-from-data-science
- https://www.mckinsey.com/business-functions/marketing-and-sales/our-insights/using-big-data-to-make-better-pricing-decisions

G.3 Legal

Data science does not have to be used solely for targeting customers and driving sales. How can we employ your data science skills in the legal sector? Great question! Data science can assist in the legal process to streamline the research process to build a case. Are there other cases with similar circumstances or characteristics to the case you are working on? Are there litigation trends that can be identified from the outcome of a particular case-law dataset? Can this information aid in diagnosing the issue at hand and quickly develop a legal strategy? Can the details of a prospective case be matched with historical cases in order to predict the amount of time or financial investment that will be required? Data science can answer these questions. Additionally, data science can aid in developing an understanding of the operational needs of the legal staff. Is there a trend in the amount of time certain types of cases are required of the staff? Are certain types of skills required for specific circumstances that could streamline the litigation process? Assessing the data associated with the details of cases from an operational perspective can aid in determining the staffing needs and how to efficiently use billable hours to strategically reduce the financial burden to increase profit for the firm.

If you are interested in positions that are within the legal industry, you should use the following keywords in your job search: structured data; data analytics; principal analyst; data analytics auditor; and legal data analyst. When you perform a job search with any combination of those keywords, you will find that employers are seeking applicants with the following skills: QL; data visualization; R; Python; Tableau; Hive/Hadoop; and Oracle.

For more details, you may start your exploration from the following links:

- https://prismlegal.com/data-science-law-an-interview-with-lexpredict/
- https://www.forbes.com/sites/markcohen1/2018/08/30/legal-innovation-is-the-rage-but-theres-plenty-of-resistance/#7002e1337cdd
- https://highperformancecounsel.com/part-3-legal-analyst-data-science-expert/
- https://www.lawtechnologytoday.org/2018/01/the-data-driven-lawyer/
- https://www.americanbar.org/groups/litigation/publications/litigation-news/business-litigation/data-analytics-new-arrow-your-legal-quiver/

G.4 Health and Human Services

Data science can be used in the health and human services sector, too. How does a local health service provider identify the needs of its local citizens? Is there a particular type of service that is needed more in one region over another? Is there a specific type of health issue that is prevalent in one area over others? Or, maybe there is an area or specific population that suffers from addiction. Data science can be utilized to identify the trends or common characteristics that shape the needs of citizens. Perhaps there is a need for increased safety or protection in an area that has a higher rate of 9-1-1 calls over others. You can use data science to review and analyze these datasets to refine the focus of a health service provider in a particular region. And, you can assist local law enforcement to identify the core areas of a community that require more attention than others – this information can provide a particular agency with an understanding of how to build an annual budget and create staffing assignments that will best serve the needs of the community.

If you are interested in positions that are within the health and human services industry, you should use the following keywords in your job search: people analytics; data strategist; data science tech lead; and data and evaluation. When you perform a job search with any combination of those keywords, you will find that employers are seeking applicants with the following skills: SQL; R; Python; machine learning; algorithms; analyzing large datasets; and predictive analysis.

For more details, you may start your exploration from the following links:

- https://datasmart.ash.harvard.edu/news/article/big-data-gives-a-boost-to-health-and-human-services-380
- https://www.fedscoop.com/hhs-data-science-colab-iterating-ahead-second-cohort/
- https://www.altexsoft.com/blog/datascience/7-ways-data-science-is-reshaping-healthcare/
- https://www.fiercehealthcare.com/aca/oig-budget-data-analytics

Appendix H: Data Science and Ethics

You might be familiar with the Hippocratic oath that all doctors and medical professionals are required to take. There is a common phrase "do no harm" that is often referenced in relation to the oath; it acknowledges an obligation of the medical professional to protect her patients, morally and ethically. Data science can be used to accomplish many positive outcomes, such as performing statistical analysis to monetize trends, to design predictive modeling, and to develop task automation and streamlining for many industries, such as corporate sales, marketing, legal, and health and social services. However, data science can also present issues surrounding privacy, access, bias, and inclusion. Data can present ethical dilemmas if proper governance and best practices are not employed. Therefore, it is also important to recognize the significance of accountability and ethical obligations in your role as a data scientist.

So, as a data scientist, how can you do no harm? It is essential for every organization that collects and utilizes data, along with each data practitioner, to establish best practices and codes of conduct to prevent ethical dilemmas and mitigate risks for both the organization and the customers the data represents. What biases could be amplified and promulgated that could potentially create negative outcomes or environments? Data collection, analysis, and use should be evaluated by monitoring the provenance of the datasets and how they are used. Social customs and legal obligations are continually evolving over time, and so must the oversight of data. In the sections below, we have presented a sample of some of the issues you can encounter as a data scientist, along with some best practices to consider. This overview is by no means exhaustive; it serves as an introduction to assist you in considering your role in the relationship of data science and ethics.

H.1 Data Supply Chain

A data supply chain consists of the lifespan of a dataset: collection, analysis, and use. Ethical issues can be presented within each step of the chain, so it is important to review each one and the potential issues that can arise. In the first step, data is collected and stored. This data can be acquired through a variety of methods, such as collecting data through the use of a particular application or retrieval from an open data source. If you have ever installed a new application on your mobile device, software on your computer, or signed up for a service, you have encountered a request to review and accept the terms of service. This is a legal agreement that contains certain rules and regulations that each user much agree to and follow in order to continue to access or use the service. The terms of service might also include disclaimers that outline the collection and use of the data through observing the activity and behaviors of each user. This is where the organization can express its intentions to collect data and seek consent of the user. Ethical dilemmas can be presented at this step in the data supply chain. Has the user been clearly informed of data collection and its use? If your organization acquired data from an open source or third party, has the original context been disclosed to you? Some applications or software might actively collect data in real time, such as a ride-share service that requires the use of location services. What data is collected and stored during this process? Are all data points essential for collection and storage? Does your data storage process properly document provenance? Is user privacy respected through proper security protocols, and has the dataset been anonymized?

The second step in the data supply chain is analysis. In this step, data is processed and analyzed – the processing of data might entail aggregation of several smaller datasets to compile one large collection for manipulation and analysis. Here, you will want to consider risks to individuals in relation to data privacy while the dataset is available for review, analysis, and manipulation. For example, if you are performing research for a retail or financial organization, how is the data accessed? Is the data encrypted? What protocols are currently employed to ensure that the data associated with a client or customer is safe and will not be inappropriately shared? If your dataset can pose security risks for both the organization and the individual it might represent, how is this handled? There are real-world cases such as data breaches within Experian and Bank of America where sensitive personal data was accessed by a third party and presented serious vulnerabilities to their customers that could result in identity theft and credit fraud. It is the responsibility of the organization to ensure the privacy and protection of the data associated with its clients. Additionally, what has the aggregation of data and the performed analysis presented? Were any biases introduced in the process? What ethical reviews were conducted during the process to reduce bias?

The last step in the data supply chain is use – how is the dataset shared after analysis has been performed and new information or knowledge has been constructed? We have presented data science skills that are required for use in machine learning and artificial intelligence. In order to create training algorithms, perform analytics, or automate tasks, a dataset must be used as the framework for these activities. It is important to consider the ethical implications of the analysis that can be performed through the use of your dataset. For instance, what if your dataset was used to construct a tool that could determine criminal recidivism rates? In this situation, you might have analyzed a large dataset of criminal profiles using predictive modeling to create a rating system that can assist in determining the severity of criminal sentencing. What type of transparency exists in the use or sharing of the data to ensure that its users and the individuals it can impact understand the potential for ethical concerns? Is there a process in place to document the use of this new tool in order to log activity in order to identify issues or other needs for improvement? Finally, is there a data access or disposal plan to ensure that control and ownership are managed with proper oversight, to prevent harm?

H.2 Bias and Inclusion

Bias and inclusion are often concerns in relation to data analytics, machine learning, and artificial intelligence. When a dataset is processed and analyzed to extract information, construct knowledge, or train a machine to automate a task, the information, knowledge, and skills are directly resultant of the dataset used. In other words, the output of data analytics is limited to the details of the input. Subsequently, if the dataset is skewed or limited to a particular population that is not justifiably representative of a whole, the analytical product can also propose limitations.

Consider the use of data science and analytics for human resources. An organization could provide you with a dataset that consists of every existing (and possibly prior) employee that contains specific information about each individual in regards to their current position, education, skills, performance evaluations, salary, and other basic profile information, such as age, race, or gender. You can use your data science skills to analyze this data in order to identify themes and develop prototypical associate profiles by role, to aid the human resources department in recruitment. However, what if the existing employee structure contains bias such as specific genders filling specific roles, specific race or ethnicity filling specific roles, or the salary range structure? You did not establish this bias, but you can aid in identifying its existence and proposing methods for limiting or preventing its perpetuation. In this case, you can play a small, yet significant, role in preventing the amplification of bias that can pose social and ethical dilemmas.

H.3 Considering Best Practices and Codes of Conduct

Best practices and codes of conduct aid in mitigating issues and reducing their impact. Essentially, they should provide a structure to train associates in how to prevent issues from occurring and how to identify and address them when they do. The development of best practices requires careful consideration of the existing ethical codes your organization currently follows, how it addresses issues when they are presented, and what protocols exist to prevent ethical issues from occurring. For example, you will want to consider if they provide sufficient guidelines to aid each individual to make informed decisions that simultaneously mitigate risk for the organization and protect the privacy of the particular population you engage with. What is the protocol for assessing data processing, analytics, and maintaining data privacy through managing storage and access? Is there an operational structure in place that outlines how to conduct pilot programs to determine social and ethical impacts? What techniques are used for collecting data? It is important to implement a schedule to review collection methods to maintain transparency and create opportunity to adapt and evolve over time as industry and social standards change. Does your organization provide a training program for all associates at all levels to provide regular education in regards to ethical considerations and how to prevent harmful practices? In many cases, there can be unintended consequences that can cause harm to a customer or the organization. What processes, if any, does your organization have in place to identify these instances? How can these cases be documented and addressed to effect change?

Follow the links provided below if you are interested in reading more about topics related to data science and ethics:

- https://ainowinstitute.org/AI_Now_2017_Report.pdf
- https://www.propublica.org/series/machine-bias
- https://www.accenture.com/us-en/insight-data-ethics
- https://royalsocietypublishing.org/doi/full/10.1098/rsta.2016.0360
- https://www.technologyreview.com/s/612775/algorithms-criminal-justice-ai/

Appendix I: Data Science for Social Good

We have presented a myriad of ways in which data science skills can be utilized within organizations for profit. A data science job will typically leverage skills to perform statistical analysis, predictive modeling, data-driven storytelling, and manipulate large datasets using Python or R (among many other skills we have presented throughout this book) in order to increase profitability, mitigate risks, and identify methods to create efficiencies. But, how can we leverage these same valuable skills for the sake of social good? How can you identify opportunities to solve real-world problems that are human-centered? What can you do to wield your data science skills to support the initiatives of mission-driven (or non-profit) organizations?

If you are motivated to utilize your data science skills to positively impact humanity through the power of technology, you can begin your search by seeking out volunteer opportunities through data science organizations, fellowship programs, and conferences. Perform a search utilizing the key phrase "data science and social good" to locate organizations and opportunities (we provided a sample of these in the links below). These programs will organize training sessions or events to focus on and further develop data science skills within the context of problems that address issues with social impact. Next, you can participate in competitions and hackathons. Many organizations solicit solutions to real-world, social problems. Typically, they will provide the dataset and it is up to you to perform the analytical and predictive tasks to offer solutions to the problems presented in the competition. Finally, you can choose to focus your professional career to deliberately seek out employment opportunities in either non-profit or for-profit organizations that are centered in human and socially conscious goals such as healthcare, human services, and environmental protection groups (read more about this in Appendix G: Data Science Jobs).

Follow the links provided below if you are interested in reading more about topics related to data science for social good:

- https://towardsdatascience.com/using-data-science-for-social-good-c654a6580484
- https://www.kdnuggets.com/2015/07/guide-data-science-good.html
- https://www.datakind.org/
- https://www.goodtechfest.com/
- https://dssg.uchicago.edu/
- https://www.drivendata.org/competitions/

Notes

1. “Announcing Amazon Elastic Compute Cloud (Amazon EC2) – beta”. Amazon.com. 24 August 2006.
2. Get started with Hadoop and Hive in Azure HDInsight using the Azure portal available at: https://docs.microsoft.com/en-us/azure/hdinsight/hadoop/apache-hadoop-linux-create-cluster-get-started-portal
3. AWS free tier details: https://aws.amazon.com/free/
4. Data Scientist Personas: What Skills Do They Have and How Much Do They Make? By Pablo Ruiz Junco. September 21, 2017: https://www.glassdoor.com/research/data-scientist-personas/

Index